The Exile Mission

Ohio University Press Polish and Polish-American Studies Series

Series Editor: John J. Bukowczyk, Wayne State University

Framing the Polish Home: Postwar Cultural Constructions of Hearth, Nation, and Self, edited by Bożena Shallcross

Traitors and True Poles: Narrating a Polish-American Identity, 1880–1939, by Karen Majewski

Auschwitz, Poland, and the Politics of Commemoration, 1945–1979, by Jonathan Huener

The Exile Mission: The Polish Political Diaspora and Polish-Americans, 1939–1956, by Anna D. Jaroszyńska-Kirchmann

SERIES ADVISORY BOARD

M. B. B. Biskupski, Central Connecticut State University
Robert E. Blobaum, West Virginia University
Anthony Bukoski, University of Wisconsin–Superior
Bogdana Carpenter, University of Michigan
Mary Patrice Erdmans, Central Connecticut State University
Thomas S. Gladsky, Saint Mary's College (ret.)
Padraic Kenney, University of Colorado at Boulder
John J. Kulczycki, University of Illinois at Chicago (ret.)
Ewa Morawska, University of Essex
Antony Polonsky, Brandeis University
Brian Porter, University of Michigan
James S. Pula, Purdue University North Central
Thaddeus C. Radzilowski, Piast Institute
Daniel Stone, University of Winnipeg
Adam Walaszek, Jagiellonian University
Theodore R. Weeks, Southern Illinois University

The Exile Mission

*The Polish Political Diaspora
and Polish Americans, 1939–1956*

Anna D. Jaroszyńska-Kirchmann

OHIO UNIVERSITY PRESS
ATHENS

Ohio University Press, Athens, Ohio 45701
© 2004 by Anna D. Jaroszyńska-Kirchmann

All rights reserved

Ohio University Press books are printed on acid-free paper ♾ ™

11 10 09 08 07 06 05 04   5 4 3 2 1

Cover photograph: A group of Polish DPs on a train heading to Bremerhaven, Germany, to board a ship to the United States, 1950. Courtesy of Victor Bik

Library of Congress Cataloging-in-Publication Data

Jaroszyńska-Kirchmann, Anna D.
  The exile mission : the Polish political diaspora and Polish Americans, 1939–1956 / Anna D. Jarozyńska-Kirchmann. — 1st ed.
      p. cm. — (Ohio University Press Polish and Polish-American studies series)
  Includes bibliographical references and index.
   ISBN 0-8214-1526-3 (cloth : alk. paper)
  1. Polish Americans—History—20th century. 2. Polish Americans—Cultural assimilation. 3. World War, 1939–1945—Refugees. 4. Refugees—Poland—History—20th century. I. Title. II. Series.
   E184.P7J29 2004
   305.891'85073'09044—dc22
                                                    2004006713

ISBN-13 978-0-8214-1527-6 (paperback)

Publication of books in the Polish and Polish-American Studies Series has been made possible in part by the generous support of the following organizations:

    Polish American Historical Association, New Britain, Connecticut

    Stanislaus A. Blejwas Endowed Chair in Polish and Polish American Studies, Central Connecticut State University, New Britain, Connecticut

    Madonna University, Livonia, Michigan

    The Polish Institute of Arts and Sciences of America, Inc., New York, New York

    The Piast Institute: An Institute for Polish and Polish American Affairs, Detroit, Michigan

Additional support for this book has been provided by the Kulczycki Prize awarded by the Polish American Historical Association

Contents

List of Illustrations ix
List of Tables xi
Series Editor's Preface xiii
Preface and Acknowledgments xv
List of Abbreviations xvii
Guide to Pronunciation xxi

INTRODUCTION 1

1. "Smoke over America, blood over Europe": World War II and the Polish Diaspora 16
2. "All I have left is my free song": The Polish Community in the Displaced Persons Camps 58
3. "Live a happy and peaceful life here": The Resettlement of Polish Displaced Persons in the United States 104
4. "So they are among brethren": Debate in the Community 147
5. "Ambassadors of our cause": Turning Points 195

EPILOGUE 228

Notes 243
Bibliography 321
Index 345

Illustrations

MAPS

Map of Major DP camps with Polish population in
occupation zones of Germany and Austria, 1945–1951   59

PHOTOGRAPHS

Following page 146:
1. Henryk Floyar-Rajchman (n.d.)
2. KNAPP delegation to United Nations conference in San Francisco, 1945
3. Front cover of *Tygodnik Polski*, May 28, 1944
4. Polish soccer team in Germany, 1947
5. Polish Educational Center in Fallingsbostel, Germany, 1947
6. School play by Polish DP students in Germany, 1948
7. Page from Polish student's album, Germany, 1950
8. Officers of American Committee for Resettlement of Polish DP's, 1949
9. Cartoon from *Dziennik Związkowy*, October 29, 1948
10. Cartoon from *Dziennik Związkowy*, October 15, 1949
11. Polish DPs who arrived aboard S.S. *General Black*, October 30, 1948
12. Delegation from PAC and PNA greeting Polish immigrants arriving in Boston Harbor (n.d.)
13. Józef Wyrwa, Chicago, 1951
14. Tadeusz Wyrwa, Chicago, 1951
15. Scouting instructors, Bantam, Connecticut, 1956
16. Girl scout troop marching in May 3 Parade, Chicago, 1952
17. Ogiński Choir, New York, 1956
18. Performance of Teatr Rozmaitości, Detroit, circa 1952
19. Władysława Wojciechowska with girls from PNA group in Toledo, Ohio, May 1955
20. Cartoon from *Zgoda*, September 1, 1956

Tables

TABLE 2.1. Polish displaced persons receiving UNRRA assistance in Germany, Austria, Italy, the Middle East, and China, December 1945–June 1947 — 62

TABLE 2.2. Occupational skills of Polish refugees in Austria, Germany, and Italy by major occupational groups, March 1948 — 63

TABLE 3.1. Resettlement of Polish refugees, July 1, 1947–December 31, 1951 — 108

Series Editor's Preface

THE GLOBAL AND REGIONAL conflicts and the convulsive social, economic, and technological changes that racked the twentieth century took a huge and gruesome human toll. In addition to the casualties of war and the victims of genocide, the events of the century produced legions of refugees and displaced persons, altering their lives forever.

In *The Exile Mission: The Polish Political Diaspora and Polish Americans, 1939-1956*, Eastern Connecticut State University historian Anna Jaroszyńska-Kirchmann provides the first full treatment of the compelling story of Polish displaced persons and refugees during and after World War II. Uprooted by the Nazi and Soviet invasions that ravaged their homeland at the outset of the war and by its postwar subjugation as a Soviet satellite, the displaced Poles commenced a journey that had two equally formative parts. In refugee camps in Europe and elsewhere, the displaced Poles first resolved to carry on their country's struggle against foreign domination. Subsequently, as part of a worldwide postwar Polish political diaspora, the displaced Poles remade the demographics, ideology, and politics of prewar Polish immigrant communities and took up a growing leadership role in the West's Cold War struggle against Soviet communism.

Jaroszyńska-Kirchmann's volume complements a growing body of historical work on refugees and asylum seekers and will be of interest to scholars and students of the Cold War period, historians of immigration and ethnicity, policymakers, immigration law specialists, and social service professionals whose practices put them in contact with contemporary immigrants not unlike the author's subjects. But this book will hold especial salience for Polish displaced persons and their families, who for fifty years have awaited a serious examination of the Polish "DP experience." Jaroszyńska-Kirchmann has written a book that not only resonates with memory but offers comparative insights relevant to our own times. In the words of one scholar, "It is well documented, objective and properly respectful to various points of view that emerged following the encounter between the DPs and those who helped them find asylum in the USA."

The Exile Mission: The Polish Political Diaspora and Polish Americans,

1939–1956 is the fourth volume in the Ohio University Press Polish and Polish-American Studies Series. The series revisits the historical and contemporary experience of one of America's largest European ethnic groups and the history of a European homeland which has played a disproportionately important role in twentieth-century and contemporary world affairs. The series publishes innovative monographs and more general works that investigate under- or unexplored topics or themes or that offer new, critical, revisionist, or comparative perspectives in the area of Polish and Polish-American Studies. Interdisciplinary or multidisciplinary in profile, the series seeks manuscripts on Polish immigration and ethnic communities, the country of origin, and its various peoples in history, anthropology, cultural studies, political economy, current politics, and related fields.

Publication of the Ohio University Press Polish and Polish-American Studies Series marks a milestone in the maturation of the Polish studies field and stands as a fitting tribute to the scholars and organizations whose efforts have brought it to fruition. Supported by a series advisory board of accomplished Polonists and Polish-Americanists, the Polish and Polish-American Studies Series has been made possible through generous financial assistance from the Polish American Historical Association, the Polish Institute of Arts and Sciences of America, the Stanislaus A. Blejwas Endowed Chair in Polish and Polish American Studies at Central Connecticut State University, and through institutional support from Wayne State University and Ohio University Press. To this list of funders, with this volume we are especially pleased to add Madonna University and the Piast Institute, which graciously stepped in to fill the void left when our former funder, St. Mary's College, ceased operation last year. Our heartfelt thanks go to Sister Rose Marie Kujawa, CSSF, president of Madonna University, which absorbed the St. Mary's students and programs, and to Dr. Thaddeus Radzilowski, president of the Piast Institute, for their enthusiastic support of this publication endeavor. The series meanwhile has benefited from the warm encouragement of a number of persons, including Gillian Berchowitz, M. B. B. Biskupski, the late Stanislaus A. Blejwas, Thomas Gladsky, Thaddeus Gromada, James S. Pula, and David Sanders. The moral and material support from all of these institutions and individuals is gratefully acknowledged.

John J. Bukowczyk

Preface and Acknowledgments

WHEN I CAME TO THe United States for the first time in 1986 and enrolled in the doctoral program in history at the University of Minnesota, I had an M.A. in history from Maria Curie-Skłodowska University in Lublin, Poland. My grasp of Polish history was strong and stemmed from countless classes, individual reading, family stories, the collective memory so characteristic of the Polish nation, as well as, for the more recent periods, any uncensored underground publications I could lay my hands on. I knew very little about the history of Polonia—Poles and those of Polish background living outside Poland's borders. But, then, I did not feel there was much to know about it. Polish history, after all, was happening in Poland, and in the eventful 1980s there was enough of it to fully capture anyone's attention. This assertion was soon challenged, as I started to discover new and exciting areas of both Polish and American history.

In 1986, I began work as a research assistant at the Immigration History Research Center (IHRC) at the University of Minnesota. Using my archival training and experience from Poland, I processed, described, and made accessible the Polish-American manuscript collections housed at the IHRC. The very first collection I worked on was that of the American Committee for the Resettlement of Polish DP's (ACRPDP). On the desk in front of me I had piles of yellowing letters from postwar Polish refugees stranded in displaced persons (DP) camps in Germany and their photographs, showing faces marked by wartime experiences of unimaginable magnitude but still full of hope for the future. And I had piles of ACRPDP correspondence revealing the tremendous organizational effort of Polish-American activists who scrambled to resettle the refugees in the United States and to find sponsors, jobs, housing, and funds. All of a sudden, I was hooked. I wanted to know more. I wanted to understand what had motivated all those Poles and Polish Americans whose letters, written several decades earlier, were now in my hands. My fascination and intellectual adventure with immigration history had begun.

I have been very fortunate to have a number of outstanding mentors and friends who guided me through the complexities of my research, the final product of which is *The Exile Mission*. I owe them gratitude for their support, friendship, and expert advice. My special thanks go to three distinguished scholars. Professor Józef Szymański was my adviser and mentor in Poland, and I thank him for instilling in me a healthy respect for primary sources and for being my friend throughout the years. Professor Rudolph J. Vecoli, director of the IHRC and professor of history at the University of Minnesota, introduced me to the richness of immigration history, guided me through the dissertation writing process, gave me a job when I needed it the most, and always encouraged and supported me in all my scholarly pursuits; I will always treasure his friendship. The late Professor Stanislaus A. Blejwas, Chair of Polish and Polish American Studies at Central Connecticut State University, whose article on the "Old and New Polonias" inspired me, became my role model as a scholar and Polonia activist.

Many others also deserve my heartfelt appreciation, and particularly Professor Roger Daniels for his encouraging words and Professor John J. Bukowczyk for giving me a chance and invaluable advice. Numerous individuals helped me in many ways at different stages of research and writing and have earned my gratitude: the IHRC staff, and especially Joel Wurl, Halyna Myroniuk, Judy Rosenblatt, and the late Timo Riippa; the wonderfully helpful archivists at the Truman Library, the Polish Museum of America, and the Polish Institute of Arts and Sciences, as well as those at the Józef Piłsudski Institute, including Iwona Drąg-Korga and Krzysztof Langowski, and at the Polish Archives at CCSU, including Ewa Wołyńska. At Eastern Connecticut State University my special thanks must go to all the helpful colleagues in my department, particularly Emil Pocock and Katie Lynch, and to the patient librarians, Anka Stanley and Greg Robinson. The Ohio University Press Polish and Polish-American series, and especially John Bukowczyk, Gillian Berchowitz, and Ricky Huard, deserve my gratitude for making the publication process professional, but open-minded and friendly. And there were many other dear friends who assisted and cheered me on along the way; I will always appreciate their support.

I would also like to thank my parents, Teresa and Józef Jaroszyński, and my brother, Dr. Andrzej J. Jaroszyński, for all their love. The one person without whom this book would not have been possible is my dearest husband Tim Kirchmann, who supported my passion with rare magnanimousness, patience, and good humor throughout the years.

I dedicate this book to all the Polish exiles and Polish Americans who carried an exile mission in their hearts always.

List of Abbreviations

ACEN	Assembly of Captive European Nations
ACRPDP	American Committee for the Resettlement of Polish DP's
AK	Armia Krajowa (Polish Home Army)
APLC	American Polish Labor Council
CCDP	Citizens Committee on Displaced Persons
DP/DPs	Displaced person/Displaced persons
DPC	Displaced Persons Commission
FON	Fundusz Obrony Narodowej (National Defense Fund)
IRO	International Refugee Organization
KNAPP	Komitet Narodowy Amerykanów Polskiego Pochodzenia (National Committee of Americans of Polish Descent)
KON	Komitet Obrony Narodowej (Committee of National Defense)
KPR	Korpus Przysposobienia i Rozmieszczenia (Polish Resettlement Corps)
KWE	Komitet Wolnej Europy (National Committee for a Free Europe)
NCFE	National Committee for a Free Europe
NCWC	National Catholic Welfare Conference
NiD	Niepodległość i Demokracja (Independence and Democracy)
NKVD	National Commissariat of Internal Affairs
NRC-NCWC	National Resettlement Council-National Catholic Welfare Conference
NSZ	Narodowe Siły Zbrojne (National Armed Forces)
PAC	Polish American Congress
PAHA	Polish American Historical Association
PAU	Polska Akademia Umiejętności (Polish Academy of Arts and Sciences)
PCIRO	Preparatory Commission of the International Refugee Organization
PIASA	Polish Institute of Arts and Sciences in America

PIC	Polish Immigration Committee-American Commission for Relief of Polish Immigrants
PIN	Polski Instytut Naukowy w Ameryce (PIASA)
PNA	Polish National Alliance
PNKD	Polski Narodowy Komitet Demokratyczny (Polish National Democratic Committee)
PPS	Polska Partia Socjalistyczna (Polish Socialist Party)
PRC	Polish Resettlement Corps
PRCUA	Polish Roman Catholic Union of America
PSK	Pomocnicza Służba Kobiet (Women's Auxiliary Military Service)
PSL	Polskie Stronnictwo Ludowe (Polish Peasant Party)
PU	Polish Union in Germany
PWA	Polish Women's Alliance
RPA	Rada Polonii Amerykańskiej (Polish American Council)
RFE	Radio Free Europe
RWE	Radio Wolna Europa (Radio Free Europe)
SD	Stronnictwo Demokratyczne (Democratic Movement)
SHAEF	Supreme Headquarters Allied Expeditionary Forces
SN	Stronnictwo Narodowe (National Movement)
SP	Stronnictwo Pracy (Labor Movement)
SPK	Stowarzyszenie Polskich Kombatantów (Association of Polish ex-Combatants)
SSR	Soviet Socialist Republic
SWAP	Stowarzyszenie Weteranów Armii Polskiej (Polish Army Veterans Association in America)
TRJN	Tymczasowy Rząd Jedności Narodowej (Provisional Government of National Unity)
UNHCR	Office of the United Nations High Commissioner for Refugees
UNRRA	United Nations Relief and Rehabilitation Administration
WRS-NCWC	War Relief Services–National Catholic Welfare Conference
ZAP	Związek Akademików Polskich (Association of Polish Academicians)
ZHP	Związek Harcerstwa Polskiego (Polish Scouting)
ZPA	Związek Polaków w Austrii (Association of Poles in Austria)

ZPT	Związek Polaków w Tyrolu (Association of Poles in Tyrol)
ZPUW	Zjednoczenie Polskiego Uchodźstwa Wojennego (Union of the Polish War Emigrants)
ZSP	Związek Studentów Polskich (Association of Polish Students)

Guide to Pronunciation

THE FOLLOWING KEY provides a guide to the pronunciation of Polish words and names.

    a is pronounced as in *father*
    c as ts in *cats*
    ch like a guttural h
    cz as hard ch in *church*
    g always hard, as in *get*
    i as ee
    j as y in *yellow*
    rz like French j in *jardin*
    sz as sh in *ship*
    szcz as shch, enunciating both sounds, as in *fresh cheese*
    u as oo in *boot*
    w as v
    ć as soft ch
    ś as sh
    ż, ź both as zh, the latter higher in pitch than the former
    ó as oo in boot
    ą as French *on*
    ę as French *en*
    ł as w
    ń changes the combinations -in to -ine, -en to -ene, and -on to -oyne

The accent in Polish words always falls on the penultimate syllable.

INTRODUCTION |||

THROUGHOUT THE EIGHTEENTH AND nineteenth centuries, the Polish nation repeatedly fought first to retain and, later, to regain its independence after expansionist neighbors Prussia, Russia, and Austria had divided historically Polish territories among themselves in three successive partitions in 1772, 1793, and 1795. The two largest Polish national uprisings—the 1830 November Uprising and the 1863 January Uprising—failed under the overwhelming military might of the partitioning powers. But no oppressors could defeat the spirit of the Polish people, whose national anthem proclaimed, "Poland is not overcome yet, as long as we are still alive." Even while continuing their armed resistance, Poles also struggled against the attempts of foreign administrations to make them forget who they were and to transform them into Germans or Russians. Poles consciously resisted the politics of denationalization and took special care to preserve and to develop Polish national culture, language, traditions, and history. Their dreams of an independent state became a reality in the Treaty of Versailles: Poland regained its independence as a new and democratic state in 1918, after 123 years of partition.

The concept of the exile's responsibility toward the homeland has roots as deep as the 1830 November Uprising, whose failure drove thousands of political émigrés out of Poland. Most of them settled in France, Great Britain, and Belgium, where they carried out activities intended to provide political and spiritual leadership to the nation. The Great Emigration (*Wielka Emigracja*), as it came to be known, produced important Polish intellectual and artistic legacies, weaving together the nation's Romantic tradition and profound patriotic feelings. The poets Adam Mickiewicz, Juliusz Słowacki,

Zygmunt Krasiński, Cyprian Kamil Norwid, historian Joachim Lelewel, and political writer Maurycy Mochnacki belong to the pantheon of Polish arts and letters.[1]

Adam Mickiewicz's contribution to the astounding output of the Wielka Emigracja included the creation of a vision and a metaphor that described the role of Polish exiles, whom he called "Pilgrims." "The Polish Pilgrims are the soul of the Polish Nation," he wrote, and the Pilgrim's vow is "to journey to the holy land, the free country." On this journey, the Pilgrims were to be guided by "star and compass": "And the star of the Pilgrims is heavenly faith, and the compass is love of country."[2] Mickiewicz's vision and other political writings of the Great Emigration laid the foundation for the exile mission, an unwritten set of beliefs, goals, and responsibilities of Polish emigrants, which placed patriotic work for Poland at the center of their duties toward the homeland. For many decades thereafter, the exile mission guided and defined the experience of émigrés in different countries, including the United States. During and immediately after World War II, the exile mission again became a motivating force for the Polish political diaspora on many continents. It also rested at the heart of the relationship between postwar political refugees and later generations of Polish Americans.

In the nineteenth century, waves of Polish immigrants to the United States had adopted the nationalistic ideology of struggle for a free Poland.[3] American Polonia considered itself the "fourth partition of Poland," whose duty was to speak for the subjugated nation.[4] The process of nationalization of the peasant masses in America took place among "contentious organizational competition in Polish immigrant communities, immigrant parishes and schools, patriot priests, the immigrant press, and the intimidating encounter with the host society."[5] The debates over the role of Polish immigrants within their own community, as well as in relationship to the Roman Catholic Church and the homeland, were reflected in disputes between American Polonia's two largest fraternals, the Polish Roman Catholic Union (PRCU, 1873) and the Polish National Alliance (PNA, 1880). An elite collection of political émigrés active in the Polish community in the United States played a particularly important role in building national consciousness among the economic immigrants. They responded to the 1879 appeal of Agaton Giller, a political exile after the January Uprising, to organize the immigrant masses for patriotic work for Poland and to persuade them to accept the exile mission. Through the activities of those early nationalists, Polish immigrants developed a strong and meaningful relationship with the homeland. Gradually, this political culture based on the ideas of exile, displacement, and injury translated itself into New World nationalism, expressed in ethnic popular culture and literature as well as in political allegiance and relationship to the American state and its policies.[6]

Although some of the first Polish communities on American soil were established by political exiles after the failed insurrections of the nineteenth century, it was the later, more massive, and largely economic immigration that gave character to the Polish settlement in the United States.[7] About 64.5 percent of Polish immigrants worked in agriculture prior to emigration. Once they arrived in America, almost 90 percent settled in urban industrial areas, performing unskilled labor in factories in the East and Northeast. Poles also found jobs in mining and smaller industries in New England and the Middle Atlantic states. Those who decided to work in agriculture settled mostly in Michigan, Wisconsin, Illinois, and Indiana, or in smaller communities in the Connecticut River valley and upstate New York. More than 2 million immigrants left the Polish territories for America between 1871 and 1914.[8] The Polish-American community, consisting of these immigrants and their American-born children, topped the 3 million mark by 1910.[9]

Polish immigrants brought with them a traditional peasant culture based on religion (overwhelmingly Roman Catholic), a strong family structure, and a sense of community. Despite some sociological predictions of social disorganization resulting from the transition from a preindustrial agrarian setting to modern industrial life, Polonia communities survived and flourished in America. They were usually organized on the parish basis and centered on the church, its organizations, and the parish school. This parish-based structure and clerical leadership supplied the community with internal cohesion, religious and civic leaders, and space in which to practice and preserve old-country beliefs and traditions. Parish schools perpetuated these traditions in the education and upbringing of the American-born generations. Family structure adhered to the traditional bonds of extended family. Families were units whose economic survival was the responsibility of each family member. Males were the main breadwinners in the marketplace, but women and children also substantially contributed to the family budget. Moreover, women were charged with the duty of preserving the traditional values and customs within the family and passing them along to the next generation.

The neighborhoods within the parish structure became important self-sustaining areas, where small businesses and services catered to the immigrant clientele. They also housed local mutual aid and insurance organizations that later gave rise to the establishment of large Polish-American fraternals, uniting thousands of immigrants under their auspices and defining Polonia's ethnic identity. These fraternals fulfilled multiple and complex economic, social, and cultural roles. While their initial goal was to provide death benefit insurance and to cover funeral expenses, they also carried out fund raising for community purposes or the homeland. By offering participants a number of positions and functions, the organizations contributed to status competition within the community and gave an opportunity for the civic involvement of the immigrants. Fraternals also advanced the vigorous development of Polonia-run press and publishing houses that tied separate communities into a lively national network.[10]

Polish Americans, the majority of whom were employed in industry, rapidly adjusted to the demands of working-class life. Together with other blue-collar industrial workers, Poles felt the impact of economic depressions, decreasing wages, and tense labor relations. The image, held by some, of a docile Slavic worker proved unfounded. Poles participated in collective labor actions during the 1880s and the 1890s and continued their involvement in strikes during the volatile first two decades of the twentieth century.[11]

The outbreak of World War I became a test of commitment to the ideals of a free Poland for American Polonia. In an enthusiastic show of support, Polish communities developed wide-ranging humanitarian aid programs and sponsored diplomatic and political actions, led by the famous Polish pianist and statesman Ignacy Jan Paderewski. They also raised about twenty-four thousand volunteers for the Polish Army in France, of whom nearly twenty thousand went overseas under the command of General Józef Haller to participate directly in the fight for an independent Poland. By the end of the war, approximately two hundred fifteen thousand Polish Americans had served in the U.S. armed forces.[12] Polonia's financial contribution to the cause of an independent Poland proved to be no less impressive. According to some reports, Polonia raised more than $50 million for the cause, while purchasing $67 million in American Liberty Bonds and earmarking another $1.5 million specifically for the Polish Army in France. All of these funds came, as one scholar noted, from "committed immigrants, most of whom held low-paying, unskilled jobs."[13]

After the Polish state was reestablished in 1918, American Polonia had to redefine many of the goals that previously had been tightly tied to the struggle for Polish independence. Although some American Poles returned to Poland following the war, the vast majority remained in the United States. Those who returned often came back disappointed with the economic and social conditions of the country as well as its political instability. In the meantime, new immigration restrictions decreased the flow of immigrants into Polish-American communities to a trickle of about six thousand a year. Polonia increasingly turned toward its own internal affairs and developed a more domestic focus. Membership in fraternals increased significantly, and the Polonia press flourished. As Polish immigrants participated in the postwar economic boom, their communities began developing a middle class based on ethnic businesses and professional enterprises. Social mobility and the acquisition of consumer goods facilitated a growing assimilation. The newspapers gradually introduced English into their pages. The immigrants deplored the Americanization of the second generation and showed concern for the growing gap between themselves and their children. Polish-American historian Karol Wachtl best expressed those anxieties over the need to redefine an ethnic identity: "We lost our way into the future. Before, all here knew where they were going: toward free Poland! But Poland went her way and we—in a different country, in an entirely different society, have to go along different routes. And what are these routes? Not entirely Polish and not quite American."[14] As James S. Pula put it, in the 1920s the signs of assimilation were unmistakable while the "mantel [sic] of leadership passed from the immigrant to the second generation."[15]

Community leaders initiated a debate on the role of American Polonia in order to find its place in a changed international political situation as well as to face the challenges of assimilation. Their response became a slogan adopted in the 1920s with the broad support of the immigrant masses: *wychodźstwo dla wychodźstwa* (emigrants for themselves), which indicated a drastic shift in focus for Polish Americans.[16] At the same time, the creation of cultural organizations, such as the Kosciuszko Foundation, the Polish Museum of America, and the first Polish Arts Clubs, attested to increased efforts to preserve not only Polish cultural heritage, but that of Polonia as well.[17]

In the 1920s Poles in Poland faced a multitude of problems stemming from the difficult task of overcoming the grim legacy of the partitions. These problems included the unification and reconstruction of the Polish economy, the building of a democratic political system, the establishment of relations with all neighboring countries, and a variety of social and educational reforms. The 1921 census showed that 25 percent of the Polish population lived in towns, and 75 percent in the countryside. Peasants constituted 64 percent of the population, and an additional 10 percent were landless agricultural laborers. Gradual industrialization resulted in a decrease of 5 percent in the rural population between 1921 and 1938. The industrial proletariat accounted for 17 percent of the population; 5 percent were professionals and intelligentsia; 2 percent were entrepreneurs; and less than 1 percent were owners of large estates.[18] In 1931 ethnic Poles constituted 69 percent of the total population; Ukrainian, Jewish, Belorussian, German, Lithuanian, and Czech minorities formed the remaining part of society.[19]

Polish society changed dramatically during the interwar decades. Perhaps the most noticeable transformations took place in the rural population, which, despite the economic hardships, showed an increased radicalization and political involvement, particularly in the southern provinces. Land reform in 1919 and 1920, limited though it was, increased land ownership among peasants. Both rural areas and towns benefited from the reorganization of the educational system, one of the most sweeping reforms in interwar Poland. The number of schools rose considerably, and illiteracy was substantially reduced.

The Polish economy eventually revived, too, albeit after a long period of struggle to integrate the infrastructures, currencies, tax systems, and financial institutions of the three partitions. During the 1920s a series of reforms supervised by Władysław Grabski introduced the *złoty* (zloty) currency, established the Bank Polski (Bank of Poland), and initiated government investments in public works and rural improvements. In the next decade the electrification campaign, construction of the seaport in Gdynia, and establishment of the foundations for the Centralny Okręg Przemysłowy (Central Industrial Region) were among the brightest achievements of the period. Although in the late 1930s Poland was still an underdeveloped country, its economy showed strong signs of improvement.[20]

After decades of suppression by the partitioning powers, intellectual and cultural life in Poland flourished with extraordinary intensity. The twenty years between the two world wars were filled with scholarly and scientific achievements, as universities became vigorous centers of intellectual life. Talented intellectuals contributed to the expansion of journalism, book publishing, theater, film, and art exhibits, which in turn received strong support from the Polish public.

The Polish intelligentsia (*inteligencja*) led the way in the development of national culture. The intelligentsia represented a specific social stratum that developed in Poland and Russia in the second part of the nineteenth century. As a result of the political and economic changes in Poland at that time, "members of the 'déclassé' fraction of the landed nobility, seeking to maintain in an urban environment their traditional style of life, had to separate themselves from the 'bourgeois' middle class."[21] They were united in sharing a specific set of values, beliefs, moral attitudes, and political behaviors formulated by a group of intellectual leaders. Among the most significant values and goals of the intelligentsia were humanistic education and creative activity. Moreover, the members of this "charismatic stratum" saw their fundamental social role in the leadership of the nation "to its destiny." Accepting the call to serve the nation as their credo, members of intelligentsia adopted a number of national causes, including the struggle for independence and social work for the benefit of the lower classes.[22] By the end of the interwar period, the intelligentsia included urban professionals, such as doctors, lawyers, and government employees, as well as teachers, scholars, intellectuals, writers, journalists, artists, and the higher ranks of the military. They continued their traditional political and cultural leadership, replete with strong patriotic and nationalistic accents.

The changes of the interwar period influenced both those Poles who were born during the partition but then experienced twenty years of freedom, and the younger generation that was fortunate enough to grow up in an independent Poland. They witnessed the social, economic, and spiritual rebirth of the nation and participated in its growth, however uneasy and troubled it was at times. For decades afterward, émigrés were inspired by their memories of Polish modernization and its accompanying spirit of patriotism, optimism, and unrealized potential.

The war that began on the morning of September 1, 1939, ended this brief period of Polish independence. Wartime brought renewed suffering and loss. The country was again divided between Nazi Germany and the Soviet Union, and Polish citizens everywhere faced unparalleled terror. Poles suffered under the extermination policies of the German oppressor, including prisons, concentration camps, prisoner-of-war camps, slave labor, and indiscriminate killing. The Polish nation responded with a widespread resistance movement that culminated in the Warsaw uprising in 1944. In the Soviet occupation zone, Polish citizens, deprived of any legal protection, were harassed, imprisoned, and deported into brutal labor camps in Siberia. The population movements that took place in the Polish territories were unprecedented. In addition to prisoners, slave laborers, and deportees, there were civilians who crossed the Polish borders in search of safety. Polish armed forces formed in the West and later in the Middle East. All in all, about 6 million Poles remained outside Polish borders in 1945. Wherever the *polskie drogi* (Polish roads) led the refugees, they established communities and tried to repair the torn fabric of their lives. They also planned for the future, keeping Polish culture alive and taking care of the education of their children.

The war became a turning point for an entire generation. The Polish postwar diaspora had already become a reality during the war. Although emigrants did not commonly invoke the term diaspora, other Polish phrases in common use expressed a similar meaning.[23] *Emigracja wojenna, emigracja walcząca*, or *emigracja niezłomna* denoted wartime emigration, characterized by a fighting and indomitable spirit. The emigrants embraced notions of an organized transnational community deriving from a common historical experience and of the exile mission that guided and motivated this community.[24]

Polish sacrifice and contribution to the Allied war effort did not secure an independent Polish state after the war. In 1945, at the international conference at Yalta, the West agreed to abandon Poland to the Soviet sphere of influence. Hundreds of thousands of Polish veterans, refugees, deportees, and prisoners faced a difficult choice: should they return to the communist-dominated homeland or embrace exile? Most did return, but many others waited in the refugee camps, displaced persons (DP) camps, or in exile communities established during the war. International efforts slowly got under way to permanently resettle a million so-called unrepatriables from various nations. About four hundred thousand Poles were resettled in four dozen nations of the world, although some displaced Poles faced hardship and despair in the DP camps for as long as nine years. During that time Poles established communities that aided everyday survival in many ways, and, more importantly, they used the DP period to install the framework of the postwar Polish diaspora and adopted the exile mission to guide them.

After the international resettlement action had dispersed the refugees into many countries on many continents, they either joined older existing Polish communities, for example, in the United States, France, Austria, and Argentina, or built their own communities nearly from scratch, as in Australia and Great Britain. Although separated by space and borders, Polish refugees still felt a strong bond to the entire postwar diaspora. They eagerly participated in debates about international events, inspired by press reports and personal letters and contacts. Veterans associations, scouting groups, and other organizations with membership in different countries cemented ties developed during and after the war. The Polish government in exile in London provided the most important political point of gravity by claiming to represent the only legal continuation of prewar authority.

Immigration and Naturalization Service statistics indicate that about fifteen thousand Polish quota immigrants were allowed into the United States during World War II (1939–45). About seventeen thousand more came within the next three years. As a result of the enactment of the 1948 Displaced Persons Act and its 1950 amendments, close to one hundred forty thousand displaced persons born in Poland, including Polish veterans from Great Britain, arrived in the United States between 1948 and 1952. All in all, between 1940 and 1953, 178,680 quota immigrants born in Poland arrived in the United States.[25] Most of the statistics for this period (including those of the Displaced Persons Commission, or DPC, a federal body responsible for the resettlement of DPs in the United States) classified immigrants on the basis of their place of birth or last residence. Therefore, the population of immigrants born in Poland usually included Ukrainians and Polish Jews as well as ethnic Poles. According to some estimates, nearly forty thousand of the new arrivals were Polish Jews;[26] it is unclear how many were Ukrainians.[27] The ethnic Polish Christians (predominantly Roman Catholics) who are the focus of this study joined roughly 6 million Polish Americans—first-generation immigrants and their offspring born in the United States—according to the 1940 census.[28]

The group of Poles who immigrated to the United States between 1939 and 1945 included an exceptionally high number of intellectuals, artists, politicians, and people representing the Polish prewar professional middle class, or inteligencja. Most often they settled in large urban areas, especially in

New York and Chicago, forming active émigré communities for the duration of the war. Polish refugees who immigrated after 1945 were usually part of a nuclear family unit, with Polish spouses and children born (usually) outside of Poland. Polish organizations in displaced persons camps in Germany and Austria, from which most of the refugees to the United States emigrated, estimated that members of the inteligencja made up only 5 to 10 percent of the Polish DP population. Farmers comprised some 70 percent of the group, and the remainder was divided between skilled and unskilled workers. A sociological study conducted in 1971 described these emigrants as rather young (the average age was about twenty-four to thirty-five years) and fairly well educated, the majority having at least some high school and close to one-third having a university degree. Some 92 percent claimed Roman Catholicism as their religion, and a majority indicated political reasons for their emigration.[29]

Polish exiles arriving in the United States during and immediately after the war joined a generation of Polish Americans who recently had gone through significant changes. In the 1930s they had come to accept a double identity, one both Polish and American. The process is best illustrated by the relationship between American Polonia and the World Union of Poles from Abroad (Światowy Związek Polaków z Zagranicy, or Światpol). Światpol was an international organization formed in Poland with the aim to unite and coordinate the activities of Polish communities abroad in the interest of Poland and its government. In 1934 Światpol organized a congress in Warsaw attended by representatives of Polonia from all over the world. To the dismay of the organizers, the American delegation to the congress, led by Francis X. Świetlik, the grand censor of the Polish National Alliance, declined membership in Światpol.[30] "Regarding ourselves as an inseparable component of the great American nation," the statement of the American delegation announced, "we take an active and creative part in every walk of American life, thus contributing to boosting the name of Poland in our country."[31] After returning to the United States, Świetlik further justified his position: "Polonia in America is neither a Polish colony nor a national minority but a component part of the Great American Nation, proud, however, of its Polish extraction and careful to make the young generation love everything Polish."[32] Miecislaus Haiman, a prominent Polish-American historian, summed up the controversy provoked by American Polonia's refusal to become a part of Światpol:

"In the eyes of the Poles in Poland and in other countries we are still only Poles while in fact we are already Americans of Polish extraction."³³

The Great Depression hampered to some extent the process of assimilation by blocking social mobility and forcing the second generation back into the old ethnic neighborhoods, where Polish Americans, "cut off from the homogenizing influences of a consumption society, . . . once again clung to their cultural forms."³⁴ First and foremost, the depression meant hard times, unemployment, and social turmoil. Second-generation Polish Americans responded to adversity by pooling community resources and relying on family economic units, but they refused to be mere victims. In 1935 Polish women in Hamtramck, Michigan, took their protest against skyrocketing meat prices to the streets. Others actively participated in strikes and union drives, which produced a number of Polish-American union leaders, such as Leo Krzycki, Stanley Nowak, Bolesław Gebert, and Stella Nowicki. The radicalizing impact of the depression was demonstrated also by the growing membership of Poles in the Congress of Industrial Organizations (CIO). By the end of World War II, the CIO included about 6 million members, of whom approximately six hundred thousand were Polish.³⁵ Finally, the New Deal cemented Polonia's traditional adherence to the Democratic Party, even though the participation of Polish Americans in party politics remained limited.³⁶ The assimilation process of the 1920s and 1930s affected the broad masses of working-class Polish Americans, resulting in their way of life being "'made in America,' just as the coal that they mined or the steel ingots that they rolled."³⁷

The outbreak of the war revived the Polish communities in the United States. American Polonia, although internally not homogenous, contributed generously to humanitarian causes, which included support for Polish refugees and prisoners as well as (whenever possible) for the Polish population in Poland. Polish Americans also took an interest in international matters that could affect Poland, and in 1944 they formed a powerful lobby: the Polish American Congress (PAC). After the end of the war, American Polonia worked for a change in immigration laws and for the admittance of European displaced persons to the United States. Polonia's activism worked within the American framework to a greater extent than it had during the previous world war. For young Polish-American men and women, military service meant accelerated assimilation.³⁸ After the war, taking advantage of generous veterans benefits and the booming economy, Polish Americans displayed noticeable upward social mobility. Greater numbers of second-generation Polish-American males moved into white-collar occupations, and women, who had entered the work force during the depression and the war years, tended to stay there. Finally, many second-generation Polish Americans left ethnic communities for the suburbs, "for a slice of the promised 'good life' and, frankly, a chance to leave their sometimes embarrassing hyphenate ethnic past far behind."[39]

During the war Polish Americans were keenly aware of the plight of Polish refugees scattered around the globe and carried out successful charitable actions through a variety of organizations. They were one of the first ethnic groups that heralded the cause of European displaced persons and lobbied tirelessly for a change in the immigration laws, which would allow their admission to the United States. After the 1948 Displaced Persons Act had been passed, American Polonia mobilized itself for an unprecedented resettlement effort. Throughout the war and the early postwar years, Polish Americans revived their long tradition of activism on behalf of Poland. Decrying Poland's loss of independence at Yalta and responding to international Cold War pressures, the majority of Polonia displayed vivid anticommunist sentiments. As U.S. citizens, they aspired to leadership in the struggle for Poland, and the DP cause became one of the important points of their mission.

The arrival of political refugees, instead of providing anticipated fresh reinforcements for Polonia, brought tension and conflict between the two groups. The refugees based their exile identity on the common experience of life in independent Poland before the war and on their wartime suffering and struggle. Neither of these experiences had been shared by American Polonia. Tensions heightened also for other reasons, some linked to the finer points of the exile mission and others connected to the social characteristics of the two populations. Lack of adequate knowledge about the history of each group, competition for political and cultural leadership, level of assimilation, class differences, social mobility, and the issue of loyalty to the Polish government in exile and to the rest of the diaspora were all factors that contributed to the friction.

Most significantly, the new arrivals did not consider themselves simply new immigrants, but rather a special category of immigrants: political refugees. This distinction had been adopted during the war and especially during the DP period of increased politicization of the refugee masses. The refugees counterposed the concept of political exile and that of the earlier economic "emigration for bread." Tapping the Polish Romantic tradition, they considered their political motivation a nobler and more legitimate reason for emigration. In their own eyes, it gave them a respectable identity, one easily compatible with the inspiring legacy of historical struggle for Poland's independence. Armed with claims to European and Polish high culture—supposedly superior to the plebeian roots of American civilization—the refugees used the exile mission to ensure the survival of their Polish identity. For example, the First Convention of the New Emigration, which took place in New Bedford, Massachusetts, in September 1950, adopted a resolution explicitly stating its character: "The new emigrants regard themselves as a political emigration and strongly denounce tendencies to define them as stateless or economic emigrants."[40] Stanisław Kwaśniewski, the author of the 1948 poem "Polscy Kombatanci," put the matter even more succinctly. "They are coming for freedom, not dollars," he wrote about the postwar arrivals, sharply distinguishing them from the turn-of-the-century peasant economic immigrants.[41]

For these political refugees the exile mission provided justification for their refusal to return to Poland and called for action on behalf of the homeland, which had been subdued by the communist oppressor. Poland's independence was central to both political and social thinking, and one's work for Poland defined the measure of one's patriotism.[42] Political action focused on lobbying Western governments and public opinion through constant reminders of the Polish nation's historical significance and its contribution to victory in World War II. The West was to be warned against the dangers of communism and informed of the hardships of life in Poland under the communist regime, for which those who had condoned Yalta were held responsible. Émigré Poles believed that they had the right to represent Polish interests in the West and that the communists' claim to power should be officially delegitimized. Some of their more detailed demands included the repudiation of Yalta, the return of Western recognition to the Polish government in exile, international guarantees for Poland's border with Germany, the return of Poland's eastern territories lost to the Soviet Union, an investigation of the Katyń massacre, and the release of political prisoners.[43] The responsibility of this work for Poland fell on all exiles. While the exile leaders conducted direct political lobbying, the rank-and-file refugees attempted to inform and influence Western public opinion. In order to increase the effectiveness of their political action, the exiles recognized the need to cooperate with older immigrant waves and strove to preserve ties to the entire postwar diaspora, both through organizational and personal means.

This focus on the issues of the homeland and the diaspora had added expediency in the first decade after the war, because of the unstable political situation. Many exiles believed that their sojourn in foreign countries would be temporary and that when another war ended the communist occupation of Poland, they would return to a free homeland.[44] The myth of impending return prompted efforts to build strong exile communities, which could facilitate necessary political action as well as preserve Polish culture. The exiles formed separate organizations to fulfill those goals as well as to meet more pragmatic needs, such as securing housing, jobs, schools for children, language classes, and loans to buy furniture and other necessities, or finding churches and ethnic support groups.

The exile mission strongly emphasized both preservation and development of Polish culture in exile. The importance of this task for the spiritual survival of the nation had been clear since the partitions of Poland in the eighteenth and nineteenth centuries. The exiles felt particularly responsible for the protection and nurture of Polish high culture: the literary language, artistic expression, as well as intellectual thought and scientific achievement. The wartime extermination of Poland's intelligentsia, the Sovietization of political and economic life, and the suppression of Polish culture gave this goal a renewed sense of urgency. The patriotic upbringing of the next generation became another significant element of the exile mission. The youth had to be prepared to return to Poland or to continue the mission in exile. Children and young people were expected to know the Polish language; to be familiar with Polish history, traditions, and customs; and to adopt patriotic attitudes toward the homeland of their parents.

A sense of history and historical memory has always been vital to the Polish experience. The memory of past glories helped the nation endure the partitions. After World War II, the exile mission recognized the momentousness of history and ranked it high on the agenda. The war effort and the refugee experience yielded themselves to placement within the larger history of the Polish nation's sacrifice and survival. Attention to history and the lessons learned from it permeated much of the exile discourse, providing examples, comparisons, and sometimes predictions for the future.

The mission's strength rested within family and community, since individuals could carry out its particular components on both the local and the personal levels. The leaders were usually members of the intelligentsia, prewar activists, and politicians, but the vast majority of rank-and-file refugees also interpreted their refusal to return to communist Poland as a political decision. In the context of Polish history and the Cold War, exile politicized the diaspora and particular communities within it.[45]

Differences between the refugees and Polish Americans intensified in the conflict-prone environment of the resettlement program. The bipolar image of the new arrivals as victims and as sturdy immigrant material, and the specific needs of the refugees proved difficult for Polish Americans to absorb, while the resettlement program stretched thin their resources and put enormous pressure on the community. Without fully grasping the significance of the wartime experiences of the refugees and the intensity of their commitment to the exile mission, Polish Americans too often acted in dismissive and patronizing ways. The refugees, on the other hand, retaliated with accusations of political inactivity, cultural backwardness, and advanced Americanization.

While the exiles' presence both energized and challenged the community, the majority of Polish Americans represented by the Polish American Congress revitalized the main elements of the exile mission derived from their earlier Polonia tradition. For example, Polish Americans' vision of the struggle for Poland did not include the myth of return nor did it rely on close cooperation with the rest of the postwar diaspora. Polish Americans were ready to assume leadership in the struggle for Poland, but as American citizens who counted on American foreign policy and who recognized the Polish government in exile as an important symbol rather than as a sovereign political authority. In the cultural realm, working-class Polish Americans felt protective of their folk culture and confined their social and cultural activities to the traditional forms and structures of the existing Polonia organizations.

The debate between the exiles and Polish Americans, which took place in the 1940s and early 1950s, polarized Polonia but also provided a unique chance to explain and to negotiate the exile mission as well as to confront their ethnic identity. The process was not easy, and in some instances the differences would never be overcome; but by 1956, American Polonia and Polish exiles in the United States had managed to negotiate many, if not all, points of the exile mission. Changes within Poland and the stabilization of the international situation reinforced the values that both groups held in common: devotion to Poland and readiness to work together on the nation's behalf.

1 ॥ "Smoke over America, blood over Europe"
World War II and the Polish Diaspora

War in Poland and the Creation of the Wartime Diaspora

> One day very early in the morning some stubborn knocking at the door woke us up. My husband, surprised, goes, opens the door and after a short conversation, comes back inside, holding a piece of paper in his hand. Looking straight at me he says: "This is my draft card to the army. Germans entered our lands without declaration; it is war...." My hands began shaking, my heart began pounding. We stood for a moment in silence, staring at each other.[1]

THE DAY WAS SEPTEMBER 1, 1939. Helena Podkopacz saw her husband for the last time. His military transport was bombed, and he was killed instantly. She was left alone in a small village in eastern Poland with two little children and an ailing mother, while German air raids on all major cities and military installations were destroying Polish ground forces. A counteroffensive on the river Bzura broke down by midmonth, and other points of defense in the country fell one after another when the Soviet army entered the Polish territories on September 17, cutting off escape routes and closing the trap on the surviving Polish forces. On September 28, Warsaw, although furiously defended by its civilian population, surrendered to the Germans, while the Polish garrison on the peninsula of Hel on the Baltic held out until October 2. The president of Poland and Polish government officials crossed the border to Romania, and, after a brief internment there, they continued on to France, where the government was reconstituted. The last Polish military unit in the field capitulated at Kock on October 5, although some guerrilla forces fought for many more months. Poland lost some sixty thousand men killed in action and another one hundred forty thousand wounded, in addition to high civilian casualties.[2] By the end of the campaign, Poland was divided into a German occupation zone in the west and a Soviet zone in the east.

The formal division of Poland between German and Soviet conquerors became a fact with the signing of a convention between them on September 28, 1939. The demarcation line that ran along the rivers Bug and San became the official frontier between the Third Reich and the Soviet Union. Each occupation zone received a different administration and became subject to the unrestrained terror of the invaders. The territories in the Soviet zone were divided into three areas. The northern area was granted to the Republic of Lithuania, eventually annexed by the USSR. The central area was granted directly to the Belorussian SSR. The southern part, containing the city of Lwów, was attached as "Western Ukraine" to the Ukrainian SSR. Fraudulent and openly coerced plebiscites organized by the NKVD (National Commissariat of Internal Affairs, the Soviet secret police) on all three territories resulted in the "official request" of the populations to admit the occupied lands to the Soviet Union, a request that was promptly granted.[3] The Polish lands under German occupation were divided into two separate areas. The western and northern parts were annexed directly into the Third Reich. The remaining, larger area formed the General Government (Generalna Gubernia) headed by Hans Frank, governor-general. The Polish population of both areas was subject to lawless and cruel Nazi terror, which increased systematically from the late fall of 1939.

Beginning in November 1939, shortly after Hans Frank took office, the Nazis undertook a systematic extermination of the Polish nation's leadership. The city of Warsaw's president, Stefan Starzyński—distinguished in his defense of the city—and thousands of other Poles were promptly arrested. The Nazis put to death about thirty-five hundred political and municipal leaders in a mass execution in Palmiry Forest near Warsaw. One hundred eighty-three professors from the Jagiellonian University in Kraków were captured as a part of a special action (*Sonderaktion*). Some were later released, but many were transported directly to death camps in Germany or were delivered to the Gestapo (the German secret police), a fate that, in reality, also meant death. These first acts of terror were then followed by arrests of members of the Polish intelligentsia, the clergy, political activists, students, and anyone suspected of having leadership skills, whose names appeared on specially prepared lists used during spring 1940 and summer of 1941. The captives were then placed in German prisons and concentration camps, especially Dachau, Buchenwald, and Sachsenhausen.[4]

Nazi authorities closed Polish universities, schools, museums, research institutes, theaters, archives, libraries, publishing houses, and presses. Poles were not allowed to own radios or to listen to Polish music. Food was rationed, and the work order included all citizens. In December 1939 Germans introduced the rule of collective responsibility that they later used with horrifying frequency; in revenge for the wounding of a German soldier, they executed 107 Poles in Wawer near Warsaw. In January of the following year, plans were laid for the building of a concentration camp in Auschwitz (Oświęcim), where some 1.5 million people were to perish by the time the war was over.[5] The terror further intensified in 1941, when an arbitrary German law allowed for indiscriminate street executions, imprisonment and torture, and street hunts (łapanki). Rural pacifications decimated the Polish population in hundreds of villages. The largest systematic action was a 1942 campaign in the Zamość region, where hundreds of thousands of Polish peasants were forcibly evicted to make room for German and Ukrainian settlers, while their children were sent to the Reich for Germanization purposes.[6]

Approximately 2 million Jews who found themselves on the territory of the Generalna Gubernia (many resettled from the area incorporated into Reich) were officially identified by a yellow Star of David worn on the clothing. Their possessions and businesses were confiscated. At the beginning of 1940 the Germans created work camps for Jews that did not differ much from concentration camps. In the ghettos created in many Polish cities, Jewish citizens were isolated and terrorized. They lived in terrible conditions, dying of hunger, brutal work, and epidemic diseases. In the spring of 1942 the Nazis began the introduction of the "Final Solution": the ghettos were liquidated, and their inhabitants murdered en masse in concentration camps. Facing the liquidation of the largest Warsaw ghetto in April 1943, the Jewish population struck back against their oppressors in a military uprising, which the Nazis suppressed with great brutality.[7]

The Polish nation responded to the Nazi terror with the formation of an extensive network of the resistance organizations. Already by the end of September 1939, the Służba Zwycięstwu Polski (Polish Victory Service)—the largest underground organization and the basis for the future Armia Krajowa (AK, Home Army)—had been established and had initiated its activities. Eventually, a large percentage of the Polish population directly participated in or supported what became the strongest resistance movement on the territory of occupied Europe. The Home Army, together with other guerrilla forces (Bataliony Chłopskie—Peasant Battalions; Gwardia Ludowa—People's Guard; and Narodowe Siły Zbrojne—National Armed Forces), participated in a number of actions, including derailing trains and blowing up bridges to slow down German military transports, executing high Nazi officials, freeing Polish prisoners, and engaging local German units in direct battles. The resistance movement also contributed to uplifting the spirits of the oppressed population through the organization of underground schools, theaters, presses, and publications, the protection of Polish national art treasures, the dissemination of information on Allied victories, or the encouragement of small acts of sabotage and slowdowns in work for the German economy. Polish resistance fighters also passed information on German military movements to the Allies. Youth from the Związek Harcerstwa Polskiego (ZHP, Polish scouting), which during the occupation reorganized itself into the storm troops known as Szare Szeregi (Grey Ranks), worked within the Home Army.[8]

When the Soviet offensive approached Warsaw in July 1944, the leadership of the Home Army decided to call for an uprising in the capital. Fighting began on the streets of Warsaw on August 1, 1944, and lasted for sixty-three days of heroic struggle to wrest Warsaw from German hands. After initial successes on the Polish side, the Nazis gradually regained control of the city, killing both Polish soldiers and the civilian population, while the Soviet army waited on the other bank of the Vistula River. Deprived of help, short on munitions, food, water, and medicines, the Warsaw Uprising collapsed in the fall of 1944. In an act of revenge, the Germans evacuated the city and undertook its systematic destruction, razing it to the ground.[9]

The Nazi occupation caused tremendous population movements that resulted in masses of Poles remaining outside Polish borders, forming the bedrock of the Polish postwar diaspora. The first waves of Poles left Nazi-occupied Poland in September 1939, and each following year brought more forced population movements out of the country.[10] In October 1939 the Polish government, after evacuating to France, reached an agreement with the

French government to raise a Polish army there. By early summer of the next year, more than forty-four thousand Polish immigrants residing in France had enlisted, joined by about forty thousand officers and soldiers initially interned in Romania and Hungary as well as some eighteen hundred who escaped from occupied Poland.[11] In June 1940 Polish forces in France numbered more than eighty-four thousand men. Of that number, more than thirty thousand were brought over to Britain after the collapse of France in 1940, and these troops were reinforced by volunteers recruited from refugees and escapees from Poland.[12] The Polish army under British command (London became the new seat of the Polish government in exile) was reorganized in Scotland as the First Polish Corps. Polish soldiers participated in battles on several different fronts. In the Battle of Britain in 1940, Polish fighter pilots accounted for some 15 percent of enemy losses.[13] The First Polish Armored Division, under the command of General Stanisław Maczek, fought during the invasion of Nazi-occupied Europe and distinguished itself in battles on the territories of Belgium and France. After the capitulation of Germany, the division was stationed in the British zone of occupation in Haren, which was renamed Maczków in honor of the Polish commander.[14]

These military units in the West were not the only Polish soldiers outside of Poland after the end of the war. Combatants captured by the Germans in September 1939 had been interned in *Oflagen* (POW camps for officers) and *Stalagen* (POW camps for noncommissioned soldiers), and prisoners in the latter were forced to work in the German economy. The total number of Polish POWs taken in the initial invasion came close to four hundred twenty thousand. In the fall of 1944 some seventeen thousand insurgents of the Home Army who had fought in the Warsaw Uprising joined the imprisoned Polish soldiers.[15] There was also a separate category of Polish citizens who had been forcibly conscripted into German military units. Most of them came from the areas that had been annexed directly to the Reich, and were considered "ethnically German." In sum, between two hundred thousand and two hundred fifty thousand Poles served in German forces during the war.[16]

The largest category of migrants from Nazi-occupied Poland included people who worked for the German war machine as slave laborers. A few thousand accepted offers of work in the Reich, compelled by deteriorating living conditions in late 1939 and early 1940 and lured by German promises of a quick return to Poland. Some decided to join family members deported to or imprisoned in Germany. Wacław Jędrzejczak's family, for example, made such a decision. After Wacław's father had participated in the September campaign, he was imprisoned in a POW camp in Germany and then was forced to work for a German farmer. Despite receiving help from their extended family, Wacław's mother and her two sons could barely support themselves. The reunification of the family in the Reich allowed them to survive the harsh economic reality of the war years.[17] But low numbers of volunteers resulted in increased physical coercion, including penalties of prison and death camps for those who refused to comply. When even those methods did not bring about the expected results, the German authorities organized łapanki, the infamous manhunts in which they rounded up hostages in the streets and transported them to the Reich. The precise number of Polish citizens of various ethnic and religious backgrounds who remained in Germany as slave laborers is hard to estimate, but historians suggest that close to 3 million of them were at some point employed in the German war economy.[18]

Political prisoners and prisoners in concentration camps constituted another large group of people deported to Germany from Polish lands. Arrests and deportations were often elements of mass actions against the Polish population, including those in November 1939 and the mass deportations to concentration camps that took place in 1942 and 1943. Until the end of the war, both civilians and members of the Polish underground fell victim to this manifestation of Nazi terror. Victor Bik, for example, was arrested in January 1944, at the train station in Częstochowa while seeing off a friend. For the next three weeks he was brutally interrogated and tortured at Gestapo headquarters and then transported to the concentration camp in Gross-Rosen. "As soon as our transport arrived," he remembered later, "even before the door of the boxcar opened, one could hear barking dogs and loud 'barking' commands of waiting SS guards, who marched us to the camp, about two miles from the railroad station." What followed was his "induction to the existence in the concentration camp":

> About 250 of us were assembled to the big hall.... For the last time I heard my name before becoming just a number. This was call to shower room or should I say to another form of torture station. Stripped of everything, each of us underwent the assembly kind of processing, executed by the inmates under ever present supervision of SS guards. First step cutting hair... and of course, shaving of all private parts. No change of razor

blade, who knows for how many victims. I received rather harsh treatment because I was perceived as "grosse bandite" on account of my blue and black back and buttocks from torture by Gestapo the day before. Next, actual shower consisting of a burst of very hot water followed by a burst of ice cold water and naked step outside and wait in the formation by five until column of one hundred was moved to the next barrack. It was winter: February 1944.[19]

In the fall of 1944, after the collapse of the Warsaw Uprising, about sixty-eight thousand Poles from Warsaw were placed in German death camps. Among them was Tadeusz Gubala, a soldier of the Home Army, who, by a lucky accident, was captured in a group of civilians. He was transported to Bergen-Belsen and made to work together with other prisoners on the railway in Lehrte during frequent bombing raids by the approaching Allies.[20] Two other young *powstańcy* (insurgents), Jerzy Bigosiński and Tadeusz G., surrendered along with thousands of other soldiers of the Home Army after the uprising and were imprisoned in POW camps in Fallingsbostel and Sandbostel, respectively. They were only fifteen and sixteen years old, and throughout the war they had actively served in the Szare Szeregi and the AK resistance.[21]

Including those Poles who served out sentences in German prisons, the total number of Polish citizens deported to concentration camps in Germany and Austria was greater than two hundred thousand. In the last months of the war, the retreating Germans imposed even more inhuman conditions and treatment on tens of thousands of Polish prisoners, who were either immediately killed or transported (often on foot or in overcrowded cattle cars) to the territory of Germany, with the intention to eliminate eyewitnesses of Nazi terror.[22]

A special category of people forced to leave Poland as a result of the Nazi occupation were those whom the German authorities had decided to subject to the Germanization process. They included families from the ethnically mixed territories of Silesia, Pomerania, and Kashubia, who were transported to the Reich and resettled under special supervision, far from any Polish slave labor communities. Some seven thousand young Polish girls were selected for Germanization and placed in German homes between 1941 and 1942. Finally, the Germans deported about two hundred thousand Polish children to the Reich with the intention of Germanizing them.[23]

living and working conditions for the Polish population in Germany Most Oflagen introduced harsh discipline and very limited food ra- : Oflag in Sandbostel became particularly famous for its lack of food ear starvation of the prisoners. Polish officers had only very restricted privileges, but, in compliance with the 1929 Geneva convention, they ,wed to develop limited forms of culture and education, such as the on of internal bulletins and the establishment of libraries, amateur ·oups, sports teams, or educational courses. The clandestine resis-)vement led mainly by the Home Army penetrated many Oflagen, sulted in the creation of small underground organizations.[24]

ᴇ laborers faced much hardship and oppression. Most were hungry reated on a daily basis, deprived of any rights or protection. They to exhaustion and experienced repeated physical punishment and ιborers could not marry, worship freely, establish schools, travel, or ι any economic activity. Arbitrary German laws subjected them to ecution for many transgressions, including sexual relationships with ɩ. The sharpest measure of cruelty was the separation of infants born . women workers in order to Germanize them or to kill the weaker ɔugh lethal injection. The same fate also awaited seriously ill adult ιls. About one hundred forty thousand slave laborers from Polish ɟ several thousand newborns perished in Germany during the war; those who survived remained either ill or crippled for the rest of s.[25]

;en-Belsen, Buchenwald, Dachau, Flossenburg, Gross-Rosen, Mau- Neuengamme, Ravensbrück, and Sachsenhausen were among the)ncentration camps in Germany and Austria, and held more than two thousand persons born in Poland. The inhuman treatment and cruelty ɔcaust victims experienced in the concentration camps defy imagina- :ematic extermination of the prisoners was intertwined with their un- us use in the German war economy, without any regard for human)ite those brutal conditions, some prisoners created small secret orga- ; within the camps, specializing in passing information and keeping irits of their fellow prisoners. Others engaged in the so-called *szkoła* ι (walking school), when university professors and other teachers ssed on their knowledge to students during walks.[26]

lian refugees also fled Poland through various channels. The majority of those persons who were temporarily out of country at the outbreak of the war remained abroad. A large number of refugees followed the retreating Polish army and government officials to Romania and Hungary in September 1939. Some—a majority of them young men determined to join Polish military forces in the West—managed to leave occupied Poland through the so-called green border, that is, by illegally crossing into Romania and Hungary. Finally, a small number of civilians were able to leave the country at the very outset of the occupation, or even later, with false passports.[27]

In order to survive, civilian refugees sought any available jobs. Young men usually joined the Polish army in the West; some Poles in France and Spain established very successful intelligence networks, working for the Allies; and others joined foreign resistance movements, for example, in France, Italy, Greece, Yugoslavia, and Albania. Others worked for different units of the Polish government in exile, for the press, or in schools. Professionals and artists tried to continue their occupations. For example, Irena Koprowska, a Polish physician, found temporary employment as a doctor in an insane asylum in France. Irena Lorentowicz, a painter, interior decorator, and stage designer who had been on a scholarship in Paris at the outbreak of the war, worked in Portugal, painting furniture for wealthy families. Others accepted any available jobs, used family resources salvaged from Poland, and called on friends and business connections in European countries.[28] Many of the Polish refugees in western Europe fled before the advancing German army and immigrated to Canada, Argentina, Brazil, Colombia, Mexico, and Uruguay. For some, the South American countries became a permanent home; a large group of them, however, gradually arrived in the United States.

Wherever a Polish exile community took shape, the refugees strove to establish some kind of organization that included cultural and political institutions, a press, book publishing, and schools. In Hungary, Romania, France, Switzerland, and Great Britain, the refugees published newspapers and literary journals, created theater groups, revived political parties, and taught Polish children and youth in networks of elementary and high schools.[29] Exiled Polish intellectuals formed a university in Paris in December 1939; when France fell, they organized several higher learning institutions in Great Britain, including a medical academy at the University of Edinburgh, a Polish teachers' college, a department of veterinary studies, a law school, a business school, a technical school, as well as a military school and an air force school.

Polish soldiers and officers interned in neutral Switzerland at the beginning of the war enrolled in three Swiss universities and received more than 350 university diplomas and degrees between 1940 and 1945. The United States, Great Britain, and Switzerland became centers of research that gathered exiled scientists and intellectuals who desired to continue their scholarly work.[30]

To sum up, as a result of forced population movements from the lands of Nazi-occupied Poland, about 4 million Polish citizens were outside Polish borders at the end of the war. Ninety percent of them were slave laborers.[31]

Poles in the Soviet occupation zone did not fare much better than their counterparts in the Generalna Gubernia. In the fall of 1939 the Soviets captured more than one hundred ninety thousand Polish soldiers and lower-ranking officers and held them in camps located in Soviet territory. The prisoners were hungry, inadequately clad, overworked, and tortured. After mid-1940, they were gradually freed from the camps and transferred as civilians to perform heavy labor for the Soviet economy. About fifteen thousand Polish officers were placed in three camps in Kozielsk, Starobielsk, and Ostaszków. Between April and June of 1940, the Soviet NKVD executed 14,552 of these officers, including 12 generals. The Germans discovered their mass graves in the Katyń Forest in 1943, but Soviet authorities denied any responsibility until 1990.[32] About three hundred fifty thousand civilian Poles were incarcerated in Soviet prisons and penal camps, accused of activities against the Soviet Union. The death toll among these prisoners was extremely high; for example the death rate in some of the harshest prisons in Kolyma or Chukotka reached a full 90 percent.[33]

Helena Podkopacz and her family lived in western Ukraine. In June 1940 they were crowded into cattle cars and transported to Siberia under inhuman conditions. They were part of one of the major deportation waves in February, April, and June 1940 that decimated the Polish population of the eastern territories of prewar Poland. Estimates differ among authors trying to appraise the total of the deported population. The most commonly accepted figures indicate that between 1939 and 1941 the Soviets deported about 1.7 million Polish citizens. About 60 percent of those were ethnic Poles, 20 percent Jews, 15 percent Ukrainians and Russians, and about 4 percent Belorussians. More than 66 percent of those deported were male. Close to three hundred eighty thousand were children, and one hundred eighty-four thousand were more than fifty years old.[34] Polish citizens, faced with brutal living and working conditions and inhuman treatment by Soviet camp officials, died of starvation, malnutrition, exposure, exhaustion, and epidemics. According to some conservative estimates, two out of every ten people deported lost their lives in Siberia.[35]

Olga Tubielewicz's husband, Jan, worked as a postmaster in Telechany in the Pinsk region. The Tubielewicz family avoided deportation until early summer 1941. In June 1941 the NKVD burst into their house at night, arrested and took away Jan, and ordered Olga to pack some bare necessities for herself, her two children, and mother-in-law. "I, my husband's elderly mother, and my children all went to our bedroom, knelt in front of the picture of the Virgin Mary of Perpetual Help, cried, and prayed.... After they took my husband, I could not move or pack anything," recalled Olga. They spent the night in cattle cars in the train station. The next morning's news electrified everyone: war between Germany and the Soviet Union had just broken out. Olga and the other deportees heard German planes circling over the station, which was a natural target for bombing. "If we die," she thought, "at least it will be in our own land." Despite the danger, the transport made it through to Siberia and to a work camp in the Altai Mountains, where the family was forced to perform slave labor in the forest.[36]

The outbreak of the German-Soviet war in June 1941 prevented the total annihilation of the deported Polish population. Entering the anti-Nazi coalition, on July 30, 1941, Stalin signed a Polish-Soviet treaty providing for the formation of the Polish Army in Russia and for the release of Polish citizens from labor camps, prisons, and exile.[37] After the news was announced to the deportees, large groups of Poles began to travel toward the south, where General Władysław Anders was forming the Polish army and setting up assembly centers. Chaos and destruction accompanied their odyssey: the Polish government in London was unable to provide any substantial aid, and Soviet officials did nothing to facilitate their movements. Hunger, violence, cold, heat, disease, and exhaustion resulted in a rising death toll as Poles arrived in the Central Asian republics of the Soviet Union.[38] Conflicts about the organization and use of the Polish army as well as the tragic situation of the civilian population resulted in the decision to move all Poles out of the Soviet Union and into Iran. During two large-scale operations in March-April and August 1942, about one hundred fifteen thousand people—including forty thousand civilians, mainly women and children—were evacuated from the USSR.[39]

The evacuees stopped first in several refugee camps in Iran, including Tehran, Ahwaz, Ashabad, Isfahan, and other places. The Polish population was in urgent need of food and clothing, but especially medical attention. Most were exhausted after the strenuous trip from Siberia and years of malnutrition and mistreatment. Red Cross hospitals quickly filled to capacity with Polish children suffering from serious diseases. The surviving children entered a system of kindergartens and schools established by devoted Polish teachers and educators, themselves refugees from Siberia. Close to two thousand children joined Polish scouting groups organized in Iran. Adult refugees had to deal with grief, look for lost family members, and plan for the future. Prewar political activists recruited new members to their parties. Scientists established the Towarzystwo Studiów Irańskich (Association of Iranian Studies) that sponsored research into the biology, geography, and geology of the Middle East, published the scholarly journal *Studia Irańskie* (Iranian Studies), and in cooperation with the University of Tehran organized a popular lecture series.[40]

Great Britain accepted about six hundred fifty Polish orphan children and some of the teachers caring for them in a refugee camp in Balachadi, India. Despite the unstable military situation in 1942, more Poles were evacuated from the Soviet Union and arrived in refugee camps in Karachi. A year later, more than two thousand Polish orphans and mothers with children were placed in a camp in Malir. Valivade became home to about twenty-five hundred Polish refugees, some of them from camps in Iran.[41]

The largest number of Polish refugee camps serving the Siberian deportees was located in the eastern part of Africa: Uganda, Kenya, Tanganyika, South Africa, South and North Rhodesia. Between 1942 and mid-1944, East Africa hosted more than thirteen thousand Polish refugees, who, like their compatriots in India, formed schools, churches, hospitals, and cultural organizations. Stefan Remiarz, for example, was only three years old when the war broke out in 1939. His entire family was deported from the Wilno area to Siberia. After his father and older brothers joined the Anders Army, Stefan and his mother were placed in refugee camps in Tanganyika, where they remained until 1948. Stefan remembers fondly his African experience, despite primitive living conditions in small huts made of clay and straw, without running water, electricity, or windows. He received excellent care and education in a Polish school, where nuns working as teachers drilled the children in Polish grammar and literature.[42] Several hundred more Polish children arrived in Pahiatua, New Zealand in 1944, where they enjoyed hospitality of the New Zealand government. There were also Polish children and women living in a large camp in Santa Rosa, Mexico, near León.

After experiencing life under Soviet communism firsthand, not many of these refugees returned to Poland after the war. Some of them remained in their countries of first resettlement; others were offered refuge in Great Britain and its dominions, Canada and Australia; and residents of the Santa Rosa camp as well as Polish orphans from India and Africa were directly admitted to the United States. Many other refugees eventually arrived in America, emigrating from other countries as the opportunity arose. Helena Podkopacz, for example, after the loss of one son to disease during the exodus from the Soviet Union and a dramatic search for another lost on the way, was sponsored by her sister and arrived in Minneapolis, Minnesota, in 1950. After a prolonged sojourn in India, Olga Tubielewicz's son was brought to the United States by the Polish National Alliance and placed with a group of other boys in Polish schools in Orchard Lake, Michigan. Olga and her daughter Roma arrived in Minnesota in 1947, sponsored by a family member who had resided in the United States since before World War I. It took another four years for her to reunite with her husband, who, having survived Soviet captivity, had joined the Anders Army. Stefan Remiarz's father decided to return to Poland, but his older brothers settled in Great Britain, and Stefan and his mother joined them there. After a few years, disappointed with poor economic opportunities, the family gradually immigrated to the United States.[43]

The new Polish army was initially formed on the territory of the Soviet Union and consisted of deportees and prisoners freed under the Sikorski-Maiski agreement of 1941. Polish General Władysław Anders took command. After leaving the Soviet Union, the army was eventually incorporated into the British forces in the Middle East and later reorganized as the Second Polish Corps. It also included the Carpathian Brigade, which already had distinguished itself in battle at Tobruk and other places in North Africa.[44] The Second Corps participated in the Italian campaign, earning fame at the battles of Monte Cassino, Bologna, Ancona, Anzio, and the Gothic Line. After the defeat of Italy, the corps performed a year of occupation duties there, and in the late summer and early autumn of 1946, was brought to England in its entirety.[45]

The composition and character of the Second Corps were notable for several reasons. A majority of its members was from the eastern territories of Poland that were annexed by the Soviet Union at the end of war. They had shared the experiences of the deportation period and felt a common hatred of Russia and communism. Heavy fighting in Italy further cemented the brotherhood of arms among the soldiers, who were fully devoted to their commanding officers and especially to General Anders. The Second Corps, "never in close touch with G.H.Q. in London, . . . evolved on its own, with its own schools, theater, newspapers and tradition."[46] The vibrant cultural life of the Second Corps put its stamp on Polish refugee communities at every stage of their exile. While still stationed in the Middle East, a large group of Polish journalists within the Second Corps began the publication of several journals directed toward both civilian and military audiences, and toward children as well. These publishing activities resulted in the appearance of both new and reprinted Polish-language books that were especially welcomed by the mushrooming Polish schools and libraries. The Second Corps also sponsored an active film group and three theater groups that offered entertainment for troops and civilians alike.[47]

During their Italian sojourn, the ranks of the Second Corps swelled with new volunteers. Tadeusz G. arrived from Sandbostel, an Oflag in which he and many other Warsaw Uprising soldiers had been imprisoned until the liberation of Germany. "I was young, ready for adventure and some sightseeing. DP Germany seemed stagnant, while the legendary Second Corps seemed to offer exciting opportunities," he recalled.[48] Some of these opportunities were, for example, high-school-level education for the soldiers in the Polish gymnasiums in Alessano, Mottola, Rome, and Porto San Giorgio, or enrollment in Italian universities, sponsored and financed by the education department of the Second Corps. Another was work for the new Polish publishing house (Instytut Literacki, or "Casa Editrice Letters," 1946-47), whose editorial staff, led by Jerzy Giedroyć, put out twenty-eight books and the first issues of *Kultura* (Culture), the most important émigré journal in the West, later published in Paris.[49] Resettled in Britain together with other Polish military units, the Second Corps became the backbone of the Polish community and Polish veteran organizations.[50] A substantial number of these veterans immigrated to the United States in the early 1950s, after the amendments to the Displaced Persons Act were passed. On the basis of that law,

Zygmunt Tubielewicz left Great Britain and joined his family in Saint Paul, Minnesota, in 1951.

The Second Corps also included units of the Pomocnicza Służba Kobiet (PSK or *Pestki*, Women's Auxiliary Service), later the Pomocnicza Służba Wojskowa Kobiet (PSWK, Women's Auxiliary Military Service). The first attempts at organizing women in the Polish military were made in France in the winter of 1940, but the fall of France and evacuation to Great Britain prevented full execution of the plan. The agreement with the Soviet government for the formation of a Polish army on the territory of the USSR did not provide specifically for women's service; the Polish command, however, interpreted the phrase "Polish citizens" eligible for service as including women. One of the motivations behind the decision to organize women into military units in September 1941, was the need to protect the largest possible group of Polish deportees. Between 1941 and 1945, about sixty-seven hundred women served in different branches of the Polish military in the West, both in the Second Corps and in other Polish military formations in France and Great Britain. Polish women completed basic military training and were employed in transportation as truck drivers and transport plane pilots, in the signal corps, in administration and billeting, as well as in kitchens and provisioning. They also staffed canteens, common rooms, and moving libraries, and organized cultural events and leisure activities. Perhaps the largest area of military activity for Polish women was health care, in which they served as doctors, dentists, and nurses. In addition to those duties, Polish servicewomen took up responsibilities for the care of mothers and children as well as for large groups of orphaned children and youth. They ran kindergartens, schools, and day-care centers and organized scouting groups and sports teams.[51] Women who served in the Home Army or other underground organizations and fought in the Warsaw Uprising also had combat experience and often were decorated officers of the Polish army.

Poland's ordeal and sacrifice in World War II reveal enormous personal suffering and tragedy. The war was a calamity of extraordinary proportions, in which human lives were lost or changed forever. But just as wars bring out the worst in some people, they also highlight the best in others. In the face of disaster, the Polish people demonstrated exceptional resilience and strength. Prisoners, slave laborers, deportees, civilian refugees, resistance fighters, soldiers, women, men, and children responded to the trials of their exile with determination and resourcefulness. Even accidental and temporary Polish refugee communities all over the world strove not only to survive but also to continue the cultural and political life of the nation. One aim was to care for the younger generations and their education. As a standard, Polish refugees established kindergartens and schools and pooled resources to provide for their children and youth. A second common element was the establishment of a press and publishing institutions, which flourished in all refugee communities.[52] The exiles also established political and cultural institutions, which, even if short lived, provided them with space to exchange ideas and to rebuild the disrupted connection to Polish culture and tradition; they also were symbols of hope in a time of loss and despair. Some Poles survived unimaginable tragedy in concentration camps or as slave laborers in Germany; others traveled the world as deportees, soldiers, or refugees in pursuit of safety. Their experiences during the war shaped their views and personalities and became absolutely central to the concept of the exile mission for the postwar Polish diaspora.

The U.S. Polish Exile Community during the War

The war years witnessed the creation of a new community of refugees and exiles from Poland in the United States. Statistics from the INS indicate that a total of 14,956 persons born in Poland arrived in the United States as quota immigrants between 1939 and 1945. Between June 30, 1945, and mid-1946 (when the influx of refugees admitted under the so-called Truman Directive began) a total of 4,806 immigrants born in Poland arrived in the United States.[53] They came largely through private channels, sponsored by friends and relatives or, in some cases, by American employers. No formal resettlement program had been organized. Initially, these immigrants remained largely invisible, as developments in occupied Poland attracted public attention. Soon, however, the refugees, who had been admitted mostly on temporary tourist visas, began creating small groups and social circles based on common experiences, intellectual affinity, as well as professional and political interests. They formed new organizations with political or cultural agendas and initiated new publications. For the most part, they remained relatively isolated from Polonia, regarding America as a temporary stop on their way back to a free

Poland once the war ended. Kazimierz Wierzyński, one of the greatest Polish poets and essayists, described that state of isolation in the following way:

> For the first five years I lived in the United States absent in this country. My thoughts were in Poland. I wrote things related to the war, I had lectures, I started "Tygodnik Polski" with my friends, and we began publishing books under the name "The Polish Library." I circulated only among Poles and watched America through the window. When after the war it turned out that a return to Poland would be a return to a country deprived of its own will, I awoke in America as if within an unknown, overlooked reality.[54]

Kazimierz Wierzyński belonged to the generation of Polish poets who gained fame in the interwar period. He was a member of the "Skamander" group connected with the popular literary monthly of the same name. The Skamandrites (*Skamandryci*) celebrated poetic freedom in the independent Polish state and consciously broke with the older tradition of nineteenth-century Romantic poetry, which had focused on national issues and demanded that Polish poets be spiritual leaders of a suffering nation striving for independence. Before the war, the Skamandryci published together in literary magazines, such as *Skamander* and *Wiadomości Literackie* (Literary News) and often met during poetry evenings in Warsaw's salons and bohemian cafés (such as the legendary café Ziemiańska) to recite their newest poems and discuss literature. Among them were Julian Tuwim, Kazimierz Wierzyński, Jan Lechoń (Leszek Serafinowicz), Antoni Słonimski, Jarosław Iwaszkiewicz, Maria Pawlikowska-Jasnorzewska, Kazimiera Iłłakowiczówna, and Stanisław Baliński. In September 1939 almost all members of the group found themselves outside of Poland. Most of them came together in Paris, where the editor of *Wiadomości Literackie*, Mieczysław Grydzewski, reestablished his magazine until the fall of France in June 1940. On Christmas Eve, 1939, Wierzyński, Słonimski, Tuwim, Lechoń, Baliński, Grydzewski, and their families spent an evening together celebrating the holiday with a traditional Polish meal, their last meeting before the war dispersed them all over the world. After the German occupation of Paris, the poets succeeded in obtaining visas to Portugal. From there, Słonimski, Baliński, and Grydzewski sailed to London; Lechoń, Tuwim, and Wierzyński traveled to Brazil, and then in the spring of 1941, to the United States, where they soon met up with another Polish exile writer, Józef Wittlin.[55]

In Paris, the Polish poets and writers had tried to define their mission as émigré artists. Similarities abounded between their situation and that of the Great Emigration to the West after the November Uprising of 1830; but in the first issue of *Wiadomości Polskie* (Polish News), poet and writer Ksawery Pruszyński distanced the new exiles from the nineteenth-century tradition:

> That previous emigration was the emigration of the defeated. This new one is an emigration of fighters [*emigracja walczących*]. That old emigration lost its army, this one is just creating it. Finally, the former emigration was the emigration of mature persons, who were never to return to their country. This new emigration is an emigration of young and very young people, who are forming the army and who, with the army, will return to the homeland.[56]

Pruszyński called on his fellow writers to respond to the tragedy of September 1939 and to provide artistic expression of Polish volunteers' experiences in the military forces in the West. The literature of the new emigration, Pruszyński wrote, had to "enter the soldiers' ranks ..., learn the art of war, fight—when they fight, perish—when they are to perish. Had we remained in the country, we should have suffered with the country, but since we crossed the border with the army—we need to fight in the army."[57]

Polish exile literature during World War II accepted this challenge. As Kazimierz Wierzyński concluded in his literary review in 1943, the Polish pen was again in the service of the Polish cause.[58] Wherever the war led Polish soldiers and refugees, they produced new writing. A large group of poets and writers joined the Second Corps and followed its route from Siberia to Iran, the Middle East, Italy, and Great Britain. Polish poets and writers followed the legacy of the Great Emigration: they, too, became spiritual leaders of the nation in exile. They, together with other intellectuals, scientists, and politicians, laid the foundation for the formulation of the exile mission, constructing bridges to the nineteenth-century Polish Romantic tradition and making struggle for Poland the most important cause of all.[59] In the United States, it was these wartime refugees and later arrivals who formed the basis of the postwar Polish intellectual diaspora.[60]

In New York, *Tygodnik Polski* (Polish Weekly) dominated the literary scene of the exile community since January 1943. It superseded Zenon Kosidowski's *Tygodniowy Przegląd Literacki Koła Pisarzy z Polski* (Weekly Literary

Review of the Polish Writers' Circle), which had been published on a duplicating machine between 1941 and 1942. The very first issue of *Tygodnik* exemplified its orientation. Jan Lechoń's front-page editorial was accompanied by a large drawing of Poland in its prewar borders, identifying the journal with the London government's political position on the issue. A short story by Kazimierz Wierzyński recalled the bravery of Haller's Army and intertwined the tradition of military sacrifice in World War I and the events of September 1939. A poem by Lechoń focused on the exile's longing for his country, and another by Józef Wittlin related the experiences of Polish Jews under the Nazi regime. Ewa Curie, daughter of Nobel Prize winner Maria Skłodowska-Curie, described her encounters with the Polish army created in the Soviet Union. Anatol Muhlstein and Stanisław Strzetelski presented essays on international politics and the Polish question. Finally, the last page featured a review of the newly published book by Arkady Fiedler, *Squadron 303*, about Polish pilots' contribution to the victory in the Battle of Britain. The issue closed with a score of announcements of lectures organized by the Polish Institute of Arts and Sciences of America.[61]

Almost all refugee intellectuals in the United States and many from the larger Polish war diaspora authored articles for *Tygodnik*, making it—next to Grydzewski's *Wiadomości Literackie* in London—the best wartime publication by Polish intellectuals in exile. Among those who contributed their work was a sizable group of women. Irena Piotrowska, Felicja Lilpop-Krancowa, and Maria Werten published on art and architecture, reviewing exhibitions and books on those topics. Irena Lorentowicz and Maria Modzelewska wrote about art and theater. Wanda Landowska, a renowned Polish harpsichord player whose concerts in the United States received rave reviews, contributed material on music. Marta Wańkowicz-Erdman wrote essays and reports from her journalistic travels. Beata Obertyńska, a soldier of the Anders Army, and Zofia Bohdanowiczowa, who sent her poetry from exile in Algiers, and the Polish-American poet Wiktoria Janda reflected women's contribution to poetry. *Tygodnik Polski* featured articles on women, for example, female deportees to Siberia and Pestki,[62] and advertised Rój, a publishing house headed by Hanna Kister in the New York City.[63] For a few months in the winter of 1944, *Tygodnik Polski* experimented with a separate section for women under the editorship of Pani Wanda (Ms. Wanda). The page discussed the same topics that one could find in any other women's journal:

recipes, beauty and fashion advice, sewing patterns, and savings in the domestic budget. Soon, however, Pani Wanda had to answer a letter from a female reader, who asked about the significance of such trivial concerns in times of war and suffering. After a run of just over two months, the women's section quietly disappeared from *Tygodnik*'s pages.[64]

Exiles to the United States were among the founders of many cultural institutions: the Polish Institute of Arts and Sciences of America, the Polish American Historical Association, and the Józef Piłsudski Institute for Research in the Modern History of Poland. These cultural organizations were designed to support and facilitate the further development of Polish culture and scholarship in exile and to represent them to the larger American society.

The Józef Piłsudski Institute was established in July 1943. Its founders included new arrivals who before the war had been closely connected to the Polish government: Ignacy Matuszewski, former minister of the treasury; Wacław Jędrzejewicz, former vice-minister of education; and Henryk Floyar-Rajchman, former minister of industry and trade. Frank Januszewski of *Dziennik Polski* (Polish Daily) in Detroit, and Maksymilian F. Węgrzynek of *Nowy Świat* (New World) in New York, represented the Polish-American press. The goals of the institute included the collection, preservation, and study of documents dealing with the history of Poland since 1863. Gradually, the institute created an extensive library, archives, and a small museum for the display of historical artifacts. The institute also carried out editorial and publishing work; organized lectures, exhibits, and occasional conferences; and sponsored research projects and scholarships. Even though it failed in its attempt to create a large international membership among Polish diaspora, the institute was able to attract a devoted group of supporters. They included recent exiles from the prewar Piłsudski circles and some sympathetic intellectuals and artists, such as Jan Lechoń, Kazimierz Wierzyński, and painter Zdzisław Czermański. Other active members during the war were employees of the Polish consulate and embassy, activists of the Komitet Obrony Narodowej (KON)—or Committee of National Defense, a Polish-American organization dating back to World War I—as well as a group of supporters connected to Detroit's *Dziennik Polski*. Refugees of the DP wave further strengthened the institute. In time the institute became a viable center for the study of Polish history, which attracted both Polish scholars and intellectuals and members from the older Polonia.[65]

The Polish Institute of Arts and Sciences of America (PIASA; in Polish the Polski Instytut Naukowy w Ameryce, or PIN) was established in New York in 1942. Polish scholars and members of the Polish Academy of Arts and Sciences (Polska Akademia Umiejętności, PAU) who found themselves outside of Poland at the outbreak of World War II were determined to continue scholarly activities disrupted by the war. They considered it their moral obligation, because the Nazis were systematically destroying Polish learning and scholarship in the homeland. Their new organization, PIASA, aimed at providing appropriate conditions for the presentation of Polish scholarship to larger American society. Among the first members and officers were such world-renowned scholars as historians Oskar Halecki, Jan Kucharzewski, and Rafał Taubenschlag, anthropologist Bronisław Malinowski, historian of Slavic literatures Wacław Lednicki, and chemist Wojciech Swiętosławski. Between 1942 and 1945 the Polish government in exile supported PIASA with a financial subsidy, enabling it to organize numerous lectures and conferences and to publish books and scientific works. From 1946 through 1951 the Polish American Congress granted PIASA a modest annual subsidy, but after that period PIASA had to look for other sources of support, mainly private gifts and volunteer work. Despite these dire financial straits, in 1953 PIASA organized the Mickiewicz Centennial, celebrating the one-hundredth anniversary of the poet's death. The results of PIASA's work were regularly published and publicized through the *Bulletin of PIASA*, replaced in 1955 by the *Polish Review*.

One of the most active PIASA committees focused on researching Polish immigration. It was soon transformed into a separate scholarly organization, the Polish American Historical Association (PAHA), with its own research agenda and separate publication, *Polish American Studies*. Both PIASA and PAHA attracted many Polish, Polish-American, and American intellectuals; and from the moment of their creation they have belonged to the most active cultural organizations within the Polish community in the United States.[66]

The story of Polish actors who were a part of the first wave of war refugees represents another example of an attempt to recreate the Polish artistic community in the United States. One of the most significant initiatives of the war years was the establishment in New York of Polski Teatr Narodowy (Polish National Theater) with the support of Koło Artystów Sceny Polskiej (Polish Actors' Circle). Their performances evoked much enthusiasm, especially among the most recent arrivals from Poland. The repertoire featured classic Polish historical dramas and comedies, occasional programs (for example, for New Year's Eve), and some new plays by Polish exile authors. By contrast, the company's artistic tours to some of Old Polonia's smaller centers did not meet with a great deal of success. Blamed for the failure was the supposedly high intellectual level of the repertoire, which did not appeal to a Polonian audience accustomed to lighter entertainment. Additionally, frequent references to wartime experiences in Poland were hard for the viewers to identify with, and high ticket prices and a lack of energetic management and marketing further hurt the ambitious theater company.[67]

In the fall of 1942 the Polish Actors' Circle announced the establishment of Polski Teatr Artystów (Polish Artists' Theater), subsidized by the Polish government in exile in London. The majority of actors who had participated in the Polish National Theater now transferred to the new company. Its nature was, however, very different. From the beginning it was designed as an artistic enterprise which would cater mostly to the tastes of recent Polish refugees who planned to return to Poland as soon as possible. The theater, despite some success, never achieved its objective of becoming a permanent center for the Polish performing arts in New York. When the governmental subsidies ended in 1945, the company ceased to exist. Most of the actors followed different career paths, including radio programs and individual tours to smaller communities in the country, or else returned to Poland.[68]

The existence of the theater during the war became an extremely important factor in the Polish exiles' life. It enabled the survival of a group of people whose careers could not have been transferred easily into a foreign environment. For example, it gave employment to a host of Polish actresses such as Jadwiga Smosarska (one of the most popular and promising film actresses in Poland), Janina Wilczówna, Zofia Nakoneczna, Lunia Nestorówna, Karin Tiche, Stanisława Nowicka, and Maria Modzelewska, an accomplished actress of the Warsaw stage.[69] But more significantly, it symbolized the efforts of the Polish people to go on despite war, exile, and terrible news from occupied Poland. In an article for *Tygodnik Polski*, director and playwright Antoni Cwojdziński described preparations for the performance of *"Pastorałka"* (Pastorale), a Christmas play based on traditional Polish folk motifs, as involving the good will and ingenuity of the entire company. The rehearsals took place in a private apartment after the regular workday, and even actors suffering from flu participated. A singer practiced in the bathroom, the only space free from interference and noise from the street. The stage designer created decorations by hand and often carried them herself to and from the car. The actors often played in small, unheated halls, to which they had to travel long distances. Still, an atmosphere of enthusiasm and ardor accompanied their work.[70]

This labor of love brought its own rewards. Irena Lorentowicz, who was the set designer and prepared all the costumes, noticed that "often laughter, loud calling, warnings for the characters on the stage, exclamations, and the sincere tears of the audience" came in instant response to the acting.[71] After the premier of each new play, professional reviews appeared in *Tygodnik Polski,* written by Jan Lechoń or Józef Wittlin. In one of them, an excited Lechoń wrote: "Anyone who has lived in Warsaw and remembers the atmosphere of premiers in the Warsaw theaters could not fail to feel at the performance of the Polish Artists' Theater . . . the rush of memories of those days and those halls."[72] During one program, "Echoes of the Polish Land," when the actors on the stage sang, "We were happy and we did not know it," several recent refugees, overwhelmed by their emotions, got up and left.[73]

The wartime exile community did not meet only during PIASA lectures or theater performances; they also created a close-knit community that was determined to recreate Polish prewar social circles in an American environment. The largest number of exiles settled in New York, and their social life centered on several key locations. One of them was the consulate of the Polish government in exile, until 1945 recognized by the United States as Poland's legal authority. There, according to Lorentowicz, "we searched each other out[;] everybody was getting pieces of news from the homeland and sharing them with others."[74] Another place for social gatherings was the Ognisko (Campfire) restaurant located next to the consulate. As one exiled writer, Aleksander Janta, commented, every day Ognisko drew a sizable crowd of Poles, as if it was a popular place in Warsaw. "Here you could find all the gossip," he wrote, "Here was the stock exchange for all political and social sensations and insinuations, here you could meet those that count and those that have just arrived, here you could learn everything about everybody."[75] The menu included strictly Polish cuisine, and the wait staff was composed of former diplomats, actors, and actresses, who had no chances for other employment in America.[76] Hotels run by Poles in the Adirondacks and in Sea Cliff on Long Island served as other gathering places for the Polish elite of wartime New York.[77]

A particular brand of elitism, social self-sufficiency, and the belief that their sojourn in America soon would come to an end resulted in refugees having only limited contact with American Polonia. Gradually, refugees and Polish Americans came to know each other on several different levels. Concerns for the welfare of the refugees, Polonia's humanitarian actions, and wartime political goals became the strongest catalysts for a closer relationship.

American Polonia and Polish Refugees during the War

As soon as the first news of the German attack on Poland reached the United States on September 1, 1939, Polish Americans manifested their support for the people of Poland. In a strong display of solidarity, Polonia organizations called for a united action on behalf of Poland. The Polish language press published a declaration, which proclaimed:

> At this historic moment the Polish American Council calls all in whose veins Polish blood flows to mobilize their moral forces, to free all their spiritual powers, to focus their thoughts and will in one direction—the victory of Poland. All of Polonia in the United States, whose sons shed blood in the battle to regain independence, stands by the Homeland in this decisive struggle. We call all countrymen to unite their hearts and minds. We call all of Polonia to a great deed.[78]

Both the rhetoric and the spirit of the declaration signified a full return to the ideals of the exile mission in its familiar formulation from the turn of the century and the World War I years, when American Polonia claimed the cause of a free Poland as its most important objective. The call to unite and to sacrifice in the struggle for Poland revived the patriotism of Polish Americans and focused their attention on the cause of the homeland.

The response to the call was immediate, and the unification of efforts instantaneous. Rada Polonii Amerykańskiej (Polish American Council), a Polish-American charitable organization, underwent a quick reorganization in order to provide the homeland with humanitarian aid in the most effective way.[79] The multitude of existing Polish-American organizations and parishes as well as the special relief committees that instantly sprang up in Polonia, comprised its ranks. At an extraordinary meeting on October 19, 1939, the Polish American Council, headed by Francis X. Świetlik, dean of the law school at Marquette University and censor of the Polish National Alliance, united all Polonia's relief efforts under its auspices.[80]

Numerous demonstrations, public meetings, and solemn masses manifested American Polonia's moral support for the Polish nation. At the conventions of several major fraternals in the fall of 1939, eloquent declarations of support and flaming manifestos entwined with spontaneous collections of donations and the formation of permanent administrative structures to coordinate humanitarian and political work. An important part of this undertaking focused on drawing the attention of the media and politicians to Poland's plight and gaining the support of the American public and the government. For example, Polonia mobilized its members through a letter-writing campaign to support Franklin Roosevelt's measures to assist the Allies, despite the official pronouncement of neutrality by the United States.[81]

Some initiatives spontaneously adopted at the outset of the war ended in failure. Collections for the Fundusz Obrony Narodowej (FON, or National Defense Fund) for Poland had to stop immediately after the American government announced its neutrality. Information centers, intended to disseminate news about the situation in Poland, turned out to be short lived for lack of organizational and financial support. Finally, efforts to recruit Polish Americans for a specially created military force patterned after Haller's Army of World War I failed to receive enough support. Reflecting internal transformations within Polonia in the 1930s, the response to the idea of a new Polish-American legion in 1939 was weak.[82]

The neutrality pronouncement by the United States dictated the main focus of Polonia's activities, which for years to come would concentrate on humanitarian aid. As Teofil A. Starzyński, president of the Polish Falcons (*Sokół*) fraternal, stated in September 1939, Polonia fully understood and accepted its position, but did not rule out the possibility of change in the future. "Poland does not need our blood yet," his declaration read, "but when she calls for it, we will offer it willingly. Today we need rather financial aid and help in propagating the Polish question in the American public opinion. Such aid we must provide."[83] Rada, the American Red Cross, and countless local relief committees received an outpouring of donations from individuals, parishes, and organizations. In mid-October 1939 the PNA leadership gave the American Red Cross a check for $150,000 for relief work in Poland. The PNA and many other organizations announced a five-cent monthly tax on each member for the exclusive purpose of aid to Poland. The Polish Women's Alliance, gathered at its national convention in September 1939, proclaimed that "the entire Polish Women's Alliance in America and all its parts ... turned into one, huge Relief Committee" and vowed to focus all its efforts on the work for Poland.[84] In Chicago a group of Polish second-generation women, mostly recipients of stipends from the Kosciuszko Foundation, created Legion Młodych Polek (Legion of Young Polish Women) under the leadership of pianist Adelina Preyss. They systematically volunteered in the American Red Cross and carried out fund-raising activities. Within two weeks from the inception of the legion, its membership had grown to one hundred women.[85]

Most of the funds collected by the Polish-American community were at the disposal of Rada, which based its organization on a network of thirty-six regional districts. By the spring of 1940, its leaders announced that the organization had collected more than $500,000; by the end of the year, Rada was gathering approximately $60,000 per month.[86] In the financial report prepared for the 1942 convention, Rada made accessible a detailed account of all the donations received between May 1, 1941, and September 30, 1942. Day after day, name after name, Rada documented the financial effort of the Polish population, whose individual donations ranged from one dollar to several thousand.[87] All in all, between November 1, 1939, and September 30, 1942, Rada collected some $1,600,000.[88]

Cooperating closely with the American Red Cross and the New York-based Committee for Polish Relief, headed by former U.S. president Herbert Hoover, Rada worked to overcome difficulties of access to occupied Poland. Although it was impossible to deliver any assistance to the Soviet zone of occupation or to the Polish population deported to Siberia, some goods were shipped to the German-occupied areas of Poland until the spring of 1940. Rada also provided humanitarian aid to Polish civilian refugees in Romania, Hungary, Lithuania, France, Switzerland, and Britain, as well as to Polish soldiers and officers in German POW camps. After the outbreak of war between Germany and the Soviet Union, followed by Soviet entry into the Allied camp, Rada was able finally to reach Polish deportees in Russia.

Assistance also was extended to the Anders Army and to refugees scattered in the Middle East, Africa, and India.[89]

After Pearl Harbor, Rada Polonii Amerykańskiej coordinated its activities with the national war effort. As Polish War Relief, Rada became a chartered member of the National War Fund, which after 1943 consolidated all fund drives.[90] Despite difficulties, Rada managed to send Polish POWs in Germany approximately twelve thousand food packages a month.[91] When the Allied invasion of Normandy disrupted delivery of the humanitarian aid in Europe, Rada focused on Polish refugees in different parts of the world, including Egypt, Kenya, Rhodesia, Uganda, Tanganyika, Palestine, and Mexico. Rada continued its activities after the war, becoming American Relief for Poland in 1946. According to Świetlik's detailed report presented at Rada's convention in Buffalo in December 1948, between October 1939 and October 1948, Rada had distributed the staggering total of $20 million in humanitarian aid.[92]

Throughout the war, Rada systematically informed Polonia of the plight of Polish refugees. Its publicity efforts were a continuation of a larger propaganda action coordinated by Community and War Chests and designed to educate and appeal to Americans in general. In his report to Rada's 1942 national convention, Świetlik reviewed Rada's accomplishments in publicity for the Polish cause. "We do not use this word," he said, "and do not talk much about propaganda, but the fact is that . . . we have done a lot to aid propaganda on behalf of Poland."[93] Dissemination of information on the Polish population outside of Poland remained a large part of that publicity campaign.[94] In the brochure *The Facts about the Polish War Relief*, published in English early in 1945, Rada presented its aims and program for the future and summarized its wartime activities and achievements. The brochure recapped the story of Polish refugees in different parts of the world as well as that of prisoners in German POW and concentration camps. Graphic pictures illustrated the suffering, death, hunger, and terrible living conditions. Some photographs showed temporary communities built by the exiles: a church erected by them in Valivade, India; a women's workshop in an African camp; and Polish medical students working at the Paderewski Hospital in Edinburgh, Scotland.[95] Another publication, entitled *Poland's Children*, focused on the fate of the "war's little victims" both in Poland and in exile; according to the brochure's authors, "the children—the most helpless victims of the war—have always been the object of [the Polish War Relief's] special attention."[96]

Expressive drawings depicting the suffering of Poles by the recognized Polish artist W. T. Benda decorated the covers of both brochures. Their poster-size enlargements hung on the walls of Rada's offices and its New York warehouse, reminders of the war's victims.[97]

One of the most successful actions carried out by Rada in cooperation with the National Catholic Welfare Conference (NCWC) involved the establishment, maintenance, and eventual dissolution of the Santa Rosa settlement in Mexico. The Santa Rosa Polish refugee camp had its origins in negotiations among the American, Polish, and Mexican governments in 1942 and 1943. As a result of an agreement between the Polish government in exile and Mexico, nearly fifteen hundred Polish civilian refugees from India (mostly women and children) found a new home in the camp near León, Mexico. The U.S. Navy offered to transport the refugees free of charge. The American ambassador to Mexico was assigned as an advisor to the Polish camp and the U.S. government demonstrated a vivid interest in the fate of these Poles who had survived the hell of Soviet deportations to Siberia. Rada became involved immediately, appropriating funds for the purchase of food and goods for the refugees who passed through American territory on their way to Mexico. Although the maintenance and administration of the camp were the responsibility of the Polish government, several American humanitarian organizations offered their financial and administrative support. Rada took upon itself the funding of education and health care programs within the camp, the State Department's Foreign Relief and Rehabilitation Operations covered the administrative costs, and the NCWC pledged financial support for the cultural, recreational, and rehabilitation activities of the camp. Rada appointed a permanent delegate to the camp to monitor and report on the needs of the refugee population. Rada's special commissions visited the camp, and substantial donations in money and in kind followed.[98]

The old, run-down hacienda in Santa Rosa soon was transformed into a flourishing and lively Polish colony.[99] In the summer of 1945, however, the Polish government in exile lost its recognition in Western countries, and the refugees turned their eyes toward the United States as a possible place of immigration. Negotiations on the camp's dissolution involved the American government and dragged on for many months filled with uneasiness and frustration.[100] PNA/PAC president Charles Rozmarek succeeded in obtaining the American government's permission to bring twenty-five orphaned boys to the United States. They arrived in the spring of 1946 and were placed in the facilities of the PNA college in Cambridge Springs, Pennsylvania. Due to the efforts of Rada and Świetlik, Roman Catholic orphanages supported by Polonia in Chicago, New York, Milwaukee, Detroit, and Buffalo accepted a group of 231 orphaned children. The NCWC also aided in that effort.[101]

The resettlement of Polish refugee children, sponsored by Polonia and led by Rada, also included thirty-one boys from Polish refugee settlements in India who entered the Polish Seminary in Orchard Lake in 1945. Two years later another group of eighteen candidates for the priesthood arrived at St. Francis College in Cedar Lake, Indiana. Another group of fifty Polish orphans came from India to America in early 1947, as a result of the efforts of the special committee to aid Polish orphans organized in Chicago.[102]

Many wartime refugees had a chance personally to experience the generosity of American Polonia, especially during the initial phase of their sojourn. The refugee wave consisted not only of intellectuals and artists; other exiles left Poland abruptly, were caught by the outbreak of the war in foreign countries without many resources at their disposal, or managed to immigrate to the United States after experiencing deportations or incarceration. Numerous professionals faced limited employment opportunities, even if they could find any legal or illegal work. There was, for example, a large group of professional women unable to support themselves in exile. Some of them were elderly women or widows; some were women with sick children or dependent elderly parents; others were the wives or mothers of Polish soldiers and officers serving in the armed forces in the West, imprisoned in POW camps in Germany, or murdered in Katyń. For them, war meant not only loss of or separation from family members, but also disabilities, illnesses, and exhaustion resulting from their experiences in the Soviet labor camps or in Germany.[103]

The refugees established the Polish War Refugee Association in the United States (Zrzeszenie Uchodźców Wojennych z Polski w Stanach Zjednoczonych), based in New York, and the Circle of Polish Refugees in the Chicago area. The association, headed initially by Stefan Zagórski, and then by Władysław Korczak, turned to Rada for help. Rada allocated some financial resources for the refugees, and in March 1941 it formed a special Executive Committee for Aid to War Refugees from Poland in the United States, headed by Walter Bayer, to coordinate the aid distribution. At the end of

August 1940, the lists prepared by the association in cooperation with the Polish consulate general in Chicago included about 250 persons living in the New York and Chicago areas.[104] A year later, a similar roster for New York contained names of 577 Polish Christian refugees. The Polish War Refugee Association's lists of persons receiving financial aid for 1944 through 1946, however, included both Polish and Jewish names, for example, Lazar Markeles, an unemployed rabbi, and Chil Trunk, a Jewish writer.[105]

The Polish government was concerned about the care of the refugees. Both Consul General Karol Ripa and Ambassador Jan Ciechanowski negotiated with Rada on behalf of the exiles. In the summer of 1941 Ciechanowski himself turned to Censor Świetlik, asking him to support an increase in aid to the refugees in New York. Responding to this request, Świetlik quoted the opinion of the Executive Committee for Aid, declaring that a thousand dollars a month was a sufficient sum for the time being. Świetlik reminded him that the type of support the refugees could expect in the United States would differ from what they might have gotten used to at other stages of their journey, when they were able to lean on the Polish government. "In the United States the refugees will have to depend on their own resourcefulness to a larger extent," he cautioned. "All refugees in Chicago, with the exception of a few individuals really unable to work, found themselves jobs and settled down nicely.... We are under the impression that the refugees from the New York area are showing less willingness to rely on themselves," he added.[106]

Beginning in September 1940, Rada allocated $150 per month for Chicago-area refugees, and $500 for those in New York.[107] Between the beginning of 1941 and the end of 1945, Rada subsidized the Polish War Refugee Association in New York with roughly a thousand dollars a month and covered some additional outstanding sums for medical emergencies and treatment. Rada's report for its second national convention in 1942 indicated that more than $21,000 were spent from the organization's funds to aid Polish refugees in America. Rada's report of 1948 showed that the help provided by the Committee for Refugees in New York exceeded $68,000.[108] In the years 1942 through 1945, the refugees could also count on some financial support from the Ministry of Welfare of the Polish government in exile. In July 1945, when the United States and other Western countries withdrew their recognition of the London government, the subsidies stopped. In December of the same year, Rada terminated its obligations toward the Polish War Refugee Association. Throughout

1946, the association's leaders wrote eloquent pleas to Rada, hoping for the resumption of payments. In the spring of 1947 the association's own funds ran out as more and more refugees landed on American shores; in the summer of 1945 alone, about two thousand persons had registered with the New York association.[109] The association dissolved, transferring its responsibilities to the newly created Polish Immigration Committee of New York.

In addition to humanitarian action, politics was another area of contact and cooperation between the refugees and Polonia. Franklin Delano Roosevelt won an overwhelming majority of Polish-American votes in 1940.[110] Convinced of the benefits of Polonia's loyalty, the president made friendly gestures toward the representatives of the London-based Polish government in exile.[111] But the support for Roosevelt and the Democratic Party that Polonia demonstrated in the first years of the war was tested when, in June 1941, Hitler's army invaded the Soviet Union. Stalin became an instant ally and the American government rushed in with material assistance for the Soviets. For the Poles who vividly remembered "the stab in the back" from the Soviet army that had invaded and annexed territories of eastern Poland during the 1939 war with Germany, accepting the Soviet Union as an ally of Great Britain and the United States was difficult indeed. In the summer of 1941 Polish prime minister Władysław Sikorski signed an agreement with Soviet ambassador Ivan Maiski, which allowed deported and imprisoned Poles in the Soviet Union to leave the country. Stalin, however, did not give any guarantees of a return to the prewar Polish borders. Sikorski's moderate position and his restoration of Polish-Soviet relations prompted a serious rift within the Polish government in exile, resulting in staunch opposition to any further dealings with the Soviets. The situation changed again when the United States entered the war after the Japanese attack on Pearl Harbor in December 1941. The constraints of neutrality had come to an end, and Polish Americans could fully demonstrate their support for the war effort. The number of Polish Americans in the American military totaled nine hundred thousand.[112] Those who did not actively serve contributed to the war economy and purchased government bonds in record numbers.[113]

The political unity of the first years of the war, however, seemed to be breaking up. On the left side of Polonia's political spectrum, a relatively small but significant group of pro-Soviet Polish socialists based in Detroit became involved in the creation of the American Slav Congress, established in April 1942 under the leadership of Leo Krzycki, a vice-president of the CIO's Amalgamated Clothing Workers of America. Krzycki was considered to have a following among left-wing Poles, centered in the Polish Labor Party and the nine thousand members of the Polish section of the International Workers Order. The CIO opted for American-Soviet friendship, support for the Red Army, and the opening of a second front. In 1943 another pro-Soviet group, the Kosciuszko League, composed solely of Polish Americans, was formed by a maverick Roman Catholic priest, Stanisław Orlemański. The most eminent spokesperson for the pro-Soviet element, Oskar Lange, a professor of economics at the University of Chicago, worked closely with both of the above organizations.[114]

The right side of the political spectrum was occupied by the National Committee of Americans of Polish Descent (Komitet Narodowy Amerykanów Polskiego Pochodzenia, KNAPP), formed in New York in 1942. The leadership of KNAPP included representatives of the Polish-American press, editors and publishers Maksymilian F. Węgrzynek and Frank Januszewski.[115] They were aided by a vocal group of new arrivals from the prewar Polish government's Piłsudski faction (called Piłsudskiites, or *Piłsudczycy*, supportive of the prewar regime, or *Sanacja*), which included such distinctive figures as General Bolesław Wieniawa-Długoszewski, ambassador of Poland in Rome and member of governmental circles in interwar Poland, Wacław Jędrzejewicz, Henryk Floyar-Rajchman, and Ignacy Matuszewski. They believed that American Polonia had not only a moral obligation to Poland but also the political means to have an impact on United States foreign policy. Shocked by the presumed lack of involvement and inaction of Rada, they formed a political lobby to promote the anti-Soviet position and to denounce Sikorski and his moderate policies. Although KNAPP's membership never surpassed two or three thousand, its impact on the increasing politicization of American Polonia at that time and on the creation of the Polish American Congress in 1944 was considerable.[116]

The Chicago headquarters of the major Polish-American organizations and Francis X. Świetlik, the president of the Polish American Council, represented a more centrist position, which included support for Sikorski and his policies and for Roosevelt as well. The turning point in the wartime relationship between American Polonia and Roosevelt's Democratic administration came in the spring of 1943. At that time, the Germans announced the discovery of mass graves of some fifteen thousand Poles in the Katyń Forest, near Smolensk. The Germans blamed the Soviets for the mass murder; the Soviets announced that the Germans had committed the crime after entering the Soviet territories in 1941. When the Sikorski government confronted Stalin and demanded a Red Cross–led investigation, the Soviets unilaterally broke diplomatic relations with the Polish government in exile. Shortly thereafter, Sikorski died in an unexplained plane crash over Gibraltar and was replaced as prime minister by Stanisław Mikołajczyk.

Historians have argued that "the impact of the Polish-Soviet split on domestic politics in the United States was considerable. Those moderate elements in the Polish community who had refrained from public and divisive attacks on the Soviet Union in response to unity pleas by the Roosevelt administration now found themselves bitterly agreeing with the KNAPP militants."[117] On the other hand, the pro-Soviet Poles vigorously attacked KNAPP and its supporters on the pages of Detroit's *Głos Ludowy* (People's Voice), the only pro-Soviet Polish daily in the country. The concern of the administration over the KNAPP-inspired anti-Soviet campaign was reflected in its initiation of the circulation of a pamphlet attacking KNAPP signed by more than thirty moderate and leftist Poles.[118]

Throughout 1943 American Polonia observed with gravity how the American public as well as the government generally accepted the Soviet side of the Katyń story and showed signs of deliberately undermining the demands of the Polish government in exile.[119] The U.S. War Department refused to launch any investigation into the Katyń massacre, despite the appeals of nine Polish-American congressmen led by John Lesinski of Michigan, Thaddeus Wasilewski of Wisconsin, and Joseph Mruk of New York. During the Big Three meeting in Tehran in 1943, the fate of Poland's eastern border was decided without consultation with the Poles. Approached by Polish Americans inquiring about the results of the meeting, Roosevelt, who was determined to keep the agreements secret, offered vague and inconclusive answers.[120] Shortly afterward, the White House allowed two controversial figures connected with the American Slav Congress, Professor Oskar Lange and the Reverend Stanisław Orlemański, to travel to Moscow on a direct invitation from Stalin. In response to widespread criticism from major Polish-American newspapers, the White House announced that the two had journeyed as private citizens and had no right to speak for the United States.[121]

Political issues concerning postwar arrangements in Europe continued to occupy public attention. The Polish-American community expressed vivid interest in assuring the existence of a sovereign and independent Polish state. Charles Rozmarek, the president of the PNA since 1939 and a rising star in Chicago Polonia, together with KNAPP leaders and some other activists from the Polish press and clergy realized that Polonia needed to establish a political presence that could exert greater pressure on Washington. As a result, the Polish American Congress (PAC) was founded in May 1944 at a meeting of some twenty-five hundred representatives of Polonia gathered in Buffalo, New York. The PAC, as a large federation of fraternal, church, and professional organizations, immediately evoked enormous enthusiasm among American Polonia. Soon the PAC claimed 6 million members and followers, and was supported by nearly all Polish-American organizations.[122]

The PAC accepted the leadership of American Polonia in a difficult moment. Roosevelt, conscious of the significance of the Polish vote in the upcoming presidential elections, agreed to meet with Mikołajczyk in the summer 1944, but demanded that the premier have no contact with Polish Americans. On August 1, 1944 an uprising broke out in Warsaw, led by the Polish Home Army, which fought against overwhelming German forces as the Red Army watched from the right bank of Vistula River. Despite the repeated pleas for help that the PAC directed to the American government, no decisive action was taken as the Germans suppressed the uprising, killing and deporting the population of Warsaw and turning the city into a sea of ruins.

The Republican Party failed to capitalize on the growing dissatisfaction of Polish Americans with Roosevelt's policies toward Poland. In October 1944 Roosevelt went to Chicago and met Rozmarek, convincing him of his good intentions regarding the Polish question. Rozmarek, the most influential political leader of Polonia at that time, was swayed by FDR's eloquence and announced his support for Roosevelt. On Election Day the Polish-American community gave Roosevelt 90 percent of their votes.[123]

International events in 1945 continued to follow an adverse course for Poland. In February 1945 Roosevelt, Churchill, and Stalin met in Yalta to formalize the agreements arrived at in Tehran and to conclude the settlement of the postwar world. The Allies affirmed that the boundary between Poland

and the Soviet Union would run along the so-called Curzon Line, which meant a loss of 178,220 square kilometers in the east, including the cities of Wilno and Lwów. Although Poland was to be compensated by the award of German lands in the west (101,200 square kilometers), Poland became the only country in the victorious Allied camp that came out of the war with a territorial loss.[124] It was also agreed that the Lublin government installed by the Soviets would be reorganized to include a broader representation of Polish society and democratic leaders from abroad. This Provisional Government of National Unity (Tymczasowy Rząd Jedności Narodowej, TRJN) was to be recognized by the Western powers and to have the responsibility to hold "free and unfettered elections."[125] The reaction of the PAC, Rozmarek, and the group of Polish-American congressmen was an immediate and vehement criticism of the Yalta agreement and Roosevelt's politics as well. Leo Krzycki, however, as president of the American Polish Labor Council (APLC) and claiming to represent six hundred thousand trade union members of Polish background, supported Roosevelt and Yalta and called on the president to reject the divisive claims of other Polish-American leaders. The APLC manifesto was signed by representatives of the auto, steel, electrical, clothing, transportation, and smelter workers unions.[126]

Both political factions of Polonia were represented at the San Francisco United Nations conference in April 1945, but their presence was symbolic. At the beginning of July 1945, the United States and Great Britain withdrew recognition from the London government and recognized the Provisional Government of National Unity formed in Warsaw on June 28, 1945. Despite hopes that Truman would adopt a tougher stance on the Polish question, the Big Three, meeting in Potsdam in July 1945, only confirmed the previous agreements. The PAC bulletin of August-September declared: "It was not Russia but *America* that broke Poland."[127] In the growing climate of the Cold War, the Yalta agreement—often referred to as the "betrayal at Yalta"—became a rallying point for the PAC and Rozmarek. Coming closer to the position taken by KNAPP, the PAC called for the repudiation of the Yalta agreement, recognition of the London government, and Allied supervision of elections in Poland. In the Cold War atmosphere and as the Left gradually lost its significance, the PAC became the voice of the majority of American Polonia, gaining in stature and support, and representing Polonia before the American government and society.

The loss of recognition was a serious blow to the Polish government in exile in London, but its leaders were determined to carry on and, recalling the nineteenth century tradition, revived the concept of the "state in exile." The state in exile, or *Mała Polska* (Little Poland) in exile, assumed a certain institutional completeness, with governmental, political, military, and social structures as intact as possible. For instance, its leaders discouraged naturalization, which was

> considered to be an act of disloyalty to the exiled Government. If an officer of the Polish Army became a British subject, for example, his name was removed from the officers' list of the future Polish Army and added to the list of the deceased. Any Pole who felt that the nature of his job justified his becoming a British subject was expected to apply for permission to the London Polish Government. They saw the preservation of the Polish character of the community, of its sense of its own Polishness, as a major task, involving the encouragement of separate Polish political, cultural, social and even quasi-military organizations.[128]

After the Polish armed forces in the West had been disbanded, many still continued to believe that, in the case of imminent war between the West and Russia, Poles would take an active part in the struggle for Poland's independence. They "considered themselves to be 'on long leave' rather than fully demobilized," a view reinforced by General Anders.[129] The state in exile concept assumed that Polish diaspora had the right to consider itself a true nation in exile, being an intrinsic part of the Polish nation in Poland, and its main goal was "the duty of struggle for independence." According to Adam Pragier, minister of information and a respected politician, the nation in exile included soldiers of the Polish armed forces, the war emigration (*emigracja wojenna*), and the old emigration, or Polonia. He further assumed that leadership over this structure belonged to the Polish political circles in London.[130]

Although the political goals of Poland's independence and a shared anti-communism brought the exiles and American Polonia closer together, neither cooperation nor day-to-day coexistence proved easy. For example, the goals of KNAPP included full mobilization of the Americans of Polish descent on behalf of Poland and their activism in support of the war effort and a just peace after the war's end. According to KNAPP's historian and cofounder, Wacław Jędrzejewicz, the organization became the arena of both confrontation and negotiation between the divergent leadership styles and methods adopted by the exiles and Polish Americans. Jędrzejewicz thought that the main reason for this not-always-harmonious relationship was the newcomers' lack of familiarity with American conditions in which the organization had to function. "One could not always utilize similar methods of work from Poland and transfer them to American soil," he wrote. At the same time, he emphasized that the differences "never related to political matters, but rather to tactical and organizational problems."[131] The tensions did not prove serious enough to threaten the activities of KNAPP. The Piłsudskiites who took upon themselves the ideological side of these activities, acknowledged the influence and resources of their Polish-American collaborators, Maksymilian Węgrzynek and Frank Januszewski. They were careful to stress the American character and methods accepted by the organization. The first manifesto of KNAPP, published in October 1942, denounced any affiliation with Polish or American political parties, underlined the organization's ideological independence, and called for the general participation of all Polish Americans. KNAPP never became the mass apolitical organization envisioned by its founders. More than ten years after KNAPP's inception, Jędrzejewicz saw three main reasons for this failure, all of them directly or indirectly connected to the group's relationship with Polonia. First and foremost, he claimed, the inadequate political proficiency of American Polonia prompted numerous emotional but uncoordinated manifestations, which carried no political significance during the war. Second, the charitable actions of Rada were perceived by many as sufficiently fulfilling Polonia's duties towards the old country. The third reason was based on the assumption that the Polish government in exile and not American Polonia should be responsible for Polish politics. In this situation, KNAPP attracted mainly older activists with roots in independence actions on behalf of Poland during World War I.[132]

In the cultural realm, many Polish Americans supported the activities of the Piłsudski Institute and PIASA through financial contributions and voluntary work. Neither organization, however, ever developed a mass Polonian membership, and, at least throughout the 1940s and 1950s, they remained largely the domain of Polish exiles and later generations of educated Polish Americans. The complicated nature of the relationship between

Polonia and the exiles also can be observed in the example of *Tygodnik Polski* and its editor, Jan Lechoń. In its first issue, published on January 10, 1943, *Tygodnik* proclaimed friendly relations with American Polonia to be one of its primary goals. The editorial read: "The one-year-old acquaintance of writers from Poland with their compatriots from America, both through private contacts as well as books and articles, has proved—despite some pessimists' croaking—that a writer from Poland and a Polish American can understand each other perfectly, that can learn from each other, and that they both desire this understanding and knowledge."[133]

The same goal of building bridges between the exiles and American Polonia was frequently repeated in subsequent issues of *Tygodnik*. Letters from the readers' section featured correspondence from Polish-American subscribers—frequently Polish-American priests—including one from Rev. S. A. Iciek, who expressed his genuine excitement over the work of so many recognized Polish intellectuals and artists and pleaded with them: "Stay with us also after the war! Keep up the weakening immigrant spirit."[134] Soon, a handful of authors ventured into Polonian communities, presenting reports from visits with miners in Pennsylvania, trips to Polish Chicago, or occasional interviews with Polonia activists.[135] Beginning in April 1944, *Tygodnik* included a page with short notes about events in the Polish-American community and paid more attention to the exploits of the Polish-American soldiers fighting with the American army in Europe. In an unprecedented move, the entire expanded issue of *Tygodnik* of May 28, 1944, celebrated the creation of the Polish American Congress in Buffalo, New York, and was devoted to American Polonia, its history, organizations, and achievements.[136] In 1946 and 1947, for reasons that included a rather thinly veiled desire to attract financial backing, *Tygodnik* made a conscious effort to reach out to Polonia. At that time Polonia activist Francis Wazeter began publishing excerpts from his radio show, *Talks with Polonia*, and distinguished Polish-American figures and business people were featured in the column Profiles (*Sylwetki*).[137]

In 1946 Lechoń wrote an extensive report on his trip to Chicago and on the author's evening of poetry organized for the Chicago audience. First, he expressed his anxiety that no one was going to attend the meeting: "For certainly everyone is tired and overworked, and not many would bother to occupy one free Sunday afternoon with my lecture." But, he added, his work for *Tygodnik* brought out numerous examples of vivid interest among American Polonia for intellectual pleasures, good books, and good poetry. When the lecture began, the spacious hall of the Polish Museum of America was filled with people. Many Polonia activists, including the busy Charles Rozmarek, were in the audience. "His presence is also a special declaration that Mr. Rozmarek properly esteems the present significance of culture and art for national life; it is a declaration and a call for others," commented Lechoń.[138] *Tygodnik*, however, struggled financially, and its editors had to look for support from other sources, both in America and abroad. Rozmarek and the PAC did not show any interest in supporting an enterprise that they considered elitist and that had no clear appeal to the broader masses of American Polonia. By the end of 1946, in private correspondence to Aleksander Janta, an angry and disillusioned Lechoń would write of Rozmarek as a symbol of "the ocean of indifference" drowning the more ambitious initiatives.[139] Despite these efforts to extend the publication of *Tygodnik*, the weekly had to be discontinued for lack of funds. The last issue of *Tygodnik* closed with the poignant quotation from Joachim Lelewel, a nineteenth-century Polish politician, historian, philosopher, and representative of the Great Emigration. Lelewel's words expressed a pure, Romantic version of the exile mission and sounded like a testament that the new exiles had a duty to fulfill:

> Exile is an indescribable affliction; one needs to experience it to learn the magnitude of its misery. There is no language that could fully depict it. It contains, however, something that lifts a person up, calling forth his strength and courage. In misfortune, a captive is made to give himself up to his fate, bound by impotence and slavery. An exile is free and able to rely on his free will and to resist misfortune. It is up to him to reject and defeat his fate, which afflicts him with so many adversities.... Moreover, an exile in his fragile freedom has the responsibility of action, stemming from his being a Pole and a human being. He took this responsibility on himself of his own accord, went into exile of his own free will, and has the means and can meet his duty.[140]

Lechoń survived in New York a few years longer, with financial support and care from both his Polish friends and some wealthy Polish-American sponsors. In 1956 he committed suicide by jumping from a New York skyscraper.[141]

Lack of knowledge about each other was, perhaps, one of the greatest obstacles in the development of closer personal relationships between exiles and Polish Americans. Kazimierz Wierzyński dedicated a moving essay, "The Walnut Tree Called Dewajtis," to Long Island Polonia, made up of generations of successful farmers.[142] Unlike Lechoń, Wierzyński did not look to Polonia only for its resources; he approached this community with genuine and warm interest. He noted the accomplishments of the Polish immigrants, their struggle for survival, and their attachment to Polish culture. He and his wife made personal friends among the old immigrants, as they did among Americans of non-Polish backgrounds. Irena Lorentowicz, on the other hand, noticeably struggled with her feeling toward Polish Americans. At first patronizing and aloof, at other times moved and enthusiastic, Lorentowicz displayed much curiosity about the lives of Polish Americans and claimed to have formed lasting friendships.[143]

The wartime group of Polish exiles included an exceptionally high percentage of inteligencja and intellectuals—the social, political, and artistic elite of prewar Poland—who felt entitled to political and cultural leadership. As they struggled to establish contacts with Polonia, they also tried to define their own role within the Polish diaspora and to adhere to the ideals of the exile mission. They considered the continuation of the Polish nation in exile their responsibility and understood that this historical role of the inteligencja was made more urgent by the extermination policies of the Third Reich. Perhaps their longest-lasting accomplishments were the cultural institutions they initiated to preserve and develop the intellectual heritage of the homeland. KNAPP, the most representative political body of the early wave, failed to attract a mass following and gradually disappeared from the political scene. However, its impact on the creation and the early policies of the Polish American Congress make it an important legacy from the exiles. Speaking with the voice of the most illustrious writers and poets, the exiles expressed the suffering and spirit of the fighting homeland, while they themselves adopted the exile mission tested during Poland's nineteenth-century struggle for independence.

This historical obligation became even firmer, as the guilt of absence overwhelmed the refugees. Władysław Gieysztor poignantly wrote about the long, meaningless, lonely, and gray days of an exile, filled with worry and anxiety: "We seem to be alive—but really I often do not know whether present life is reality or fiction. Poland and our people in Poland are so far. ... Far away are reality and painful concern for the beloved people and land—far at the end of the world!" After nights of troubling nightmares, Gieysztor still encouraged an equally depressed friend to be strong and full of faith, since Poles in Poland suffered so much more:

> The threat of death looms over them day and night—and we are safe here. We have food—they starve. Their hardship is greater than ours. This is all true. But they fight, they are together, at home; they see Polish sun, listen to Polish skylarks sing. Polish storks return to them, not to us each spring! They take their strength from the aromas of the Polish land!
>
> They do not know what the madness of hopeless longing can do to the Polish soul. What the blindness to foreign beauty, foreign sun means. They do not know how deep is the torment of the gray refugee days, days outside of life.[144]

Irena Lorentowicz revealed the agony of listening to the news about the Warsaw Uprising and the city's lonely struggle in 1944: "We lived through it with despair and fear from afar, we 'happy,' we 'free.' ... Nights of waiting, nights of hope. We hear the echoes, safe behind the ocean, undeserving, unharmed, fed full, worthless refugees."[145] Feelings of guilt accompanied the realization of their gradual loss of legitimacy to speak for fighting Poland. For example, Jerzy Paczkowski, himself a poet of the Skamander generation who had fought in the Polish resistance movement organized in France, in 1942 wrote a bitter response to a poignant war poem in which Kazimierz Wierzyński called for sacrifice in the struggle. Paczkowski accused Wierzyński of fighting the enemy with rhymes, when others fought with grenades; of chiseling his poetry during walks in a safe New York park while others were left behind to do "the dirty work."[146]

The exiles tried to reestablish this legitimacy after the war had ended, but the homeland found itself in the chains of a communistic regime. While the ranks of the Polish postwar diaspora were swelling with veterans and refugees from Siberia and the DP camps, *Tygodnik Polski* revisited the concept of the exile mission, defined around the exile community as a "free voice" of the Polish nation. The author of the 1946 editorial "Emigration Speaks for the Country" (most likely Lechoń himself) admitted that even though the current emigration probably would never equal the genius of the nineteenth-century Great Emigration, their goals made it a close successor. While living in freedom, the author wrote, the exiles needed to devote themselves to the homeland and "to our brethren, imprisoned and silenced." United in the struggle for Poland, Polish exiles could "not only help our countrymen immediately, but also speed up the moment of freedom, without hope of which our life would not be worth living even a day longer."[147] Numerous other references to the Great Emigration and to political exiles of the past directly called for the conscious "continuation of the national mission" and placed post–World War II exiles as heirs of the Polish Romantic tradition.[148]

After the end of the war, the exiles faced the task of redefining their place in American Polonia and in the larger American society. They had to give up their self-inflicted isolation based on the assumption of a speedy return to Poland. Their institutions, cut off from government funds, struggled for financial survival or totally disappeared. Some exiles did eventually return to Poland: poet Julian Tuwim from the United States in 1946, Antoni Słonimski from London in 1946, and Władysław Broniewski from Germany in 1945. Irena Lorentowicz returned in 1960. Some died in exile: anthropologist Bronisław Malinowski in 1942, and KNAPP activists Ignacy Matuszewski and Henryk Floyar-Rajchman in 1946 and 1951, respectively. A handful committed suicide: Wieniawa-Długoszewski in 1942, and Lechoń in 1956. Others blended into the new, broader wave of political refugees arriving on American shores after the war.

2 ‖ "All I have left is my free song"
The Polish Community in the Displaced Persons Camps

Formation of the DP Camps

> Thursday, April 12, 1945, was just another prisoner-of-war day, although there were rumors that parts of the wider area around us might be already in the Allied hands. . . . In mid afternoon, I left my barrack for a little while, and when I was coming back it happened. I heard bullets buzzing through the air and saw a bent figure in a khaki uniform running on the other side of the barbed-wire fence in the direction of one of the observation towers. It seemed that he had a machine gun in his hand. Then a huge tank rolled through the middle of the roll-call area, with an armored car at its side and we knew immediately what it meant. We were free![1]

AFTER LONG MONTHS OF captivity, Leokadia Rowinski could rejoice with the other women of the Warsaw Uprising who were liberated from the Oberlangen POW camp along with her. The women sang, cried, prayed, and planned for the future. Soon, however, their happiness gave way to anxiety and even despair. As Leokadia and her friends pored over the suddenly available newspapers, they understood that "there was no place in the world for the likes of us. We had no country and no home to return to."[2] The brutal and confusing reality of the Cold War thwarted the euphoria of freedom. The decision whether to repatriate to communist-dominated Poland or to embrace exile became the most difficult and painful choice that the refugees faced after the war. While waiting for repatriation or emigration, they stayed in displaced persons camps, which international organizations had created on German, Austrian, and Italian soil. For many of them, the sojourn in the DP camps lasted several months to several years.

The Polish Community in the Displaced Persons Camps | 59

Map 1. Major DP camps with Polish population in the occupation zones of Germany and Austria, 1945–1951. Map by Emil Pocock, Department of History, Eastern Connecticut State University, and the author

Poles were just a fraction of the approximately 10 million people who remained outside the borders of their home countries. In May 1945 "Europe was on the move."[3] Large numbers of refugees immediately undertook strenuous journeys home, either walking or catching rides on military transports, and the roads of devastated Europe filled with multilingual masses. Governments of western European countries promptly organized transport of their nationals, and the French, Danish, Belgians, Dutch, Norwegians, and Italians quickly found themselves on their way home. Among those who awaited repatriation were large contingents of Poles, Jews, Ukrainians, Russians, Bulgarians, Estonians, Lithuanians, Latvians, Czech, Slovaks, Hungarians, southern Slavs, and many other nationalities.[4] Their homes were in a part of Europe that was changing dramatically before their eyes, while borders moved, new communist governments formed, and the victorious Soviet army reigned unchallenged.

Before any transportation to central and eastern Europe could be provided, the destitute refugees needed immediate care: shelter, food, clothing, and medical attention. In the early period after liberation, care for the refugees was supervised by the Supreme Headquarters Allied Expeditionary Force (SHAEF) Displaced Persons Branch.[5] Shortly thereafter the United Nations Relief and Rehabilitation Administration (UNRRA), an international organization created in the fall of 1943, took over SHAEF's functions.[6] In addition to relief work among the refugees, UNRRA's main goal was the repatriation of the refugee population to their respective countries. Between the fall of 1945 and the end of 1946, UNRRA repatriated about 8 million people of different nationalities to their homelands. By June 1947 UNRRA had completed its activities,[7] and at this time its responsibilities were taken over by the Preparatory Commission of the International Refugee Organization (PCIRO), a new international agency assigned to the task of resettling the remaining DP population. The International Refugee Organization (IRO) began its operations in July 1947 and completed them in December 1951.[8] Since that time, refugee problems have been handled by the Office of the United Nations High Commissioner for Refugees (UNHCR).[9]

In May 1945 nearly 1.9 million citizens of prewar Poland were in Germany: about 1.2 million in the British, American, and French zones of occupation and seven hundred thousand in the Soviet zone.[10] Over 90 percent had been slave laborers in the economy of the Third Reich. The remaining 10 percent included prisoners of Nazi concentration camps and prisons, former POWs, and Poles who had been slated for Germanization. In the last stages of the war, several thousand soldiers of the Holy Cross Brigade (Brygada Świętokrzyska) of the National Armed Forces (Narodowe Siły Zbrojne, or NSZ, a right-wing anticommunist military organization), who had left Poland under the pressure of the incoming Soviets, found themselves on the territory of Germany, as did inmates of concentration camps and prisons evacuated before the onslaught of the Red Army. Former *Wehrmacht* (German army) soldiers who had been forcibly conscripted from the population in Silesia and Pomerania were still in Germany, as was a smaller group of Poles deported from the territory annexed by the Soviet Union. Polish armed forces stationed in Germany in the spring of 1945 included about sixteen thousand soldiers and officers, representing the First Armored Division under the command of General Stanisław Maczek; the First Independent Parachute Brigade (Samodzielna Brygada Spadochronowa); Division 131 of the British Air Force of Occupation; and Polish land forces that had fought as part of the French army. Most of these units participated in occupation duties in various parts of Germany.[11] The ranks of Polish civilian refugees in the Western zones soon swelled with those who had escaped from the Soviet zone of occupation and escapees from Poland who had illegally crossed the border. These numbers increased further through the high birth rate among DPs.[12]

Most Polish displaced persons, like those of other ethnic groups, lived in assembly centers, or camps, created and supervised by UNRRA. According to UNRRA statistics, there were more than 250 camps in December 1945, and more than 700 in July 1947.[13] Some Poles who could walk and who were determined to get back home as soon as possible set off on their way to Poland in the summer months of 1945. No coordinated repatriation action began until the fall, when train transports became available. By the end of December 1945, UNRRA had repatriated about 150,000 Polish DPs and provided care for 438,643 Poles in the territory of Germany and Austria. Statistics for December 1946, after the major repatriation action was over, showed that 278,868 Polish displaced persons remained in the DP camps of Germany, Austria, and Italy. All in all, between November 1945 and June 1947, some 549,998 Polish DPs were repatriated to Poland from the three Western occupation zones of Germany and 11,676 from Austria.[14]

Most of the available data on the internal structure of the Polish DP population comes from the period after the mass repatriation was over and the IRO had begun to compile statistics that could be used in the resettlement of the remaining 166,000 persons born in Poland. In 1947 data on the age structure of the Polish DP population indicated 9.5 percent were below two years of age; 6 percent were between two and seven; 4.5 percent were between seven and fourteen; 3 percent were between fourteen and eighteen; 69 percent

TABLE 2.1. Polish displaced persons receiving UNRRA assistance in Germany, Austria, Italy, the Middle East, and China, December 1945–June 1947

NATIONALITY	DEC. 1945	MARCH 1946	JUNE 1946	SEPT. 1946	DEC. 1946	MARCH 1947	JUNE 1947
Polish	438,649	476,964	369,284	341,968	276,785	193,331	166,181
Total	736,014	827,699	773,248	781,359	746,283	720,604	624,749

Total for December 1945–September 1946 does not include displaced persons in Italy, for whom nationality breakdown is not available.

SOURCE: George Woodbridge, *UNRRA: The History of the United Nations Relief and Rehabilitation Administration* (New York: Columbia University Press, 1950), 3:423.

were between eighteen and forty-five; 7 percent were between forty-five and sixty; and 1 percent were more than sixty years of age. There were more men than women in all three Western occupation zones.[15] Data compiled by the IRO in March 1948 showed that 38 percent of Polish men had a background in agriculture and farming, about 30 percent were skilled workers, and about 6 percent were professionals. Many Polish women (33 percent) worked in agriculture and service, and, of these, almost 19 percent were domestic servants. Some 7 percent of Polish women had professional backgrounds. By comparison, the 1948 report estimated that the Polish group in the American zone included about 10,000 skilled farmers and the same number of unskilled agricultural workers; 10,000 skilled artisans and workers; 4,500 people in the professions; and 7,000 persons in various white-collar occupations.[16] A different report, from the summer of 1949, assessed the class structure of the Polish DP group as follows: 68 percent farmers; 12 percent workers; 15 percent craftsmen and artisans; and 5 percent professional middle class (inteligencja).[17] A registration of inteligencja undertaken in all three Western zones in 1946 revealed that the group included 3,500 commissioned officers, 2,870 civil servants, 1,480 economists and merchants, 640 teachers, 520 civil engineers and technicians, 340 lawyers, 260 medical doctors, 240 journalists, and 180 artists.[18]

DPs of the same ethnic background immediately began to seek out their fellow nationals. Separation into nationalities proceeded spontaneously but was also encouraged by the occupation and UNRRA administrations for reasons of convenience and control. Clusters of Balts, Ukrainians, Poles, or Slovaks formed in various locations and, as the word spread, attracted more

TABLE 2.2. Occupational skills of Polish refugees in Austria, Germany, and Italy by major occupational groups, March 1948

MAJOR OCCUPATIONAL GROUPS	MEN	WOMEN
Professional and managerial	3,537	1,812
Professional	2,337	1,128
Semiprofessional	488	571
Managerial and office	712	113
Clerical and Sales	1,850	1,453
Service	1,332	4,823
Domestic service	39	3,297
Personal service	1,018	1,522
Protective service	275	4
Agriculture, fishery, forestry, and similar occupations	21,072	8,567
Skilled	16,836	3,712
Manufacturing	8,318	3,514
Nonmanufacturing	8,518	198
Semiskilled	3,724	409
Apprentices	335	74
Helpers	671	380
Laborers	1,400	390
No previous work experience	4,683	3,961
Total	55,440	25,581

SOURCE: Louise W. Holborn, *The International Refugee Organization, a Specialized Agency of the United Nations: Its History And Work, 1946-1952* (London: Oxford University Press, 1956), 305.

and more of their countrymen. Initially, Jews were placed together with DPs of other nationalities. Prompted by the so-called Harrison report and responding to the pressure from Jewish organizations and Jewish DPs themselves, American and British authorities organized separate Jewish centers beginning in the fall of 1945.[19] Separate camps ensured that DPs of the same background could find comfort and support, and develop national cultures in exile and common political programs. Both the military and UNRRA/IRO teams found the day-to-day management of ethnically homogeneous camps less troublesome. This arrangement reduced opportunities for ethnic animosities and conflict, and allowed repatriation actions and emigration programs to be executed more easily.[20]

The separation of ethnic groups, however, was never total. Many camps continued to house refugees of different nationalities, and most large cities had several camps, giving the DPs ample possibility to interact. These interactions often reflected the multiethnic makeup of prewar Poland. For example, DPs who could read Polish borrowed books from Polish libraries and subscribed to the Polish press. Ukrainian, Belorussian, and sometimes Jewish students attended Polish schools, and foreign student organizations at German universities often gave mutual support. Scouting and sports became another arena for collaboration and exchange of friendly visits.[21]

Differences among ethnic groups, generally rooted in the complicated past, often had deepened during the war years and were revived by competition for better living conditions in DP camps or for available resettlement opportunities. DPs of different ethnic backgrounds understood, however, the basic need to present a common position before international agencies, occupation authorities, or forced repatriation efforts. For example, some Russians and Ukrainians slated for repatriation to the Soviet Union found refuge and false papers in Polish camps. Polish and Ukrainian journalists organized meetings during which they discussed the situation of the DP press and the most important DP issues. Meetings of the International Bureau for DP Collaboration (Międzynarodowe Biuro Porozumiewawcze DP) attracted representatives of as many as ten different ethnic groups and debated common issues of DP camp life, emigration opportunities, and cultural exchanges. They also worked on ways to improve interethnic relations and to secure a positive DP image, necessary for successful emigration.[22]

Conditions in the DP Camps

Displaced Poles undertook community-building efforts immediately after liberation. Both SHAEF and UNRRA provided an organizational framework, but grassroots initiatives accounted for the spontaneous creation of the first Polish communities, which mushroomed all over Germany despite very difficult conditions. One of those in charge of organizing a DP camp was

Wacław Sterner, an officer of the Polish Home Army and a soldier in the Warsaw Uprising in 1944. Captured after the suppression of the uprising, he was a prisoner in the German Oflag in Sandbostel until its liberation in May 1945. The British military authorities appointed Sterner *komendant* (officer in charge) of a hastily assembled displaced persons camp in Buchhorst, which housed over five hundred Poles and small groups of French and Hungarians. People found refuge in the chambers of a brick factory's blast furnace and in the unwalled wooden shelters used for drying bricks. Sterner remembered that in those first weeks

> People camped there like nomads, in conditions contrary to any basic human needs.... There were no sanitary installations whatsoever. The entire area was covered by several dozen little campfires. Pots or kettles with water stood on bricks over [these fires] for people to prepare meals or warm water to wash or to do laundry. A striking sight was a large number of women. Taking advantage of the cloudless weather, they cooked, washed, sewed, and hurried around the grounds of the brick factory. Altogether it resembled a huge Gypsy camp.[23]

Another Polish former POW, Jan Michalski, spent the entire war in a German Oflag. He also was recruited for the post of DP camp komendant. His new assignment was Geesthacht: a large territory of shabby wooden barracks built for foreign workers around a munitions factory that had been almost completely destroyed by bombing. About two thousand Poles lived there along with a large group of Yugoslavs, also former slave laborers for the Reich. The camp was closed before winter because the barracks in Geesthacht and in neighboring Krümmel did not have any heating.[24]

Some DPs had more luck, if only temporarily. A third camp in that same area, in Spackenberg, boasted a clean and neat settlement of small one-story houses surrounded by little gardens, built before the war for young couples—members of the *Hitlerjugend*, the Nazi youth organization. The camp had a spacious old *Kulturhaus* (community center), which included guest rooms, a theater hall, and a large kitchen with adjoining dining hall.[25] In terms of the general living conditions of Polish DPs, however, Spackenberg was the exception rather than the rule.

The largest Polish camp in Germany was Wildflecken, where more than twenty thousand Polish DPs lived at any given time. Truppenlager Wildflecken, hidden in the mountains and forests of northeast Bavaria, had been an SS training camp. It resembled a town made up of huge military facilities and covered an area of about fifteen square miles.[26] Poles quartered there gave Wildflecken a new name, Durzyń, which derived from the name of the *Durzyńcy*, a Slavic tribe that had lived in that part of Bavaria in the fifth and sixth centuries AD before being pushed to the east by German tribes.[27] The scale of operations in Durzyń can be illustrated by just one example: the camp bakery prepared more than nine tons of bread daily.[28] At Durzyń UNRRA/IRO worker Kathryn Hulme was struck by the bleakness of the large rooms filled with dozens of iron beds assigned for single men. Other halls were partitioned with stacked-up luggage to create family cubicles. Families who shared such quarters usually hung army blankets to make additional "dividing walls." Hulme saw those "khaki labyrinths" as "the last ramparts of privacy to which the DP's clung, preferring to shiver with one less blanket on their straw-filled sacks rather than to dress, comb their hair, feed the baby or make a new one with ten to twenty pairs of stranger eyes watching every move."[29]

Another large Polish refugee community in Germany was formed in Haren on the river Ems, where the Polish First Armored Division was stationed, after the British authorities expelled the German population from the town. In June 1945 Haren was renamed Maczków in honor of the revered commander in chief, General Stanisław Maczek. Between 1945 and 1947, when the division was transferred to Great Britain, an entirely Polish town council governed a population consisting of military personnel and their families as well as civilian DPs. The town boasted its own Roman Catholic parish as well as its own schools, theater, publishing house, police, fire brigade, and hospital. Maczków earned the name "the capital of Little Poland," the state in exile created by Polish refugees in occupied Germany. In the American zone of Austria, the Polish camp in Ebensee played a similar role.[30]

The training centers of the Polish Guard Companies (*Kompanie Wartownicze*) in the American zone in Germany were a different type of large Polish DP community. These units, employing DPs and organized in a military fashion, were formed in 1945 to relieve American soldiers from some of their occupation duties, such as guarding military supplies, constructing and conserving airfields, and maintaining military installations and vehicles. By the fall of 1945, 75,000 Polish men were employed in these formations. Between 1946 and 1947 the number fluctuated around 40,000, and dropped to about 11,500 in March 1948. The mere existence of Polish Guards units became a bone of contention between the Polish government in exile and the Soviet Union, which saw them as hampering repatriation. The Soviets even accused the Guards of housing "fascist elements" among the DPs. In order to accommodate these protests and to emphasize the civilian character of the units, the American military changed the color of the guards' uniforms from khaki to black and replaced badges bearing the word "Poland" with the letters "CG" (Civilian Guard).[31]

The training center for Polish Guards in Mannheim-Kafertal (named "Kościuszko" by the Guards) distinguished itself with its high degree of internal organization and activism, encouraged and facilitated by the American military. The Polish Guards published their own newspaper, *Ostatnie Wiadomości* (Latest News), and, due to their secure pay, could sustain many cultural and social initiatives. The financial basis of the Guards' activities was the *Fundusz Społeczny* (Social Fund), which collected 2 percent of the Guards' salary. Money from the fund supported numerous causes, such as DP welfare funds and Polish schools.[32]

In general, living conditions in Polish DP camps varied in different locations throughout the entire DP period. For example, a report on the camps in northern Bavaria prepared in November 1947 for the Polish Union in Germany revealed multiple problems with housing for Polish DPs. The authors of the report indicated that only one camp, in Coburg, had decent housing. At the Amberg military base, the buildings were dirty, worn out, lacking adequate sanitary installations, and very overcrowded. Wooden barracks at the Weiden and Hohenfels camps were unsuitable for winter weather.[33] Moreover, frequent transfers from camp to camp hurt DPs and became a source of frustration and bitterness:

> DPs transferred to a different camp almost always get buildings in condition not suitable for living. Making them into adequate living quarters requires a lot of work and money. Recently, just a month ago, relatively well-organized camps from Auerbach and Flossenburg were transferred to the dirty and damaged military buildings in Amberg, with electrical installations destroyed, toilets clogged, pipes and taps in bathrooms partially missing, huge and undivided halls for families to live in, and no outlets for stoves to heat the halls during the coming winter.[34]

Population transfers from camp to camp were the scourge of refugee existence. At first, UNRRA moved DPs as camps were established and reorganized. After UNRRA launched its repatriation action, however, DPs interpreted frequent moves as a not-so-subtle attempt to make their lives so unbearable that they would volunteer to return to Poland. DPs charged that UNRRA officials tried to unsettle and destroy DP community structures to compel them to repatriate, and complained of UNRRA's abuse of power and mistreatment of refugees.[35] Unfortunately, the ordeal did not end after the IRO took over, although transfers from camp to camp lost their political dimension. Now camps were being closed and consolidated because of emigration. New transition camps functioned as temporary stops in which DPs waited for emigration processing.

Next to living conditions, food was the issue that was of utmost importance to the malnourished camp inhabitants. Problems with the quantity and quality of food remained high on the agenda of all DPs, whether they lived inside or outside the camps. The average daily calorie intake for DPs fluctuated between two thousand and twenty-five hundred in 1945; it dipped to less than sixteen hundred in 1947 and 1948 and increased again to two thousand the following year.[36] The undernourished DP population often received food that included only small amounts of meat and shortening and an inadequate supply of vegetables. Fruit was virtually unobtainable. Complaints about shipments of rotten food or of just one type of food for an entire week echoed throughout all the camps.[37] Parcels from the Red Cross and CARE, an international humanitarian organization, improved the situation slightly, and were distributed to the DPs either in full or after being divided into separate products.[38] Despite a ban on black market activities and the prosecution of those apprehended, many DPs traded food products with the local German population. Theft of food from German farms also became a problem in some areas.[39] Some smaller camps with land available for cultivation established little gardens to supplement the DP diet. In later periods of the camps' existence, DPs were allowed and encouraged to establish their own cooperatives to improve the food situation. Camp inhabitants also focused a lot of attention on the proper functioning of the camp kitchens. For example, during a meeting in the Polish camp at Altenhagen on August 8, 1945, nearly two hundred people participated in a "kitchen crisis" that investigated the honesty and qualifications of the cook and the camp director.[40]

Clothing was yet another nagging problem for the Polish DP population. Most slave laborers had only rags at the time of liberation, and concentration camp prisoners had only *pasiaki*, the striped camp uniform. UNRRA/IRO provided a certain amount of secondhand clothing for their charges (in part confiscated from the German population), but the supply never came close to the demand. The DPs themselves had to improvise. The skilled hands of Polish women dyed and fitted German military coats, converted sheets and blankets into usable outfits, and used any other available piece of fabric, including parachute silk, for children's or adults' garments. Shoes were harder to produce in the camps, so DPs acutely felt any shortage of seasonal footwear. Soldiers from the Second Corps organized clothing and shoe drives and shipped the shoes to the impoverished camps in Austria.[41] American Relief for Poland and the NCWC sent parcels from the United States. Despite all these efforts, the condition of the DP wardrobe remained below reasonable standards and became a source of frustration for those who were getting ready to emigrate. "I took a coat, a radio, and clothes on credit, not to look like a DP from Europe," wrote one Polish DP already resettled in the United States, expressing a widespread feeling that DP clothing had become a visible symbol of their misfortune and poverty.[42]

In the period directly following liberation, the health needs of the displaced persons became particularly pressing. A very high percentage of DPs suffered from malnutrition and exhaustion, and many children were affected by anemia and rickets. There were numerous cases of tuberculosis, venereal disease, heart disease, dental problems, and outbreaks of typhus. In time these health problems diminished, in large part due to an effectively functioning network of UNRRA health care centers and hospitals, as well as the efforts of the Polish Red Cross.[43] Other types of care, such as counseling and intervention for crisis situations, depression, and posttraumatic disorders that required professional attention, were mostly unavailable. Some dangers to the refugee psyche stemmed from the prolonged sojourn in the camps: the lack of privacy, the paternalism of charitable organizations, idleness, and uncertainty about the future.[44] Many contemporary witnesses reflected on the mood of discouragement and melancholy prevalent in the camps. The collective symptoms observed in the European DP camps after the summer of 1947 (when the major repatriation action was already finished, but resettlement schemes were not yet fully developed) were described as "DP apathy." It manifested itself in various neurotic behaviors, a rising crime rate, absenteeism from work, procrastination, and a decreasing interest in camp affairs, entertainment, and cultural events.[45] The UNRRA personnel, for the most part not qualified for this type of social work and preoccupied with the problems of day-to-day existence, were not able to address such problems.[46]

The DPs themselves had to transform the camps into communities. Concerns about peace and morality in the camps remained high on the agenda. In the first few months following liberation, some DPs, acting on long-repressed feelings of hatred, took justice into their own hands, meting out revenge to the oppressors and killing at least several dozen Germans. Cases of plunder and theft from German businesses (mainly food and clothing), underground production of illegal papers and moonshine, and trade on the black market usually received disproportionate attention from the German authorities and press. Polish DPs often protested against German accusations and stereotyping of the DPs as a criminal element, and objected to particularly harsh prison sentences for minor crimes.[47]

The truth of the matter was, however, that within the camps violence, petty crime, and the abuse of alcohol, were on the rise, especially during the first two years after the end of the war. The number of extramarital relationships and births of children out of wedlock also increased. Concerns about morality led the clergy, schools, and social organizations to sponsor campaigns under the banner of the "struggle with crime and demoralization." Both the Polish DP press and social organizations signaled the urgent need to counteract individual behaviors that hurt the image of the community and presented it in an unfavorable light to outsiders.[48]

Personal conflicts and infighting particularly plagued camp life. Unavoidable in any large population, they thrived among people suffering from a lack of meaningful occupation and frustrated by their ambiguous situation. In DP camps, gossip that would be totally harmless in a different place and time could turn deadly. Because qualification for emigration depended on multiple and detailed screenings by the immigration authorities, allegations of collaboration or an unfounded denunciation from an undisclosed source could block a DP's chances for emigration.[49] The Polish DP councils tried to deal with the inundation of accusations in their own way. Special disciplinary committees, which included persons of uncompromising character, remained busy with investigations of malevolent charges.[50] *Okólnik* (Circular), a publication of the Polish Union in the U.S. zone of Germany, recommended as a good example the policies of one DP camp council president who demanded that accusers repeat and support their charges during public meetings for everyone to judge: "Very shameful moments: a gossiper, 'pressed to the wall,' twists and fidgets, trying to find justification, but the pillory of public opinion is terrible. There is no mercy, and memory is long. When a gossiper is identified, he has to work on righting [his] wrongs in order to regain his good name. Nothing goes unpunished."[51] In Ludwigsburg the disciplinary committee issued statements that announced the results of investigations and required false accusers to retract their accusations publicly.[52] Ill will, revenge, jealousy, or bitterness caused by the accuser's own misfortune stood behind most cases of unfounded incriminations.

Although conditions of life in the camps were the first concern of the DPs, the camps were gradually transformed into communities, and DP organizations took on new functions. DP leaders consciously politicized the DP masses and prepared them to embrace the exile mission.

Building the Community

Following the concept of Little Poland in exile, the Polish government in London strongly discouraged repatriation and tried to retain abroad as large a representation of the Polish nation as possible. Liaison officers were first charged with the task of carrying out antirepatriation propaganda on behalf of the government. These officers were recruited from the Polish forces under British command stationed on German territory.[53] Later, after these positions had been eliminated, London Poles communicated directly with DP leaders, sending them instructions and directives, and assuming supervision over DP organizations.[54] Camp governments and a multitude of DP organizations played major roles in the transformation of coincidental groups of refugees into effectively functioning communities. Many individuals were motivated in their activities by a conscious sense of responsibility for the displaced Polish masses. The nineteenth-century exile mission called for work for Poland and for the preservation of all things Polish by Poles abroad; DP leaders invoked and revived this mission in the conditions of postwar displacement. Work that initially aimed at making the difficult life in the DP camps more tolerable, gradually acquired historical significance as the political situation put the displaced population at the forefront of the struggle between communism and the free world. The exile of Polish refugees became their symbolic statement to the international community.

The leaders of the displaced Polish community were mostly surviving members of the inteligencja. The Nazi authorities had targeted that social stratum during the war because they understood its leadership tradition embedded in Polish history. Members of the inteligencja, particularly those who participated in the resistance movement, were prosecuted vigorously and placed in German prisons and concentration camps as political prisoners. The Oflagen supplied a large group of commissioned officers, as well as draftees and volunteers of 1939 who in civilian life had worked in the professions. The creative energy that had been pent up during years of submission and slave labor could finally be released and put to good use. Lack of employment and the boredom of DP camp life were trying for individuals used to being active and productive. Their abilities and leadership skills could be utilized for the good of the community, so they threw themselves into organizing groups of refugee Poles into Polish communities in exile. Their activity brought a sense of normalcy after the nightmare of the war and helped to relieve the grief, frustration, and loneliness of the postwar period.

When the newly approved komendant, Jan Michalski, arrived in Geesthacht, his camp at Sandstrasse already had elected a camp committee to serve as an executive body. Only reluctantly did the council give up its authority to the new military commander and accept a more limited role as a camp council, an advisory body to the komendant and his deputy. In the following months, the power struggle between the camp council and the officers in charge abounded in drama.[55] The authority of the komendant, however, was supported both by the Allied military government of the occupation zones and by the Polish liaison officers. In the American zone of Austria, Polish officers from the Murnau Oflag in Bavaria organized several local Polish refugee centers, and in the British zone a group of Polish liaison officers from the Second Corps helped to establish camp councils in Karyntia.[56]

In practice, a camp komendant in the early period of the DP camps did not have much legal power, which rested instead with the occupation armies; but the responsibilities of these komendanci, although vaguely defined, were extensive. The internal organization of the camps; the registration of displaced persons; and relationships with the military and UNRRA as well as with the local German government and population all remained in the hands of the komendanci. The effectiveness of their work and the authority of their positions depended almost entirely on individual personalities and experience in dealing with large and diversified groups of people. By the end of 1945, when UNRRA took over the management of the camps from the military, the position of the officer in charge had gradually disappeared.

UNRRA/IRO employees, in close cooperation with the occupation authorities, headed the camps' administration but usually left enough space for self-government by camp councils (*rady obozowe*), executive boards (*zarządy obozowe*), or committees (*komitety obozowe*) elected by the DPs themselves.[57] The specific structure of governing bodies in Polish camps, as well as their names, differed from camp to camp and changed as time went by. The relationships between the elected camp authorities and UNRRA employees also differed. For example, a report from a meeting of Polish camp representatives in Northern Bavaria in May 1947 assessed the relationships between DP governments and UNRRA workers as ranging from "nonexistent contacts" (Furth/Bay), to "hostile" (Auerbach/Pegnitz), to "indifferent" (Weiden-"La Guardia"), to "friendly" (Aschaffenburg).[58] The report also made it clear that UNRRA interfered with the DP councils' functions and tried to limit their authority. For example, the council in the Polish DP camp in Coburg protested an UNRRA welfare officer's claim of the power to decide on expenditures from a council fund established from individual DP contributions and ticket sales to cultural events.[59]

The responsibilities of self-governing bodies in Polish camps were very diverse and often depended on the size of the camp and the degree of organization within its population. Their main duties included organization and support of the militia (camp guards) and civil courts, as well as control over the economic well-being of the DPs, that is, the maintenance of kitchens and systems of distribution for food and material goods. The councils were also responsible for cultural and educational activities in the camps. Council members presented the needs and demands of the camp population to the military, UNRRA, and the IRO, and generally acted as brokers between the DPs and any outside authorities.

Elections for the councils were an important exercise in democracy. Detailed reports from council meetings indicate that great significance was attached to protocol and that minute infractions of the bylaws caused vehement opposition and frequently resulted in demands to repeat the elections. Bureaucracy flourished, and the governing bodies grew in size, assigning posts in numerous committees to anyone willing to serve. Personnel changes occurred frequently, either because of abuse of power or through repatriation and emigration. According to a report from the Polish camp in Ludwigsburg covering the nine-month period between October 1948 and August 1949, the camp committee convened eighteen times in regular sessions and organized three additional plenary meetings and two informational meetings. Every day the chairman of the committee held a conference with the executive director (*kierownik*) of the camp to discuss current problems. Several special commissions were elected: an examination commission to determine the legality of the committee's activities; a disciplinary commission to deal with problems of order in the camp; a commission to control the repertoire of the theater and movies; a commission to carry out new elections in the camp; and, finally, an appeals commission. During the time covered by the report, about thirty people held posts in the Ludwigsburg camp government.[60]

The Ludwigsburg camp committee also had the authority to give out concessions for private "businesses," such as canteens or little stores for the camp inhabitants, to assign extra supplies to boy and girl scout troops, to make loans to private persons, to prepare papers for those ready to emigrate, and to organize cultural events and national celebrations. Additionally, Ludwigsburg's camp government organized information services, for example, the reading of news through the camp megaphones. Special initiatives, such as making crosses and nameplates for cemeteries where Poles were buried, also needed the camp council's approval and support.[61]

In 1946 the city council in the Polish DP camp in Durzyń adopted laws regarding mandatory work for all camp inhabitants. Every DP between the ages of sixteen and fifty was obliged to work for the camp one day a week without regard to any official position they held within the community. Only pregnant women, mothers with children below ten years of age, the sick and the crippled, and school-aged youth were released from this duty. Those caught avoiding work for the community were punished by the cancellation of extra rations of cigarettes, coffee, or dried fruit. Camp governments assigned similar one-day-a-week work duties to the inhabitants of Hohenfels (Lechów), Weiden-"La Guardia," and possibly other camps.[62] It is difficult to determine how or even whether those laws were implemented and how long they functioned in Polish DP communities in Germany.

Discipline and safety within the camps received special attention from the camp governments. Most camps had guard units made up of young men trained and supervised by a leader with a military background. One of the militia's most important functions was to unload trucks with UNRRA supplies and to protect their contents in camp warehouses. Other duties included patrolling the camp area to prevent black-market activities by DPs or the German population, detecting thefts and alcohol distilleries on the camp grounds, as well as watching for roaming groups of former SS troops. Militia teams did not carry weapons, but some of the more energetic officers did manage (at least in the first weeks after the end of the war) to arm their "boys" with handguns.[63]

From the first days of freedom, Polish DPs organized religious life within the camps, building improvised chapels or at least field altars. The need for spiritual care and religious expression was great. Throughout the war, the Nazis had persecuted the Polish Roman Catholic clergy.[64] At the end of the war, there were about 900 Polish priests in Germany, 761 of them liberated from wartime imprisonment in the Dachau concentration camp. By the end of 1945, about 250 priests had emigrated to different countries and some 100 had returned to Poland. The remaining group immediately plunged into religious service. In June 1945 the pope appointed Józef Gawlina, the Field Bishop of the Polish Armed Forces in the West, an ordinary for the Polish refugee population and entrusted him with a mission to organize religious care for the displaced Poles.[65]

Priests often worked around the clock to meet the needs of tens of thousands of inhabitants in many different camps. Since they did not receive any pay for their work from international organizations, their support depended on the generosity of the DP congregations. The statistics for the British zone for the year 1947, cited by *Naród Polski* (Polish Nation), illustrate the scope of the priests' commitment: 126 Polish priests served 255 camps with a total population of nearly 140,000; they taught religion in 125 elementary schools, 13 high schools, 101 kindergartens, and 168 special classes; and they cared for patients in 78 hospitals.[66]

Among the most needed services were weddings and baptisms. The Nazis had not allowed prisoners or laborers to marry, and many people had to wait for the official recognition of their relationships. In the atmosphere of long-awaited freedom, some young people felt that they had to make up for lost time. Others, who had lost their families in the war, wanted to start new lives.[67] The DP population in general showed a large increase in birth rates. According to a report from the Polish DP camp in Hohenfels, the camp parish registered 914 weddings and 890 baptisms during the first four years after liberation.[68] A great majority of Polish DPs participated in Roman Catholic services, and many were active in numerous religious organizations, including church choirs and Caritas, a charitable group started by the Catholic clergy in Germany. The Hohenfels camp could boast of six different religious organizations, and Altenstadt had nine. Some camps had more than one chapel, and services were celebrated twice a day. Additional religious education for the DPs and their children was also available, and some priests succeeded in organization of pilgrimages to religious shrines in Germany and Italy.[69] The responsibilities of priests increased even more as emigration began and refugees asked for "certificates of moral standing" that could attest to their piety, Christian values, and involvement in the church. They were also swamped with requests for birth, marriage, and death certificates—essential documents for emigration processing.

Polish priests also organized schools and taught religion to Polish children, prepared them for sacraments, and provided religious instruction and activities, such as scouting. Special publishing houses put out hundreds of thousand copies of Catechisms, prayer books, holy pictures, and hymnals. The religious press included at least eight different newspaper titles aimed at general readers as well as children and military personnel.[70]

The influence of the Polish clergy in the DP camps was considerable. Despite a certain degree of anticlericalism among some members of the intelligentsia, the peasant majority of the DP population followed the leadership of the priests. Through their own wartime suffering, Polish priests shared a bond with the people and a deep understanding of the problems faced by the DP population.[71] The Polish clergy consciously participated in the strengthening of the exile mission by tying religious feelings and traditions to patriotic messages. Most of the national celebrations incorporated religious elements. Priests were invited to honorary committees, led invocations and prayers, gave speeches, and celebrated solemn masses included in the program. On the other hand, members of DP organizations, such as the Home

Army Association or Scouting, prepared public declarations of appreciation, support, and loyalty to the Roman Catholic Church for its activities in exile as well as in Poland.[72]

Civic leadership in DP camps belonged to a number of organizations that strove to build and rebuild refugee community structures despite the difficulties of displacement and the hostility of some UNRRA officials. After years of horror and chaos, the DPs yearned for an internal organization that could provide them with the semblance of a normally functioning society. They also needed representation. The microcosm of the refugee world had to withstand the multiple pressures from complex levels of authority: the military in the occupation zones, international and charitable organizations, local German or Austrian officials, representatives of national governments and repatriation missions, and recruitment officers during the resettlement stage. The DPs protected themselves by establishing associations that could look after the interests of all or particular groups of DPs. Moreover, these organizations provided outlets for the pent-up energy and activism of a large leadership group. They offered companionship and camaraderie, and they reunited members of similar social and professional circles. Most of all, however, these DP organizations built a sense of the exile mission, explained it, and propagated it within the community; in this way, they politicized the masses and transformed them into conscious political refugees.

Zjednoczenie Polskie w Niemczech (Polish Union in Germany, PU) was the largest Polish organization in the three occupation zones in Germany. From mid-1945 on, Polish DPs had spontaneously created local organizations in individual camps for the purpose of self-help and representation of their interests to the occupation authorities. In the British zone, local and regional initiatives coalesced into a single organization, Główna Komisja Porozumiewawcza Środowisk Polskich (Main Commission for the Coordination of Polish Communities), formally established at a meeting of local representatives in Bardowik-bei-Lüneburg in October 1945. In August 1945 Zrzeszenie Ośrodków Polskich Bawarii Północnej (Union of Polish Centers in Northern Bavaria) became the first regional organization for Polish DPs in the American zone. Similar unions formed in southern Bavaria, Hessen, and other areas, and in December 1945 in Durzyń came together as Zjednoczenie Polskie w Amerykańskiej Strefie Okupacji Niemiec (Polish Union in the American Zone of Occupation in Germany). The French zone did not produce a separate organization but joined the activities of the American centers. As a result of cooperation between the British and American zone organizations, the Polish Union in Germany came into being in January 1946 and became the single representative of Polish DPs in all zones of Germany.[73]

The structure of the PU had five levels. The first level was that of the individual camp and its government; the second took in camps located within the same town or in the nearby area. The third coincided with the administrative and military divisions within an occupation zone; the fourth represented a zone in its entirety; and, finally, the fifth level included the all-zone Supreme Council of the PU with its executive commissions.[74] This complicated and extensive organizational pyramid slowed down the process of decision making and engulfed it in bureaucratic red tape. On the other hand, because the structure of the PU reflected that of the administrative and military divisions within postwar Germany, the organization could better represent the interests of the Polish DP population at each level. Despite the constant process of closing camps and transferring people from place to place, this structure allowed some degree of continuity in organizations and activities. Last but not least, it created positions for all who were ready and willing to serve in the Polish Union's ranks.

The membership of the PU included both individuals and organizations, and assumed that each Pole (without regard to citizenship) who lived in a DP camp was automatically a PU member. Those living outside the camps had to register with the PU authorities to obtain membership.[75] At the beginning of the PU's existence, its activities were financed mostly by donations from the Społeczny Komitet Pomocy Obywatelom Polskim w Niemczech (Social Committee to Aid Polish Citizens in Germany), an organization with its headquarters in Great Britain. The majority of its financial transactions were carried out in cigarettes, which were a form of currency at that time in Germany.[76] A decrease in cigarette donations and the reform of the German mark in July 1948 threatened the economic basis of the PU. The PU executive committee issued a dramatic appeal to all members, explaining the difficult situation of the organization and pleading for membership dues, which were established at one German mark a month for an employed person and twenty pfennigs for an unemployed person.[77] The following years brought further budget cuts resulting from dwindling membership and declining profits from subscriptions to the *Orzeł Biały* (White Eagle), a PU sponsored journal.[78]

The emigration of Polish DPs from the territory of Germany systematically deprived the PU of its members, and these changed conditions called for a redefinition of the organization's goals and structure. In 1951, the PU transformed into the Zjednoczenie Polskich Uchodźców w Niemczech (Union of Polish Refugees in Germany), an organization based on individual membership and designed to unify all those who could not or did not want to emigrate from Germany.[79]

The Polish Union was the largest and most significant organization which shaped the internal life of Polish DP camps. Practically all DP associations sooner or later entered the PU and relied on its financial and organizational support. The PU leaders represented Polish DP interests to the UNRRA/IRO authorities and remained in direct contact with the Polish government in exile in London.[80] They also represented Polish DPs from Germany and their problems in the broader forum of the Polish postwar diaspora. In November 1946, during a meeting in Brussels, representatives of Polish war refugees from all over the world established Zjednoczenie Polskiego Uchodźstwa Wojennego (ZPUW, Union of Polish War Emigration), unifying Polish war refugees into one international organization. The largest delegation at the Brussels meeting came from Germany.[81]

Perhaps the most significant and urgent area of work for the PU and the entire Polish DP population was welfare. UNRRA and IRO material support left gaps that had to be filled by the ethnic groups themselves. The Polish community in Germany met the goal of care for the most needy among them on several different levels. Regional groupings of Polish DP camps formed special commissions, and, in November 1948, a separate Referat Opieki Społecznej (welfare division) created by the executive committee of the PU took over control of the welfare issue. The PU organized frequent collections for impoverished Polish students, summer camps for children, widows and orphans of Polish soldiers, handicapped veterans, Polish inmates in German prisons, the elderly, those unable to work, and patients in hospital care.[82] The PU approached the Polish government in London for funds and appealed to other charitable organizations, including Rada Polonii. It cooperated closely with the Polish Red Cross, Społeczny Komitet Pomocy Obywatelom Polskim w Niemczech, the National Catholic Welfare Conference, Caritas, Fundusz Społeczny Kompanii Wartowniczych (Welfare Fund of the Polish Guards), Fundusz Społeczny Stowarzyszenia Polskich Weteranów (Welfare

Fund of the Polish Veterans Association). Reports of the PU indicate that the aid received from various sources in the years 1945 and 1946 far exceeded the levels of aid available for the following years, as the Polish Red Cross and Rada Polonii decreased their involvement and as emigration drained the human resources of the Polish DP camps. The financial situation of the remaining DP population made the collections for charitable purposes very difficult.[83]

Some smaller welfare organizations focused on work with particular target groups within the Polish community. For example, Polska Pomoc Społeczna (Polish Welfare) in Stuttgart secured both material and legal aid (screenings, applications for DP status, emigration procedures, and job searches) for Poles in the Württenberg and Baden areas who lived outside DP camps and were deprived of IRO support.[84] In 1947, after the closing of camps in the Western occupation zones to escapees from behind the Iron Curtain, Komitet Pomocy Uchodźcom (committee to aid refugees) aimed at helping the new arrivals.[85] A report from northern Bavaria emphasized the special need to care for Poles in hospitals and prisons. The report gave the example of one Captain Jan Passowicz, who had remained in the hospital since the end of the war. He had been wounded in the 1939 campaign and later fought in Egypt and Italy until being captured and imprisoned. "He does not have any family who could take care of him," the report read. "For more than two years he has been condemned to insufficient food and clothing; he does not receive any cigarettes and does not have anything to read." The report also called for care for inmates who found themselves in prison as a result of "demoralization caused by long stays in forced labor camps or concentration camps." They were doing "truly hard penance for their guilt," the report continued, and were in dire need of help to "return to an honest life after they leave prison."[86]

Local welfare committees were also active within individual camps. According to a report from the Hohenfels (Lechów) DP camp, each member of its welfare committee had about one thousand persons in his or her care: "Each lady [from the Committee] has a certain number of barracks to visit twice during the week, looking after the children and asking whether there are any problems that [the Committee] could solve." Committee members prepared lists for the distribution of goods, cared for the sick in the hospital, worked to obtain artificial limbs and special shoes for the handicapped, and decided on financial aid for families in particularly hard conditions.[87]

With the passing of time, the need to care for those who could not emigrate from Germany became even more apparent and urgent. In 1948, for example, the PU issued a report identifying welfare problems resulting from increased emigration:

> People who are young, healthy, single and have job training leave to settle in the free world.... The old people, the sick, those burdened with families, and those without job training stay behind, because countries admitting immigrants treat the DP masses in a purely selfish, human-market-like way, instead of with a humanitarian and social attitude. The ratio of the young and healthy to the old and unable to work gets worse almost by the hour. So far the healthy ones have helped the sick ones, and there is care from the IRO, as well as from Polish social and charitable organizations. However, this help is becoming insufficient. The governments of the Polish centers, impoverished after the reform of the German currency, remain in difficult a financial situation and can hardly solve the welfare problem. Those who need help include people who are blind, deaf, mentally ill, terminally ill—especially those with TB—handicapped, and old people who can't work. These people lost their health in concentration camps, as political prisoners or fighting for Freedom and Independence, or in POW camps..., or as civilian laborers forced to work in Germany.[88]

In these circumstances the PU authorities adopted a number of decisions making welfare issues their first priority.[89] The Polish-American press received repeated appeals for help from American Polonia. The fear of being left behind at the mercy of a hostile German administration was overwhelming.[90] Care for those in need and self-help also became the main goals of the PU's successor, Zjednoczenie Polskich Uchodźców w Niemczech.[91]

One of the most interesting initiatives of the PU was the establishment of a citizens' court. The Polish Union's bylaws for the American occupation zone formulated the court's main goals as deciding in cases that involved Poles committing acts "contrary to the recognized customs of Polish public life; harmful to Polish organizational life; and violating public interests of the Polish emigration."[92] The court was to make pronouncements in matters of ethics and defamation relating to the PU members and activists. The PU Supreme Council had the power to appoint judges and counselors of the court for one year. The details of the court's activities and responsibilities were regulated by the court's own bylaws.[93]

The court's design is in itself another indication of a conscious effort to organize the Polish DP community in Germany in an orderly fashion. Through the court, people who had survived in abnormal conditions and with an undetermined status could assume agency and strive for some semblance of normalcy. Forced to function in a reality defined by military authorities, international agencies, and hostile local administrations, Polish DPs clung to their own independent institutions, even though their range of effectiveness and their legality were rather limited in practice. The PU, in close contact and cooperation with the Polish government in exile in London, consciously supported the implementation of the ideals of the exile mission, including the concept of creating Little Poland in exile. Educational goals and directives aimed at the patriotic and anticommunist upbringing of the Polish youth also came from the political circles of the London Poles.[94] Leaders of the PU and the Roman Catholic Church, while performing the everyday functions of their offices, imbued the DPs with the political meaning and dimension of their experience, propagated ideals of the exile mission, and modeled attitudes and behaviors to be adopted in the diaspora after the resettlement.

DP Organizations

The PU was not the only organization performing the double function of meeting the needs of refugee existence and spreading the exile mission. A multitude of other DP organizations were active in Polish DP camps, including trade unions, schools, scouting organizations, publishers, cultural and sporting organizations, veterans associations, and political parties. All of them carried out some elements of the exile mission and were particularly visible during large national celebrations observing anniversaries of historical events. Respect for history also drove Polish DPs to frequently evoke the lessons of the national past and to secure protection for the records documenting their DP experience.

In 1946 the PU in the American zone initiated a Polish Council of Trade Unions (Polska Rada Zawodowa) in order to coordinate the activities of professional associations. The council contributed to the establishment of two mass unions for farmers and workers. Its journal, *Załoga* (Crew), provided information to all Polish trade unions in Germany.⁹⁵ The Trade Union Council's stated ideological goals corresponded to the exile mission of the Polish postwar political diaspora:

> The decision of the masses of Polish emigrants to remain in exile in 1945 was a result of the occupation and annexation of the eastern territories of our country by Soviet Russia. It was the only way to express in front of the Western allies our protest against the violence done to our country. There was also a tendency to create a center for independent political thought and struggle for the rights of the nation. The basic tasks then, in addition to current organizational and political problems, included groundwork preparing the Polish emigrant masses to work in professions and to resettle successfully abroad. If conditions for survival of the Polish communities abroad are positive, Polish immigrant groups will be able to fulfill their duties in the broader politics of the struggle for independence.⁹⁶

The practical goals of the trade unions and professional associations included verification of members' qualifications, issuance of proper papers and documents for emigration processing, and, above all, continuing education and vocational training. Trade unions sponsored vocational classes and published textbooks and other educational materials. Union activities connected people of the same profession and gave them a chance to continue their vocations in at least a limited way.⁹⁷ Perhaps the most explicit function of the trade unions was protection of a professional middle class whose future in exile was especially difficult and unclear, since emigration schemes openly favored blue-collar workers. Trade unions also were an arena in which to exchange ideas and to offer assistance to those in need.⁹⁸

The first trade union to be established (November 1945), and in many ways the most active one, was Zrzeszenie Kół Techników Polskich (Association of Circles of Polish Technicians), which united engineers and others with technical and mechanical professions and trades in the American zone of occupation. The association verified the qualifications of about three hundred members in 1946 and focused on educational activities, considering them most beneficial for those emigrating abroad. Polish engineers taught in the Polish Technical College in Esslingen, organized courses in many DP centers through the association's section for vocational training, and published textbooks prepared by the publishing section. The association also remained in close contact with a similar Polish organization of international scope in London.⁹⁹

Two organizations with mass membership conducted their activities among skilled workers and farmers. Związek Rolników Polskich (Union of Polish Farmers) formed in April 1947 and in the summer of that year claimed a membership exceeding twenty-seven hundred people. Its headquarters in Durzyń coordinated the organization of agricultural courses for more than a thousand participants and provided professional literature on farming and agriculture.[100] Beginning in 1947, Związek Rzemieślników i Robotników Polskich (Union of Polish Artisans and Workers) issued documents for more than fifteen hundred of its verified members. These documents became the basis of admission to labor unions in several countries of resettlement.[101]

Three other active professional associations—Zrzeszenie Prawników Polskich (Association of Polish Lawyers), Zrzeszenie Wydawców i Księgarzy (Association of Publishers and Booksellers), and Syndykat Dziennikarzy Polskich w Byłej Rzeszy (Syndicate of Polish Journalists), were all established in 1946. The Association of Polish Lawyers considered its major goal to be legal representation for Polish DPs and members of the Guards in the courts of the military governments. In addition, the lawyers, whose union was officially recognized by all administrative and occupation authorities, provided legal advice for Polish inmates in German prisons and for escapees from Poland who did not receive DP status and were charged with illegal crossing of the German border. In order to curtail crime among Poles, the lawyers worked on creating a register of Poles charged with crime in Germany. In 1947 the association had more than a hundred members.[102]

The Association of Publishers and Booksellers, although numerically considerably smaller (about thirty members in 1947), sustained a number of important activities, such as the organization of a network of retail bookstores and a wholesale business. Realizing the significance of documenting the history of the DP period, the association compiled a bibliography of all Polish publications in the territory of Germany and sent single issues of many of them to Polish libraries abroad.[103]

Members of the Syndicate of Polish Journalists initiated a similar action to preserve the historical documents and records of the Polish community in DP Germany by sending archival documents to Polish research centers in the United States. The syndicate controlled the quality of the Polish press in Germany and defended its interests, especially in the face of closings of Polish newspapers and their numerous financial and administrative problems.[104]

Other, smaller professional associations included Koło Profesorów i Asystentów Polaków (Circle of Polish Professors and Teaching Assistants) in the American zone; Zrzeszenie Artystów Plastyków Polskich (Association of Polish Artists); Związek Pisarzy Polskich w Niemczech (Union of Polish Writers in Germany); and Stowarzyszenie Artystów Sceny Polskiej (Association of Polish Performing Artists). Their activities involved a wide variety of tasks, such as organization of exhibitions and performances, licensure of theater companies and repertoire control, publication of works by scholars and writers, and free courses conducted by Polish professors after the closure of the UNRRA-sponsored university in Munich.[105]

The extensive and active network of Polish schools that began to cover DP Germany almost immediately after the fall of the Third Reich played a crucial role in the community-building process.[106] The movement to organize kindergartens, elementary schools, high schools, and courses for adult education became a spontaneous and enthusiastic effort by the entire community. A good illustration of this process was the establishment of the DP school in the Polish camp in Geesthacht. Its Polish population set out to build a school for the children shortly after the camp began to function. The parents raised the modest building with their own hands, as the children eagerly made their own preparations for the opening of the school:

> One freckle-faced boy promised a whole box of white and colored chalk. A petite girl, maybe seven years old, shyly said that she had found a bell by the brick factory. It could be used to ring for recess. Another girl offered to make a broom from birch twigs, after she removed any leaves that could litter. Still another one offered to make wicker trash baskets. One of the older girls announced that she and her friends had vowed to make sure the school was always clean and tidy.[107]

Two professional teachers who had served as officers during the 1939 campaign were recruited from the former POW camp in Bad Schwartau near Lübeck. The furnishings and some school equipment came from a nearby German school. But the lack of Polish textbooks became a serious handicap; teachers had to prepare many teaching aids by themselves. Another problem was the diversity of the youth population, which often included children between seven and fourteen years old, all illiterate. To make up for the years lost in German captivity when all education was strictly forbidden, the school program was very intensive. Teachers, however, claimed that the enthusiasm of the children was overwhelming: "The kids not only learned with great eagerness, but were also spirited and curious, asking many questions and willingly participating in conversations and discussions. The children simply inhaled all the information with extraordinary speed. Within one week, they could master material designed for a month. And with excellent results, too."[108]

The first stage of the schools' development, roughly from liberation through the summer of 1946, was characterized by the spontaneous organization of schools in DP camps in the three Western occupation zones. By the fall of 1945, 437 elementary schools with about thirty-eight thousand students were functioning in all three Western occupation zones of Germany; more than thirty-five thousand students were attending middle schools and high schools; and about fourteen hundred students were receiving college-level education.[109] The Head Office for Polish Schools in Germany (Centrala Szkolnictwa Polskiego w Niemczech) functioned as a coordinating body, until its president accepted an appointment in the Ministry of Education of the communist government in Warsaw. In June 1946 representatives of Polish teachers from the three Western zones gathered in Maczków and formed the Central Committee for Schools and Education (Centralny Komitet dla Spraw Szkolnych i Oświatowych). They also founded Zrzeszenie Polskich Nauczycieli na Wychodźstwie w Niemczech (Association of Polish Teachers in Emigration in Germany), which was loyal to the Polish government in London and rejected the overtures of the Warsaw authorities.[110] Until the dissolution of the pro-Warsaw Centrala in the summer of 1946, the schools were caught between dual educational organizations.

The Cold War context and ideological tensions between the pro-London and pro-Warsaw factions influenced the curriculum of the Polish DP schools. Although they all followed prewar school programs and often reinforced practical aspects of education, teachers paid special attention to patriotic messages. In 1945 the Polish government in exile published a special guide for the organization of Polish schools and education in Germany, establishing an ideological basis for the education and patriotic upbringing of Polish youth.[111] The London instruction identified the main goals of the education system as "saving [the youth] for Poland and Polishness [*polskość*]" and ensuring their "upbringing as Polish citizens of the best character."[112] While discussing goals of the education system for young adults and adults, the same instruction also emphasized civic training:

> The objective of social and educational work is not only a person enlightened by a certain sum of knowledge, but a new person, internally restructured. A person who deeply feels his spiritual bond with the entire nation and its new destiny. A person who clearly realizes the needs and conditions in which that destiny could be fulfilled. A person, finally, whose desire for activity embraces not only his own needs but also the general good.[113]

All schools included classes in the Polish language, Polish literature, Polish history, and Polish geography. Teachers connected to the pro-Warsaw Centrala also made a conscious effort to incorporate patriotic elements into the curriculum, although their rationale was different from that espoused by the pro-London faction. Frequent references to the beauty of the Polish land, invocations of Poland's glorious past, and introduction to the richness of Polish customs and traditions were designed to awaken love and yearning for the homeland and to increase the desire to repatriate.[114]

In the second period of their existence, Polish schools in Germany faced a challenge and a direct threat from UNRRA, whose officials perceived the Polish educational system in Germany to be an obstacle to their repatriation efforts. UNRRA repeatedly moved schools and teachers, persecuted educators, and even tried to close the entire system.[115] The establishment of the IRO in 1947 was welcomed with great relief. The best situation for Polish DP education existed in the British zone, where the Polish Central Advisory Council and Regional Advisory Councils had been established. Representatives from all DP ethnic groups formed education boards. School personnel were paid from the budgets of the German counties, but without the possibility of intervention in the schools' internal affairs by the German administration. Neither the American nor the French zones had any special institutions supporting DP educational systems. Full power and control over the DP camps remained in the hands of the IRO, which did not display much interest in DP schools and provided no financial backing for DP educational activities. Schools depended heavily on donations from a multitude of Polish organizations abroad, as well as from Polish military organizations.

Statistics for January 1, 1948, indicate that a total of 260 Polish schools of all levels (kindergartens, elementary schools, continuation schools—or *szkoły dokształcające*—vocational schools and training courses, high schools, and high schools with vocational training programs) functioned in the British, American, and French zones of Germany. At that time some 16,721 students were enrolled in the schools, and 976 teachers provided instruction. In the 1947-48 school year, schools in the British and American zones underwent consolidation, forming educational institutions in larger centers in order to secure better living conditions (including boarding houses for the youth), a sufficient number of specialized teachers, and stricter control over the curriculum and level of instruction.[116] Despite increasing emigration, some Polish schools functioned throughout the 1950-51 school year.[117]

Some Polish students pursued a college education in Germany and Austria. They established their own Związek Studentów Polaków (Polish Students Association) and self-help student organizations (Bratnie Pomoce Studentów Polaków). Beginning in the spring of 1948, 2 percent of the total number of German college admissions were allotted to DPs. Out of that number, Polish candidates received 40 percent of the placements.[118] Data for March 1, 1948, indicate that 351 Polish students were enrolled in colleges in the British zone, and 457 in the American zone. The disciplines most favored by the Poles included law, economics, medicine, and chemistry. Between 1946 and 1948, thirty-five Polish students graduated from German colleges with master's degrees, and fourteen with doctoral degrees.[119] Polish DPs established their own technical college in Esslingen, which offered education in two departments: mechanical engineering and architectural engineering. Between 1945 and 1948 the Esslingen college was housed in the old German *technische Hochschule,* and students could use its laboratories and workshops for practical classes. At the end of 1946 the college reached a peak enrollment of 278 students, who were housed in a nearby "student center" dormitory. The IRO later moved the Polish Technical College to Ludwigsburg, then to Karlskaserne, and finally closed it in June 1949.[120]

Responsibility for the development of Polish DP children and youth rested not only on the school system but also on other organizations, most prominently Polish *harcerstwo* (scouting).[121] Scouting troops and the entire scouting structure were revived immediately after the liberation of Germany by the activism of a relatively large number of Polish prewar scouting instructors. The scout's pledge called for service to God and Homeland, and that pledge also remained a beacon for the entire Polish political emigration.[122] Patriotic upbringing and a respect for Polish traditions, culture, and history became the backbone of scouting. At the same time, scouting provided DP children and youth with activities that created an atmosphere of camaraderie, friendship, collective work, and relaxation so desperately needed in the difficult and stressful environment of DP Germany. By the end of 1945, close to 25,000 boy and girl scouts belonged to harcerstwo and were led by 120 scoutmasters. Repatriation and emigration reduced those numbers in subsequent years. Between 1948 and 1949, all three zones combined had about four to five thousand scouts.[123] Statistics from January 1, 1948, indicate that there were 2,747 scouts and 35 instructors in Chorągiew Wisła (Vistula Troop), the highest organizational unit, which encompassed all three occupation zones.[124]

The scouts participated in summer camps and trips, helped to organize religious and national celebrations, published the journal *Mówią Wieki* (Centuries Speak), cared for Polish graves, and arranged classes in various practical skills. In the Polish DP camp in Heilbronn, for example, scouts organized a celebration in honor of the creator of Polish scouting, Andrzej Małkowski. The entire camp participated in the blessing of the scout community center and the opening of a kiosk with books and newspapers that was in the care of the scouts. The artistic program included a recital in dancing and singing, declamations, a theater performance, and a gymnastics show.[125]

Between five and eight thousand scouts belonged to Polish DP scouting in Austria in 1945 and 1946. The largest troop unit was Chorągiew Jagiellonów (Jagiellonian Troop) from Salzburg. The scouts from Austria enjoyed summer camps for hundreds of children and youth. They also developed close relationships with the scouting organizations of other ethnic groups, such as the Yugoslavs, Hungarians, French, Russians, and Ukrainians.[126]

The extensive and vigorous network of the Polish press, which had sprung into existence immediately after the liberation of Germany, brought the Polish DP community, scattered in a multitude of large and small camps, together with those pockets of Poles living outside the camps. An article in one Polish daily, *Biuletyn Informacyjny Dziennik Polski* (Information Bulletin Polish Daily) from Brunswick, captured the spontaneous and enthusiastic beginnings of the camp newspaper in 1945:

> Watenstadt Camp, April 22–23, 1945. Already a few days before the arrival of the American forces, we waited for good news.

> On the morning of April 11, after an entire night of artillery fire, German troops give up resistance and hang out white flags. American troops take over Watenstadt amongst the indescribable enthusiasm of our countrymen.
> Immediately, during those first days we begin organizational and social work. Poles replace the German administration of the camp.
> On April 13 the first issue [of the Bulletin] prepared on the typewriter is published on a duplicating machine and gets snatched by the camp's inhabitants eager for the Polish word. Due to intensive work ... the next issue is run off the duplicating machine. Circulation increases to 100 copies. The editorial board forms and takes over the former post office for the needs of the Bulletin.
> The circulation rises. The informational bulletin which comes out under the title *Dziennik Polski* achieves 500 copies within 5 days and this level continues through issue number eight. Issue number nine has two pages and 800 copies. Issue number 10 has 1000 copies, is published in Brunswick, and reaches the most remote areas of the region, evoking everywhere the intense enthusiasm of the Polish people.[127]

The beginnings of other camp bulletins were similar. The daily camp press supplied DPs with basic information, adopting the character of "expanded radio bulletins" as one report on the state of the Polish press in Germany and Austria remarked.[128] The subsequent development of the press was rapid and impressive. By the fall of 1946 all occupation zones in Germany and Austria boasted a plentitude of local and camp papers as well as newspapers and journals that served the entire DP community. In the American zone of Germany the Polish press agency (*agencja informacyjna*) in Munich, headed by Jerzy Ptakowski, issued weekly informational bulletins used by the entire Polish press.

The leading journal *Polska* (Poland), published by Klaudiusz Hrabyk in Ludwigsburg, distinguished itself by the high intellectual level of the writing and by its special care for the quality of the printed material. *Polska* also had the highest circulation of any Polish-language journal (fifteen thousand copies available in all the zones of Germany and Austria), and it openly propagated the ideals of the exile mission. In June 1946 UNRRA unexpectedly withdrew its authorization and demanded that the journal be closed. The main motivations for the liquidation of *Polska* were its political character, its antirepatriation stance, and its open criticism of the Warsaw regime and the Soviet Union. A few days later UNRRA canceled food rations for a group of journalists editing *Polska,* sentencing them to a diet of potatoes and herring. After soldiers of the Second Corps presented the persecuted journalists with a truckload of supplies, the American military raided the Dom Dziennikarza (Journalist's House) in Eppstein, searching for evidence to indict them on black-marketeering charges.[129] In the fall of 1946 UNRRA closed two other large journals: *Pismo Żołnierza* (Soldier's Newspaper) and *Biuletyn Informacyjny* (Information Bulletin) of Ingolstadt.[130] After September 1, 1946 no journal or newspaper could be published without a license from UNRRA authorities, who used strict political guidelines for the selection process. More than 50 percent of camp bulletins did not receive an UNRRA license and ceased to exist.[131]

In the British zone at the beginning of 1946, the number of local camp bulletins reached 75 only to drop to 40 within the next six months after several closings by UNRRA and the military authorities. Despite all these problems, in 1946 Poles in the British zone published such popular weeklies as *Jutro Pracy* (Working Tomorrow: Mülhelm-Köln, 3,500 copies); *Wczoraj i Jutro* (Yesterday and Tomorrow: Wentorf, 500 copies); and *Nasze Życie* (Our Life: Lippstadt, 800 copies). Dailies included *Kronika Dnia* (Daily Chronicle: Peckelsheim near Dossel, 620 copies): *Dzienny Biuletyn Radiowy* (Daily Radio Bulletin: Lübeck, 500 copies); *Dziennik Informacyjny* (Information Daily News: Maczków, 350 copies); *Echo Dnia* (Daily Echo: Osnabrück, 350 copies); and *Wiadomości* (News: Lippstadt, 200 copies). *Informacja Prasowa* (Press Information), a bulletin of the Polish press agency in Quackenbrück, headed by Witold Olszewski, supplied information for the flourishing press of the British zone.[132]

Although the primary function of the Polish DP press was undoubtedly the dissemination of general information, in 1945 and 1946 several journals served more specific audiences within the community. In the British zone an illustrated journal for children, *Promyczek Szczęścia* (Sunbeam of Happiness), was published in editions of more than 3,000 copies. Youth had a separate magazine, *Młody Polak* (Young Pole), and the scouts had their own *Strażnica* (Watchtower), edited by Tadeusz Starczewski in editions of 8,000 copies each. Polish armed forces published the popular weeklies *Defilada* (Parade) and *Dziennik Żołnierza* (Soldier's Daily, the journal of the First Armored Division) as well as *Spadochron* (Parachute, the journal of the First Parachute Division).[133] The Polish Guards training centers put out their own press, including *Nasze Myśli* (Our Thoughts), *Ostatnie Wiadomości* (Latest News), and *Świetlica Kompanii Wartowniczych* (Community Center of the Polish Guards, the journal of the Kościuszko company in Mannheim-Kafertal).[134] The Polish Association of Former Political Prisoners of German Concentration Camps (Polski Związek byłych Więźniów Politycznych Niemieckich Obozów Koncentracyjnych) published *Na Szlaku* (On the Trail) and *Biuletyn Organizacyjno-Informacyjny* (Organizational-Informational Bulletin); the Polish Veterans Association had their own *Wspólnymi Siłami* (With Common Effort); and *Wiadomości Prawnicze* (Legal News) was published by the Association of Polish Lawyers in the British zone.

Other journals, such as *Polska Chrystusowa* (Christ's Poland), had a religious character. *Przegląd Sportowy* (Sports Review) was a magazine of the Federation of Sport and Gymnastic Associations *Sokół* (Falcon). Finally, the Polish Repatriation Mission of the Warsaw government published *Słowo Polskie* (Polish Word), available to the DPs in all three zones. *Pokrzywy* (Nettles), the only satirical magazine in DP Germany, featured cartoons and humorous stories and poems.[135] Polish DPs also published literary and scholarly journals, bulletins with news on publishing and trade unions, organizational bulletins, resettlement and emigration news, and so on. Many of them were short-lived, and most had an unattractive appearance resulting from their use of low-quality paper and primitive duplicating machines; but all served to inform, educate, amuse, and connect the Polish community, which craved the Polish printed word after years of war and isolation.[136]

Reform of the German currency in July 1948 pulled the rug out from under the Polish press. Many newspapers and journals disappeared. Within a week after the reform, the weekly *Kronika*'s circulation dropped from about thirty-two thousand copies to just a few thousand.[137] In an appeal for support of Polish organizations in Germany, the Polish Union in the American zone also pleaded for support of the Polish press:

> The Polish press found itself in a difficult financial situation, and, if there is no support from the community, the press will be doomed to liquidation. If a person can't afford to subscribe to a newspaper alone, let him subscribe together with his neighbors. It is impossible to live nowadays without information about what is going on in the world. A newspaper is not a luxury, it is a necessity in every civilized home.[138]

The disappearance of the Polish press could not, however, be reversed. In order to preserve the remaining publications, in December 1948 Polish Union officials wrote to the Syndicate of Polish Journalists at the request of the Polish DP camps in the Greater Hesse area, asking them to "adjust the Polish press in the American occupation zone to the needs and interests of the majority of Polish DPs in that territory." The letter further suggested moving the focus of these publications away from the political aspects of the exile mission and turning it toward the more practical concerns of the DPs:

> The reason for the low readership of Polish newspapers lies in the fact that they contain too many articles on great political issues and cultural and economic problems on an international scale, and not enough articles dealing directly with the Polish DPs' lives (the activities of the IRO, resettlement questions, activities of the Polish Union, activities of social and professional organizations, the dispositions of the German and American authorities relating to DPs living outside camps, and so on).[139]

Financial limitations coupled with press licensing forced the Polish press to close practically all journals and newspapers in the French zone and to reduce their numbers drastically in the American and British zones of Germany. Seven journals received the required licenses, but by early 1949 only three still survived: a popular weekly, *Kronika* (Chronicle, subsequently closed in May 1949); the Polish Guards' journal *Ostatnie Wiadomości*; and a Catholic weekly, *Słowo Katolickie* (Catholic Word).[140] Unending financial problems, population movements in the camps, a diminishing readership base, and the emigration of many journalists contributed to the systematic extinction of the Polish press in DP Germany in the late 1940s.[141]

The publishing business, spearheaded by the Association of Publishers and Booksellers, flourished in the Polish community following the liberation of Germany until the new licensing laws forced most of the press and book publishers to close. By 1947 the number of published books had climbed to between 350 and 370,[142] including textbooks for Polish schools, masterpieces of Polish classic literature, works of the "lighter sort," and books by émigré writers and poets writing in the DP camps.[143] Book catalogs were published and made available to individuals and organizations as well as to community centers in the camps. Almost every camp had its own library and reading room, where DPs of Polish, Ukrainian, Jewish, Latvian, or Lithuanian backgrounds checked out books. In addition to these small libraries with a limited number of books,[144] some relatively large book collections existed, such as the one in the Ingolstadt camp that boasted nearly ten thousand books on the shelves and more than four thousand books in storage.[145]

The achievements of the Polish press and publishers were presented to society at large during the Exhibition of Polish Cultural and Educational Publications Printed in the American, British, and French Zones of Germany between April 1945 and June 1946, which took place in Wiesbaden in July 1946. The initiative enjoyed great success: some fifty-five hundred people visited the exhibition. Some of the inscriptions in the exhibit's guest book, written in Polish, German, and Ukrainian, testify to the impact and importance of the Polish printed word as well as to the appreciation the DPs had for the publishing work done within the community. Polish inscriptions carried references to the exile mission. "I am leaving this place deeply moved—it was a great surprise for my ill soul," one of the messages read. Other comments revealed profound feelings of pride and patriotism: "The Polish nation should be proud of its sons"; "I am proud to be Polish"; and "I wish the creators of this imposing exhibit of the press of Little Poland in Exile could soon organize a similar exhibit in a Free and Great Poland."[146]

The significance of the Polish press and publications for the Polish population in the DP camps was extremely high. Its important role was clearly understood by the DPs themselves. In his report on the Polish press in 1946, Jerzy Grot-Kwaśniewski wrote:

> The Polish press and publications are one of the most positive elements of the struggle for our rights, as people and as Poles.
> In the current situation, obstructed by political games, the Polish press and books are, for the refugees, like a true and honest friend who brings information, remembers the past, educates, and advises, filling time with usefulness.
> Without any exaggeration, both the press and books are a real attraction among us. The hunger for the Polish press and Polish books is still not satisfied.[147]

Polish-language publications became a powerful medium used to spread the exile mission. Journals and newspapers carried a plentitude of material on

Polish history and cultural traditions. They reconnected the refugees to the past of victories despite subjugation and called for the preservation of memory and spirit. They also commented on more recent events by recounting political and personal stories of the German occupation and of Soviet atrocities committed during the war. The political situation in the world and especially in Poland remained the steady focus of much of the writing. As the Cold War lowered the Iron Curtain, Polish refugees wrote and read about their decision to stay in the West as a symbol of resistance to the unjust Yalta system. These patriotic messages came in a form accessible to all, since the variety of publications offered the audience comfortable reading choices. For children who had left Poland many years before or had been born outside of its borders, Polish publications became the only source of the written, literary Polish language.

For a large group of Polish intellectuals, DP publications meant contact with the greatest achievements of Polish intellectual thought and with the literary tradition of the past as well as an opportunity to continue their own work in exile. The journals published a fair number of new works, essays, poetry, and short stories. Polish DP readers also received new book publications by, among others, Tadeusz Borowski, Bogdan Hofmański, Jan Dobraczyński, Ferdynand Goetel, Jan Komski, Ryszard Białous, and Henryk Goldring. In addition, several new books for children and stage plays for scouts came out under the auspices of the Polish press and publishing in Germany.[148]

Other aspects of the cultural life of the Polish DP community transmitted many of the same patriotic messages. Like DPs of other ethnic backgrounds, Poles organized national celebrations and patriotic rallies commemorating historical events in their homeland.[149] Two of the most significant were May 3, when the Polish community observed the adoption of the Polish constitution in 1791, and November 11, when Poles commemorated the regaining of independence in 1918; but most camps included a larger number of celebrations on their calendars. For example, in Ingolstadt Polish DPs celebrated May 3 Constitution Day, the anniversary of the Polish victory over the Teutonic Order at the Battle of Grunwald (July 15, 1410), All Saints' Day (November 1), Independence Day (November 11), the anniversary of the Lwów defense (usually November 22), the Christmas Eve sharing of the wafer, the Warsaw Uprising anniversary (August 1), Soldiers' Day (August 15), and a St.

Stanisław Kostka fête (November 13) organized by the scouts and school youth. During the November and May celebrations, the organizers raised funds for welfare and education.[150] Speeches, rallies, performances by theater groups, folk-dance groups, and choirs, and recitations by school children and scouts embellished the artistic programs. They became occasions to review the achievements of the Polish community in exile and to chart out new directions for the future. The April 1949 manifesto of the Polish Union in Germany appealed for collective participation in the celebration of May 3 Constitution Day: "Fellow Citizens! We appeal to all of you here, in exile, in your forced emigration, to express your national status, love for your Homeland, and your firm faith in regaining Freedom and Independence. Let May 3 be a day celebrated solemnly by each, by even the smallest group of Poles. Everywhere where Polish hearts are beating on this day of beautiful and special anniversary, Polish banners should shine and Polish speech and song should sound far and wide." On May 3, the PU traditionally raised funds to support Polish schools and educational programs in the DP camps.[151]

These national celebrations transmitted the ideals of the exile mission and politicized the DP masses. Patriotic manifestations frequently included demonstrations against the postwar political arrangement that had brought Poland under the communist regime. This, in turn, meant expressing hostile attitudes toward the Soviet Union. The occupation authorities and UNRRA often discouraged these patriotic rallies and many other cultural events organized by the ethnic communities.[152] On the other hand, the interpretation of the political situation and demonstration of political sympathies sometimes caused controversies within the camps themselves, polarizing Polish DPs along the political spectrum.[153]

National observances were only one expression of the culture flourishing in the DP camps. As one scholar noted, "DP camps soon became showcases for a wide variety of cultural activities—in literature, art, music, the theater—that stressed the underlying theme of national uniqueness."[154] Several theater groups performed within the Polish DP community. The PU launched its own theater company, Teatr Zjednoczenia Polskiego (Theater of the Polish Union), in November 1947; by March of the following year, it had staged twenty-four performances for some sixty-five hundred persons, but then disbanded for lack of funds.[155] Most companies traveled from camp to camp and performed variety acts. Leon Schiller, a famous Warsaw theater director from the prewar years, headed the only professional theater, which was supported by the Second Armored Division in Maczków.[156] Almost every DP camp at one time or another had its own local amateur theater group that put on popular plays and shows. In 1948 the Ingolstadt Polish DP camp enjoyed performances by the company "Gałązka Rozmarynu" (Rosemary Twig) and by their own theater group named in honor of Stanisław Wyspiański, in addition to amateur performances and several shows by scouts and youth sporting groups.[157]

One of the most successful cultural events in DP Germany was the exhibition of Polish arts and crafts "Polish Work Abroad," organized in October 1947 in Munich. It displayed an imposing number of artifacts produced by the DPs in the camps in a wide range of genres, including religious objects, charts and maps prepared during vocational courses, books and newspapers published within the community, folk art and costumes, handicrafts, and tools. The goal of the exhibit was not only to present the achievements of the community to its own members, but to build up its image to outsiders and to demonstrate that Polish DPs, after years of enslavement by Nazi invaders and despite the "psychic injury" of the war years, had managed to overcome their experiences, collected themselves again, and found "their way out of the blind alley where they had been driven by destiny. The two years stay on foreign earth which they want to leave at any price has not been without profit. During this period they worked on themselves, learned, improved their knowledge in old professions and acquired new ones."[158] The exhibition was organized under the auspices of Florian Piskorski, the delegate of the Polish American Council, and aimed at creating a favorable climate for the emigration of Polish DPs abroad.[159] As had the successful press exhibit of the previous year, the Polish Work Abroad exhibit generated a lot of interest and received a very warm reception from large numbers of DPs of various nationalities.

Polish culture in its most vigorous and spontaneous form manifested itself in the many cultural activities and entertainments organized within DP camps by the residents themselves. DP cultural committees usually attracted the most artistically inclined groups of people.[160] In the Polish camp in Arolsen, DPs could use their community center (świetlica) to read the Polish press and play chess, checkers, or table tennis. The DP Club offered dances to the music of the DP band in the evening as well as ballroom dancing lessons.[161] Lechów organized "Lechów Days," marked by an exhibition of artifacts made during the vocational courses. The camp also had two choirs, religious and lay.[162] Many camps had improvised movie theaters where DPs could watch movies distributed by the YWCA and participate in lectures and discussions after the shows.[163]

Sports proved to be an important part of DP life in Germany, providing an outlet for the energy of people forced to spend their days in idleness. Years of captivity and hard labor had weakened the physical strength of many and especially hampered the health and development of the youth. Polish DPs paid exceptional attention to sports activities for scout troops and school-aged youth and children, organizing sports and gymnastics sections in almost all DP camps. Adult sport teams multiplied. Overcoming economic hurdles (such as lack of team uniforms, sporting equipment, and prizes for the winners of competitions) became a measure of creativity and energy.[164] Sometimes, camps supported more than one team for a given sport. For example, three volleyball teams and two table tennis teams defended the colors of the Ingolstadt camp.[165] In other events, the track team from Arolsen successfully represented the camp in regional competitions in Korbach.[166] Sports facilities in the camp Weiden-"La Guardia" housed a tournament between the home soccer team and a joint representation from the camps in Coburg, Amberg, and Regensburg.[167]

Sokół (Falcon), a Polish sports and patriotic organization with historical roots in the period of the partitions, coordinated sporting activities in all three zones of Germany. After being established in Dachau in 1945, Sokół carried out its traditional mission expressed in the ancient Latin slogan *mens sana in corpore sano* (a healthy spirit in a healthy body), paying equal attention to the physical development and the moral standing of athletes.[168] Polish sporting groups took part in many tournaments with other ethnic groups and military teams within regions or zones. In the summer of 1948 the International Committee of DPs and Political Exiles in Germany organized an international Olympic competition in Munich, securing the participation of athletes from seventeen different ethnic groups. The IRO supported the Olympics and provided equipment, housing, and extra food rations. Polish athletes trained for this special competition in Ingolstadt.[169]

All the activities that structured life within the camps and allowed DPs to participate in a variety of groups fulfilled an extremely important function in the community-building process. They provided relaxation, entertainment, and education and conditioned proper physical development. Most importantly, they also created the aura of a normally functioning society. Polish women were instrumental in making sure that their families achieved a level of comfortable and peaceful existence within the deprivation and frustration of DP life. Throughout the war years they were a large part of the labor force and the imprisoned population, and together with men they shared the tragedy and despair of loss and displacement.[170] Róża Nowotarska, a Polish DP press journalist, noted that "in the abnormal life of the DP camps, women lead the most abnormal lives of all." While many men worked outside the home, she continued, women were supposed to organize homes in conditions more suitable for a military camp. This overwhelming responsibility was to blame for the relatively low participation of the Polish women in an active social and organizational life in the Polish community in Germany:

> Among the nineteen Polish centers in the American zone (including thirty-two camps) only four camps (not centers) have organized women's circles. Out of those only two can boast of really significant achievements.
> With the number of women larger in this zone than the number of men, men show considerably more initiative.[171]

Reports summarizing the achievements of different Polish DP organizations indicated the lack of an organization for women that could unify their activities at the zone level. Women's circles in the camps in Durzyń, Coburg, and Munich stood out as the lone exceptions.[172] In 1946 the Polish Union for the regions of southern Bavaria and Swabia appealed to all camp councils for the creation of women's circles and for the appointment of a woman deputy to each council to represent the female population of the camps. The recommended program for women's organizations included care for expectant mothers and newborns, organization of day-care centers and kindergartens, education in hygiene and health care, care for the sick, counseling for women in crisis, and organization of vocational and general education courses and classes for women.[173] The Association of Polish Women in Durzyń worked out standard bylaws that could be accepted by women's organizations in other camps and issued an appeal stressing the need for unity among Polish women:

> The future of Polish generations rests in the hands of a Polish woman—a mother, a caregiver, and a worker. Let us unite in the name of the well-being

of those whom fate gave into our care; let us work, study, and support each other. Let the thought of common good unite us.

There are no class or economic differences among us. We are all equal; we are united by the immensity of our suffering and the irrevocable loss of our loved ones. We are tied together by the common fate of the exiled.

Let us join hands and begin our work, so that one day we may return to Poland, to the Homeland that no one and nothing can wrest from our hearts![174]

Charges of inactivity on the part of Polish women ran counter to numerous examples of women working in DP schools and kindergartens and leading scout teams. Women found employment in camp kitchens and hospitals and were members of welfare committees. They took vocational classes and learned foreign languages. Although cases of women heading camp councils, as in the Fallingsbostel camp, were rare, their absence from camp governments and administration resulted less from the inactivity of Polish women than from a very traditional understanding of female roles by Polish men.[175] The example of Teresa R., the mother of an eight-month-old baby, illustrates the point. Teresa applied to the camp council in Ludwigsburg for the job of block inspector, recently vacated, which would provide her with much-needed income and would allow her to care for her child at the same time. The president of the council responded that in his opinion and in the opinion of the entire council, women should not be employed as block inspectors. Teresa's petition was denied.[176]

The picture of community life in the Polish DP camps would not be complete without mention of two other types of organizations that established networks in all three zones: veterans organizations and political parties. The Stowarzyszenie Polskich Weteranów (Polish Veterans Association) existed in the American zone, and the Stowarzyszenie Polskich Kombatantów (Association of Polish ex-Combatants, SPK) functioned in the British and French zones beginning in the fall of 1946. They united soldiers of the Polish Armed Forces in the West stationed on German soil, Polish September POWs, participants in the resistance movement, and Home Army soldiers of the Warsaw Uprising. Close to thirty thousand members belonged to veterans organizations in the three zones of Germany. The SPK's program echoed the ideals of the exile mission and included preservation of the principle of a free and independent Poland both among the Polish diaspora and in other nations around the world. It also urged cooperation among its members and unity within Polish communities in exile. Finally, it vowed to spread historical information about the participation of the Polish nation in World War II and its contributions to the Allied victory.[177] The Home Army soldiers' circles (*koła akowskie*), formed in the three zones between late 1945 and 1947, were smaller veterans organizations.[178] The Polski Związek byłych Więźniów Politycznych Niemieckich Obozów Koncentracyjnych (Polish Association of Former Political Prisoners of German Concentration Camps, or *kacetowcy*), created in 1945, was geared initially toward self-help and publishing activities. In the spring of 1947 the association had four thousand members in the American zone, four thousand in the British zone, and about four hundred in the French zone of Germany.[179]

The majority of DPs remained loyal to the Polish government in exile in London, and some especially active DPs participated in the establishment of political parties within the DP camps. These included Stronnictwo Narodowe (National Democratic Movement, *endecja*), Stronnictwo Ludowe "Wolność" (People's Movement "Freedom"), Polska Partia Socjalistyczna (PPS, Polish Socialist Party), Stronnictwo Pracy (SP, Labor Movement), Liga Niepodległości Polski w Niemczech (League of Poland's Independence in Germany), as well as some smaller and less active parties, such as Ruch Chrzescijańsko-Społeczny (Christian Social Movement). Endecja and the League of Poland's Independence had the largest membership and competed for influence within other DP organizations. The leadership of all parties came from the ranks of prewar activists who carried on traditional Polish political thought in exile, but it is unclear how large or how active the actual membership in any particular party was.[180]

Polish DPs in Germany created a strong and multidimensional community based on the activities of numerous social, political, cultural, and religious organizations, educational and legal systems, professional and veterans associations, as well as a flourishing press and book publishing. These self-organized communities attained the character of a well functioning society in exile, despite the lack of support from any state. The Polish DP community existed in opposition to external factors such as UNRRA's pressure to repatriate, administrative chaos, and complex bureaucracy, all of which often thwarted DP initiatives but did not stop the community-building process. When repatriation had been completed and emigration to the West began, the ranks of the most active leaders thinned, but there were always people willing to pick up where others left off. Preserving the community despite the changing international situation became a conscious political goal of Polish DPs. The social, organizational, and cultural structure of the Little Poland in exile built in the DP camps was to become a model that the refugees could replicate in their countries of resettlement. The DP camps were a training ground that prepared a cadre of leaders who gained important organizational and ideological experience during the time they spent there.

The exile mission was part of all stages of the tenuous community-building in the DP camps. The mission required that the decision to remain in the West be framed in political terms. DPs presented their choice as being motivated by the international politics that had allowed the Yalta agreement. In a symbolic protest, they would not return to communist-dominated Poland, becoming a living reminder about the injustice suffered by their homeland. Consequently, they placed themselves at the forefront of the Cold War both as its victims and as the most dedicated of anticommunist fighters. The refugees monitored international political changes, reported on the situation in Poland, and debated both the history and the future of their homeland. They remained loyal to the London government. While in the DP camps, the refugees worked for the creation of a world Polish diaspora built along personal as well as organizational lines. No matter what country the DPs chose for their resettlement, they were to become politically united and alert to the goal of service to Poland in exile.

Community involvement provided the key to the politicization of the refugees as a group. The vast majority of DP organizations adopted political as well as social goals and put them into effect through a wide range of activities. The historical ideals of positivistic *praca u podstaw* (work at the foundations) provided a solid example. The refugee inteligencja readily accepted its traditional leadership position, giving shape and impetus to organizational life. The refugees cared for the sick and destitute, and secured an education and a patriotic upbringing for their children. Their attachment to the Roman Catholic Church strengthened and added cohesion to the initiatives of local communities. Networks of personal relationships established in the camps later could be transmitted and recreated in the countries of resettlement.

The historical and cultural dimensions of the exile mission manifested themselves strongly in the refugees' effort to make their sojourn in the DP camps part of the usable past. The refugees established links with Poland's past through the adoption of historical names for their DP communities that would carry special meaning for the DPs and sound more "like home." The streets in larger camps also had Polish names commemorating important events, ideals, and individuals from the Polish past and signifying the Polish character of the communities. These name changes happened both spontaneously and as part of a conscious policy of the Polish Union in Germany, which recommended adding Polish names to the German ones.[181] With an acute awareness of the historical moment, Polish DPs commemorated victims of the war, raised monuments, and organized and cared for cemeteries.[182] Realizing the future significance of the DP period in Polish diaspora history, they collected and preserved archival materials documenting their experience.[183] The camps and their legacy were not to be dismissed as a "peculiar vacuum between ... yesterday's nightmare and the unknown ... tomorrow."[184] Vigorous press and book publishing, arts and crafts fairs, support for Polish schools and college students, all carried the element of pride and care for the national culture in exile.

The immigrants who entered the United States, Canada, and other Western countries in the late forties and fifties were not the "same" people who had left their homelands as a result of the war.[185] Wartime suffering and the DP period were crucial and formative experiences that influenced refugees' adjustment in their countries of resettlement in a most significant way. Polish refugees from the European DP camps carried with them not only hopes for a peaceful future, but also the exile mission that was the centerpiece of patriotism within the Polish families, local communities, new countries of resettlement, and the entire postwar diaspora.

3 ∣∣∣ "Live a happy and peaceful life here"
The Resettlement of Polish Displaced Persons in the United States

Creation of the Postwar Polish Diaspora

"AFTER COMING TO THIS free country, it seemed as if the world had opened up to me. Only one who has lost his freedom could appreciate its true significance," wrote Helena Podkopacz after arriving in America in 1950.[1] She was one of nearly a million refugees of different ethnic backgrounds who became resettled in more than forty-eight countries. The International Refugee Organization was in charge of this operation, which lasted almost six years and involved the cooperation of foreign governments, businesses, voluntary agencies, and ethnic communities. The resettlement of DPs took on different organizational forms and social characteristics in each country. In some cases it progressed relatively smoothly, managed with the full understanding and cooperation of both the refugee and local populations. Other resettlement programs quickly turned into failures that produced new waves of emigrants trying to escape conditions considered unfair and intolerable. In all, the IRO resettled 357,635 Polish displaced persons in forty-seven countries around the world.[2] These emigrants formed the foundation of the Polish postwar political diaspora.

Before the immigration programs, or schemes, could result in successfully resettled DPs, the atmosphere of hopeless waiting in the DP camps had to be turned into a flurry of activities focused on the best way to leave Germany. As Kathryn Hulme observed

> The scramble of the DP's to get out of Germany was at once heartbreaking and humorous. The camp bulletin boards listing all the current avenues

of escape made you think of some kind of macabre stock market that dealt in bodies instead of bonds. The DP's read the job offerings and rushed to qualify. When, for example, we posted the advance news that Canada would accept qualified tailors, everyone who had ever sewed on a pants' button was a master tailor. Our DP nurses with diplomas from Leningrad, Warsaw and Kiev swore they had done a bit of tailoring before they studied nursing.[3]

DPs rejected because of their age, health problems, or number of dependents often gave in to despair. Some fell into depression; there were cases of suicide. Most missions looked for skilled and unskilled laborers. DPs who had worked in professions had to lie about their work experience; higher education could be a reason for rejection, despite the fact that the IRO publicly denied that it was "skimming off the cream."[4] Those who had passed the numerous tests administered by the immigration missions could still face humiliation as they were forced to flex their muscles or show the calluses on their hands. Families had to face painful and dramatic decisions when only some members qualified for emigration for reasons of health, age, or required work experience. Field workers anxiously observed how the camps were aging and "growing sadder as the old people, the cripples and the ailing would be left behind, with the masses of children of the too-large families that were seldom selected." As the transports of qualified refugees were readied for departure, it became obvious that "country after country [was] reaching in for its pound of good muscular workingman's flesh."[5]

Toward the end of 1946, the Belgian government was the first to begin negotiations with the occupation authorities in Germany to recruit refugees for work in coal mines. The news of those first opportunities for emigration and work electrified displaced persons from the British and American zones, and the arrival of the Belgian mission felt "like a clean breeze blowing through stagnation."[6] At first, preference was given to young, healthy, single men, although later men with families were also accepted. By the end of 1949, nearly 32,000 refugees (including 10,378 Poles) had gone to Belgium, but close to 7,500 of them had returned to Germany. Many of the returnees expressed dissatisfaction with the working and living conditions offered to them in Belgium. Some hoped to find better conditions in other countries that had just initiated new resettlement programs.[7]

A large contingent of Polish DPs (60,308) emigrated from the DP camps to Australia, whose resettlement scheme went into operation in September

1947. Initially preference was given to Balts, but when their resettlement proved successful, the Australian government raised the quota and relaxed the selection criteria. In 1950 Australia began admitting refugees from areas other than Germany, Austria, and Italy; as a result, two hundred Poles from Lebanon found their home on the continent. The Australian resettlement program, based on two-year work contracts that the DP's had to fulfill before being allowed to move on, drew some criticism. After a period of initial adjustment, however, DP arrivals succeeded in establishing strong and lively immigrant communities in Australia, fully participating in the life of the country that had admitted them.[8]

Canada, which admitted close to 47,000 Poles, France, with almost 12,000, and the Netherlands, with approximately 3,000, were other countries that refugees eagerly chose as immigration destinations. Smaller groups of Polish DPs migrated to South American countries, including Argentina (6,563), Brazil (7,770), Paraguay (1,433), and Venezuela (2,814). Israel admitted 54,904 refugees who listed Poland as their country of citizenship.[9]

The United Kingdom admitted about 165,000 Polish servicemen and women who had served in the Polish armed forces under British command during the war. They arrived in Great Britain from Germany and Italy where they had served as occupation forces, as well as from the Middle East.[10] In 1946 the British government established the Polish Resettlement Corps (PRC, or in Polish, Korpus Przysposobienia i Rozmieszczenia, KPR), which "was intended to be a purely transitional arrangement designed to help those Polish troops who felt unable to return to Poland to resettle in civilian life in Britain."[11] Poles could enroll voluntarily in the PRC for two years and obtain language and vocational training while waiting for job placement. General Stanisław Kopański, the former commander of the Carpathian Brigade in the Middle East who headed the PRC, soon found out that securing employment and accommodations would not be easy. While in the PRC, most of the troops lived in numerous camps throughout Britain, with conditions ranging from adequate to spartan. Polish workers faced discrimination by some British trade unions, such as the National Union of Mineworkers and the National Union of Agricultural Workers, that were determined to keep labor competition away from their industries. A large group of the prewar inteligencja (according to War Office records, about twenty thousand within the PRC) had a very hard time finding suitable employment because of advanced age or professional qualifications that were unfamiliar to the British employers. Prevocational courses organized by the War Office offered Polish officers training in deep-sea fishing; farming; forestry; the mechanical, building, and electrical trades; and other skills, such as watch repair. In the fall of 1949 the corps disbanded after 114,000 Poles had passed through its ranks.[12]

Between 1946 and 1948 the United Kingdom also accepted another share of refugees: more than 84,000 "European Volunteer Workers" (including 35,780 Poles) under immigration schemes called "Balt Cygnet" and "Westward Ho!" In 1946 Balt Cygnet recruited 2,500 Baltic women to work in British hospitals. Westward Ho!, which absorbed Balt Cygnet a year later, opened the doors for men and women of many different nationalities from the European DP camps. A separate operation known as "Pole Jump" brought the dependents of Polish veterans from the Polish Resettlement Corps to the UK, fulfilling the War Office's obligation to reunite soldiers with their families. In 1947 and 1948 approximately 40,000 Polish family members were moved from Europe, India, the Middle East, and East Africa where they had been left behind in refugee camps, cared for by the IRO. In addition, other Commonwealth countries, such as the Union of South Africa, Northern and Southern Rhodesia, Ceylon, Kenya, and Tanganyika, took in more than 1,500 refugees.[13]

While these resettlement programs were being carried out, the communists in Poland succeeded in firmly clenching their grip on political power. The refugees observed with horror the confrontation between the communists and Stanisław Mikołajczyk's Polskie Stronnictwo Ludowe (PSL), or Polish Peasant Party. Mikołajczyk was the first deputy premier and minister of agriculture in the Provisional Government of National Unity, a body agreed upon at the Yalta summit. He also was the only government official who previously had served in the London government in exile. In June 1946 a referendum on changes in the government, economy, and borders was held in an atmosphere of violence and intimidation. Although its results were rigged, the referendum still revealed both the extent of anticommunist opposition and the determination of the communists to quench it. In January 1947 nationwide elections, a recommendation of the Yalta conference, finally were carried out. They, too, proved fraudulent. The communists captured an electoral majority, absorbed the remnants of the socialist party, and announced a mandate to rule the country. Fearing for his life, Mikołajczyk fled Poland in the fall of 1947. By the end of 1948, not only Poland but also Hungary, Czechoslovakia, and other

TABLE 3.1. Resettlement of Polish refugees, July 1, 1947–December 31, 1951

Country of destination	Number	Country of destination	Number
Argentina	6,563	Netherlands	2,969
Australia	60,308	New Zealand	847
Belgium	10,378	Northern Rhodesia	310
Bolivia	510	Norway	232
Brazil	7,770	Pakistan	3
Canada	46,961	Panama	8
Chile	516	Paraguay	1,433
Colombia	31	Peru	103
Costa Rica	41	Philippines	1
Cuba	148	Southern Rhodesia	97
Dominican Republic	31	Spain	9
Ecuador	66	Sweden	563
Eire	32	Switzerland	76
Ethiopia	46	Syria	4
France	11,882	Tanganyika	280
French Guyana	62	Tunisia	167
French Morocco	166	Turkey	8
Germany	46	UK	35,780
Guatemala	16	Union of South Africa	111
Hong Kong	2	Uruguay	241
Israel	54,904	USA	110,566
Italy	27	Venezuela	2,814
Kenya	184	Miscellaneous	177
Luxembourg	77	Not reported	54
Mexico	15	Total	357,635

Breakdown into nationalities according to specified country of citizenship, last habitual residence, or ethnic group. Data includes refugees departed for resettlement.

SOURCE: Louise W. Holborn, *The International Refugee Organization, a Specialized Agency of the United Nations: Its History And Work, 1946–1952* (London: Oxford University Press, 1956), 438.

countries of the Soviet bloc had been placed firmly under communist control and had launched far-reaching social and economic reforms.[14]

Poland was irrevocably behind the Iron Curtain. As the Cold War intensified, European refugees saw themselves—and were seen by others—as a symbol of the anticommunist opposition and as leaders in the struggle for freedom. When filling out their emigration applications, they cited political reasons for their decision to remain in exile. The Polish government in exile aspired to provide leadership to the postwar diaspora in its exile mission and claimed to represent the only legal continuation of prewar authority. The Polish Constitution of 1935 provided that in case of war, a retiring president would appoint his successor. This provision was invoked in 1939 when President Ignacy Mościcki, interned in Romania, resigned his office and appointed as his successor Władysław Raczkiewicz, then in Paris. Since 1944 Prime Minister Tomasz Arciszewski had been President Raczkiewicz's designated successor. However, when Raczkiewicz fell seriously ill in the spring of 1947, he signed the appointment of August Zaleski, former minister of foreign affairs, as his successor. Despite the protests of Arciszewski and his supporters, Zaleski took the oath of office in June 1947.

Initially, the government based its activity on prewar political parties reborn in exile. They included Stronnictwo Narodowe, a dominant party of the Polish right; Polska Partia Socjalistyczna, traditionally oriented toward independence (*niepodległość*) and relying on connections to the Socialist International; Stronnictwo Pracy; Stronnictwo Demokratyczne (SD, Democratic Movement); and Stronnictwo Ludowe "Wolność" (People's Movement "Freedom"). In 1945 the younger generation of political activists founded Niepodległość i Demokracja (NiD, Independence and Democracy) whose headquarters was in London. This new party soon proved to be one of the most energetic. It devoted much effort to keeping the Polish question alive on the international scene, and through veterans groups and other organizations it built up intra-diaspora cooperation. The Piłsudskiites did not form a separate party, but their influence was felt through their participation in the military and other governmental structures.

Finally, Polskie Stronnictwo Ludowe quickly gained both power and visibility in émigré politics. After fleeing Poland in the fall of 1947, Stanisław Mikołajczyk and the other members of the PSL leadership in the United States, Kazimierz Bagiński and Stefan Korboński, became instant celebrities. Received by President Harry S. Truman and members of the American government, the Department of State, and the Congress, Mikołajczyk aspired to single-handedly represent the interests of the Polish nation to the West. Both the government and the Polish political parties in exile saw Mikołajczyk as competition because of his access to high-ranking international politicians and his support from international peasant organizations.[15]

The need to counterbalance the PSL's growth stimulated efforts to unify the political scene in London, but the old political divisions proved strong. In the spring of 1947 President Zaleski approved the new government based not on the traditional political parties, but on a variety of social and cultural organizations. In 1949 the prewar parties responded by creating a London-based opposition called Rada Polityczna (Political Council). At the beginning of 1950 the Political Council formed its official representation for the United States, located in New York City and led by Stefan Korboński.[16] Between 1949 and 1954 several politicians attempted, but failed, to unify the government, and until 1972 the Polish government in exile was divided into two competing groups: the increasingly alienated Zamek (Castle), led by Zaleski, and the opposition Rada Trzech (Council of the Three), based on the political parties.[17] Although rocked with political discord and internal competition, the government continued to serve as an important symbol of legality (*legalizm*) and continuity of prewar authority in exile. London became a political point of gravity for the entire postwar diaspora, despite the fact that sometimes its political attitude of *niezłomność* (indomitable, uncompromising stance) drew criticism and caused dissent.

The exile mission as represented by the government in exile became a compass for a number of transnational Polish organizations headquartered in London, for example, the Association of Polish ex-Combatants, Polish scouting, Polish schools in exile (Polska Macierz Szkolna), as well as professional organizations for journalists, writers, and teachers. The Polish press published in London, particularly *Dziennik Polski i Dziennik Żołnierza* (Polish Daily News and Soldier's Daily News) and *Wiadomości Literackie* became opinion-making newspapers in the diaspora.[18]

Organization of Resettlement in the United States

Polish Americans had been aware of the plight of Polish displaced persons in Europe from the moment Allied forces liberated the territories of Germany and Austria. In June 1945 Censor Francis X. Świetlik, president of Rada, visited Polish refugee communities in Europe, including the DP camps. The report he published upon his return stressed the urgent need for humanitarian help, and Rada immediately set out to provide and distribute aid through its offices in Lisbon, and later in Switzerland.[19]

These charitable actions did not overshadow the political dimension of the refugee question. Polish Americans, through the voice of the increasingly politically aggressive Charles Rozmarek of the PAC, expressed their anger and disappointment at the consequences of the Yalta agreement. As the Cold War intensified, Rozmarek and the PAC saw the refugee question as being intrinsically tied to the international situation. Holding the United States partly responsible for the "betrayal at Yalta," Rozmarek called for the improvement of conditions in the DP camps, for putting an end to UNRRA's coercive repatriation practices, and eventually, for new immigration laws that would allow European DPs into the United States. In September 1945 Rozmarek appealed to Secretary of State James Byrnes to stop the forced repatriation of Poles. He pleaded with him to "[p]ermit displaced Poles in Germany to remain in their camps until such time as when Russian troops and secret police are withdrawn from Poland so these unfortunate victims can return to their homeland without fear of imprisonment, deportation into Siberia or death."[20] On behalf of the PAC, claiming to represent 6 million Polish Americans, he also petitioned for a congressional investigation into camp conditions and the treatment of Polish DPs by UNRRA.

The American government, facing international pressure and intense lobbying by many American ethnic groups, and especially Jewish Americans, felt compelled to respond to the DP question. On December 22, 1945, President Truman issued a directive allowing approximately forty thousand persons to enter the United States between the spring of 1946 and June 1948. The so-called Truman Directive did not solve the DP problem, but it further mobilized public opinion as well as ethnic groups ready to lobby for the acceptance of America's "fair share" of refugees.[21]

In the fall of 1946 Rozmarek and other Polonia activists went to Europe and spent almost two weeks visiting displaced persons camps. With this eyewitness evidence, he then launched an extensive and vocal campaign against UNRRA, which was widely echoed in the American press. The PAC's offensive against UNRRA coincided with the establishment of the Citizens Committee on Displaced Persons (CCDP), designed to lobby for special immigration laws. In close cooperation with the CCDP, and apparently moved by Rozmarek's eloquent pleas on behalf of DPs, Representative William G. Stratton of Illinois sponsored an appropriate bill in April 1947. It proposed the annual admission of one hundred thousand DPs as nonquota immigrants for four years.[22] While the DP bill slowly made its way through Congress, American Polonia demonstrated the highest level of mobilization for the DP cause. The Polish-American press informed its readers about new developments almost daily, and PAC leaders actively lobbied in Washington, D.C. Rank-and-file Polish Americans organized numerous letter-writing campaigns urging the passage of the new law. After a protracted struggle, President Truman signed the bill into law on June 25, 1948. The bill allowed 205,000 DPs to be admitted between July 1, 1948, and June 30, 1950. These numbers were to be mortgaged against quotas for each nationality group. The cutoff date for eligibility for displaced persons status was set at December 22, 1945. The act gave priority to farmers willing to work in American agriculture (30 percent) and to persons from the Baltic countries annexed by the Soviet Union (40 percent).[23]

As soon as the law began to take effect, Polonia turned its attention to lobbying for the extension and liberalization of the 1948 DP Act. A project of special significance for Polish Americans was a provision for the admittance of 18,000 Polish soldiers from Great Britain to the United States. Rozmarek again led Polonia in a campaign for the DP cause, and in 1950 amendments to the DP law finally were passed. The Baltic and agricultural preferences were dropped, "quota mortgaging" was liberalized, the number of DPs to be admitted was raised from 202,000 to 341,000 (including Polish veterans from Great Britain), and the whole program was extended through July 1, 1951. Moreover, the cutoff date for DPs, marking the last moment they could enter Western zones and be eligible for DP status, was advanced from December 22, 1945 to January 1, 1949.[24]

During the four years that the DP Act was in effect, 337,244 displaced persons entered the United States and were resettled under the auspices of the Displaced Persons Commission (DPC). The DPC was responsible "for carrying out the provisions and purposes of the [DP] Act and for formulating and issuing regulations for the admission into the United States of eligible displaced persons and displaced orphans and coordinating all the operations to the end of accomplishing the purpose of the statute." The commission was to systematically report on the progress of the program and make a final report to the president and Congress.[25] The DPC established thirty-four state displaced persons commissions and committees in order to coordinate the work.

The centerpiece of the DP law was the requirement of an assurance from a sponsor, either an individual or a voluntary agency recognized by the commission. The two most important features of an assurance were guarantees of employment and housing for the DPs upon their arrival in the United States. The obligation was not legally binding, but was based on moral grounds. Sponsors could name specific persons they wanted to assist or they could sign assurances for unnamed displaced persons. In the latter case, the field staff in Europe would match the sponsor's criteria (nationality, gender, general occupation, age, family size, and so on) with available applicants in the DP pool.[26]

The system relied heavily on the contributions of voluntary agencies. These were religious, ethnic, relief, welfare, or nonsectarian organizations, which worked through their constituencies and provided a connection between the public and the sponsors on the one hand, and the federal authorities in Europe and the United States on the other. Probably the most significant role of the voluntary agencies was the location of resettlement opportunities and the finding of sponsors. An important contribution was the issue of blank assurances, that is, assurances that did not name any particular DP and were to be filled out in Europe, while the agency took the responsibility of securing jobs and housing. These assurances were transmitted to the DPC headquarters and the cases followed until final resettlement. As the DPC report put it, "through sponsorships, the voluntary agencies pumped life-blood into the program and got it going."[27]

Three major Polish-American voluntary organizations took on responsibility for the resettlement of Polish displaced persons. Rada Polonii (after 1946 under the name of American Relief for Poland) and the Polish Immigration Committee (PIC) were both affiliated with the National Catholic Welfare Conference (NCWC). The American Committee for the Resettlement of Polish DP's (ACRPDP), an organ of the PAC, was the only organization accredited directly by the DPC. The three resettlement agencies represented a continuation of the wartime humanitarian and postwar legislative efforts of American Polonia. Due to their activities, some 130,000 DPs born in Poland arrived in the United States under the DP Act between June 1948 and June

1953.[28] Polish citizens of Jewish or Ukrainian background immigrated mostly through the efforts of Jewish or Ukrainian organizations, such as the Hebrew Sheltering and Immigrant Aid Society or the United Ukrainian American Relief Committee. Smaller numbers of ethnic Poles came with the assistance of the Church World Service and other nonsectarian agencies. For example, the Polish National Catholic Church Relief and Resettlement Center, affiliated with Church World Service, brought about a thousand DPs to the United States and provided them with care in the first period of resettlement.[29]

The NCWC was established in 1920 "to protect faith of Catholic immigrants" and served as a liaison with Congress and the presidential administration.[30] The War Relief Services (WRS) agency of the NCWC cared for the refugees in Europe, and the Catholic Committee for Refugees attended to their needs in the United States. After the Truman Directive went into effect in January 1946, the NCWC slowly began to build its policies and organizational network for the admission and resettlement of DPs.[31] The poor performance of the Catholic agencies handling the resettlement of DPs in 1947 resulted in the reorganization of the WRS-NCWC and the development of a national-scale plan of action. As a result, the board of bishops authorized a new National Resettlement Council (NRC) in November 1947, led by Father Edward E. Swanstrom. Catholic resettlement committees were set up in 120 dioceses throughout the country. Their role was to "educate their parishioners on the displaced persons problem, secure proper legislation, identify potential sponsors, raise funds, and follow up with assistance once the displaced persons arrived."[32]

The resettlement of Polish DPs became the most challenging task for Rada, a task that, despite Rada's undeniable merits in the war years, surpassed its organizational abilities. Rada's slow reaction to DP resettlement prospects, competition with other resettlement groups within Polonia, and the additional focus on direct aid for Poland drew fire from many Polish Americans. Criticized for its cooperation with the communist authorities in Poland and for creating a competitive atmosphere among Polish-American organizations interested in the refugee resettlement, Rada faced numerous difficulties. When relatively few Poles arrived under the Truman Directive, voices demanding united action by Polonia became even stronger.[33] Responding to the mounting pressure, in January 1948 Rada established a special committee for DPs. Józef Kania, the president of the Polish Roman Catholic Union of America (PRCUA), accepted the committee's leadership.[34]

In May 1948 Kazimierz Dąbski of *Nowy Świat,* a persistent fighter for the DPs, published a series of passionate articles attacking Rada's inactivity. Instead of calling for improvements, Dąbski began to distance himself from Rada. "The DP matter is first and foremost political. Rada Polonii, which works in Poland and has to have contacts with the Moscow government, can't be impartial where people hated by Soviet agents are concerned," he stated. The Polish-American Congress, Dąbski continued, as it prepared for its second national convention, should take over the DP problem and come up with the energetic resettlement program.[35] Indeed, during its convention in May 1948, the PAC formed the American Committee for the Resettlement of Polish DP's and declared the DP problem one of the most urgent points on the agenda for the near future.[36]

The DP question found a prominent place in F. X. Świetlik's extensive report on Rada's activities and plans for the future, which was presented during Rada's national convention on December 4 and 5, 1948, and in which Świetlik attempted to prove Rada's unique qualifications to carry out the resettlement program. He concluded: "Rada Polonii is fully qualified to lead the resettlement of Polish DPs, especially because in our opinion it is a strictly charitable, humanitarian effort—and not, as some would like to see it, a political matter."[37]

Despite the controversies that surrounded Rada's leadership and its resettlement program, the grassroots level involvement of Polish Americans within particular Rada districts remained strong. Policy conflicts between Rada and the PAC, accentuated by the personal rivalry between Rozmarek and Świetlik, had relatively little impact on the actual workings of their resettlement agencies. Some activists even served in the leadership of more than one agency at the same time.[38] According to the Rada's report for the period between October 1948 and April 1950, Rada sponsored about sixteen thousand Poles.[39] Rada's districts in New Jersey, New York, Wisconsin, Minnesota, Detroit, and Boston demonstrated special achievements in the number of resettled immigrants and in the variety of assistance offered to them.[40]

The second organization affiliated with the NCWC, the Polish Immigration Committee of New York, was inseparably tied to the tireless efforts and strong personality of Father Felix F. Burant. Father Burant, pastor of the predominantly Polish St. Stanislaus church in New York, had been involved in aid to Polish immigrants since 1924. During World War II Father Burant served as a chaplain in the U.S. armed forces with the rank of colonel. After returning to his pastoral duties, Burant focused his attention on the situation of Poles detained in Ellis Island and slated for deportation. Using all his influence and contacts, Burant and a group of his coworkers not only supplied those Poles with religious care and moral support but also tried to secure their release. In August 1946 Father Burant, alarmed by the increasing numbers of Poles who unsuccessfully attempted to immigrate to the United States (many of them were stowaways from Polish ships or people with inadequate immigration documents) and were being deported to communist Poland, presented Rada with a proposal to create a special body that could systematically offer help to the Ellis Island detainees. "The Immigration Committee is a post war necessity," Burant wrote to Rada headquarters. "Knowing conditions on Ellis Island as I see them, I must admit that the Polish immigrants detained are the least attended to." In October 1946 Burant received from Rada's board a recommendation to form a committee that would take care of the Polish refugees on Ellis Island and of all other Polish refugees in New York area. Rada agreed to support Burant's committee financially, assigning $ 1,300 per month to its activities.[41]

The committee, formally organized in February 1947, adopted the name American Relief for Poland—Immigration Committee and promptly set up its new offices.[42] While continuing care for the Ellis Island detainees, the committee also included care for incoming immigrants in its objectives. Like Rada and the ACRPDP, the PIC provided assistance at the ports of debarkation, transportation to temporary shelters, clothing, food, medical attention, and short-term financial aid. Further assistance included help in seeking employment, making contact with Polonia organizations, directing immigrants to language and vocational training, and enrolling children in schools and kindergartens. The PIC also handled inquiries from people interested in sponsoring immigrants. In order to promote its cause, the committee developed a large-scale publicity campaign, utilizing all available media and means. Under the DP law, securing assurances and clearing them with the NCWC were among the most urgent and important tasks.[43]

The Ellis Island detainees were just one of the special categories of Poles entering the United States at that time in addition to regular transports of DPs from Germany. The PIC had to assist, for example, a large group of more than fifteen thousand Poles with American citizenship who had been repatriated from Poland to the United States in the spring and summer of 1947. Those people often had no remaining relatives in America, did not speak English, and had no financial resources.[44] Another group of migrants in dire need of immediate help were Poles on transit visas traveling to South American countries. Their "layover" in New York, while waiting for a ship, sometimes lasted up to several weeks. In the meantime, they received no governmental or other assistance. The committee provided them with some financial resources, food, shelter and warm clothing.[45] The PIC also attended to the needs of Polish soldiers from Great Britain coming on affidavits of support as a part of the Polish quota, students sponsored for stipends by American colleges, as well as Polish fiancés arriving under special provisions for war brides.[46]

The PIC's cooperation with Rada proved difficult. Świetlik found in Burant an able, but doggedly independent associate. While relying on the financial and organizational resources of Rada, Burant followed his own policies and looked for support from a vast variety of organizations, including Rada's competitor, the PAC. In the summer of 1947, the tensions escalated, and in November 1948, the PIC, still formally a part of Rada, joined the NCWC as a separate entity.[47] A final split became inevitable. In February 1949, without any communication with Rada, Burant's committee incorporated itself under the name American Commission for Relief of Polish Immigrants (in Polish, Polski Komitet Imigracyjny—the Polish Immigration Committee or PIC).[48] According to the PIC's historian, from 1947 to September 1952 the PIC, under the auspices of the NCWC, was able to obtain assurances for 17,893 refugees from Germany, Austria, and Italy; 4,592 refugees from Great Britain; and 1,065 for "out-of-zone" refugees from various countries.[49]

The American Committee for the Resettlement of Polish DP's came into existence during the second national convention of the Polish American Congress held in Philadelphia in May, 1948. In June the ACRPDP was incorporated as a nonprofit organization under the laws of the State of Illinois and gained official recognition and accreditation from the U.S. Displaced Persons Commission, the Advisory Committee on Voluntary Foreign Aid, and the International Refugee Organization. The ACRPDP became the only Polish-American independent agency of national scope that could send its representatives abroad and issue its own assurances without the necessity of securing individual affidavits.[50] The first authorities of the ACRPDP included many established Polonia leaders who were active in all larger Polish-American organizations and provided a strong cross section of support for the ACRPDP's actions. Judge Blair F. Gunther accepted the chairmanship of the committee. Edward E. Plusdrak, a Chicago attorney and a PAC activist, served as the secretary-treasurer, and the board of directors included: Adela Lagodzinska, the Reverend Walerian Karcz, Jan A. Stanek, Józef Pawłowski, Franciszka Dymek, and Tadeusz Adesko.[51] The ACRPDP relied especially heavily on PNA structures, channeling the alliance's resettlement effort.[52] The ACRPDP organized twenty-six state division committees and many local groups whose main concern was the procurement of housing and jobs for the displaced persons. The central offices located in Chicago planned, directed, and coordinated work of the state divisions and maintained systematic contact with governmental authorities and all interested agencies.

The ACRPDP had official representatives in charge of its bases of operations in Germany and Great Britain. From the fall of 1949 onward, Colonel Bolesław Wichrowski was intensely active on behalf of the committee in Frankfurt, Germany. Franciszka Dymek, director of the ACRPDP and vice-president of the PNA, remained in Europe for six months in 1949 and 1950, visiting DP camps and representing Polish DPs to the authorities, as well as establishing useful contacts and collecting data.[53]

Despite constant financial problems, Judge Gunther's report of 1952 stated that "at the time of the expiration of the Displaced Persons Law, December 31, 1951, the American Committee for the Resettlement of the Polish Displaced Persons obtained assurances, guaranteeing employment and housing for in excess of 35,000 persons."[54] In 1950 the ACRPDP obtained recognition from the State Department to resettle 18,000 Polish former servicemen from Great Britain and their families. Some 11,500 eventually came, and the remaining 6,500 slots were later made available to displaced persons still in Germany following the DP Act's expiration.[55]

The Experience of Resettlement

The Displaced Persons Commission's *Second Semiannual Report to the President and the Congress* of August 1949 stated that "resettlement is a long-range program which begins with the displaced person overseas and terminates when the goal of American citizenship is attained." The same report described successful resettlement as a mental process in which the displaced persons gradually lose the feeling of displacement, while at the same time the "displaced person" identification also disappears from the thinking of the American people.[56] From an organizational point of view, the resettlement process presented itself as a tremendous challenge to a community with limited resources and no previous experience in carrying out operations of that scale. More importantly, for both DPs and Polish Americans, the resettlement effort, with all its organizational shortcomings and chaos, became a time of establishing first relationships and sorting out first impressions.

Most DPs traveled on American ships that took them from Bremenhaven, Germany, to the ports of New York, Boston, and New Orleans. Some DP groups flew into the United States or Canada and then rode the train to further destinations. The welcome DPs received from governmental and voluntary agencies immediately after disembarkation became their first memory of America. Exhausted by the long journey, sometimes ill, and always anxious about the future, the displaced persons had to deal with confusing immigration regulations, foreign officials, language barriers, and overwhelming trepidation about meeting sponsors and organizing the beginnings of their new lives. Polish-American resettlement agencies tried to ease the tensions of that moment by providing their friendly assistance to the newcomers. Polish Americans representing resettlement committees as well as those who worked directly for the NCWC or DPC participated in welcoming ceremonies on the piers on a regular basis.

Some arriving DP groups enjoyed the special attention of governmental officials and the press. Crowds received the SS *General Black*, the first ship bringing DPs to the United States under the Displaced Persons Act. According to *Dziennik Związkowy* of November 3, 1948, the *General Black* entering the New York harbor was decorated in festive flags and banners. Port sirens and sirens of all the ships wailed, as American army planes circled above the ship and the port water cannons shot fountains of water in the air. Three smaller pilot ships met the *General Black* before it entered the port, bringing in scores of dignitaries and reporters. The official program took place on the deck and included speeches of Ugo Carusi of the DPC, New York mayor William O'Dwyer, Attorney General Tom Clark, and Francis Cardinal

Spellman. All the larger Polish-American organizations sent representatives, with Charles Burke speaking on behalf of the PAC.[57]

The port of Boston also became the scene of many large demonstrations of support for Polish DPs. Close to two hundred Polish Americans awaited the arrival of the SS *Marine Flasher* in January 1949. To their dismay, the ship brought only twenty Poles, which raised questions about the effectiveness of Polonia's resettlement agencies.[58] Half a year later, however, Boston witnessed a ceremony welcoming the fifty-thousandth DP—who happened to be Polish—Józef Bujak and his family. Again, the DPC's Ugo Carusi, Massachusetts governor Paul Dever, and other governmental officials graced the festivities with their presence.[59] The very last DPs—also Poles—were Józef Żyłka and his family, whose visa had number 339,000; they not only met representatives of the DPC and the governors of New York and Illinois, but were also invited to the White House and spoke to President Truman.[60]

The everyday operations on the piers usually proved less festive and much more tedious. Representatives of Polonia spent long hours waiting for transports and assisting with the processing of the immigrants. In New York, Polish women organized a canteen with sandwiches, coffee, and sweets for the children. Charles Sepucha, a worker with the Massachusetts DP Commission in Boston, secured benches for the waiting room in which DPs spent hours waiting for customs and other examinations.[61] DPs in need of immediate medical attention received care, and those planning to travel farther were transported to railroad stations. Train transports arriving in Chicago, where large numbers of DPs were sponsored, found Polonia delegations awaiting them on the platforms. Frequently, some representatives traveled out of the city to make the last stage of the journey together with the DPs and to prepare them for arrival in Chicago. PAC activists met the special train bringing the first group of Polish DPs sponsored by the ACRPDP miles before it reached Chicago. They quickly set up a provisional office, informed immigrants about their sponsors, and distributed welcoming gifts from the PNA: five-dollar bills and issues of *Dziennik Związkowy*. To further facilitate assimilation into Polonia, PAC and PNA leaders provided them with information about their respective organizations and advised them to join as soon as they got settled in Chicago.[62]

Receiving incoming transports went more easily when the sponsors themselves showed up to take care of the DPs. The situation became complicated if DPs came either on blanket assurances from the resettlement agencies or on so-called "courtesy" assurances from people who were willing to provide their signatures, but who relied on the organizations to care for the DPs. In some cases, sponsors simply withdrew their support, claiming unforeseen difficulties in securing jobs and housing. DPs who found themselves without sponsors required the assistance of Polish-American volunteers until a job and a place to live could be found for them.

In order to provide the DPs with temporary shelter, Polonia either purchased or rented "DP houses" and apartments. The Illinois state division of the PAC purchased a house in Chicago that could accommodate several families; but because of the housing shortage in the city, it had to rent another one in 1951. Bonawentura Migała, a member of the Illinois PAC division, served as an administrator of both houses.[63] In New Jersey, Rada's District 5 operated a sixteen-bedroom house, which, between fall 1949 and fall 1950 lodged more than 351 Polish DPs. Rada's District 8 in Buffalo used a house provided for DPs by the Catholic diocese, in which up to ten families at a time were put up. Similar arrangements in Detroit proved insufficient, and Rada's District 34 petitioned the headquarters for the funds necessary to secure another shelter.[64]

As immigrants filled DP houses in excess of their capacity, new arrangements had to be made. DPs coming to the Chicago area frequently found themselves guests in the private house of Charles and Wanda Rozmarek. Wanda Rozmarek served as the head of the PAC Illinois DP department from its inception in 1948 until the expiration of the DP law. Over a period of more than four years, Wanda Rozmarek devoted all her time and energy to the resettlement cause. She met DPs personally at the train stations at all times of the day and night, drove them around the city to their sponsors, cooked for them, ran errands, and actively looked for jobs. Rozmarek's house accepted about four hundred DP families for a temporary stay. Her private phone number was passed around among DPs waiting for departure in Germany. All the expenses Wanda Rozmarek covered herself; and on top of this, she and her husband donated two thousand dollars to DP funds.[65]

The majority of Polish DPs were sponsored by Polish Americans and joined older Polish communities in the largest urban centers of the Northeast and Midwest. Some, however, traveled to sponsors in locations where Polonia was either not as numerous or nonexistent. The Polish press sometimes published reports on the experiences of the DPs, citing both positive and negative examples. An American farmer from McDonald County, Missouri, shared her impressions of the Polish family she had sponsored as help on her 420-acre farm. "There is nothing this family won't do, and the entire group wants to help," wrote Mrs. Wiggin. "It makes my heart rejoice having had the privilege of bringing to America this fine Polish family."[66]

A Polish couple sponsored to work as a chauffeur and a domestic in Nashville, Tennessee, depicted their first encounter with their sponsors as seen through DP eyes. Zdzisław J. and his wife were filled with anxiety and hope when they arrived on the train in Nashville. Because Zdzisław knew English, they were able to locate their lost luggage and telephone their sponsor, Mr. John D. Zdzisław and his wife felt very encouraged by the friendly welcome and conversation with Mr. D. on the way to the house as well as during their introduction to his family, who listened to their wartime story with great attention. However, when dinner time came, the travelers, clad in their nicest clothes to make the best impression, discovered that their meal was served in the servants' quarters. "The joyful feeling that we had ceased to be second-class people suddenly fades away," wrote Zdzisław. "During dinner we stay quiet and a little bit sad. . . . It would not have taken too much to invite us to the table just for this one night. To let us feel the hospitality of people caring for people." In the evening Zdzisław and his wife again discussed the events of the day:

> Were we right to expect different treatment at the table from our employers? After some thinking we decided that we weren't. Their lack of invitation seemed suddenly so trivial when compared with the risk they had taken in sponsoring two unknown DPs from Germany, that we finally laughed at our own extravagant expectations.
> They took a poker-type risk. They performed a Christian deed of helping thy neighbor, and now we need to earn their respect. And the most important is that thanks to their help we are not DPs any more.[67]

The Polish Immigration Committee sponsored some special projects, experimenting with group resettlement schemes. The idea gained the support of the NCWC as a quick and efficient resettlement option. The most spectacular and successful example was the resettlement of 735 young, single Polish men, mostly former members of the Polish Guards, on farms on Long Island.

The initiative to sponsor Polish DPs came from farmers' cooperatives in Suffolk County, uniting Polish-American farmers active in the New York state division of the Polish American Congress. The first was the Eastern Suffolk Cooperative, which pledged sponsorship for 250 DPs in April 1949. The goal was to receive the first transports before July 15, just in time for harvest. In a series of meetings in different locations in Suffolk County, representatives of the PIC (headed by Father Burant and Walter Zachariasiewicz), a PAC delegation, and local activist Judge Henryk Zaleski of Riverhead discussed organizational matters with the farmers and pastors of larger Polish-American parishes. By the end of the month, more than seven hundred assurances signed by Polish-American farmers and priests as well as a fair number of American farmers, were sent to the NCWC representation in Germany. The "Long Island Operation" evoked the interest of the DPC and the support of congressmen John Lesinski and Francis E. Walter, who ensured that some DP groups would travel by air in order to speed up their arrival.[68]

Beginning in the first hot days of July, transports of Polish Guards heading for Long Island farms drew the attention of Polish-American as well as mainstream American media, which praised both the good presentation of the "boys in black uniforms" and the devotion of the Suffolk County farmers.[69] Completed in September 1949, the "Long Island Operation" was proclaimed a success. An IRO delegation that visited some of the farms released an interview with the general manager of the Long Island Fertilizer and Produce Company, which employed some of Polish DPs. "These boys are better than all right in their energy, their attitude, their eagerness to make good. They are going to make substantial citizens of this country," he commented.[70] *Nowy Świat*, which had been following the operation since its inception, began to publish a regular column, "Among Polish Farms of Suffolk County, L.I.," through which the readers could trace the progress of the resettlement. It also informed readers of signs of revitalization of the community's life: a celebration to commemorate the German invasion of Poland attracted close to a thousand people, including DPs and local government officials; Polish entertainers incorporated Suffolk County into their artistic tours; and the press announced the first weddings between Polish men and Polish-American women.[71]

Because some Guards had suffered delays that excluded them from resettlement on Long Island, smaller groups of young Polish men were directed to work on farms and in agricultural plants in other states, among them Texas, Florida, Connecticut, Nebraska, and Montana. The "Texas Operation," also cosponsored by the PIC and the NCWC, resettled about a hundred men, mostly on farms but also as drivers and craftsmen.[72] According to PIC records, in 1950 the number of group resettlement plans sponsored by the PIC increased. They included "Long Island Operation Number Two," with 597 assurances; the "Shade Tobacco Operation," with 732 assurances; and the "Rockland County Operation," with 90 assurances.[73] Not everywhere, however, did former Polish Guards find conditions as good as those in Long Island. In Montana, for example, the farm work turned out to be only seasonal and left groups of Poles both without jobs and without the support of Polish-American communities.[74]

The resettlement of some Polish DPs in Louisiana also created serious problems. Poles were a part of a group of about five thousand DPs, including a large percentage of Balts and Ukrainians, who came to the South as agricultural laborers. The American government showed keen interest in directing incoming DPs to work in the South, which was not affected by the overcrowding the Eastern and Midwestern industrial centers had experienced. In January 1949, Kazimierz Dąbski, previously employed on the editorial board of *Nowy Świat*, embarked on an official tour of the Southern states to explore resettlement possibilities for Polish DPs there. His organizational base became Miami, Florida, which boasted an active Polish-American community.[75] But by April, during the meeting of the PAC Illinois state division in Chicago, the deplorable conditions of life in the South became a topic of a heated discussion. Polish DPs "live like slaves," announced Wanda Rozmarek: "We must rescue them . . . because these are brothers and sisters of ours." The meeting decided to extend help to DPs in the South and, whenever there was a chance, to bring them to the Chicago area.[76]

On May 3, 1949, the story about the exploitation of DPs in Louisiana broke out on a national scale, as newspapers published a report by the Reverend Carl Shutten, a Catholic pastor in New Orleans, and the Reverend J. Stanley Ormsby of the NCWC, who had visited 150 displaced persons in the vicinity of New Orleans. The report stated that the DPs were living in "desperate conditions, without sufficient food, clothing, and going rapidly into debt at the sugar company commissaries."[77] As the press began sending reporters to the sugar plantations, Harry N. Rosenfield, commissioner of the

DPC initiated an investigation. The reports he received from Lawrence E. Higgins, the Louisiana Commissioner of Welfare, Senator Guy J. D'Antonio, the Louisiana governor's representative on displaced persons, and Wilmer Grayson from the Louisiana Department of Agriculture all indicated that "the situation is very much exaggerated and that isolated instances were used to generalize."[78] The common opinion was that only a few DPs, who were not farmers and could not manage life on sugar plantations, had voiced dissatisfaction. Higgins commented that "the whole affair has been a 'Great Deal about Nothing,'" while Grayson concluded that "[t]he DPs are even a little better off than our own farmers."[79]

The Reverend Dr. Joseph B. Koncius, the president of the Lithuanian Relief Fund of America, conducted a separate, private investigation and sent his report directly to President Truman. Alarming letters received by the Lithuanian- and English-language press had prompted him to undertake the trip to Louisiana personally. His investigation was by no means limited to Lithuanian DPs; many Polish-sounding names were included in the report. Surveying the housing facilities of the DPs of different nationalities, Koncius found that "[t]he homes provided for the majority of Displaced Persons living on sugar plantations are not fit for animals. They cannot be called houses, but shanties. ... rough boards and in many instances from the inside of these shanties I saw holes through which bugs were crawling and rain could beat through."[80]

Koncius pointed out that some DPs were being paid below the minimum wage and then only on fair days, which brought their weekly earnings to the poverty level. DPs were allowed to use only company grocery stores, which offered them food on credit. Excessive costs for the modest furniture provided for the houses were subtracted from the paychecks, perpetuating DPs' debts. Koncius concluded: "In hundreds of camps I visited [during the DP camp tour in Europe, 1945–46] I found some of the shacks of the Displaced Persons here in New Orleans worse than any of the DP Camps in Europe, and the food conditions here not much better than [those of] the Prisoners of War whom I saw in Germany."[81]

As a result of the scandal, the Louisiana State DP Commission was created to prevent similar situations in the future. The NCWC reviewed 300 cases resettled in the New Orleans area, and approximately 150 were transferred elsewhere. All the NCWC cases destined for Louisiana which had not yet arrived there were also rerouted to other states.[82]

Resettlement in rural areas, strongly encouraged by the government, captured the imagination of some people of good will, such as the Reverend Jan Śliwowski. Śliwowski was a Roman Catholic priest who had spent several years working among Polish refugees in a refugee camp in Tanganyika. After returning to the United States, he devoted all his energy to the goal of bringing as many of those refugees as possible to America. In 1948 he purchased an eighty-acre farm near Syracuse, New York, that could support about ten people, and had plans gradually to buy more farms in that area. "If I am not able to sponsor my people from Africa soon, I will take a number of DPs from Germany," he wrote in his letter to *Nowy Świat*. In rousing words, Śliwowski appealed to Polish Americans for financial support of his project in the name of "our suffering brethren."[83]

The reality of resettlement in rural areas, however, was often discouraging. Those DPs who found themselves in regions without any Polish population felt the need for relations with their own ethnic group. The frustrated author of a letter to the ACRPDP, resettled with his family in a small town without any Polonia community, repeatedly requested addresses for the nearest centers of "some Polish Associations." He wanted to break out of his isolation and tried dramatically to plug into the mainstream of Polish-American life. "Remember once and forever," he wrote to the committee, "that people like me, though arriving here not a long time ago, are not savages ... but are people like all of you." Moreover, he interpreted the tragic experiences of the war as improving the survivors' characters and making them more altruistic than "millions of U.S. citizens, also of Polish background, living only for themselves and their businesses."[84]

In order to meet the DP law's agricultural criteria, some DPs either claimed a farming background or accepted job offers on farms without having any previous experience. This situation quickly became a source of dissatisfaction for both DPs and their sponsors. A report from Rada's District 34 noted that the unfriendly attitudes of some farmers to Polish DPs in Michigan stemmed from the fact that in one case a lawyer and in another case a professor had been sent to farms. Neither of them, the report indicated, had carried out their responsibilities adequately and they harmed resettlement prospects for others.[85] For nonfarmers resettled in rural areas, life brought feelings of isolation, bitterness, and anxiety. "I can speak English with the help of a dictionary," wrote a thirty-seven-year-old radio electrician from a farm in Indiana. "In Europe I was advanced in English; unfortunately, here, by the cows, I forgot more than I had learned during those seven months. I spent six years in German captivity but I felt morally [sic] better."[86]

The ACRPDP received numerous job offers from Polish-American farm owners in many different states. Farmers were usually willing to sponsor either young single men or young married couples who could provide immediate help with farm work. There were also some single Polish-American farmers who looked forward to meeting Polish displaced women. An example of a marriage offer came in correspondence from Joseph A. of New York State. Joseph wrote to the ACRPDP: "It is hard for me on my farm without a lady of the house [*gospodyni*]. When the first transport comes from Germany, please, choose for me a pretty lady, because I want to marry her. I am enclosing three photographs of me and my farm." In another letter (all of them left without a response by the committee), Joseph expressed willingness to come to New York to get introduced to the right candidate for a wife. "I would marry a Polish woman," he added, "or a Lithuanian one if you ran out of Polish."[87] This example is, of course, extreme; but in the face of shrinking ethnic communities, some Polish Americans gladly welcomed a new influx of Poles, counting on establishing their families within their own ethnic group.[88]

The DP Commission identified the problems of rural resettlement in its second semiannual report to the president and the Congress, and fully acknowledged these difficulties in its final report. The movement of DPs from farms to the cities, according to the report's findings, followed the same patterns as the movement of native-born Americans in the United States. Some of the factors affecting the shift included declining employment opportunities in farming, higher wages in the cities, inadequate financial arrangements of farmers in some areas of the country, and relative isolation on the farms.[89] Jan Olejniczak, in his report on the resettlement operation sponsored by Rada, also commented on the voluminous correspondence the headquarters had received from DPs resettled in the countryside. The letters asked for help in finding jobs in the city (preferably Chicago) and justified the need to move with a variety of reasons, such as

> The work is too hard; they [DPs] are not qualified for farm work; without knowing English they have problems communicating with sponsors and others in a foreign environment; they want to send children to Polish

schools; they would like to be close to a Polish church; they do not have adequate living conditions, wages, etc. Each such complaint is thoroughly investigated by Rada and diocese's NCWC director. . . . The majority of those complaints are unfounded, and the situation described by DPs is far from reality, but they still want to be resettled in the cities, where, as their DP acquaintances inform them, one can make "big money."[90]

The job market in the cities, however, left much to be desired and the "big money" myth was certainly an unattainable dream to the newcomers as well as to many Polonians. After the wave of strikes, labor unrest, and layoffs following the reconversion from wartime production in 1946, the economic situation generally improved, but difficult conditions continued in some industrial regions with a heavy Polish-American population, such as Detroit, Michigan. Strikes and rising unemployment reduced the opportunities for DPs to find well-paying jobs in that area. When the government put limits on automobile production in the early 1950s, the unemployment rate in Detroit skyrocketed. According to some estimates, about seven hundred Polish families who had arrived under the DP Act in Detroit found themselves without means of support and facing hunger. In January 1952 the local Polonia, centered on Rada's District 34, launched a free kitchen dispensing one meal a day to the DPs. Some DPs were sent to Chicago in search of jobs. District 34 received a monthly subvention from Rada Headquarters and used the money for short-term loans to those in the worst situations.[91] The ACRPDP letters from Michigan and other areas occasionally mentioned displaced Poles' participation in some of the strikes, as well as the loss of income due to strikes and layoffs.[92]

An especially dramatic situation faced those displaced persons who could not find jobs matching their education and profession. Both the IRO and the resettlement agencies admitted that all systematic efforts to successfully employ professionals in their specialties had failed. Difficulties faced by teachers, lawyers, physicians, dentists, veterinarians, scholars, journalists, artists, and other professionals included language barriers, the negative attitudes of American licensing authorities, legal obstacles (citizenship requirements), and lack of retraining programs. In its report, the Massachusetts DP Commission followed the resettlement of twenty-six DP attorneys and jurists in the state. "It is a bit sad," the report read, "that these attorneys, who are, of course, educated men who enjoyed a definite status in their home communities, have been definitely down-graded as to employment; eight of them found employment as dishwashers and kitchen help, eleven as laborers and factory hands, and the others as housemen or janitors."[93]

The Polish community encountered the same types of problems. A good example was that of a married couple who looked in vain for jobs other than housemaid and factory worker. Both of them were renowned scientists with impressive lists of scientific publications in foreign languages enclosed in their resumes. Similarly, many officers and soldiers of the Polish army from Great Britain had to accept low-paying factory jobs as unskilled workers.[94]

A report of the Pennsylvania Commission on Displaced Persons revealed a number of reasons why some employers only reluctantly hired DPs:

> Approximately 250 employers have been appraised of the displaced persons program as a source of labor by our local offices. Reaction was one of indifference due to: No critical need, language barrier, time lag in recruiting workers, interpretation of government security regulations in defense plants, and unfavorable experiences of employers with displaced persons mainly due to improper placement resulting in displaced persons working in jobs far below skill or social level. Also, tendency to "job hopping" after arrival in this country.[95]

Complaints about "job hopping" appeared in many reports on the effectiveness of the resettlement program. The Massachusetts DP Commission commented that the DPs' "excess of mobility has been a source of irritation to many citizens."[96] The final report of the DP Commission identified the movement of DPs to different jobs after only a short time with their sponsors as the number one reason for unsuccessful resettlement cases. The DP Commission explained "job hopping" by, among other things, the desire of people who had been subjected to regimentation in practically all aspects of their lives for many years to move according to their own decisions. "Part of the restlessness of the displaced person," the report indicated, "like that of a newly returned soldier, is the normal reaction of the individual to want to move under his own decision—using his new freedom—without regimentation."[97]

The problem of mobility affected the Polish resettlement program. Rada's report pointed to this tendency as harmful to the resettlement process and implored the Polish press to appeal to DPs to persevere in their jobs. The report concluded: "Traveling from one state or city to another proves that these DPs are not trying to adjust to the conditions of life in the country which welcomed them."[98] "Job hopping" ideas, however, did not always come from the DPs themselves. In Minnesota Rada's District 10 experienced a crisis due to intervention from probably well-meaning but not well-informed representatives of the local PNA group. Rada had resettled a young Polish woman named Maria as a domestic with American sponsors in Brainerd, where her adjustment seemed to be progressing in a satisfactory manner. After a few weeks, Maria was approached by a PNA representative from Minneapolis who insisted that she should move to the Twin Cities, where she could earn better money working at Dayton's department store. Maria's sponsor, who had counted on her working for him longer, was upset by the PNA's interference and called for mediation. The girl agreed to stay in Brainerd. Unfortunately, the arrangement proved to be a fiasco. Soon, the sponsors noticed that Maria was "now sullen and dissatisfied and practically of no use to them." The responsibility to clean up the mess fell on District 10, which arranged for Maria's transfer and protested to the PNA national office the "tactless" behavior of their local group.[99]

Among the most difficult problems encountered during the resettlement process were unexpected medical emergencies, leaving the newly arrived DPs at the mercy of Polish-American communities. Detroit's Polonia enlisted the help of their Polish-American physicians, who saw many patients gratis and offered free x-ray services and eyeglasses.[100] Polish-American doctors donated care or offered discounted rates in other Polonia locations. Sometimes the costs of medical treatment became so high that it required much effort to find ways to cover the expenses. This happened, for example, in one Minnesota case, when a Polish DP family of three resettled in Mankato. They were ineligible for public assistance because of lack of legal residence but experienced a series of medical emergencies. After unsuccessfully appealing to the NCWC for funds to cover the costs, the Minnesota DP Commission referred the entire matter to Francis J. Nahurski, the head of Rada's District 10 in Minneapolis, hoping to be rid of the problem by transferring the responsibility to the local Polish-American community.[101] Another publicized case pertained to Jan Kołpak and his family, who had been sponsored by the ACRPDP. During the ocean passage Kołpak suddenly fell ill, and the first diagnosis after the ship had arrived in New Orleans was mental illness. The immigration authorities began proceedings to deport the Kołpak family back to Germany.

Only the quick intervention of the ACRPDP, which covered the costs of Kołpak's hospital stay and posted a one-thousand-dollar bond, saved the family from being boarded back on the ship. As further medical tests proved, Kołpak was not mentally ill, and the family successfully resettled in Chicago.[102]

It cannot be denied, however, that wartime experiences could and, indeed, did leave profound emotional wounds on many DPs.[103] Some refugees could not easily adjust to the new environment. Cases of alcoholism were noted. ACRPDP records contain correspondence with the Immigrants' Protective League about a neglected Polish child whose parents—DPs—were reportedly having drinking problems. In another case, a pastor from one of the southern states wrote about two Polish DPs employed by the parish for the maintenance of church property. "Both of these men are industrious, capable and personable and have done well the tasks assigned to them," the pastor commented. After some time in Texas, both DPs started to drink and provoke fights. The pastor, asking for help, recommended a change of environment to a place where they could live among their countrymen and avoid loneliness and despair.[104]

Some DPs went through breakdowns not always registered in medical statistics. There is no firm evidence of the scope of this problem among Polish displaced persons. ACRPDP correspondence with DPs contains only a few letters relating to this question. In one of them, a DP from Chicago asked the committee to provide him with security because of an alleged communist conspiracy against his life. In another, a patient in a psychiatric hospital claimed that American physicians were holding him there in order to carry out experiments on his body. A third letter was from a thirty-five-year-old man who, after coming to America with his family, allegedly murdered his wife. Initially, the man was put in jail, then he was placed in a psychiatric ward. From there he wrote to the committee requesting legal help, money, and cigarettes.[105]

The two most important and difficult challenges facing Polish-American communities during the resettlement process were attracting sponsors and collecting the money necessary to carry out operations. In both respects, Polonia activists had to demonstrate endurance and resourcefulness while appealing to the hearts and pockets of Polish Americans. The search for sponsors remained always in the forefront of the program. Many people felt uneasy about signing assurances and dealing with the legal implications of sponsorship. The public needed education about the responsibilities and rights of sponsors. In order to dispel anxieties, the press published explanations prepared by Polonia lawyers, who also often spoke at meetings and gatherings. Attorney Edward E. Plusdrak, secretary of the ACRPDP, made available to the press a letter from Edward M. O'Connor of the DP Commission elaborating on the public charge feature of the DP law. The letter was published in full in English, followed by explanations in Polish.[106] Wanda Rozmarek went on the radio to reassure the public: "Sponsors have no legally binding obligations toward the DPs . . . so-called assurances are just a formality, that can be signed by anyone, whether rich or poor."[107] The press also announced that resettled DPs had the right to sign assurances even before they took their "first papers." This explanation was followed by stories about DPs bringing over other DPs and encouraging continuation of this trend.[108]

Polish-American organizations accepted the challenge of signing large numbers of assurances. As early as July 1948, the PNA had pledged ten thousand assurances, and in November of the same year, the first two thousand were presented to the ACRPDP. During just one meeting of Chicago's Charitable Association, women members signed thirty assurances, moved by an eloquent plea of Franciszka Dymek.[109] By 1951 Dymek herself had signed three times the number of assurances allowed for one person and was reprimanded by the DP Commission. Wanda Rozmarek claimed to have signed close to a thousand assurances for DPs and 150 for soldiers.[110] The press regularly published long lists of sponsors who had signed assurances and included appeals for more efforts. In the heat of the battle for more assurances, one Polonia activist in New Jersey went so far as to announce that anyone who provided housing and a job for a DP would receive ten dollars. The announcement immediately resulted in a scandal, and the entire offer had to be revoked.[111]

The need for money also affected the resettlement program. Although volunteers performed nearly all the tasks, funds were needed to meet some operational expenses, such as office supplies, postage, and gas. The bulk of collected money went to cover DPs' inland transportation, small loans to families, food and warm clothes for those without any means, as well as rent for DP shelters and houses. A collection "for the DPs" became a part of any social gathering, picnic, meeting or cultural event. Installation dinners, anniversary celebrations, and private birthday parties or baptisms brought on spontaneous collections averaging between twenty and a hundred dollars. Organizations earmarked certain funds from their resources and handed checks to the representatives of the resettlement agencies. Polish-American bankers, entrepreneurs, and industrialists came forward with more substantial donations. Most of the collected money represented small donations from individuals sympathetic to the DP cause. An exceptional example was a seventy-year-old Polish-American woman from a small town, who sent three hundred dollars for the PIC and became the topic of Peter Yolles's *Nowy Świat* essay about devotion and sacrifice in Polonia.[112]

The initiatives of the PAC Illinois division illustrate the scale and scope of the effort. Before the DP Act came into effect, the Illinois division had assigned twenty thousand dollars to cover the costs of bringing a hundred youths to America from the DP camps. After the law was announced, this sum became the seed of the Fundusz Wysiedleńczy, the DP Fund. Beginning in 1948, during every year of the resettlement program, the Third of May demonstration in Chicago—the largest annual show of power by Chicago Polonia—included a special collection for the DP Fund, announced and advertised as the main collection of the day. The division also sponsored a summertime Dzień Polonii (Polonia Day), with a picnic and outdoor activities. The main cause adopted by those celebrations became the DP Fund.[113] In 1950 the division organized a large fifty-dollar-a-plate banquet in Chicago's Palmer House, which turned out to be the talk of the season in the community. The money from the banquet improved the finances of the DP Fund. A year later, however, the division had to accept thirty-five thousand dollars from the PNA to help cover inland transportation for the DPs and assist in the maintenance of two DP houses in Chicago.[114]

In many other Polonia communities, organizations carried out collections of furniture, housewares, clothing, shoes, books, and toys to facilitate DP adjustment in the first period after their arrival. DPs were often invited to Thanksgiving dinners and Christmas parties organized by Polonians. The PIC in New York paid special attention to the care of the DP children, helping to place them in schools and day care centers, and arranging for free summer camps.[115]

The resettlement effort by American Polonia has to be regarded as successful. The community had no previous experience in actions of that scale and no existing mechanisms that could be utilized during the program. The voluntary agencies involved in resettlement had to learn their lessons as the ships unloaded new transports of displaced persons. The financial resources of the resettlement agencies were limited at best, and giving decreased as the community pressed on in a ten-year effort on behalf of Poland. The Polish population in Poland, affected by the devastation, poverty, and destitution resulting from the war, became a natural competitor for Polish-American charity and care. Moreover, the intricacies of the DP law made resettlement complicated from both legal and organizational points of view. Ethnic resettlement agencies struggled to adapt to the law's requirements and limitations within a restricted period of time. The pressure of time and impending deadlines caused much of the work to be done in a hasty manner. The resettlement agencies counted on sponsors to continue to care for refugees, while the agencies themselves had to accommodate new transports. In too many cases efforts to provide adequate information failed, and sponsors were ill informed about their rights and obligations, as were the displaced persons themselves.

Despite these problems, the seasoned, although overburdened cadre of persons active in the Polish-American community accomplished an amazing amount of organizational work in difficult conditions. Polish-American women, particularly, invested enormous amounts of time and energy in the resettlement and care of DPs. Wanda Rozmarek, Franciszka Dymek, and Adela Lagodzinska[116] led them by personal example. Polish-American women were in the forefront of the program both as sponsors and as rank-and-file volunteers. They located jobs and housing and conducted fund raising. They met newly arrived DPs on the piers and train stations, made sandwiches and coffee, collected clothing, kitchen utensils, and furniture, and donated toys for the children. The very fact that some 140,000 refugees born in Poland were resettled in the United States in a period of about six years is in itself a telling achievement of American Polonia. Despite the many obstacles, time pressures, inexperience, and resource limitations, Polish Americans rose to the task in order to allow their compatriots to "live a happy and peaceful life" in the United States.

For the refugees, the resettlement period brought important experiences. It was the time to gather first impressions about America and American society, and become familiar with American Polonia. It was also the time to search each other out and restore ties severed by the migration process.

The New Emigration

From the time of their arrival in the United States, the refugees began the implementation of an important part of their mission: the reestablishment of the exile community, often termed the New Emigration (*Nowa Emigracja*) in contrast to the established Polish-American community or Old Polonia (*Stara Polonia*). In the early years of the resettlement period, postwar Polish immigrants displayed a strong tendency to create their own separate organizations. The most characteristic organizations for this phase were the self-help (*samopomoc*) associations formed by the refugees immediately after their arrival and geared toward addressing needs stemming from their recent immigrant and refugee status. Other associations focused on particular points of the exile mission, for example, the development of Polish culture in exile, the patriotic upbringing of the children, and the preservation of Polish history. Political and veterans organizations championed the cause of Poland's independence and preservation of diaspora ties.

Stowarzyszenie Nowych Amerykanów (Association of New Americans) in Milwaukee, Wisconsin, and Samopomoc Nowej Emigracji (Mutual Aid Association of the New Polish Emigration) in Chicago, Illinois, were excellent examples of self-help associations. The former was established in 1948, and reached out to Poles who arrived under the DP Act. Its main goal was self-help: information for the newly arrived, aid in difficult economic conditions, English language classes, and assistance in solving problems related to resettlement in the Milwaukee area. From its inception, Stowarzyszenie developed a particularly vigorous cultural activity in the Polish language. It organized meetings and picnics, and produced amateur theater performances, specializing in comedies and variety shows that utilized the acting talents of its own members. It also sponsored visits to Milwaukee by popular Polish performers touring larger Polonia communities, mostly groups formed by exiled prewar Polish artists. Stowarzyszenie formed its own male choir, a sports club with a winning soccer team ("Polonia"), and a youth circle. More than three hundred people participated in some of the more popular events.

In order to accommodate large audiences, including members of both Old Polonia and the New Emigration, Stowarzyszenie used the facilities of the Polish Falcons and other Polonian organizations in Milwaukee. Cooperation with Old Polonia was especially noticeable during more formal occasions, such as the traditional Christmas celebration of sharing a wafer (*opłatek*); invited guests included representatives of all the major Polonian organizations, and official speeches promised closer ties between both groups.[117] In 1951 Stowarzyszenie and new immigrants who formed a separate PNA group explicitly invited Old Polonia to their summer picnic, considered to be the best occasion to "get to know each other better." It is telling that another summer picnic organized three years later had the same goal.[118] In time, however, the organizers of Stowarzyszenie's cultural events began to complain about the indifference of Old Polonia to their efforts. By 1954 the overall visibility of Stowarzyszenie had decreased considerably. The pages of the Milwaukee *Kuryer Polski* instead featured more announcements from the local chapter of SPK, which had taken over many of Stowarzyszenie's previous functions.

The Chicago-based Samopomoc Nowej Emigracji, organized on a basis similar to that of the Milwaukee Stowarzyszenie, proved to be longer lived; this is not surprising, considering the sheer size of the Chicago Polish community. Established in 1949, the Samopomoc emphasized information and other services directed specifically to new immigrants. Designated members held evening office hours in the organization's headquarters, taking care of numerous problems plaguing the newly arrived. They assisted with job and housing searches, translation of documents, sponsorships, applications for war reparations, and financial aid. The cultural program included lectures and presentations on a broad variety of topics and an immensely popular Żywy Dziennik (Live News), which drew crowds of new and old immigrants. In a move characteristic of the new organizations, Samopomoc established its own library with publications in both Polish and English. Its headquarters also played a role as a community center for the new immigrants, who were invited to stop by for a game of chess or to discuss current international political situation. It frequently organized popular dance parties and shows featuring Polish artists. Samopomoc was a member of the Polish American Congress, and cooperated with numerous other New Emigration and Old Polonia organizations.[119]

Among the many artistic and cultural organizations, the Ogiński Choir deserves special attention because of both its longevity and its success as a new organization. The choir was founded in Wildflecken, the largest Polish DP camp in Germany, in 1945. Two years later it transformed itself into an all-male choir. When Captain Feliks Ciejko left Wildflecken for America in 1949, as the first of the choir's members to emigrate, he made a solemn promise to bring the entire choir to the United States. He found a sponsor, Ben Rogozenski, a Polish American from Port Washington, Long Island. Shortly thereafter, thirty-five members of the choir with their families, more than sixty people altogether, arrived in New York. Despite the dispersion of the members, who often had to travel long distances to the choir's rehearsals and reconcile the time demands of refugee life with a full schedule of performances, the choir flourished. It was invited to perform on numerous occasions for both Old Polonia and New Emigration. In a gesture of friendship toward Old Polonia that was applauded in the Polish-American press, the choir joined the Seventh District of the Polish Singers Alliance of America. Over the years, the choir also included second-generation Polish Americans, eager to keep up Polish song and music. In 1995 the choir had twenty-four members—some of them sons of the founders, and a few other recent Polish immigrants—and remained as active and popular as ever. The ages of members ranged from twenty-five to seventy-five years of age. With great fanfare, the choir celebrated its fiftieth anniversary.[120]

As part of the explosion of New Emigration organizational activity in the early 1950s, the refugees formed a multitude of theater groups. The initiatives undertaken in Chicago, traditionally fruitful ground for Polish-American theater, aptly illustrated the changes in the cultural life of the community. Nasza Reduta (Our Redoubt) was a new theater group active under the direction of Lucjan Krzemieński and Elżbieta Dziewońska-Krzemieńska between 1950 and 1973. The theater attracted exiled Polish actors and actresses and played mostly for the postwar immigrants. The repertoire included classic dramas by both Polish and émigré authors, together with a few English-language dramas translated into Polish. Nasza Reduta occasionally cooperated with Old Polonia's directors and actors but mostly presented work of a "generational character" while, according to some members, it resisted turning support for Polish art in exile into a heavy patriotic duty.[121] In 1953, Nasza Reduta announced a competition for "best contemporary drama," which brought in over thirty works. Despite the organizers' suggestion that the works highlight relationships between the New Emigration and the host society, only one drama accepted that challenge. The other works set their action either during the war or in communist Poland. The play "Uśmiechnij się

Giocondo" ("Smile, Gioconda"), by Hanna Peretiakowicz of London, which focused on DP life, was staged by Nasza Reduta in December 1953.[122]

Other theater groups active in Chicago were similar in character to Nasza Reduta; they included Teatr Dramatyczny (Dramatic Theater) of Wanda Zbierzowska-Frydrych, Teatr Aktora (Actor's Theater) of Władysław Salicz-Płoskoń, Radiowy Teatr Wyobraźni (Radio Theater of Imagination) of Robert Lewandowski, and Teatr Ref-Rena (Ref-Ren's Theater) of Feliks Konarski and Nina Oleńska. Smaller performing groups specializing in stand-up comedy and variety shows, such as Wesoła Czwórka (Jolly Foursome) and Wesoła Lwowska Fala (Jolly Lwów Wave), also gained popularity. In other Polonia communities, the new immigrants either formed new theater groups or reinvigorated existing ones. Polonia centers such as New York, Detroit, Los Angeles, and Boston could all boast some degree of artistic success in theater.[123]

The new immigrants' continuing concern for the patriotic upbringing of their youth expressed itself in the support of Polish Saturday schools and the scouting movement, both of which were characterized by the increased involvement of Polish women activists. The example of the Polish Saturday school in Buffalo, New York, organized in 1955, effectively illustrates the trend. The new immigrants' efforts to create a school in Buffalo in the early 1950s initially met many obstacles. Interest among families freshly arrived in the area was low. There were no teachers and no money. The school was finally formed thanks to the support of the local SPK and Polish-American clergy. The first teachers included veterans of the DP camps' educational system. Soon, the school had about two hundred students, both from Old Polonia and New Emigration. When the school celebrated its tenth anniversary in 1965, it was already a well-known institution, represented at all local ethnic celebrations.[124]

The postwar wave brought to American shores many devoted scouting leaders who previously had distinguished themselves in their work with young people in the DP camps. For example Jerzy Kuncewicz, who had been deported to Germany after the fall of the Warsaw Uprising, worked both in DP schools and in Polish harcerstwo. After arriving with his wife and three children in Connecticut in 1951, he joined Związek Młodzieży Polskiej (Association of Polish Youth), a New Emigration organization in Bridgeport. Soon thereafter, he ran into other scouting instructors from the DP camps, and they together decided to start the first Polish scouting troops in Connecticut. Kuncewicz and others led weekly scout meetings in a hall made available to them by the Old Polonia Orzeł Biały (White Eagle) PNA group in Bridgeport, staged performances and occasional programs, participated in national celebrations, and spent vacations at scout camps and jamborees. The Connecticut group remained in close contact with scouting organizations established by other exile nationalities, such as Ukrainians, Latvians, Lithuanians, Hungarians, and Romanians.[125]

The initiatives and relentless energy of the scouting instructors resulted in the formation of local scout troops for girls and boys, and became the foundation of the Polish harcerstwo organization in the United States.[126] Between 1949 and 1977 approximately twenty thousand young people went through its ranks. They met periodically at national jamborees and participated in the cultural lives of their communities. Financial support for the movement came from various fund-raising activities as well as from the Circle of Friends, composed primarily of scouts' parents. The American branch of harcerstwo was part of the postwar diaspora organization headquartered in London.[127] The pages of the chronicle of the first girl scout group, established in Chicago in 1951, illustrate the organization's ideological profile. Both the scout leaders and the girls wrote credos and expressed their motivation for work in harcerstwo. "Harcerstwo is ... fortitude of spirit!" wrote one of the two female organizers of the team. "Let's not forget that the time will come when one will have to choose between the comforts of America and hardship and work in the country of our Fathers, in the free Homeland. Let us live to see this time and let us select the latter road!" A teenage girl scout chose for herself this credo: "Through Harcerstwo—to a Free and Independent Poland!"[128]

The history of harcerstwo in the United States after the war lists close to 140 female names and short vitae of many devoted scouting leaders. One example is scoutmaster Władysława Wojciechowska, born in Warsaw in 1921. During the first month of war in 1939, together with other girl scouts (*harcerki*) in Warsaw she participated in the distribution of bread and first aid to the population of the city and served as aide in the Institute for Deaf and Mute Children. In October 1939 Władysława took a special wartime scouting oath and immediately became active in Szare Szeregi (Polish underground scouting in the resistance movement). Risking her life, she distributed underground publications and pasted posters on the walls of Warsaw. She also worked as a courier (*łączniczka*). In the spring of 1940 Władysława was arrested by the Germans and imprisoned in Mokotów, Aleje Szucha, and Pawiak, the harshest of Gestapo prisons. But even there she continued her resistance activities. Together with her mother, she was later transported to the concentration camp in Ravensbrück, Germany, where she became a member of a clandestine scouting team, for which she was punished by a transfer to another concentration camp in Flossenburg after five days on an infamous death march. Władysława survived the war, and after the liberation of Germany in 1945, she was instrumental in the re-creation of harcerstwo in the American and British occupation zones. In the United States since 1950, she organized several girl scout troops, Saturday schools, and summer camps for children of different age. She was also active in the PAC, serving as its Ohio director; the Home Army Association; and the SPK. Together with her husband Marian Wojciechowski, for seven years she was the co-owner of the Polish-language newspaper *Ameryka-Echo* in Toledo, Ohio.[129]

Many other new immigrant organizations had an educational or professional character. In 1950 Polski Związek Akademików (Polish Academic Association) was established by Polish college students and graduates, and soon developed into a nationwide organization. Another association, Nowa Polonia (New Polonia), based in Chicago, launched a program of modest scholarships for college students. Koło Byłych Wychowawców i Wychowanków Polskich Szkół Średnich z Niemiec (Circle of Former Teachers and Pupils of the Polish High Schools from Germany) sponsored an ambitious program of public lectures on Polish history and culture, as well as Saturday schools in the Polish language for children in Chicago. Lectures, courses, and discussions also were important features of the programs adopted by some professional organizations, such as Stowarzyszenie Prawników Polskich w Stanach Zjednoczonych (Association of Polish Jurists in the United States) and Związek Lekarzy Polskich na Wychodźstwie (Association of Polish Physicians in Exile). Many organizations strove to develop their own libraries and reading rooms stocked with books and newspapers in the Polish language.[130]

The veterans community, strengthened by more than eleven thousand soldiers with their families who arrived from Great Britain between 1950 and 1953, formed their own organizations. The Association of Polish ex-Combatants came to life in 1945 and 1946 as an organization with welfare goals and social and educational programs intended to facilitate the transition of the Polish Armed

Forces in the West from military to civilian life. SPK also expressed political aims because its establishment was a "logical consequence of the decision... to remain in exile as a sign of protest against giving Poland up into the Soviet slavery as well as for the continuation of the struggle for the rights of the nation."[131] During the first five years of its existence, SPK developed its units in twenty-two countries. In the United States, Polish veterans were initially encouraged to join the Polish Army Veterans Association in America (Stowarzyszenie Weteranów Armii Polskiej, SWAP), an Old Polonia organization started by Polish veterans of World War I. Conflict between the newcomers and the leadership of SWAP, however, resulted in the creation of a separate SPK unit for the United States in 1952. The SPK developed strong community ties to all of Polonia. Its leadership cooperated with the PAC in policy matters pertaining to the homeland, and local chapters often helped in the formation of new Saturday schools for Polish children or the revitalization of existing ones and in the organization of national celebrations within communities.[132]

In addition to the SPK, other veterans organizations claimed the exile mission goals, including the political struggle for Poland's independence, propagation of knowledge about the Polish contribution to the Allied victory, continuation of battlefield bonds, and care for disabled comrades-in-arms. There were among them Stowarzyszenie Lotników Polskich (Association of Polish Pilots), Związek Polskich Spadochroniarzy w Ameryce (Polish Airborne Forces Veterans Association in America), Samopomoc Marynarki Wojennej (Polish Navy Veterans Association of America), Okręg Armii Krajowej na Stany Zjednoczone (Home Army Veterans Association), Stowarzyszenie Saperów Polskich w USA (Polish Sappers Veterans Association of the USA), and Stowarzyszenie Byłych Żołnierzy 1. Dywizji Pancernej (First Armored Division Veterans Association).

Veterans networks in diaspora proved particularly strong. Several veterans organizations active in the United States were part of larger world organizations, which periodically met at international congresses, formulated common policies, and exchanged information. The military traditions of the past Polish emigration waves and wartime experiences bound veterans to the exile mission in a special way. Pride, awareness of the significance of their contribution, and the conscious political motivation in the refusal to return to communist Poland were best expressed in some former soldiers' objection to the very term "refugees":

> Without undue questioning of the good will of those who use these terms, one must still admit that such terms as "refugee immigration" and "refugees" in no instance should be applied to the Soldiers, Sailors, and Pilots of World War II. . . . [By using those terms] one neglects and obliterates the role and significance of this immigration [and] annuls its political reason and sense.
>
> We Soldiers, Sailors and Pilots did not "take refuge" from anywhere and we are not "refugees." We did, however, refuse, after a hard and bloody soldiers' service, to return to Poland, to our own homes. We manifested this way and protested against selling Poland to the enemy and against treason on the part of the Allies.[133]

The American SPK quarterly, *Kombatant w Ameryce*, was not limited to conveying the organization's news and local matters. Subscribers could find information about world affairs with special emphasis on the situation in Poland. In the United States the veterans, wearing their unit uniforms and displaying banners, were visible participants at all community observations, on American holidays such as Memorial Day, Independence Day, and Armistice Day, as well as at Polish national celebrations.[134] Their presence provided a link between the past and present, and evoked images of Poland's military history, while symbolizing hope for the future.

A new organization of special significance was Polskie Stowarzyszenie Byłych Więźniów Politycznych w Stanach Zjednoczonych (Polish Association of ex-Political Prisoners in the United States), uniting all those who had suffered in Nazi prisons and concentration camps as political prisoners (kacetowcy). The mission of the kacetowcy, apart from the common political and patriotic duties declared by basically all New Emigration organizations, focused on lobbying to obtain reparations from the German government, as well as on the care for ailing, disabled, or poverty-stricken colleagues all over the world. They also lobbied the American Congress to allow the United States to accept additional groups of refugees and political prisoners from behind the Iron Curtain.[135]

Veterans organizations were not the only ones to take upon themselves the care of World War II victims in the postwar diaspora. Separate organizations of war invalids, established in Polish communities on many continents, made help to the disabled their main goal. The condition of those who remained in Germany because they could not qualify for emigration generated special concern. An excellent example of community organizing on their behalf was Komitet Niesienia Pomocy Polakom Pozostałym w Ingolstadt (Niemcy) (Committee for the Care of Poles Remaining in Ingolstadt, Germany), initiated in Chicago in 1953. After receiving a call for help from the Polish population of the liquidated DP camp in Ingolstadt, more than eight hundred persons in all, the committee made an effort to locate Poles in the Chicago area who at some point had lived in the Ingolstadt camp. In the first months of its existence, the committee obtained more than a hundred addresses and enlisted the help of more than half of the Ingolstadt ex-DPs. After teaming up with Stowarzyszenie Samopomocy Nowej Emigracji, the committee launched a vigorous campaign to secure funds needed to help the families and children of the Ingolstadt Polish community.[136] The situation of Poles in Germany would be of continual concern throughout the 1950s. Frequent articles in the Pomost section of New York's *Nowy Świat* reminded readers of the need for material help as well as Polish publications and textbooks to counteract de-Polonization of the younger generation. The Polish Immigration Committee remained in close contact with Poles in Germany, channeling funds and sponsoring immigrants to the United States.[137]

The creation of many small organizations by the New Emigration, duplicating programs within the same community, evoked frequent criticism. Some saw them as adversely affecting the unity of all of Polonia. One letter to the editors of the popular "Dział Nowej Emigracji" in *Dziennik Związkowy*, from Hammond, Indiana, read: "It seems to me that many newcomers want to fulfill their ill-conceived organizational/oratorical ambitions, and this affects the organizational coherence of the Old and the New Emigration."[138] The proliferation of new immigrant organizations encouraged some consolidation efforts. For example, from 1953 on several smaller organizations from New York State periodically combined their energies arranging "interorganizational social parties," as well as observances of national holidays.[139] Similarly, several Chicago-based organizations united for an annual Christmas opłatek celebration for all their members.[140] The president of the New York Home Army Circle and the Polish Airborne Forces Veterans Association even authored a project to "federate" all veterans organizations. He argued: "The existing organizations of the new emigration are vegetating. The membership is dwindling. Dealing with the difficult living conditions requires so much time that even several hours a week for voluntary work are hard to find. The work itself has no impetus. Hardly any organization is able to leave behind its particularisms and give the community something on a good level. The boards, overburdened with their own as well as their members' work, are losing the initiative."[141]

Although the veterans federation did not come into being, another similar initiative was more successful at uniting new immigrant organizations of the East Coast. Zjednoczenie Polaków w Ameryce (Union of Poles in America), established in New Jersey in 1953, coordinated actions of separate organizations, especially in regards to the aid to Poles in Germany and political goals of the New Emigration.[142]

Unlike the organizations of the older American Polonia, which centered around parishes, the organizations of the New Emigration remained mostly lay in character. There seems to be no easy explanation for this phenomenon, especially given that the overwhelming majority of the refugees claimed an attachment to Roman Catholicism. One possibility is that those who settled within older Polonia communities and attended Polish-American churches relied on the active network of existing parish organizations and saw no need to create new ones.[143] Parishes served as shared space, and religious devotion remained a strong part of the newcomers' lives. Saturday schools often used parish facilities for their classes, veterans organizations had chaplains assigned for each of their posts, and most celebrations incorporated solemn masses or began with special prayers. There were also cases of the self-help organizations being established within local Polish-American parishes, such as Koło Nowej Polonii (Circle of the New Polonia) in Bayonne, New Jersey.[144]

The settlement of refugees outside of Polish sections of urban areas and far from Polish churches must have been, however, a factor in the decrease of refugees' involvement in Polish-American parishes. The declining living conditions in inner cities and the scarcity of well-paying jobs available to their residents caused refugees to move farther away from the ethnic enclaves. Some sociological studies indicate that only about 39 percent of new immigrants in the early 1970s belonged to a Polish-American parish and that about 22 percent did not belong to any parish.[145]

The centrality of the parish, characteristic of Old Polonia's community life, ebbed in favor of lay and professional associations, based on emotional rather than geographic ties to the community, and advocating the ideals of the exile mission. They were led by the inteligencja, who, although attached

The Resettlement of Polish Displaced Persons in the United States | 145

to Roman Catholicism as their religion, assumed leadership roles following the traditional responsibility of their class and showing less need for clerical leadership accepted by the peasant immigrants before them. The priests, who held the posts of chaplains in veterans organizations, worked with Polish scouting, or participated in national celebrations were often Poles who shared the refugee experience and remained loyal to the exile mission. Some members of the intelligentsia might also have shunned parish activism because it was dominated by Polish-American folkways unfamiliar to the newcomers. Some newcomers searched for additional forms of religious expression and interests. For example, *Dziennik Związkowy*'s New Emigration section regularly published information on the activities of the Chicago-based Polskie Katolickie Stowarzyszenie Uniwersyteckie "Veritas" (Polish Catholic Academic Association "Veritas"), featuring lectures and talks on religious and church-related matters by Polish priests and lay intellectuals.[146]

Cooperation between the organizations of Old Polonia and the New Emigration grew slowly, but steadily, as they often shared common space and resources. Observances of national holidays became an especially fruitful common ground. Programs commemorating national anniversaries or honoring national heroes gained cosponsorship from many local organizations, and traditionally included speeches of representatives of both Old Polonia and the New Emigration. If followed by parties and dances, they provided favorable conditions for blending and forming relationships. Special gestures of good will further fostered the cooperative spirit prevalent in many localities. For instance, Chicago's Legion Młodych Polek (Legion of Young Polish Women), which distinguished itself in its work for Polish refugees both during the war and the resettlement, funded a banner for Chicago's Armia Krajowa in 1950. The dedication of the banner, well-attended by the entire community, combined with celebrations commemorating the Warsaw Uprising and became an occasion for a public display of friendship and declarations of cooperation in the future.[147] New immigrant organizations also manifested their support for the Old Polonia traditions by participation in parades and programs honoring the Third of May Constitution and General Pułaski, which for decades were one of the highlights of Polonia's life in the United States. Although typically marching under their own banners, new immigrants presented themselves and were seen as an intrinsic part of the entire Polish-American community. Unnoticeable to the larger American society, however, was an undercurrent of tension and resentment, which divided the Polish-American community. Challenged by each other to redefine their identity, Polish Americans and refugee Poles engaged in a lively debate, which was to shape their mutual relationships in the years to come.

1. Henryk Floyar-Rajchman, one of the founders of KNAPP and the Józef Piłsudski Institute in New York. Courtesy of the photographic archives of the Józef Piłsudski Institute, New York

2. In 1945 KNAPP sent a delegation to the United Nations conference in San Francisco. *Left to right:* Lucjusz Kupferwasser, Wacław Jędrzejewicz, Franciszek Januszewski, Walenty Porański, Ignacy Matuszewski, Józef Piech, Wacław Gawroński. Courtesy of the photographic archives of the Józef Piłsudski Institute, New York

3. The front cover of *Tygodnik Polski* from May 28, 1944, designed by painter Zdzisław Czermański, shows a family in Poland secretly listening to the proceedings of the Polonia congress in Buffalo, during which the Polish American Congress was established. Portraits of Tadeusz Kościuszko and Woodrow Wilson adorn the walls. This entire issue of *Tygodnik Polski* was devoted to American Polonia.

4 (*below*). Polish soccer team before a game against British armed forces team in Germany, 1947. Courtesy of Victor Bik

5. Teachers and students of the Polish Educational Center in Fallingbostel, Germany, 1947. Courtesy of Victor Bik

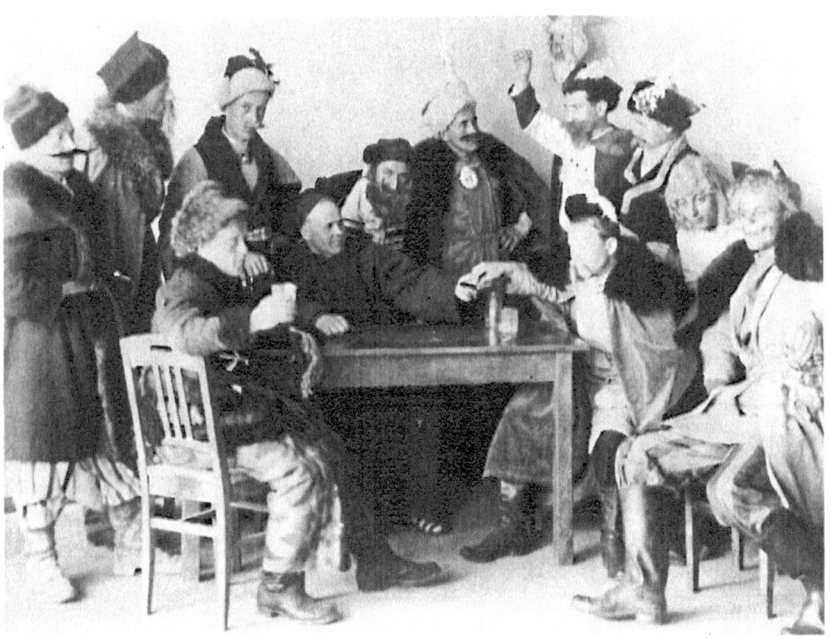

6. A scene from a school play staged by the Polish DP students in Germany, 1948. Courtesy of Victor Bik

7. Before emigrating from German DP camps, some Polish students kept albums, which their friends could sign *pro memoriam*. A page from A. Błaszkiewicz's album bears the inscription "Love God and Poland" and carries the image of a young 1944 Warsaw Uprising soldier against the background of Poland's coat of arms—a white eagle. Patriotic symbolism accompanied this expression of the exile mission in the diaspora. Courtesy of the Józef Piłsudski Institute, New York

8. Officers of the American Committee for Resettlement of Polish DP's during a meeting in April 1949. *Left to right:* Charles Rozmarek, president of the PAC; Rev. Valerian Karcz, director; Judge Blair F. Gunther, chairman; Edward E. Plusdrak, secretary-treasurer; Frances Dymek, Joseph Pawloski, and John A. Stanek, directors. Courtesy of the Immigration History Research Center, University of Minnesota, Minneapolis

9. A cartoon from the first page of the *Dziennik Związkowy* (October 29, 1948) shows a group of Polish DPs (*polscy wysiedleńcy*) arriving on American shores welcomed by Polonia in the United States, which extends the greeting "Welcome, Countrymen!" The inscription over the cartoon is a traditional Polish welcome phrase, "Czym chata bogata, tym rada," indicating a host's readiness to share with guests. Courtesy of *Dziennik Związkowy/Polish Daily News*, Chicago

10. A cartoon from the first page of the *Dziennik Związkowy* (October 15, 1949) shows Chicago Polonia (*Polonia chicagoska*) welcoming a representative of Polish DPs (*polscy wysiedleńcy*) in front of the newly purchased "D.P. House" (*Dom D.P.*). They exchange traditional Polish greetings: *"Szczęść Boże"* (God bless) and *"Bóg zapłać"* (May God requite you). The inscription above the cartoon reads: "A week from tomorrow, all roads lead to the D.P. House." Courtesy of *Dziennik Związkowy/Polish Daily News*, Chicago

11. Polish DPs aboard the S.S. *General Black* organized a choir, which entertained passengers by singing Polish folk songs during the long trip from Germany. The choir members are seen with representatives of Polonia, including Józef Onka, director of Rada Polonii; Karol Burke of the PAC; and Feliks Popławski of *Dziennik Dla Wszystkich*. Courtesy of the Immigration History Research Center, University of Minnesota, Minneapolis

13. Józef Wyrwa in Chicago, 1951. Courtesy of Tadeusz Wyrwa

12. A group of representatives from the PAC and PNA welcomed Polish DPs who arrived aboard the S.S. *General Bundy* in Boston Harbor. First row, *left to right:* Stanisław Blinstrub, Eugeniusz Olszewski, Mieczysław Łada, Łucja Olszewska, Maria Blinstrub, and Karol Burke. Courtesy of the Immigration History Research Center, University of Minnesota, Minneapolis

14. Tadeusz Wyrwa in Chicago, 1951. Courtesy of Tadeusz Wyrwa

15. Scouting instructors at the scout camp in Bantam, Connecticut, 1956. *Left to right:* Władysław Misiąg, Jerzy Maderski, Henryk Półtorak, Jerzy Kuncewicz, and Leon Dembowski. Courtesy of Jerzy Kuncewicz

16. A scout troop marches in the May 3 Parade in Chicago, [1952]. Courtesy of the Immigration History Research Center, University of Minnesota, Minneapolis

17. Members of the Ogiński Choir after a performance during the visit of General Tadeusz Bór-Komorowski in New York, [1956]. The general is in uniform, standing first from the left. Courtesy of Ogiński Choir

18. A scene from a performance of the Teatr Rozmaitości in Detroit, [1952]. The actors are Regina Engelhardt and Jan Madurowicz, and the play is a popular Polish nineteenth-century romantic comedy, "Damy i Huzary" ("Ladies and Officers"). Courtesy of the Immigration History Research Center, University of Minnesota, Minneapolis

19. Władysława Wojciechowska (*standing, center*) with a group of girls from the PNA group in Toledo, Ohio, during a Memorial Day celebration, May 1955. Courtesy of Maryann and Marian Wojciechowski

20. A front-page cartoon from *Zgoda* of September 1, 1956, entitled "The Polish American Congress Appeals for a Return to Moral Principles." PAC president Charles Rozmarek, portrayed on the left, presents both U.S. party platform committees with a list of demands: an appeal for freedom for the captive nations, a final recognition of Poland's western border on the Oder and Neisse rivers, free elections in Poland, and the repudiation of the Yalta agreement. The background depicts a metaphorical representation of nations under the Soviet yoke. Courtesy of *Zgoda*, Chicago

4 ⫶ "So they are among brethren"
Debate in the Community

Images of Displaced Persons

AS THE EXCITEMENT OF THE first DP transports arriving in America subsided, Polish Americans and refugee Poles faced another challenge: that of learning how to live together within the same ethnic community. Despite hopes and expectations to the contrary, everyday experience soon revealed that the groups differed in many important aspects.[1] Tensions grew, manifesting themselves in personal conflicts between sponsors and DPs, as well as between leaders of Polish-American and newly created New Emigration organizations. The debate centered around Polishness and Americanization, history and class, refugee versus ethnic status, the exile mission, and the responsibility of Polish immigrants toward their homeland. Much of the debate took place in the pages of the Polish-language press, which welcomed letters from both sides and encouraged an exchange of ideas, but it also spilled over into organizational life and contacts between individuals. In the course of the debate, Old Polonia and the New Emigration reevaluated their respective identities and negotiated a concept of Polishness, one that incorporated the main elements of the exile mission and corresponded to the Cold War context within the United States.

Since the end of the war, leaders of American Polonia, while constructing an intense political lobby for the change of immigration laws, also had mobilized rank-and-file Polish Americans behind the DP cause. In order to muster the support of Polonia, the press and other organizations tried to educate Polish Americans about displaced persons through news and feature articles on life in the DP camps. Their publicity supplemented the publicity developed by the Citizens Committee on Displaced Persons, a special-interest organization formed to lobby for changes in immigration law and designed to reach the entire American public. As a result, the Polish-American community received a particular image of the DPs, one intended to evoke both sympathy and a sense of responsibility on the part of Polonia.

The CCDP's program was supported by a million-dollar-plus fund and led by expert publicists. The CCDP produced hundreds of publications distributed to the public in hundreds of thousands of copies. Magazines, newspapers, Sunday supplements, and newsletters received direct contributions or advice and consultation, together with "fact sheets" prepared by the committee. The CCDP sponsored several movies dealing with the subject of displaced persons and paid special attention to radio publicity:

> Documentaries, panel discussions, statements of prominent people, spot announcement and dramatic sketches and interpretations, for which stage, screen and radio personalities volunteered their services, were recorded by the Committee. These recordings, eventually numbering into the hundreds, were then sent free of charge to most of the radio stations in the United States with a permission to play them when and as often as they wanted.... The recordings ... were played thousands of times as a public service by the radio stations.[2]

The main goal of that publicity campaign was to be "moving and provocative, spurring the audience to action as well as informing it."[3] In order to reach the American public, the CCDP campaign focused on the very existence of the DP population, and combated ethnic and religious prejudice. The committee's propaganda addressed issues of security in the Cold War and worked to dispel concerns about jobs, housing shortages, and other anticipated burdens on the American postwar economy.[4]

Polish Americans, of course, were not immune to the massive publicity effort launched by the CCDP. However, the propaganda available through their own ethnic media had many accents, which differed from those of the CCDP campaign. Active during the war in Rada's relief efforts, Polish Americans were well aware of the refugees' experience. Throughout the war, Rada had kept Polonia informed about refugee issues. It had succeeded in developing a sense of obligation, which prompted generous donations to the humanitarian effort; but after the war, the donations decreased sharply, as Polonia showed signs of fatigue and as the refugees' needs had to compete with the needs of the impoverished population in Poland.⁵ Rada, as well as all other organizations interested in the refugee problem, had to find new ways to energize and involve Polonia on behalf of the exiles. Most concern related to the quality of people who were to join the Polish-American communities. Therefore, publicity within Polonia focused on several major facets: the victimization of DPs, the positive aspects of the community-building process in the DP camps, the dismissal of fears about DPs as "demoralized," and the presentation of the "DP problem" in personal and human dimensions. Although well-intentioned, these efforts produced an image of DPs ridden with internal tension, ranging from helpless and mistreated victims to sturdy, energetic, and ready-to-work immigrant material. Simultaneously, Cold War political dimensions required stressing America's responsibility for Yalta and the DP's uncompromising anticommunism.

Francis X. Świetlik's trip to Europe in the summer of 1945 became an occasion for Rada Polonii to make the displaced persons' needs known within the Polish-American community. The trip resulted in the publication of a brochure that was written in a very matter-of-fact tone and included many statistics and details of humanitarian aid distributed to the refugees. It also featured numerous pictures taken in the camps. In one of them, a young woman with a desperate face clutched a sad-eyed baby. In another, a former prisoner of war, still wearing his military uniform, buried his face in his hands in a gesture of disconsolation. Groups of DPs posed in front of desolate camps fenced with barbed wire. Some photographs reminded readers about wartime sufferings: Świetlik and his party examined the crematorium at Dachau. Świetlik also provided his own poignant commentary. "At the time of my visit I found the spiritual conditions of the people at a low ebb," he wrote. "The uncertainties regarding the fate of missing members of their families and of their former homes in Poland, the confinement in the camps, and the lack of any useful occupation or recreation combined to create an air of despondency and discontent."⁶

The PAC leadership chose to present the DP problem in both a humanitarian and a political framework. The PAC delegation's trip to Germany in the fall of 1946 provided much-needed eyewitness evidence of UNRRA's mistreatment of DPs and their deplorable living conditions. The pages of the Polish-American press filled with reports on the desperate situation in the camps.⁷ On December 1, 1946, shortly after Charles Rozmarek's return to the United States, an estimated five thousand persons had a chance to listen to the PAC president's report from his trip during a gathering organized in the Ashland Boulevard Auditorium in Chicago. Rozmarek's speech lasted more than an hour and captivated the audience. After hearing details of UNRRA's brutality and the harsh living conditions, the audience adopted a resolution calling for a change in the immigration law that would allow the refugees into America. The PAC Illinois Division presented Rozmarek with a thousand-dollar check earmarked for aid to displaced persons. As the press noted, the atmosphere during the rally was uplifting and full of energy.⁸

Rozmarek, continuing his campaign against UNRRA, often depicted Poles as victims of persecution that was initiated by this organization, but all too frequently was carried out by the American military. The Polish-American press exploited this theme regularly. For example, an article in the New York daily *Nowy Świat* deplored the impotence of the DPs in the face of UNRRA's administrative machine: "Families, women, and children, rattle in the trucks, together with their bundles, carried from one corner of the country to another. They drive this human load like sacks of sawdust. There, we still have some space in the barracks for a hundred sacks; it's enough to pour in or pour out a little. Here are the barracks—get off! From a distance one can see the laundry drying on the wire fences."⁹ Dependent on UNRRA and its officials for all essentials and waiting for the nations of the world to open their doors to them, the displaced persons' faces were "drawn by long captivity and oppression," their eyes "full of sadness, pain, and uneasiness about the future."¹⁰ The image of the displaced persons' faces repeatedly appeared in correspondence published in the Polish-American press. An article entitled "D.P." read:

> It looks toward us: the hopeless, gray, and distrustful face of a human being called "D.P." . . . The face of a person with a past he would rather forget forever, and, what's worst, a person without a future in which he could build a new life on the granite of hope and faith. The face of a man abandoned, useless now, whose best years pass unfruitfully, who can't graduate from college, start his own business, or find a job to secure his old age. The face of a man who can't build a home for the woman he loves and who is afraid to give a new life to a child to spare his offspring the fate of a homeless wanderer, the curse of a man without a homeland.¹¹

Some pieces of poetry by the exiles themselves also emphasized a similar atmosphere of despair and hopelessness. A poem "Refugees' Religion" by Tadeusz Nowakowski depicted displaced people giving up efforts to receive asylum in any countries of the world; as crowds awaited admittance to see consuls, Polish refugees asked only "for citizenship in Heaven."[12]

The victimization of Polish displaced persons received wide coverage in the Polish-American media. The press reported on frequent searches organized in Polish camps by the military and described the brutalization and humiliation of the DPs.[13] A report on the ruthless behavior of American MPs in the Austrian camp of Ebensee appeared under the title "A Picture from the Depths of Misery of the Homeless People in Austria."[14] In February 1947 *Nowy Świat* published a series of sworn testimonies by displaced persons on the abuse and brutality of the American military in the DP camps. The series, entitled "From the Abyss of Polish Misery. A Brutal Trampling of Human Dignity. The Heartbreaking Complaint of Homeless People, Oppressed by the American Soldiers," included descriptions of incidents of Americans using excessive physical force during searches, refusing to allow medical help to a man having a heart attack, and being responsible for the death of children exposed to severe weather during transport in unheated cattle wagons.[15]

Other examples illustrated the psychological hardships of Poles, humiliated both by the allied armies and by the hostile Germans. In the article "Poles Are Second-Class Soldiers in the American Occupation Zone in the Reich," the author criticized an order from the American military to dye the uniforms of the Polish Guards so that they differed from American uniforms. "According to the Americans . . . we are not worthy to wear the same color uniforms as they are," commented one member of the Polish Guards.[16] Reports on German police raids on DP camps and the persecution of Poles by Germans employed in the occupation administration, as well as incidents of the German civilian population's hostility supported by the Allies, must have shocked readers and magnified the picture of DP suffering.[17]

The image of Poles as victims of life in the DP camps returned with full force in discussions about the demoralizing influence of the camps. Numerous voices on both sides of the ocean warned of the dangers of a prolonged stay in DP limbo. As one of the articles noted, "[I]dleness and a lack of activities and responsibilities are the greatest threat to our countrymen; they are in danger of complete demoralization and distortion of character." Although the DPs deserved to rest after the war's end, the protracted lack of activity resulted in "drunkenness, [and] became the reason for the lowering of the moral standards, and even crimes."[18] Polish displaced persons were also regarded as vulnerable to mixed marriages that could result in the "loss of our blood" and the denationalization of the offspring.[19] Children born out of wedlock and brought up among a foreign population could suffer complete assimilation,[20] while Polish youth in the camps could experience "despondency and stunted physical growth."[21]

The main goal of these stories about the despair and oppression of Polish DPs was not only to familiarize American Polonia with the sad facts of life in the DP camps but to evoke compassion for their compatriots. Personal letters and appeals from DPs and veterans published in the Polish-American press were designed to appeal to the hearts of Polish Americans in the most direct way. One of them read: "Dear Editor! I beg you, please, print these words; maybe there will be someone willing to give us a hand, maybe someone's heart will respond to my desperate plea, maybe someone will understand the misery of an exiled countryman who can't return to his Homeland. I beg you, I ask your help, I knock on human, Polish hearts."[22] In the fall of 1948 *Nowy Świat* initiated a regular section entitled "Letters from the Abyss," featuring personal stories and letters from the refugees. In an earlier period, the Association of Friends of the Polish Soldier (Zrzeszenie Przyjaciół Żołnierza Polskiego) had published fragments of numerous letters from Polish veterans asking for affidavits of support to come to the United States.[23]

The image of displaced persons as victims was supplemented by evidence of their agency. The press releases that talked about oppression at the hands of UNRRA and the military also made known that Poles fought back with all the means available to them. DPs staged protests and appealed to the authorities, as they did in the so-called Murnau incident. On January 7, 1947, the Polish population of the Murnau camp received an order to evacuate, despite sub-zero temperatures. The DPs refused to move. The American military used physical coercion and weapons to remove people from their homes.[24] Polish DPs also reported abuses to the Polish American Congress, Rada Polonii, the press, and the authorities in charge. They collected sworn testimonies about events in the camps and gathered evidence of the misuse of power.[25] In desperation, they staged rebellions—as in the case of Altenstadt—or initiated hunger strikes.[26]

These actions to mobilize American Polonia for the DP cause in the period before mass resettlement also stressed many other, more positive aspects. The *Nowy Świat* editors made a conscious effort to solicit correspondence directly from the DP camps and used it as an effective means of mobilizing Polonia for the refugee cause. In March 1948 Kazimierz Dąbski of *Nowy Świat* wrote to the Polish Union's general council in Germany, notifying the council of the positive change in climate toward the DP issue and stressing that the advent of a new immigration law was nearing. It was time to prepare Polonia to support and welcome the DPs as soon as possible, Dąbski wrote. The best people to do it would be the refugees themselves; they could send over letters describing the achievements of DPs in their social and organizational work in the camps and in this way convince Polonia of the DPs' high moral and social values. The correspondence would then appear in a special section of *Nowy Świat*.²⁷

Dziennik Związkowy systematically informed its readers about the progress of the community-building process in DP camps. Brief notes about the establishment of Polish organizations, the legal and educational systems, the press, and self-government proved that Polish DPs had organized themselves into communities despite all the hardships.²⁸ Reports from the PAC delegation's visit in Germany brought additional details on life in DP camps, as well as comments on the positive impressions made by the "thriftiness and providence of the Polish population, who, with enormous work effort, managed to turn the DP camps into acceptable living environments."²⁹ During a meeting with former POWs in Ingolstadt, "the sight of those hollow-cheeked, but dignified and noble soldiers ... filled the hearts of the delegation members with both sadness and pride."³⁰ Longer treatments of the situation in DP Germany and detailed coverage of Polish communities in some larger DP centers were also featured in Sunday supplements of *Nowy Świat*.³¹ Personal stories and letters from DPs stressed their willingness to work, honesty, thriftiness, and piety. Many letters emphasized that refugees seeking sponsors were ready to accept any job offered to them. For example, a letter from Jan Obrębski, an engineer and a DP in Ludwigsburg, read: "So let our dear compatriots from beyond the ocean know that free food chokes us and the free camp roof weighs heavily down on us. We want to work. Eight, ten, twelve, or eighteen hours a day.... We want to be useful.... We'll cast away our scholarly degrees joyously. We will stand in the workplace as plain workers.... We want to be soldiers of freedom and work."³²

Direct responses to the charges of corruption, demoralization, high crime rates, and low moral standards were especially significant in Polonia's internal publicity campaign. They addressed questions that were difficult and subject to various interpretations. To let them go unanswered might fan the fears of future sponsors and damage the DP support base among Polish Americans. One article, published in the London *Dziennik Polski* and reprinted in *Nowy Świat,* blamed the UNRRA and American military policy of forcing Polish DPs to return to Poland for spreading hostile propaganda about the DP population. The author complained, "If one reads the American *Stars and Stripes,* one could be under the impression that Polish camps are full of either thieves and bandits or reactionaries and fascists."[33] A good illustration of this kind of propaganda was an article on DP morality published in *Die Neue Zeitung,* an American newspaper in Germany, and cited in *Dziennik Związkowy.* The author of the article pointed to wartime experiences as dehumanizing and brutalizing. He concluded: "Long years of slavery bore in some persons the cynicism of people deprived of hope. Treated as criminals, they finally began to feel like criminals."[34]

Politics and international haggling over the DP problem also were identified as sources of prejudice about displaced persons, who were considered to be an impediment to postwar peace and prosperity. Ironically summarizing some negative opinions of DPs, Jan Kowalik from Ziegenheim, Germany, wrote with bitterness:

> Some say that DPs are people who eat white bread and delicate salmon, drink real coffee and real moonshine. They occupy themselves with nothing but theft, fights, and murders, and they do not want to go back home, for fear of work and justice.
>
> Others say that DPs were influenced by the conditions they lived in and that they are not worse people than natives in Germany. . . .
>
> Still others consider DP centers the nests of subversive propaganda, and shelters for traitors and collaborators.[35]

Such opinions must have been widespread among Polish Americans, since General Józef Barzyński, representative of Rada for DP matters in Europe, addressed them directly in his correspondence for *Nowy Świat.* "The majority of the population is religious, disciplined, and honest," Barzyński wrote. Even though there was a lot of talk about criminality among Poles in Germany and about their participation in the black market, he continued, such rumors were greatly exaggerated and proved the ill will of people who spread them. Individuals who went to jail were often guilty of nothing more than illegally crossing the border during their escape from Poland. The term "black market activities" frequently referred to the "crime" of exchanging cigarettes for some food products from German farmers. Such offenses resulted from "abnormal life conditions." The general concluded: "Let a man eat to the full, and he won't go to the 'black market.' Let him have work, he will become an exemplary citizen."[36]

DPs writing to Polish-American newspapers used similar arguments to counter the charges of black marketeering. Zbigniew Łukaczyński reminded readers of the high rates of infant and child mortality from malnutrition in DP camps. "When parents . . . try to buy some food from a German farmer, they usually fall into the hands of uniformed and non-uniformed German police," while German farmers involved in trading never face any charges, he argued.[37] The authors of another article pointed out that the black market in postwar Germany was a normal and unavoidable occurrence: the currency had no real value, yet any type of product exchange or bartering qualified as illegal activity.[38]

Although criminal elements did exist within the Polish DP community, advocates emphasized the fact that offenders with jail sentences had already disqualified themselves from any chance of emigration, since all candidates for immigration underwent a thorough screening.[39] Many inmates of the camps made pleas for the formation of a central screening organization made up from DPs themselves, who would identify and prevent the emigration of undesirable people, since "one unsuitable person who [went] to the United States could close the door for a hundred honest people."[40]

The internal campaign to mobilize Polonia for the DP cause appealed to the political and civic consciousness of Polish Americans. The Polish American Congress did not miss any opportunity to stress that displaced persons were the moral responsibility of the Allies because "if not for American-British diplomacy, they would have been able to return to their homeland . . . a long time ago." The PAC's statement continued: "It is [because of] our diplomats' work that those Poles became refugees. . . . In other words, the fate of the Displaced Persons . . . is a political question, remaining within the framework of our moral responsibility."[41] Despite the constant pressure from

UNRRA—suspected by the DP community either to have been infiltrated by the communists or, at least, to be catering to their demands—Polish displaced persons displayed staunch anticommunism. The Polish-American press reported on the hostile reception of communist repatriation missions in the DP camps. The results of a questionnaire distributed among Polish DPs in the French zone also indicated that communism in Poland was the main reason for the refugees' refusal to return home.[42] The DPs celebrated Polish national holidays forbidden in communist Poland and gave speeches proclaiming loyalty toward the London government and a hatred of communism. After thousands of Czech refugees escaped to the American zone of Germany from Czechoslovakia in 1948, Polish DPs, despite their own hardships, organized a committee designed to help the anticommunist Czechs.[43]

The Polish-American press tried to present the DPs in a more personal and human dimension through letters and appeals from the displaced persons themselves. In addition to requests for help or sponsorship, Polish displaced persons expressed their gratitude and appreciation. "We would like you to understand us," one of the refugees from Brogans, Austria, wrote, "and to continue your support by giving us a chance to work among you without oppression and in freedom."[44] The newspapers often printed thank-you letters from the camps, full of expressions of appreciation for humanitarian help, monetary donations, and Polish books and newspapers. In order to counteract the effects of the excessively depressing coverage, some humorous pieces on different aspects of life in the DP camps also showed up in the press. Written by the DPs themselves, the humorous stories sought to put a human face on the refugees and their everyday existence. Our experiences are tragic, they seemed to say, but we are simply people, looking for something positive and funny in the worst dire straits.[45] Those who managed to get to the United States before the passage of the DP Act, frequently joined the campaign, reporting to the press on conditions in the camps and hoping to "shed light on the DP matter from the point of view of the DPs themselves."[46]

By the time the DP Act was passed and the first transports arrived, American Polonia had received a bipolar image of DPs. One side of it portrayed the DPs as helpless victims of the war and of persecution by UNRRA and the occupation authorities. The other side presented them as energetic builders of communities in exile, ready to contribute substantially to American society and Polonia. Their anticommunism made them a particularly welcome addition to society and appealed to the atmosphere dictated by the Cold War. The propaganda campaign did not cease with the passage of the DP Act in June 1948. Its character, however, changed. It emphasized sponsorship and relations between sponsors and newcomers. It also had to address new issues stemming from direct interactions between displaced persons and established Polonia, as well as the rules and conditions of resettlement in the United States.

Sources and Manifestations of Tensions

Inadequate knowledge of the other's history became one of the sources of misconceptions that affected relationships between Polish Americans and refugee Poles. The majority of refugees saw America through the lenses of immigrant letters and stories, presenting the old, familiar picture of the "Promised Land" and "streets paved with gold." Even if that image had not been previously reinforced, the power of the United States revealed during the war convinced the doubtful. Military victories and political leadership among the Allies spoke for themselves. Most of all, the material support received through CARE packages, UNRRA, and IRO, pointed to the affluence of American society.

Polonia was a part of this vision. Six million Polish Americans sounded like a powerful and influential group, capable of a strong showing on behalf of the old country and countrymen. Some people could remember Haller's Blue Army of World War I or Polish-American investments in the Polish economy during the interwar period. Much more recent memories included the charitable work of Rada Polonii and packages with goods prepared by fellow Poles in Chicago, Detroit, and other large Polish-American communities. For Polish refugees and POWs, parcels from Rada received at various stages of their journeys were often the only tangible link with American Polonia. This aid made them feel cared for and instilled a sense of indebtedness toward Polonia. Rada acquired the aura of a powerful organization among DPs, who might have developed excessive expectations of further assistance. Publicized tours by Polonia dignitaries speaking about their efforts to change the immigration law and to open doors to the refugees—and the success of this lobbying—added to the impression of power and influence.

The Cold War brought the matter of European refugees to the forefront of the battle against communism. The Cold War rhetoric presented the Polish-American ethnic group in the United States as particularly entitled to speak for the victims of communism, adding prestige and strengthening its position in the eyes of the refugees. The traditional understanding of Polonia's role as the "fourth partition of Poland" once again regained its validity. The "free voice of the Polish nation" could be heard only through the political commitment of six million Polish Americans.

As Polonia's power and its political responsibility raised the hopes of the refugees, few realized how little they really knew about everyday life in Polish-American communities in the United States. The Displaced Persons Commission, in cooperation with voluntary agencies and particularly with the American Friends Service Committee, IRO, the YMCA and YWCA, and the Red Cross, sponsored a limited orientation program geared toward familiarizing displaced persons with basic knowledge about the United States, its government, and its social and political arrangements. The program never became a mandatory step in immigration processing and, due to financial restraints, developed on a larger scale only after 1950. According to the DP Commission's final report, only 25 to 30 percent of displaced persons took advantage of the orientation program.[47]

Publications by the Polish-American press sent directly to the DP camps played a much more significant role. From the beginning of 1948 all Polish camps and committees in the American zone of Germany had received free copies of *Nowy Świat* and Buffalo's *Dziennik Dla Wszystkich*.[48] *Nowy Świat* in particular became a medium of communication between Polonia and the DPs. It not only supplied information but also offered its pages to the refugees themselves by publishing descriptive letters and reaction commentaries sent from Europe. DPs depicted their lives in the camps, pleaded for help, and sometimes defended their reputation. Many commented on the deep appreciation for that service and considered *Nowy Świat* their "window to the world."[49]

Polish DPs understood the need to find information about America. In the May-June 1946 issue of *Świat i Kraj*, published in Nuremberg, the editors wrote: "'America,' 'the United States,' 'the USA' used to be concepts very distant to us.... And overnight we are neighbors. Neighbors or, rather, guests of America. We encounter Americans every day and—let's be honest—we struggle with Americanism." As the authors further explained, that "struggle" did not stem as much from language barriers as from unfamiliarity. In order to make the relationships between the DPs and the administration of the American zone easier, *Świat i Kraj* began publication of a series of articles on various aspects of American life.[50]

Among the DPs, the Polish Guards serving in the American Army had a better opportunity to gain knowledge about the United States and Polonia. In July 1947 the educational department in the Kościuszko training camp in Mannheim-Kafertal published a Polish-language brochure entitled "Bases of American Liberty." It contained a collection of the most significant documents and speeches in American history, including, among others, the Declaration of Independence, the preamble to the Constitution, the Gettysburg Address, the Monroe Doctrine, and President Wilson's Fourteen Points. A year later, a short history of Poles in America was also printed, based on Bolesław Wierzbiański's study published in London in 1946.[51] It is impossible, however, to determine how many Polish Guards benefited from those materials.

The Polish DP press, which often based its information on that of the Polonia press, sometimes published correspondence from refugees already resettled in the United States. These letters brought the DPs eyewitness accounts from the point of view of fellow DPs focused on the practical side of establishing themselves in America. Correspondence from Janina Muklewicz, writing from Austin, Texas, provided a representative example. From the outset of her letter, the author sought to dispel the myth of America: "Not for everyone, and in the least degree for postwar refugee immigration, is America a 'Promised Land.'" After traveling through eleven states, Muklewicz tried to capture the "American character," warning that behind American friendliness and kindness she detected a "my-home-is-my-castle" attitude. She also reported on the life of other DPs she met in Chicago:

> Some are content, and some disappointed. Most, however, experienced disappointment. They have to work hard to make thirty to fifty dollars a week. After work, since they do not know English well enough and they want to obtain citizenship within three years, they have to go to school. So, practically, they are out of the homes between 7:00 AM and 9:00 PM. Their earnings are sufficient for food and clothes. They also can save a few dollars for emergencies. But their quarters are very poor. The furnishings include usually a few chairs, a table and a bed. Furniture is expensive here.... But beginnings

are always difficult! They live for the hope that their lives will get better in time.[52]

Other letters published in *Kronika* also described the harsh reality of life in America, concentrating on high prices, job scarcity, and the necessity of learning the language. The port reception organized by Polish Americans received praise and appreciation, but everyday contacts with Polonia revealed problems:

> Relationships with Polonia here are difficult also because of differences in outlook. Polonia, although it admits ties to the "Old Country," as they call Poland here, has no ties other than memories. They are completely Americanized. First questions asked the newcomers have to do with their willingness to stay here permanently and get American citizenship. Attempts to make sure that children speak good Polish are met with surprise. Any non-American matters are considered uninteresting, and the overall attitude toward the new immigrants is rather reluctant.[53]

It is impossible to determine the scope of readership of either the Polonia press or the DP press in the camps and thus to assess how widespread their impact was, but it seems that information on America and Polonia was rather limited. Prior to arrival in the United States, only a relatively small percentage of refugees could gain any real knowledge about the history and everyday life of their compatriots in America.

American Polonia also had rather limited knowledge of the changes in Polish society that had taken place after Poland regained its independence in 1918, although the Polish-American press did follow major political and economic changes in Poland. As with all immigrants, regardless of their ethnicity, their memories of the old country became confined to the image of a native village around the turn of the century. Immigration restrictions in the 1920s and the minimal influx of new immigrants before World War II, as well as infrequent travel possibilities, were responsible for this time capsule image of the old country. One example, cited by Aleksander Hertz, was the story of an elderly woman who demonstrated with pride the benefits of indoor plumbing to a newly arrived nephew, commenting, "I'll show you now something you have never seen in Poland."[54] Searching for an explanation, Hertz, a sociologist by profession, concluded that America had taught old immigrants to embrace the concept of success. As they increasingly experienced economic success and a relatively affluent Polish-American lifestyle, they also developed a patronizing attitude toward their compatriots left in Poland. America meant both social and economic advancement to them, the apparent proof of which was the political guidance and charitable help offered to Poles and Poland.[55]

The anxiety and tension between the exiles and Polish Americans were often the result of misinterpretation or even abuse of the resettlement program's rules and the sponsor-DP relationship.[56] Sponsors expected that DPs would be qualified for jobs and would stay in them for a longer period of time. Many sponsors anticipated some display of gratitude on the part of DPs, and, in extreme cases, demanded free work from them in order to compensate for imaginary costs connected with the sponsorship. From the DPs' point of view, sponsors were obliged to support them in any way possible, including free room and board for an extended period of time. If the promised job either did not materialize or turned out to be inadequate, DPs expected sponsors to secure a different one. Inevitably, such misinterpretations of the law resulted in cases of exploitation, resentment, and open conflict.

Letters to the American Committee for the Resettlement of Polish DP's reveal many examples of the resettlement-related confrontations between DPs and their sponsors. In one case, an argument broke out between a DP woman and her sponsor, the owner of a gift shop. The woman claimed that her sponsor was exploiting her work; the sponsor accused her of ingratitude, slovenliness, and theft.[57] Another DP woman wrote to the ACRPDP looking for protection from her sponsor, a Polish-American farmer from Oregon who repeatedly made unwanted sexual advances. He also demanded money and free labor in return for signing assurances for her and her son and repeatedly threatened to send them back to Europe. The woman worked for her sponsor for three weeks without pay, but refused to become his mistress and left the farm. She later sought protection in the nearest Polish-American organization and complained to the ACRPDP.[58] *Ameryka-Echo* published a letter from a reader who condemned the dishonest practices of a woman who sponsored young male DPs and placed them in her house, charging five dollars per bed, which they sometimes had to share with other newcomers. After the DPs figured out that they had been exploited and left, the "ingenious patriot" was furious and raged about their ingratitude.[59]

Some sponsors had good reason to complain, too. An elderly couple wrote to *Ameryka-Echo,* asking for advice on their relationship with a DP family whom they had sponsored from Europe. According to their letter, the DPs had lived with their sponsors for six weeks, enjoying free rent, food, and occasional gifts in the form of new clothes for the woman and the child. When the man began to work and earn a living, however, the sponsors asked them to look for different housing. His wife demanded that the sponsors find them a new place and continue to support them. She threatened to take them to court if they refused.[60] "Dział Nowej Emigracji," a running self-help and information section for new arrivals in *Dziennik Związkowy,* also addressed the problem of excessive demands for care and support that DPs had been directing to resettlement and other ethnic organizations: "Polonia, and especially resettlement committees, secured sponsorships for jobs and housing, received the arrivals in the harbors, helped with transportation, and found such work as was available under conditions of mass resettlement. There, their role basically ends. No one can demand that they take care of the sick, provide persons with free books, give out loans, look for engineer positions for technicians, or take legal action to obtain compensation in individual cases.... In normal life people have to take care of all such matters by themselves."[61]

The lack of initiative and resourcefulness demonstrated by some DPs, *Dziennik Związkowy* commented, stemmed from years spent either in the army or in the DP camps, which stifled individual initiative and made people dependent on free care and services. But there were also other reasons for the excessive dependence of some refugees on local Polonia. In the Greater Boston area, the clause providing that displaced persons might not become public charges was too often incorrectly interpreted as a need to avoid at all costs referral to any social agency or use of the services of a professional social worker. Instead, problems of health, childcare, maladjustment, and financial difficulties were handled by well-meaning but often uninformed individuals with limited resources. Such cases frequently gave rise to misunderstandings and ill feelings and resulted in generalizations hurtful to both Polish Americans and DPs.[62]

There were also other sources of conflict, as seen in letters from DPs and sponsors to the ACRPDP. One Polish DP complained of mistreatment and harassment by his Polish-American sponsor because of his German wife, whom he married while in the DP camp.[63] A Chicago sponsor told his story of a conflict with a Polish DP family. The author of the letter had suggested that his DP friend join the Polish Army Veterans Association of America, to which he himself belonged, but the DP had refused. Later, the same DP had refused to apply for the U.S. citizenship. Probably considering such an attitude unpatriotic, the sponsor demanded that the whole family move out of his house.[64]

Some Polish Americans, who had worked hard in America to achieve economic security, resented the newcomers for their seemingly easier success: newly purchased houses, cars, radios, and even bicycles for their children. Sponsors also criticized the DPs for spending money on going to the movies as a form of entertainment.[65] Sponsors advised the ACRPDP to show more firmness and less compassion in the recovery of funds advanced for transportation. Addresses of firms where the DPs worked were sent to the committee in order to locate some indebted DPs. The author of one of the letters, after describing the wealth and newly purchased possessions of a DP family, added, "From disease, hunger, and war, and such DPs, save us Lord."[66]

But examples of harmonious relations between sponsors and DPs also could be found in letters to resettlement agencies and in the Polonia press. A young electrician who had settled in a small town where he could not find a job lived at his sponsor's expense: "My sponsor is very good to me and shows me an honest Polish hospitality.... Staying with this patriotic Polish man without a job is for me a psychological torture."[67] Some sponsors loaned money to help the DPs start their own businesses. One seventy-three-year-old retired miner offered to sell his lifetime collection of seven thousand stamps to get money for the DPs' needs. In another case, neighbors wrote to the ACRPDP requesting that it extend the repayment term of a loan to a DP woman living in hard conditions.[68] Some DPs expressed their deepest gratitude to the ACRPDP for help: "We are surrounded by truly good people here," they wrote, "and they are so nice to us.... We are very grateful to the ladies and gentlemen from this organization, and God bless you that you helped us to get out of that German hell."[69]

When the resettlement program was in full swing, not many people realized that refugees constituted a very distinct category of immigrants that required special care and treatment. As a matter of fact, these wartime refugees and DPs became one of the first populations of forced migrants ever to be the subject to scientific studies in such disciplines as psychology, psychiatry, sociology, and social work. The results of these studies indicate that refugees are more at risk psychologically than are voluntary migrants, but this knowledge was largely unavailable to the people who engaged in DP resettlement in the late 1940s and early 1950s.[70]

Clinical studies conducted on groups of refugees that included displaced persons in various countries in the late 1940s and early 1950s suggest that refugees displayed certain characteristic behaviors after their arrival in countries of permanent resettlement. For example, during an initial period lasting for several months, the refugees often demonstrated heightened activity, enthusiasm, and a positive, accepting outlook for the future. About six months after their arrival, the refugees entered a new and longer stage, called by some the period of "psychological arrival." At this point some refugees began to suffer from "personal disequilibrium," which manifested itself in a mix of paranoid behaviors, anxiety, depression, and somatic complaints. Some studies indicated that refugees became more aware of the differences in customs and of their own losses in the idealized past. In some cases, the third stage of "social displacement syndrome" included the "impairment of interpersonal and social skills manifested by contradictory tendencies of social withdrawal or hostility and tendencies to relate."[71] Similar reactions were confirmed in the population of European refugees who arrived in New York City before the DP Act was inaugurated.[72] Long-term studies on refugee adjustment demonstrated that after the initial period, and for one or two years after their arrival, refugees displayed "an impressive drive to recover what [had] been lost," often through obtaining additional education, entering retraining programs, changing jobs, and moving to different areas. After four or five years, the major part of refugee adjustment was considered complete. After this period, changes happened less frequently, and discouragement set in as the refugees resigned themselves to their new situation. After ten years, the refugees achieved a certain stability, which, despite their efforts and determination, produced a status lower than the one they enjoyed in the old country.[73]

These psychological phenomena also can be observed among voluntary migrants, especially if one assumes that any migration "represents an interruption and frustration of natural life expectations, with all the related anxieties and potential damage to the self-concept. Migration induces cognitive stress, forcing the immigrant to change his familiar images and build a new cognitive map."[74] However, even though the symptoms may be similar, refugees experience them more frequently and in a more acute form.⁷⁵ One of the major factors that can increase the danger to the psychological well-being of refugees is the prolonged period between flight and definite resettlement, a period filled with anxiety and uncertainties; the damaging impact of refugee camps is by now widely acknowledged.⁷⁶ How much the psychological characteristics of the DP refugee population could have affected their relations with other immigrants still remains an open question.⁷⁷

The resettlement process, with all its pitfalls, was only one source of the tensions that began to arise between Polonia and the refugees. Real or perceived class differences became another. Members of Polish-American communities had expected to welcome to America socially compatible individuals. They had expected them to lead a life of hard labor and sacrifice, much like their own experience. An excellent illustration of this attitude is found in a series of cartoons published in *Dziennik Związkowy* between June and September 1948 and commenting on the Polish-American effort to bring Polish war victims into Polonia communities. They showed masses of poor, ragged people crowded on ships bound for American shores, very similar to the turn-of-the-century immigrants who had arrived from Polish villages. The women in those pictures wore babushkas, the men bushy mustaches, and everybody carried shapeless bundles with a few possessions rescued from the war.⁷⁸ A year later, in October 1949, *Dziennik Związkowy* published another cartoon, announcing the opening of the *Dom Wysiedleńców* (DP House) in Chicago. In this picture, *Chicagoska Polonia* (Chicago Polonia), metaphorically portrayed as a beautiful woman draped in classical Greek-style clothing, handed bread and salt to the representative of *Polscy wysiedleńcy* (Polish DPs), in a traditional gesture of welcome. The figure of the Polish DP did not resemble the people from the harbor. He was a handsome, middle-aged man, clean-shaven and dressed in a three-piece suit and a tie; a typical member of the Polish inteligencja.⁷⁹ Within one year, the social image of Polish DPs had undergone a considerable transformation in the eyes of American Polonia.

Polish Americans, with their roots in the peasant immigration of the turn of the century, occupied mostly blue-collar jobs. Although after the war more second-generation Polish-American males began to move into white-collar jobs, Polonia's life-style remained working-class and centered on traditional urban ethnic communities. Polish displaced persons of working-class or agricultural backgrounds had no problem integrating into blue-collar Polish

America.[80] For example, a DP from a rural background sponsored by distant relatives whom he had never met before, reminisced about his Polish-American family's difficult economic conditions. They were poor, he said, but they all worked very hard, especially the mother, who kept the whole family together by her determination and drive. "We fit together nicely," he added, "I had lots of admiration for them all."[81]

Another DP wrote a letter to *Nowy Świat* describing his first impressions of a Polonia-organized dance in a New York Polish National Home. After entering the dance hall, Serafin Dobczyński froze at the sound of Polish polka music: "I stood in the corner of the hall with my eyes closed. I found myself for a moment in my native village near Białystok." The music and the atmosphere of the dance brought back familiar memories and helped him feel "at home"—home, that is, from about twenty years before. After that time, Serafin wrote, the polka had been replaced in Poland by more modern dances, such as the tango, the rumba, and the foxtrot: "I thought that I would be able to see that beautiful dance, polka, in the theater only. Instead, the polka immigrated to the U.S. and thrives here proudly together with our people."[82]

The situation was different for the numerically smaller, but more vocal, refugee intelligentsia, who during the war had been a natural target for the extermination policies of the Third Reich. Lawyers, doctors, architects, engineers, teachers, scholars, scientists, civil servants, professional army officers, politicians, actors, and artists, as well as industrialists and businessmen, were numerous among the prisoners from German concentration and POW camps, slave laborers, and civilian refugees who became displaced persons after the war. Their skills were not easily transferable in the conditions of the American economy, and, to make matters worse, most had reached middle age by the time of their arrival in the United States, which further hampered their chances for successful adjustment and retraining. The majority had to accept any manual labor that was available. America did not represent social and economic advance for them, but rather made them feel déclassé.[83] They complained about their loss of status and the waste of their skills and education, and grew nostalgic about their life before the war. Many looked for ways to improve their job situations and move out of the blue-collar world. To them, the working-class life-style of Polish America seemed unfamiliar and second rate. They decried the Polish Americans' lack of sophistication and education, their peasant ways, their folk culture and Polish language far removed from the literary ideal. They demanded respect and tried to regain their leadership positions, if not within broader American society, then at least within Polonia. The intelligentsia counterpoised the assimilation, loss of language, and Americanization of customs observed among Polish Americans with the notion of the superiority of European culture and the purity of their Polishness. This condescending attitude evoked a strong response from Polish Americans, who "tried, through threats and ridicule, to 'teach them how to work.' They mockingly called them 'princes,' 'barons,' or 'masters' for their middle-class dress, their educated speech, and their predilection for Polish military titles, a pretense reminiscent of a Polish aristocratic past that peasant immigrants had tried to escape."[84] These tensions were reflected in the debates printed on the pages of the Polish American press, as both sides presented their arguments and attempted to persuade others to understand them and to change their attitudes.

Some voices in the debate recognized the special needs of the refugee intelligentsia and their value to the community. Ignacy Matuszewski, who was a member of the first wave of wartime refugees, had successfully transferred from his prewar position as minister of the treasury to a postwar position as a political activist within KNAPP and journalist for *Nowy Świat*. In a 1947 series of editorials entitled "A Burning Question," Matuszewski fairly distributed blame for the frictions within the community. According to him, the professional middle class that had landed on American shores was guilty of snobbery and uppishness. Polonia, on the other hand, was unjustly prejudiced toward this group of refugees who had come out of the war with tremendous losses and who felt helpless in America. Polish Americans shut them off from employment opportunities within the community and condemned them to the "baptism of poverty" that they themselves had experienced after arriving in the United States many years ago. Matuszewski warned: "People, either middle aged or even older, experts, specialists, who went through the gehenna of either German or Soviet captivity—or both—will not pass that baptism successfully, as did their predecessors who came here individually and in normal times. They will simply perish. They can be our benefit. They are our assets that we give up."[85]

Peter P. Yolles, one of the most popular journalists on the staff of *Nowy Świat*, whose essays were widely read and commented on within Polonia, was also one of the most outspoken, as well as controversial, participants in the debate. He introduced readers to the problems of refugee professionals by depicting his conversation with a middle-aged Polish lawyer, who had asked him for help in getting a job. The lawyer knew French and German, but no English. He had no work experience other than his profession and had never done any manual labor. His health was poor. "How do you imagine finding a job?" asked Yolles. "I can't imagine it at all," was the lawyer's response. "That's why my situation is so tragic. Nobody needs me, I am no good for anything. Intelligentsia . . . it's an overwhelming burden that no one needs."[86] Yolles continued this theme in relation to festivities in honor of Jan Lechoń, one of the greatest Polish poets, who had been exiled in New York since the beginning of the war. Polonia has a responsibility to Polish scholars and artists, argued Yolles, and this responsibility should not be treated as charity, but rather as a patriotic duty that requires special care for the creators of the highest national culture.[87] One *Ameryka-Echo* reader expressed a similar sentiment: "Poles born in America as well as those who settled here a long time ago, should be ashamed of the fact that we cannot utilize in a proper way our countrymen who arrive here with good education, through securing for them adequate positions in the economic and intellectual life of America."[88]

Not everyone shared these sentiments. Feliks Tontarski of Watertown, New York, wrote to *Ameryka-Echo:* "I suspect that a lot of refugees who have nothing to do with honest work crowded themselves into those camps. Many such petty 'gentlemen' [*pankowie*] and 'dames' [*paniusie*] with a generally good education arrive here and they look down on the older Polish immigrant who sponsored them and earned everything with his own hard work."[89] Leonidas Dudarew Ossetyński also filled his correspondence to *Nowy Świat* with images of Polish professionals, artists, and aristocrats thrown into physical work and complaining about their fate. The series of essays on the adjustment of newcomers to California's Polish-American community had the common title "Let's Not Be Ridiculous" and showed little sympathy for the loss of status experienced by intelligentsia.[90]

One of the fiercest arguments in the pages of the Polish-American press followed the publication of an article entitled "Polski Dom w Ameryce" (Polish Home in America), in London's *Dziennik Polski* and reprinted in the Polonia press. Zygmunt Nagórski Jr., a well-known Polish journalist and writer, described in it his Easter visit to the home of a Polish-American physician near Philadelphia. The article began with a biting depiction of a chaotic party, with several radios blasting at the same time and men in suspenders but without sport coats playing cards. Nagórski continued:

> If someone had wanted to transfer the atmosphere of a Polish country cottage directly to the United States, he could not have succeeded more than did the clan of my host. Nothing really had changed—it's true, there is a refrigerator and a television set. There is also a modern car in front of the gate. But these are purely superficial signs. People, their life-style, and way of thinking are the same. . . .
> It is equally hot inside as it would have been in the cottage behind the stove. No one opens the windows, because it is unhealthy. Countless holy pictures with maxims adorn the walls. The table is full of food, but lacks virtually anything other than sausage and cabbage! People eat when they want, what they want, and with what they want. . . . In the beds, the sheets are anything but clean. Generally, however, all this is very moving in its attachment to Polish tradition, to the tradition of Easter, which none of those people ever had celebrated in Poland.[91]

Yolles, outraged at the arrogance and ignorance of Nagórski, called him unprofessional, a liar, and a tactless coxcomb. He also pleaded with his readers not to close their doors to other refugees, because Nagórski was an ungrateful exception. Soon *Nowy Świat* published an explanation and apology from Nagórski. The description had been grossly exaggerated, Nagórski admitted, and he had plenty of admiration both for Polonia and for his gracious host. Nagórski further pointed out that the intent of the article had been to evoke a reaction that could initiate changes in the marginal position of Polonia within American society, because it deserved more recognition. These ineffective and awkward excuses did not convince the editors of *Nowy Świat*, who enclosed a chilly commentary about the weakness of the author's apology.[92]

The waves caused by Nagórski's article had hardly subsided when Detroit's *Dziennik Polski* published another article, which became a source of fierce controversy. Written by Jan Langiewicz, "Poradnik dla przybywających do Stanów Zjednoczonych" (Guide for Those Arriving in the United States) made fun of American life-style and culture, warning newcomers of American crudity and lack of sophistication.[93] Even though Polish Americans were not mentioned by name, the article struck Polonians as arrogant and the criticism as undeserved. Again, it was Peter Yolles who responded on behalf of Polonia in a series of essays entitled "O wysiedleńcach" (On Displaced

Persons). After condemning the prejudiced attitudes of journalists looking at America (and Polonia) from the position of "European superiority," Yolles offered his own version of a guide for newcomers. He set out to teach and instruct displaced persons how to behave in order to fit in, to succeed, and, by avoiding trouble, to ensure that more DPs arrived from Europe. Despite his apparent good intentions, Yolles's guide lacked an understanding of the refugees' situation and amounted to offensive, patronizing advice. Yolles wrote that even before they began their journey to America, the DPs should have instilled in themselves the values of duty and responsibility: "duty to behave in such a way so that they do not disturb the lives of their hosts, and to accept the hospitality offered to them with gratitude and appreciation." He explained that "[the DPs'] hatred towards us will be a natural thing ... A hungry man envies a well-fed man, one without a place to live considers the one with a house to be a sinner." He also instructed newcomers to forget about what they had lost in Poland, to stop feeling sorry for themselves, and to accept any job, because even American presidents often had humble beginnings. He advised the refugees to show humility.[94] In the final part of the guide, Yolles addressed the refugees directly, compiling a the list of dos and don'ts:

> First of all, be patient! Do not try to be an instant millionaire or a great success. When you find a job, do not try to undermine others, intrigue, or gossip; do not show how smart you are; do not climb up on others' backs....
> Do not think that by being a European, you are better than they.... REMEMBER THAT YOU ARE AN INVITED GUEST....
> Do not found your life on crying and martyrdom.... Your hosts know and sympathize, but do not think that you have any special rights, because you have suffered....
> Do not talk about what you had and who you were in Poland. This does not make an impression on anyone and will not gain you friends....
> Do not demand recognition for not returning to Poland. YOU ARE NOT DOING ANYONE ANY FAVORS. You could have returned on your own responsibility....
> Work! Work hard.... If you get a position and an honest job that will earn you your daily bread, be grateful and happy....
> Do not bring with you your old concepts.... Do not get into politics. ... Be loyal to America.[95]

The response from outraged refugees was quick and strong. Many readers referred to their war experiences as a time of particular suffering, which was not understood fully by the Polish-American community. Maria Plater-Zyberk of Devon, Pennsylvania, concluded that Yolles had caused more harm than good through his essays on displaced persons. Addressing Yolles's specific arguments, she appealed to readers not to treat a refugee as a guest, but as "a valuable person and a worker," ready to contribute to America. "Do not teach him hard work," she implored, recalling years of slave labor and exploitation in the German war economy; Poles coming to America did not need to be instructed about life's hardships; what they had gone through matched any imaginable ordeal. She also objected to Yolles's call to keep quiet about the past: "Listen sometimes to his [the refugee's] stories: you could find new knowledge and learn from him, too!"[96] Magdalena Roszkowska of Waterbury, Connecticut, protested against the claim that refugees came to America with hatred in their hearts and she despised the call for humility. "You ask us," she wrote to Yolles, "to 'forget.' No, we can't forget. We would have to be born again to do it.... You claim that we have no special rights. It's true, Mr. Yolles. Only God can be the judge of our deeds." She concluded: "So, the little guide with instructions for Polish DPs should perhaps be published in a bit different tone.... We did not bring you shame fighting for Poland. We will not bring you shame here, in America."[97]

Yolles did not respond directly to the letters, but returned to the problem repeatedly in later years. In an essay of June 3, 1949, he revealed an initiative to publish a guide for sponsors, in order to introduce them to the refugees' problems and background. In another piece, he appealed for more care and understanding for DPs, more warmth and love, as if they were "an adopted child, an orphan."[98] Despite obvious efforts to promote harmonious relationships between the two immigrant waves, Yolles's essays were typical of the confused and patronizing attitudes of some older Polonians. In 1950 Yolles again attempted to speak for Polish Americans in Pomost (Bridge), a regular *Nowy Świat* section devoted to matters of interest to newcomers. There Yolles published an ill-fated series of "Conversations with Uncle Sam." Adopting the persona of "Uncle Sam," the journalist used the metaphor of an uncle who had bought a DP a new suit. "What do I expect? I will be brutally honest. I expect gratitude. Nobody bought me a suit for forty-seven dollars." A few paragraphs later he explained: "My dear one ... I am talking about ... freedom, not about a suit."[99] Like Yolles's previous articles, "Conversations with Uncle Sam" provoked immediate responses. The "suit metaphor" was rebutted by a DP who wrote to "Uncle Sam": "The world expects greatness from you...., and finds in you a salesman."[100] Other newcomers followed with their own "conversations with Uncle Sam," presenting the problem from their own points of view. Their correspondence continued to appear in Pomost long after the original "Uncle Sam" disappeared from the section after a month-long run.[101]

The exiles challenged Polonia on the issue of assimilation. The changed character of Polish communities and the transformed identity of Polish Americans received extraordinary attention. The debate over the shape of ethnicity continued from early 1947 into the beginning of the 1950s with unabated intensity. Accused of "Americanization" and scorned for their loss or deformation of the Polish language, Polish Americans faced the need to reexamine what it meant to be Polish in America. The exiles, on the other hand, bound by the demands of the exile mission and concerned about retaining the purity of their Polishness, found it necessary to understand the forces of assimilation and to think of effective ways to counteract them. One aspect that received special attention was the language problem and the readership of Polish books and newspapers. Forms of ethnic culture, reflected in participation in and design of cultural events, such as concerts, theater performances, lecture series, commemorative exhibits, or ethnic celebrations, became another aspect discussed within the Polonia community. Finally, the issue of membership in traditional Polish-American organizations and the adoption of certain forms of ethnic activism also demanded negotiation between Polish Americans and the exiles.

The "Polonian" language used in Polish-American communities was a sign of assimilation easily discernible to the ears of the refugees. They made fun of it, but they also showed concern for the preservation of literary Polish in the exiled communities. Humorous pieces about the experiences of a DP freshly arrived in Chicago, written for *Dziennik Związkowy*, were a prime example of this attitude. The author, "Marcelko," wrote an imaginary letter to his friend still waiting to emigrate from a DP camp in Europe: "Poles live everywhere around us, and one can run errands in the post office or in the stores using the Polish language. I hear there are Americans living in other parts of the city who do not speak Polish, but I have not been there yet. Since even in the factory one hears almost exclusively Polish, you should not be surprised that I have forgotten all one hundred words of English that I had learned in school in [the DP camp at] Wentorf."[102] Continuing his letter, Marcelko admitted that both he and his wife had problems with many unfamiliar words in the Polish language that they had to use in Chicago. In order to master them, they studied together as if they were working on a foreign language. Marcelko gave examples of such expressions, quoting English words "adjusted" to Polish pronunciation and grammatical rules. In another letter, Marcelko again wrote about language problems, but this time he defended Polonians and their old-fashioned Polish—full of obsolete rural dialects and "assimilated" English phrases—by pointing to the amount of time elapsed since their departure from Poland. He stressed, however, that his wife put a lot of effort into making sure that their children did not litter their pure Polish with Polonian or English additions.[103]

The Polonian version of Polish also was in official use in the Polish-American press and radio. Aleksander Janta, a writer and journalist who had arrived in America in the last years of the war, deplored the quality of the Polish language on the Buffalo radio station and in the popular *Dziennik Dla Wszystkich*, where he had found temporary employment. In his work as an editor, he felt overwhelmed by the trend toward the use of "Polonian" instead of "Polish" and hopelessly ineffective in his efforts to improve the language in *Dziennik*, although he also did see some humor in awkward direct translations from English or stubborn "adjustments."[104] The influx of Poles educated in Poland had the potential to ameliorate the linguistic level of Polonia's press and other publications. Many refugees followed Janta's footsteps into the editorial boards of the Polish-American press; almost every newspaper employed at least one newcomer who could write in proper literary Polish. The correspondence from exiles that was frequently published in the press also brought examples of correct, educated, and modern Polish.[105] The Polonian dialect, however, held a strong position. For example, in the early 1950s, Milwaukee's *Kuryer Polski* initiated a column written by "Majk" (Mike), a fictional Polish American who spent most of his time in bars discussing both local matters and world developments with his drinking buddies. The language that Majk used was a caricature of Polish and American slang, deformed to the point of being hardly intelligible. Readers protested this use of jargon and caused an offended Majk to announce a strike and suspend the column. This, in turn, resulted in a show of support for the colorful humorist—including support from Peter Yolles of *Nowy Świat*. Majk returned to the pages of *Kuryer Polski* and continued to update his readers on the opinions expressed in his favorite local bar.

In their letters to the Polish-American press, the exiles appealed to other newcomers to cultivate correct Polish and warned against Polish-American language mixtures. They also condemned the use of English among Poles and Polish Americans, even in public settings that included non-Polish Americans.[106] There were, however, exceptions. Aleksander Janta, who was involved in the Polish Cultural Clubs movement, first in the Buffalo area and then nationally, expressed an opinion not always shared by Polonians or by newcomers. According to him, it was "not important whether an American of Polish descent could speak Polish if he had nothing to say in this language; it would be much more valuable if he, even not being able to speak Polish, had something important to say on behalf of Poland, or on Polish subjects."[107] Through the use of English in Polish ethnic organizations, Janta saw a way to bring back Polish-American youth of the second and third generation who had gravitated away from the ethnic communities. The use of English instead of Polish could also help to gain the attention of mainstream American society and, following the expectations of the exile mission, to educate it about Polish national culture, traditions, and achievements.[108]

The exiles accused Polish Americans of giving only weak support for Polish books and the Polish-language press. Considering the existence of the Polish-language press and publishing houses as a norm of community life in exile rather than as an achievement, the newcomers expressed outrage over low readership within Polonia. DP writers and journalists looking for publishers for their books received disappointing responses citing the difficulty of finding a demand for Polish-language literature. "How is it possible?" one author exclaimed, "In Germany, where there was just a handful of Poles, books were published in various cities and people purchased them; and here, with four millions of Poles [sic], one can't even dream about marketing Polish literature?"[109] Refugees who settled in Polish communities in Canada expressed similar sentiments. A reader of *Pomost* from Canada noticed the absence of Polish-language newspapers and books in Polish homes, either because of lack of interest or because of prohibitive subscription costs. Because millions of our countrymen had been silenced, he wrote, exiles had a duty to keep up the heritage and speak out for them.[110]

Some Polish Americans joined the debate about falling readership. Józef

Bronowicz of Toledo, Ohio, in his letter to *Ameryka-Echo*, agreed with the earlier criticisms. "Our Polonia is nowadays almost completely Americanized," he admitted. Polish Americans preferred the American press, and, even if they subscribed to Polish newspapers, they frequently left them unread. Libraries of Polish-American organizations also provided few choices for readers. Bronowicz concluded that the only hope for the preservation of Polish language and tradition was in the wave of refugees, but "not at once. First, they have to familiarize themselves well with Polish-American life and get to know our young generation, and that takes time."[111] This conciliatory attitude differed greatly from the more aggressive stance of Leonidas Dudarew Ossetyński. In response to the refugees' charges of low readership among Polish Americans, he posed a question about the newcomers' own actions: how many DPs claiming "higher culture" themselves bought Polish books and subscribed to the Polish-language press? How many of their children, who, after only five years in America could hardly speak Polish, would maintain their Polish heritage? Instead of offering criticism, the DPs should take part of the blame on themselves and act to offset the assimilation process in the community, Ossetyński charged.[112]

The discussion of language and readership was part of a larger debate on assimilation within the Polish-American community. Challenged by the newcomers, Polish Americans reexamined assimilation and assessed its impact. Peter Yolles set off the debate in the pages of *Nowy Świat* in a series of essays entitled "Americanization." He addressed what he saw as three different types of Polishness, corresponding loosely to the three generations of immigrants. He concluded that even though their Polishness was not alike, all could retain ethnic consciousness within the social and cultural framework of what it meant to be an American citizen.[113] When *Nowiny Polskie* (Polish News) in Milwaukee published an article reproaching Polish Americans for making their Polish names more English-sounding, Yolles defended them, claiming that "Polishness does not depend on a name" and treating their actions as a human response to the demands of real life in America.[114] Yolles's article was immediately followed by a reader's rebuttal maintaining that name changes were proof of an inferiority complex and a lack of character.[115]

J. P. Zajączkowski examined the arguments of those who supported ghettoization and the preservation of pure Polishness in isolation from American influences, as well as the arguments of those who admitted that assimilation was unavoidable and could be a positive force in shaping ethnic identity. Responding to Yolles's claims about Polish-American identity, Zajączkowski wrote: "Such freaks are unknown to sociology in the long run.... There is no, absolutely no basis to assume that the abnormality known as 'Poles of American background' could exist much longer." He continued: "A fully shaped person, one who emigrated, cannot be anything other than a Pole"; any attempts to renounce Polishness would do irreparable damage to that person's psyche and result in alienation and loneliness. Zajączkowski, however, did acknowledge that the development of children had to differ: "We must bring these children up as Poles and only Poles," he argued, although with sensitivity and sensibility, holding "wide open for them the gates to the world they live in."[116]

The cultural life of Polonia, as expressed in numerous celebrations in local communities, became another object of criticism by the exiles, who sought to introduce into Polish-American communities higher forms of national self-expression. One of the most outspoken critics was Aleksander Janta. He lamented the identification of Polish culture with "folk dance, folk song, food and prayer."[117] He also decried "somber taverns and gloomy gathering places, patriotic and religious ceremonies, mournful in tone and atmosphere," that lasted for long hours of tedious speeches and unsophisticated artistic programs.[118] As president of the Buffalo Polish Cultural Club and, later, national president of the American Council of Polish Cultural Clubs, Janta advocated the adoption of an ambitious plan to foster knowledge of and appreciation for Polish national culture within existing Polonia communities, particularly among alienated second- and third-generation Polish Americans and the larger American society. The 1955 national convention of Cultural Clubs became an occasion to demonstrate a new model of ethnic celebration. Designed by Janta, the celebrations included founding of the Polish Room at the University of Buffalo, the donation of valuable archival materials on Polish history to the university library, lectures by prominent Polish and American scholars, an English-language performance of a nineteenth-century Polish drama, and the publication of a commemorative program with essays on assimilation and ethnic culture.[119] In his 1957 essay "Barriers into Bridges," Janta further elaborated on his vision of promoting Polish culture. He suggested close cooperation with learning centers, such as universities, libraries, research institutes, and museums, and recommended launching a score of projects documenting and popularizing Polish history and culture.[120]

New initiatives were developed also on a more local level. For example, Polish exiles united in Milwaukee's Stowarzyszenie Nowych Amerykanów (Association of New Americans) tried to fill what they saw as a "cultural void" in Polonia by sponsoring variety shows and performances by theater groups and singing ensembles. Most of the performers came to Milwaukee from Chicago and from other major centers of Polonia life and represented scores of Polish artists who had immigrated to the United States during and after the war. Despite these efforts—as well as reportedly high artistic quality of the events—rented halls were often left with rows of empty seats, prompting the association to decry the lack of support from older Polonia and to ask itself a dramatic question: "Why bother?"[121] At the same time, many newly arrived refugees considered the entertainments preferred by Polish Americans to be unappealing and vulgar. One illustration of this attitude was a fictional description of a visit to a Polish club named for Adam Mickiewicz, a famous Romantic Polish poet of the nineteenth century. A Polish-American uncle who had sponsored his DP nephew took him to the club shortly after his arrival. Contrary to the nephew's expectations, however, the club was not devoted to the popularization of Mickiewicz's poetry. It was "dark from cigarette smoke and filled with noise, the singing of drunken men and women, and some annoying music."[122]

Cultural leadership was an important element of the exile mission, but it was a difficult one for the exile leaders to achieve under the conditions that prevailed in America. Within the framework of the mission, most of the exiled intellectuals could identify themselves with the refugee wave and lay claim to represent this group, but they had little following among established Polonia. Their own efforts to venture into Polonia were rather limited. Acting from a position of cultural and often class superiority, they found it difficult to understand Polonia's own history and interests. Deprived of a broader readership base, they often felt alienated and isolated as they strove to redefine their place in exile.

Józef Wittlin—a prominent Polish writer, poet, and essayist—delivered a speech entitled "Sorrow and Grandeur of Exile" at an American branch meeting of the international P.E.N. Club, Centre for Writers in Exile, in 1957. In it, Wittlin attempted to construct a positive program for émigré writers experiencing the "misfortune of political emigration." "The life of the exile," Wittlin declared, "like the life of any other person, speeds onward to its end, but an exile, as it were professionally, moves backwards. Hence, often serious and even tragic conflicts arise. It happens that the émigré lives in a complete vacuum which his imagination fills exclusively with phantoms of a dead world."[123] The overwhelming nostalgia for things bygone is further reinforced by the "sentimental considerations" of the "restricted society" in which exiled writers live and in which they find primary audience for their work. The dangers of this arrangement, however, may be balanced by certain benefits of isolation: "solitude cools our passions, but also sharpens our perspicacity."[124] Pointing to the search for universal values as redeeming the work in exile, Wittlin concluded with both bitterness and hope:

> Amidst the horror of life, amidst Hell on Earth, time and again there suddenly awakens in us an unconscious nostalgia for something that is not Hell or horror and exile, and not even our native soil, and who knows whether it is not the mission of writers and artists to grasp and express these very longings and presentiments of man. I believe that working in exile, under conditions of more or less forced anonymity, we may come near those artists who in the Middle Ages were preparing the soul of man for another, no longer an exile's existence, where no one asks the question "how do you spell your name?"[125]

Another Polish émigré scholar, Wacław Lednicki, sought to identify opportunities for Polish intellectuals to play an active role in America and to fulfill the obligations of social and cultural leadership that traditionally came with membership in the Polish intelligentsia. He saw the role of a Polish intellectual as that of a representative of Poland and her thousand years of history and tradition vis à vis American society, which he considered particularly ignorant of things Polish. Participation in American life was a condition *sine qua non* for this duty. With a great dose of arrogance, Lednicki also observed that the old economic immigrants had "for years been accustomed to associate their Polonism only with poverty and social humiliation." Therefore, Lednicki argued, work to acquaint Old Polonia "with their rightful historical and cultural background, of which the Polish immigrants have no slightest reason to be ashamed," constituted a worthwhile vocation for the Polish intellectual in exile.[126]

Another Polish émigré, sociologist Aleksander Hertz, after fifteen years in America and having made a conscious effort to familiarize himself with various aspects of American life and culture, admitted to a certain degree of acculturation. He could not, however, imagine his full social assimilation, because he identified himself too strongly with the Polish intelligentsia, whose tradition he saw rooted in the high culture of old Europe. Although recognizing the revolutionary impact of American civilization on the development of the world, Hertz confessed: "I realize that after so many years of life spent in America I have not reached spiritual identification with American civilization. I feel in it both lonely and foreign."[127] Feelings similar to those expressed by Wittlin, Lednicki, and Hertz—nostalgia and alienation, a search for identity and calling, a struggle with the émigré condition and foreignness—became a recognizable part of many other poetic and literary works by Polish exiled authors in the postwar diaspora.[128]

The exile mission, which defined the issues of cultural goals and cultural leadership, put the most emphasis on political work on behalf of Poland. The concept of political involvement became a significant source of differences between the two groups. The refugees proudly called themselves political exiles and repeatedly invoked their mission to work for Poland's independence and to preserve the Polish nation in exile. Although American Polonia's history did include political activism in the Romantic tradition and participation in the military struggle for Polish independence, Polish Americans were in the eyes of the refugees "only economic immigrants"— peasants and not soldiers—too assimilated to American culture and too detached from recent political events to lead the struggle for Poland. Melchior Wańkowicz, for example, for whom Polish Americans were "eaten through by spiritual erosion" and "corroded by the civilization of materialism," saw their value in the struggle for Poland only as American citizens. It was the political emigration, however, that had to provide them with direction and political culture in order to politicize Polonia and renew its commitment to Polishness.[129] American Polonia, however, had no intention of stepping down and giving up leadership to the newcomers.

The vehement anticommunism of both groups facilitated cooperation and provided common ground. The exile mission demanded that the new immigrants not cease in their protests against Yalta, considered to be a betrayal in which Poland's wartime allies abandoned her to the Soviet Union. As one

Nowy Świat reader put it, "[E]migration was and is an unceasing protest against selling Poland into slavery."[130] Consequently, the exiles had to voice arguments against Yalta and to assert the truth about Poland constantly and at every occasion.[131] The Polish American Congress articulated similar sentiments, making anticommunism a catalyst for closer political collaboration.

What separated the two groups was their attitude toward party politics linked to the London government in exile. Party leaders in London formulated policies, constructed alliances, broke into smaller parties and factions, or created new ones. The government made appointments and prepared programs that could have been implemented immediately, had the international situation changed and had the government returned to Poland. Many of those activities had symbolic meaning and were designed to prove to the free world the illegitimacy of the communist government in Poland and to continue the prewar authority of all those who never accepted the Warsaw regime.[132] Critics of party politics saw the London government circles as a pathetic make-believe game invented by a useless and embittered group of men who were out of touch with reality and who could not move on with their lives. In a 1949 essay on Polish London, Melchior Wańkowicz, a writer and journalist, condemned the excessive ghettoization of the exiles, the infighting, and the ideological control that resulted in ostracism of those who dared to show more open-mindedness or to question party lines.[133]

Observing the internal divisions and infighting within London governmental circles, American Polonia grew increasingly concerned about their negative impact on the unity of the diaspora and on the representation of Poland's interests to Western governments. Polonia's leaders perceived themselves to be most effective while acting within the structures of American politics and asserting their rights as American citizens. They despised what they saw as the divisiveness of the London government and its political parties and factions. Proclaiming symbolic loyalty to the legal authorities in exile, they reserved the right to remain independent and free of the political confusion resulting from party politics. The Polish American Congress repeatedly criticized party politics, declared its disinvolvement in the power struggles, and expressed its satisfaction with all efforts toward unification. The transplantation of party politics onto American soil was generally considered a threat to unified support for the PAC and its independent politics. Numerous voices in the pages of the Polish-American press called for the total abandonment of party activities in the United States and concentration on the PAC's work. Those refugees who tried to carry out party activities were accused of shattering the unity of American Polonia.[134]

Despite those declarations, both the PAC and other Polish-American organizations in the United States not only closely followed but actually became directly engaged in London politics. For example, in December 1947 in Chicago, Charles Rozmarek on behalf of the PAC and Stanisław Mikołajczyk on behalf of Polskie Stronnictwo Ludowe signed an official agreement regarding mutual cooperation, according to which the PSL could utilize PAC structures and press for their work. The agreement drew major criticism from both the London government and Polonia organizations such as KNAPP and PRCUA, which considered Mikołajczyk morally and politically compromised. Rozmarek's move permanently severed relations between the PAC and KNAPP and resulted in Józef Kania's leading the withdrawal of the PRCUA from the PAC ranks during its second national convention in Philadelphia.[135] American Polonia—and especially important parts of its leadership—could not remain totally indifferent to the internal divisions within the London government. Although political sympathies toward the various quarrelling parties in London were of decidedly secondary significance, they introduced additional tensions between exile activists and Polish-American leaders.[136]

Average Polish Americans felt distant from London and its political agendas. Frequent changes in alliances, and never-ending constitutional arguments seemed complex and confusing. Aleksander Janta gives one example of the disorientation of Polonia's leaders. Following a lengthy presentation by General Tadeusz Bór-Komorowski, in which he harshly criticized President August Zaleski and voiced support for the opposition Political Council, a well-meaning Polish American asked him on behalf of American Polonia in Buffalo "[W]hat can we do to help our dear President Zaleski?"[137]

The political parties active in the United States did not seem to be able to attract vast masses of supporters from among the DP population. Instead, they became the domain of a small group of prewar Polish political activists looking for an outlet for their political energy.[138] Exile politics, however limited its practical impact, carried an important symbolic meaning, fulfilling the exile mission's goal of re-creating the Polish nation in exile, complete with democratic political structures at all levels. Political parties were established in countries of settlement all over the world and their frequent communication strengthened diaspora ties and involved them in a common political discourse.[139]

Organizational separation often deepened the divisions between Old Polonia and the New Emigration. As exiles formed their own organizations, Polish Americans criticized the refugees for their perceived lack of involvement in the life of Polonia. The Polish-language press abounded in appeals to the newcomers, encouraging them to join older organizations. These appeals revealed a sentiment that viewed the influx of refugees as a revitalizing force for the aging organizations. Polish Americans justifiably expected that displaced persons would readily join the existing organizational structure of Polonia and strengthen it through support of traditional programs and activities. The membership influx, however, proved smaller than predicted. The Polish American Labor Council of Chicago, while acknowledging the involvement of some DPs, accused the majority of isolationism, inactivity, and pursuit of only material gains.[140] The press and its readers asked, "Where are the newcomers and what can be done to attract them to the organizations?"[141] Rada Polonii published "The Ten Commandments for Displaced Persons," which included a point about the necessity of joining a Polish fraternal organization and a Polish parish.[142] Some refugees already active in Polonia called on others to get involved and to continue building on the strong foundations laid by older Polonia. Leonidas Dudarew Ossetyński repeatedly chastised the newcomers for their lack of support for Polonia's "work for Poland" in California.[143]

The refugees responded to these allegations in many different ways. One young immigrant cited the practical problems faced by newcomers who were unfamiliar with the language, struggling financially, and overwhelmed by America.[144] Zygmunt Nagórski argued that the new immigrants had needs and goals that differed from those of Old Polonia and that, at least temporarily, they needed to form their own organizations, which could better address their problems.[145] And Aleksander Janta, recalling his own experiences working for a couple of prestigious Polish-American foundations, emphasized their set ways of doing business, their unwillingness to introduce any changes, and a particular personal style of leadership, often incomprehensible (or unacceptable) to "outsiders" like himself.[146] Despite criticism or efforts by activists on both sides, postwar immigrants continued to form their own organizations, separate from existing ethnic institutions. The anticipated process of gradual fusion, increased cooperation, and acceptance of comparable goals and methods, proceeded slowly and reluctantly.

The issue of leadership of organizations in Polonia erupted in controversy in 1952. Some Polish-American organizations, which initially had invited all newcomers to join their ranks, later undertook steps to limit the new immigrants' opportunities to reach leadership positions. For example, during the third national convention of the Polish American Congress in Atlantic City in 1952, a resolution was passed requiring all convention delegates to be American citizens. The new immigrants perceived it as discrimination directed against them and voiced their protests.[147]

The split within the veterans organizations had similar roots. In June 1949 the councils of the Stowarzyszenie Weteranów Armii Polskiej (SWAP, Polish Army Veterans Association), a group established by former soldiers from World War I, and the Stowarzyszenie Polskich Kombatantów (SPK, Association of Polish ex-Combatants), a post–World War II international organization with its headquarters in London, came to an agreement on cooperation in the United States. Recognizing the long history and many achievements of SWAP, as well as affinity of goals, SPK decided to forgo the establishment of a separate SPK branch in the United States, as had been done in other countries of postwar diaspora. Instead, it called on its members to join existing SWAP organizations. According to Stanisław Gierat, the deputy of the SPK for the United States, by December 1951 about fifteen hundred World War II veterans had joined SWAP. This number, however, had to be considered relatively low because it constituted only about 7.5 percent of all former soldiers who had settled in the United States. Some World War II veterans hesitated to join SWAP, alarmed by the provision in the organization's constitution that restricted positions in the supreme council (*zarząd główny*) to those having five years of membership. Both the SPK headquarters in London and its New York delegates hoped that the national convention of SWAP, planned for early summer of 1952, would address that problem and carry out amendments accommodating the World War II veterans.[148]

The eagerly awaited eleventh national convention of SWAP that took place in Utica, New York, between May 30 and June 1, 1952, astonished the veteran community. Not only was the SWAP constitution not changed in favor of the newcomers, but new amendments indicated a harder line on the part of the old SWAP leadership. A five-year waiting period was required for holding office in either the supreme council or the district councils, and all officers had to be American citizens. Moreover, the new constitution stipulated that the blue Haller army uniform was officially accepted as the organizational uniform of the SWAP. These changes caused a stir within a vocal portion of the World War II veteran community, which perceived them as discriminatory and a flagrant attempt to limit their influence. The SPK leadership in London announced that the 1949 agreement between the SPK and SWAP was no longer in force, creating the possibility of the formation of a separate veterans organization on the territory of the United States.[149]

The SWAP leadership responded to these accusations of ill will and discrimination by downplaying the significance of the changes. They called for unity and blamed the discord on a minority of disaffected newcomers, identifying them as power-hungry elements connected to the Polish prewar political and military establishment.[150] Nothing, however, could counteract the rift that cut deep across the veteran community. In September 1952 a group of members of Post 201, New York, consisting of World War II veterans, announced their withdrawal from SWAP. In a lengthy open letter published in the Polish-American press, they stated their reasons, which included discrepancies between the resolutions of the SWAP national convention and the text of the newly printed constitution. World War II chaplains who formed SWAP Post 200 also announced their withdrawal from the organization. Posts in Cleveland and Milwaukee took similar actions. The pages of the Polish-American press became the venue for a public debate on the issue. For example, members of SWAP District VIII (Worcester, Massachusetts), consisting of fourteen different posts, proclaimed their dissatisfaction with the results of the national convention as discriminatory toward World War II veterans, but they vowed to fight the changes on constitutional grounds. The remaining members of New York Post 201 took a similar position and decided to continue their membership in SWAP. The majority of calls for a separate organization for World War II veterans came from the exile circles, but even they were not uniform, with many strong voices opting for the maintenance of one organization. Despite the prevailing opinion that the Utica resolutions indeed did discriminate against the newcomers, some of the refugee veterans perceived a lack of unity as too great a threat to the strength and vitality of the entire veteran community and, in the long run, to the fulfillment of the exile mission.¹⁵¹ Nevertheless, in 1953 the SPK in the United States came into being with a little more than one thousand members and gradually grew, establishing posts in many states.¹⁵²

Sprawa Wyrwy

Both veterans and other exiles faced the most important test of their loyalty to the exile mission in connection with *sprawa Wyrwy* (the Wyrwa affair). The main issues were loyalty to the Polish government in London, allegiance to the government of the United States, trust in America's leadership in the struggle against communism, and the concept of military readiness of the diaspora during the Korean War. With exceptional sharpness, the Wyrwa affair revealed ideological rifts between Polish Americans and the more radical members of the exile community. In the end, the Wyrwa affair challenged the convictions of all exiles and forced them to identify their positions on difficult questions of political loyalty, citizenship, and immigrant responsibility.

The debate on the case of Tadeusz Wyrwa was played out in the pages of the Polonia press and later was fully documented in the memoirs of his father, Józef Wyrwa.¹⁵³ Both Wyrwas had fought during World War II in the Polish guerrilla forces of the Home Army, earning ranks as officers. Józef had been part of the famous group under the command of Major Hubal since 1939, and after Hubal's defeat Józef continued on with the Home Army guerrilla formation active in the Kielce region.¹⁵⁴ Tadeusz joined him in active duty in 1941, when he was only sixteen years old. After the seizure of power by the communists, both Wyrwas were arrested and imprisoned. They managed to escape and lived for a while under assumed identities. As the political situation worsened and as their cover became more uncertain, the father and son decided to leave Poland. They crossed the border illegally in March 1947 and were arrested and sentenced to six months in prison by the authorities in the American occupation zone of Germany. They succeeded in escaping from this new distress and they soon reached the Polish DP camps, where they were provided with false papers identifying them as former war prisoners. For a couple of years Józef worked in the Polish DP school system as a teacher and Tadeusz attended school. In the summer of 1949 both Wyrwas found themselves in a DP transport heading for the United States and were resettled in Chicago.

186 | *"So they are among brethren"*

In August 1950 Tadeusz Wyrwa, twenty-five years old at the time, received a draft order from the American Army. He refused to join, justifying his decision with the argument that he was a Polish officer obliged to follow only orders of the legal Polish (that is, London government) authorities. According to the account published by Józef Wyrwa, the American draft officer was at that point joined by a Polish-speaking officer, who exclaimed, "I know you, DPs, communists, subversives! You came to America to gobble, but you're not eager to work. Why aren't you going back to Poland?"[155]

The American press, including the *Chicago Tribune*, *Chicago Sun-Times*, and *Herald-American*, publicized Wyrwa's refusal to serve and commented on the ingratitude of displaced persons, causing a stir in Polonia circles. *Dziennik Związkowy* promptly followed with a condemnation of Wyrwa's position, claiming that Wyrwa's attitude harmed the "good opinion about Poles, who were and are ready to fight for the United States." It concluded, "Wyrwa should know that here, especially in times such as the present, guests of his kind are unwelcome. Everybody who wants to benefit from the welfare of this country has to be also ready to defend it."[156] *Kuryer Codzienny* of Boston echoed the same argument and added, "All who come to a foreign country have the duty to follow its written and moral laws. If they do not wish to comply—they need to leave the country."[157]

Responding to the publicity, Tadeusz Wyrwa published an open letter in *Dziennik Chicagoski* in which he explained and justified his position, stating, "I am a Polish citizen and I intend to stay one." He also reminded readers of Poland's contribution to World War II and of her abandonment and betrayal by the Allies. "What is the guarantee that also after the coming war Poland will not be betrayed . . . ?" he asked. He continued

> In what name then are the United States authorities now calling Polish citizens to fight in Korea in the American Army? Let them announce, as President Wilson did during World War I, that one of the war's goals is the establishment of an independent Poland.
>
> Let them withdraw recognition of the pro-Soviet government in Warsaw and return recognition to the legal Polish government in London, and then not only I, but very many Poles, as well as representatives of other Central and Eastern European nations will volunteer to fight against Russia under their own banners and under the orders of their native legal governments![158]

Both Old Polonia and New Emigration journalists joined the debate, providing a framework for the opinions of readers, who began to send in their own comments. Peter Yolles of *Nowy Świat* drew a clear line between Wyrwa's understandable (although not acceptable) "act of psychological despair" resulting from the betrayal at Yalta and the patriotic duty of Polish Americans. He defined the Wyrwa affair as having no impact on the attitudes of Polish Americans and condemned the young soldier for, metaphorically speaking, not lending a hand to a neighbor whose house was on fire. "Wyrwa would have done better," Yolles wrote, "had he volunteered and taken an oath—and at the same time published a press statement explaining that he was doing it DESPITE the fact that America betrayed Poland."[159] Józef Karasiewicz of Detroit's *Dziennik Polski* tore into Yolles in a series of passionate articles, defending Wyrwa and attacking opportunism within Polonia. "I am an American of my own free will," declared Karasiewicz in one article, explaining further that his main duty was to make sure that America remained fair and just, and stood for democracy and respect toward other countries' freedom, as it had in the pre-Yalta past. "If America had been today the way it was a hundred years ago," he continued, "Wyrwa's brave action would have probably received popular support. It would not have hurt Polish immigrants, but rather gained them more respect."[160] Karasiewicz remained among the loyal few who defended Wyrwa from beginning to end.

Klaudiusz Hrabyk (in the United States) and Zygmunt Nowakowski (as a London correspondent of *Dziennik Polski*) represented the viewpoint of the DP wave and both argued for Wyrwa. Hrabyk reminded the readers that only an official agreement between the United States and the legal Polish (London) government could release Wyrwa from his oath. With regard to the accusation of ingratitude on the part of the DPs, Hrabyk skillfully turned the argument around. The refugees certainly felt grateful, he wrote. The United States, however, also should be grateful to be presented with a chance to right the wrong of Yalta, offering the safe haven to at least a handful of Poles while the entire Polish nation suffered in the yoke of communism.[161] Nowakowski was even more straightforward, identifying Wyrwa as a spokesperson for all political exiles in the Polish diaspora and accusing America of a lack of clearly defined goals in its foreign policy in Asia.[162]

The debate heated up further. Readers joined the discussion on Wyrwa, and their letters appeared in Chicago's *Dziennik Związkowy* and *Dziennik*

Chicagoski, Boston's *Kuryer Codzienny,* Detroit's *Dziennik Polski,* Toledo's *Ameryka-Echo,* and Milwaukee's *Kuryer Polski.* The editors of *Nowy Świat* opened the newspaper's pages to readers, inviting them to participate in the "court over Wyrwa" (*sąd nad Wyrwą*). The authors of letters were split in their opinions. Most of the newcomers supported Wyrwa and decried America's betrayal at Yalta. Aleksander Moc wrote to *Dziennik Związkowy* about expectations of gratitude: "Poles feel the responsibility to be grateful to America of Wilson and Hoover, and they have proved it in many ways. But no country that participated in Tehran and Yalta has the right to demand gratitude from the Poles."[163] Kazimierz Wiedzielski from Alligator, Mississippi, scolded: "First, recall Yalta and Tehran and right the wrongs toward Poland. . . . The present threat to America and England is also the result of Yalta and Tehran."[164] Zofia Deszcz from Washington, D.C., wrote, "Mr. Wyrwa's action did more for Poland than all of American Polonia with its telegrams to Washington. He touched a wound that still hurts and reminded those who should keep it in their memory that Poland and Poles do exist."[165]

Others were highly critical of Tadeusz's decision. While the press published information about DP volunteers in the American Army who were ready to fight in Korea, Józef Kaczmarek from Buffalo, New York, wrote

> I am one of the former DPs, newly arrived from Germany. While reading about the Wyrwa affair I had to conclude that he brought us, DPs, shame. He did not show bravery, but demonstrated a lack of understanding of his obligations. We have in Buffalo a society, "Polonia," organized by the New Emigration. I am appealing to the members of this society to pass an appropriate resolution condemning such behavior [like Wyrwa's] in order to prevent others from refusing the military duty.[166]

There were also Polish Americans who objected to Wyrwa's stance. For example, one World War II veteran even questioned the effort to bring Polish former soldiers to America under the amended DP Act. "Have those who support Wyrwa's position come here only in search of better living conditions at a time when our colleagues bleed, fighting for freedom of the entire world? . . . We do not need 'Wyrwas' in the United States," he wrote.[167] Others did not share his harsh opinion. Wacław Śpiewak from New York City explained that

[o]ne has to be a good Pole to understand Wyrwa. He has no choice. Soldiers of the Home Army took a special oath. The death penalty awaited those who broke it during the war. Nobody released Wyrwa from that oath. We, Americans of Polish descent, need to be consistent. Wyrwa is a political refugee who can't go back to Poland. Our responsibility is to feed him, show him good heart, give him time to look around our country of freedom and learn to love it, the way we all love America. Give him a fair chance.[168]

The first convention of the New Emigration, which took place in New Bedford, Massachusetts, in September 1950, adopted a resolution expressing solidarity with Tadeusz Wyrwa and stating that because the "Western democracies had so far done nothing to restore Polish independence," the new immigrants "declare[d] that the struggle for freedom for South Korea only, with the omission of hundreds of millions from other nations, is an insult to the states and nations given up into Bolshevik slavery."[169] The exiles were still far from unanimous in their judgment of the Wyrwa affair. Józef Wyrwa noted instances of hostility and condemnation from members of Chicago's Polish émigré and veterans circles and what he referred to as "a dubious position" taken by the London government's political delegation in the United States, located in New York City. Unfortunately for both Wyrwas, the debate on Tadeusz was not limited to the press. Józef Wyrwa reported that they had received numerous anonymous letters and phone calls filled with threats and invective, and had been repeatedly fired from factory jobs.[170] In this situation, both Wyrwas gratefully received favorable comments in the Polish press in Great Britain, Australia, and Germany, as well as a show of support from a group of new immigrants in Argentina. The Association of Polish War Refugees, a leading postwar diaspora organization, also announced its support for Wyrwa.[171]

As could be expected, the Wyrwa affair provoked a reaction from the London government. The government announced that without the consent of the legal Polish authorities, no Polish citizen could serve in a foreign army and that in the current situation volunteering to serve in any foreign forces was against the interests of the Polish state.[172] An almost simultaneously published interview with General Anders (reprinted from London's *Dziennik Polski* by *Dziennik Chicagoski*) revealed the general's strong belief that the Korean War might turn into an international conflict in which Polish émigré soldiers could participate within Polish units formed in the West. "The road to Poland," said the General, "does not lead through the foreign legion and foreign uniforms."[173] The belief that Korea would lead to more than a local conflict was widespread.[174] In its appeal "To the American Polonia," the PAC also maintained that Korea was "the first signal of the third world war." Addressing directly American Polonia as well as the DPs, the PAC called on them to fight under the American flag because "He who wants to fight for Poland—must fight on the side of the United States. He who fights in the United States' ranks—fights also for Poland."[175]

In the meantime, in order to close existing legal loopholes, the U.S. Congress took action and after a short debate passed an amendment to an existing law regarding compulsory military service by foreigners residing in the United States, which took effect in June 1951.[176] In January 1952 Tadeusz Wyrwa again received a draft notice. Having no intention of complying, he applied for a visa to leave the United States but was refused, as were all males of draft age. Upon consultation, the representatives of the Polish London government in New York suggested that Wyrwa give up his position and observe the law. In February 1952 Wyrwa stood before the draft commission and once more refused to join the army. Shortly thereafter the FBI investigated the matter and arrested him. Wyrwa was released on bail and awaited trial.

This time, the reaction of Polonia was much less supportive of Wyrwa. The majority of commentators, both in the United States and in the larger diaspora, emphasized that Wyrwa unquestionably had broken the law. In the anticommunist fervor of the Cold War, Ignacy Morawski of *Nowy Świat* even warned that attitudes like Wyrwa's might be welcomed by Moscow. The Polish government in London, pressed for some concrete action on behalf of Wyrwa, offered no real support.[177]

Józef Karasiewicz of *Dziennik Polski* continued to mobilize public opinion within Polonia, attempting to turn the suit against Wyrwa into a showcase that would bring international attention to the Polish question. Waiting for his impending court date, Wyrwa also sought a broader audience for his views and convictions. Summoned for help, readers of *Dziennik Polski* sent in donations to hire "a good attorney" for Tadeusz. "Will Polonia stand up to the opportunity to defend Wyrwa in such a way as, for example, the communists and other radicals did in the case of Sacco and Vanzetti?" asked Karasiewicz. The readers stated their own reasons for contributing to the fund. A Polish-American organization, Komitet Obrony Narodowej (KON, Committee of

National Defense), wrote, "We, ... American citizens of Polish descent, offer to T. Wyrwa our moral support for his determined position. T. Wyrwa is defending in this way the Polish question, which was ignored at the allies' conferences in Tehran and Yalta. We think that the Wyrwa affair is a Polish and international matter."[178] A Polish-American doctor who sent a donation explained that he was sorry to hear about a young Polish refugee refusing to serve in the American army, but he wanted him to have a fair trial, one that could give him a chance to present and defend his views publicly. Altogether, readers collected more than eight hundred dollars for Tadeusz's legal expenses.[179]

The case failed to turn into a spectacular debate of the Polish question within the American legal system. Despite the wishes of the defendant and his father, the attorneys managed to have the case dismissed in September 1952 on the grounds of Tadeusz's long service as an officer in the Polish Home Army, classified as an American ally during World War II. The closing of the case received only modest attention in the Polonia press. An isolated article in New York's *Sprawa Polska* commented on this "conspiracy of silence," calling the Wyrwa affair a test "of the moral and political standing of the émigré community." The article concluded that the exiles had demonstrated a "shallow opportunism" as well as a lack of familiarity with the American political system, and it made pessimistic projections about the questionable moral values of the new emigrants.[180] Disappointed and embittered, both Wyrwas left the United States in 1952 and settled first in Spain and then France.[181]

By any account, Wyrwa's attitude must have been considered extreme and uncompromising. From the beginning of the affair, his stance never enjoyed unanimous support, even from his own refugee cohort. Those who had supported him in the first stage of the affair mistrusted the goals of American foreign policy and believed that the "betrayal at Yalta" justified his action. The prospect of an international conflict that would affect Poland's political future had further strengthened the belief that exile was only temporary and that refugees needed to remain loyal to the Polish authorities in London. The government in exile had encouraged this position. Two years later, the argument of Wyrwa's supporters changed. Poles and Polish Americans mobilized by Józef Karasiewicz and *Dziennik Polski* wanted to turn the Wyrwa affair into an international forum for the presentation of the Polish question to the American public and to the world.

Wyrwa's attitude certainly struck a nerve with Polonia and the entire diaspora. The "court over Wyrwa" became more than a judgment over the controversial attitude of a young Polish war hero. It was a debate on the understanding of the main tenets of the exile mission, including loyalty to the government in exile and the concepts of an exile army, and political institutions. The attitudes of the participants in the debate depended on the centrality of either Poland or the United States to their world view. The Wyrwa affair effectively challenged the formulation and principles of the exile mission in the Cold War United States. Its epilogue became a symbolic acknowledgment of the fact that, in order to be useful, the exile mission had to be negotiated and reconstructed by each new wave of immigration and each new generation of Polonia. It proved that the exiles in the United States had negotiated for themselves a compromised—but perhaps more pragmatic—version of the exile mission, one that gave symbolic support to the London government but approved of the political leadership of the United States in the anticommunist struggle. The Cold War emphasis on the need for unity, which had already come to the surface in the SWAP-SPK conflict, further silenced potential pro-Wyrwa arguments.

The larger debate that took place within the Polish-American community in the 1940s and early 1950s had special significance. It involved many groups and individuals within the community, including sponsors, neighbors, family members, activists and leaders of large and small ethnic organizations, veterans, and journalists. After sharing in the refugee experience, combat, and the resistance movement during the war, women felt entitled to express their views equally. The confrontation between Polish Americans and refugee Poles prompted both groups to express their views publicly and to exchange opinions on the complex problems of assimilation, community life and leadership, and their relationship to the homeland. The Polish-language press became a unique forum for the debate, confirming its formative role in the community by providing encouragement, space, and a framework for the discourse.

Although the debate was sometimes considered a divisive force breaking up the unity of Polonia, it would be a mistake to see the tensions as only a destructive influence. On the contrary, many positive elements resulted from the debate and became a basis for reconciliation. Both groups had to redefine their identity. Polish Americans responded to the challenge of more active leadership in political lobbying on behalf of Poland and adopted many points of the exile mission, including greater involvement in the postwar diaspora. They also welcomed the revitalizing influence of the newcomers in the areas of arts and culture. The refugees had to readjust their mission to the conditions of life in a new country and to develop new ways of implementing it. The Wyrwa affair was just one example of changes in the understanding of the mission.

A characteristic feature of the debate was its appeal to the entire Polish postwar diaspora. Some of the press articles that stirred American Polonia were either first published in other Polish centers abroad or later reprinted in the newspapers in London, Paris, Sydney, or Toronto. This sharing of ideas strengthened the concept of the diaspora and the exile mission. Nor was the debate limited to the intra-ethnic relationships, but rather offered Polonia as a whole a redefined position vis-à-vis the larger American society. In the framework of the Cold War, Polonia could use the vehicle of anticommunism to move closer to the mainstream. The very presence of exiles was a symbol of protest against the Yalta system and underscored Poland's contribution to the Allies' victory in World War II. Their wartime experiences in the captivity in the Soviet Union, connections to the diaspora, and focus on international politics and lobbying on behalf of Poland provided Polonia with powerful arguments in the Cold War discourse. As resettlement was completed and the tensions connected to it were eliminated, this international Cold War context rendered perhaps the most effective ground for reconciliation.

The Korean War did not bring on an international conflict that could resolve the Polish question. The Cold War, however, presented many strong motivations for unity within the ethnic community. Many began to interpret the rift in Polonia as the work of communist agents aiming to weaken the Polish-American lobby on behalf of Poland. For example, Stanisław Michalski, a new immigrant, explained the obstacles faced by the refugee intelligentsia in their efforts to find better employment by alluding to a vaguely defined conspiracy to deprive Polonia of effective leadership.[182] The language used to call for the resolution of conflicts illustrates the impact of Cold War rhetoric: the enemy was waiting to benefit from the frictions; the divisions were a communist provocation and an attempt to break the strength of emigration, while the Polish question on the international arena demanded unified efforts. Both sides were asked to give up their animosities before the enemy could use them.[183] The death of Stalin in 1953, the political thaw behind the Iron Curtain, and détente between East and West required increased attention. The New Emigration and Old Polonia in the United States stepped up their efforts for political cooperation, which were further accelerated by the 1956 events in Poland and Hungary.

5 ⫶ "Ambassadors of our cause"
Turning Points

Politics of the Mission

THE EXILE MISSION MADE political activism the foremost duty of refugees. No one questioned the need for political activity, although according to writer and politician Stanisław Mackiewicz, the exiles could be divided into Poles and Poles-politicians, and the proportions between these two groups were unclear.[1] Underscoring the same point, Zbigniew Chałko, a journalist and a poet who settled in Chicago, wrote in 1950: "After Yalta . . . the functions of ambassadors became directly transferred onto the refugee masses . . . , and hundreds, thousands, maybe tens of thousands of former tailors, druggists, chimney sweepers, . . . sergeants and privates—are great ambassadors of our cause."[2] While the exile leaders engaged in more direct political action, the rank and file could render them their support, inform and influence Western public opinion, and attest to the exile mission through their everyday personal attitude. In times of need, the rank and file mobilized, not only participating in actions designed by the politicians but also spontaneously undertaking their own initiatives.

Three main centers of influence vied for leadership of the diaspora in the area of politics. The first was Zamek, whose leader, August Zaleski, claimed constitutional legitimacy for his presidential authority. The second center of political influence was the opposition to Zamek: the Political Council (1949-54) and later the Council of the Three (1954-72), both based on prewar Polish political parties, which rejected the authority of Zaleski. Last, but not least, Stanisław Mikołajczyk's Polski Narodowy Komitet Demokratyczny (PNKD, Polish National Democratic Committee), active from 1950 onward, gathered some of the PSL, SD, and SP politicians (mostly settled in the United States) and, according to its creators, presented a democratic alternative to the other two political émigré centers.[3]

The diaspora was greatly concerned with the internal divisions within the government in exile, which was expected to represent the interests of the Polish nation as well as those of the émigrés. Any attempts at unification of the government were greeted with enthusiasm, and pressure to negotiate in good faith came from many different directions. Throughout the early 1950s, several émigré leaders took on this challenge, including the popular generals Władysław Anders and Marian Kukiel, but their efforts failed.[4] In the United States, some exiles were directly involved in the government's politics. For example, when in late 1951 President Zaleski appointed a new Rada Narodowa (National Council), eleven of its seventy-six members lived in the United States. The Political Council also had separate chapters in the United States and France.[5] American Polonia, reluctant to become entangled in exile politics, continued to keep its distance; but in August 1951 the PAC, too, appealed—albeit in vain—for the creation of a broad representation of "free Poles" from the government, the Political Council, and Mikolajczyk's group.

Strong incentives for unification came from the American government, which planned on playing East and Central European émigré politics as a card in the Cold War. The main agency active in émigré politics was the National Committee for a Free Europe (NCFE; in Polish, Komitet Wolnej Europy, KWE). The KWE, established in June 1949, officially was a private, apolitical organization intended to provide support for democratic leaders in exile. In fact, however, most of its funds and directives came straight from the CIA and the State Department.[6] Under KWE guidance, all émigré groups representing exiles from behind the Iron Curtain—except Poles—formed National Councils in Exile. The divisions within the Polish group proved insurmountable. Because no single existing political body had gained the KWE's approval, at the end of 1951 the KWE directly approached various Polish leaders in order to put pressure on them to establish a unified political representation. The American maneuvers strongly underscored the urgency of the situation, but were not enough to force an agreement.[7]

General Kazimierz Sosnkowski, living in Canada, became a political figure whose prestige, popularity, and political skill propelled him to undertake a new attempt at unification. After a successful visit in the United States, where, at the height of the Korean War, presidential candidates Dwight D. Eisenhower and Adlai Stevenson had received him, Sosnkowski arrived in London in December 1952. While the diaspora watched with hope, Sosnkowski engaged in a series of political talks. As a result, in mid-May 1953 Zaleski announced his resignation, effective June 1954, after the expiration of his seven-year term. In the spring of 1954 representatives of Polish political parties signed the so-called *Akt Zjednoczenia* (Act of Unification), vowing to cooperate within the government and the new Rada Jedności Narodowej (Council of National Unity). The diaspora greeted the signing of the act with an outpouring of support and enthusiasm, expecting Sosnkowski to be Zaleski's replacement. Despite his previous promise, however, Zaleski changed his mind and decided to remain in office, and his newly appointed government rejected the Act of Unification. In response, pro-unification politicians created the Tymczasowa Rada Jedności Narodowej (Provisional Council of National Unity) and appointed the Rada Trzech, which was to act in the capacity of an executive office. In August 1954 Tomasz Arciszewski, Władysław Anders, and Edward Raczyński began their term as the new opposition triumvirate.[8] The split within the Polish government in exile was final. It continued until Zaleski's death in 1972.

Despite the distractions of internal quarrels and altercations, in the early 1950s the émigré circles undertook a number of initiatives designed to bring the Polish question to the attention of the Western powers. The initiatives had a mostly European basis and character. Polish émigré politicians voiced their concerns over the safety of Poland's western borders with Germany as well as what they perceived as a continual German threat. Some advocated the creation of a union of nations behind the Iron Curtain to counteract Soviet influence in this part of Europe. During the Korean War, Polish politicians probed the possibility of forming a Polish military force in exile. Most such initiatives were limited to talks with Western officials, if access to them became available, and to the filing of official notes and memoranda, including some presented to the United Nations. Some initiatives, however, clearly went astray, as did the so-called Berg affair of 1950 to 1952 or the controversial Operation Spotlight between 1954 and 1956.[9]

Some U.S.-based Polish émigrés became active in two competing groups created in 1951 by exiles from nations behind the Iron Curtain: the Conference of Eastern and Central European Countries, led by the Slovak politician

Juraj Slavik, and the Committee of Central and Eastern Europe, led by a Hungarian, Ferenc Nagy. In 1954 the two organizations combined to form the United National Committees and Councils in Exile. Within days the KWE, determined to have full control over exile politics, created the Assembly of Captive European Nations (ACEN). ACEN received wide press coverage, and its representatives enjoyed access to high government officials in the United States. ACEN's sessions were concurrent with those of the United Nations, and the UN became the main target of ACEN's resolutions and memoranda.[10] The real political influence of ACEN and other representations of Eastern and Central European exiles proved, however, illusory and remained only symbolic.

A more consequential creation of the KWE was Radio Free Europe (RFE; in Polish, Radio Wolna Europa, RWE). Its Polish desk (since 1952 based in Munich, Germany, and led by Jan Nowak-Jeziorański) produced programs that could be heard all over the world, including Poland. In time, RFE became one of the most powerful centers of opinion making in the entire Polish diaspora, cooperating with many recognized politicians, leaders, and intellectuals in exile.[11] Paris-based *Kultura*, a monthly edited by Jerzy Giedroyć and other preeminent Polish émigré journalists, became another significant center of political and cultural influence. *Kultura* and its editors presented political opinions independent from any party line and often challenged the views of the *nieprzejednani* (the indomitable) in London. *Kultura* distinguished itself by displaying far-reaching expertise in international affairs and demonstrating greater sensitivity toward the changing needs of the Polish nation in Poland.[12]

Although the influence of the Polish émigré political opinion-making centers in Europe was definitely the strongest, the United States remained an exceptionally important area for at least two major reasons. First, the United States' role in the Cold War made it the most desirable ally in émigré politics. Second, the American government proved to be the most willing to use exile politicians in its Cold War strategy. The Polish American Congress dominated relationships with and representation before the American administration and society. Polish émigré political organizations, although numerically rather small, strove to achieve visibility within Polonia and vied for influence within the PAC. Mikołajczyk's early successes were challenged by the New York-based Political Council, whose leaders were invited as guest speakers to the third national convention of the PAC in Atlantic City in 1952.[13] NiD, as a new party distancing itself from prewar politics, also gained acceptance by American Polonia, including the PAC's influential Charles Rozmarek.[14] Generally, the nuances of émigré politics were of no real concern to average Polish Americans or to their leaders, who frequently and publicly criticized London's infighting. The exiled politicians understood that, in order to be effective in the United States—unlike in the diaspora's other countries of settlement—political initiatives had to be supported by the entire American Polonia.

The escalating Cold War provided particularly favorable conditions. For example, in the early 1950s stories of daring Polish pilots who defected from Poland in Soviet-built planes electrified the Polish-American community. In each case, the pilot received a hero's welcome and was sponsored to remain in America under political asylum. The reception of escapees from behind the Iron Curtain gave American Polonia the opportunity to manifest its anticommunism and support for the politics of the United States.[15]

As some authors have observed, "the anticommunist impulse, while it could exploit fears of a foreign conspiracy and produce administrative, legislative, and judicial action aimed at aliens, did not flow primarily along nativist channels."[16] Instead, the influx of new immigrants of Central and Eastern European origin, themselves victims of communism and Soviet expansionism, provided ethnic groups with a cadre of "veritable trenchermen" attempting to "move the United States toward a policy of facing down the Russians and liberating Eastern Europe."[17] While the Polish-American left suffered greatly during this period and never again resumed its position within Polonia, most Poles and Polish Americans who openly declared their vehement anticommunism moved toward the American mainstream. In perspective, the mood of anticommunism and McCarthyite zeal "offered many immigrants the means to scale the walls of ethnic prejudice" and made "joining the Cold War consensus . . . the surest means of affirming their patriotism."[18]

The Katyń Massacre investigation became one of the issues that in the early 1950s unified American Polonia and gave it, at least for a brief period, political visibility and clout. The PAC, led by Rozmarek, sponsored the action, with the participation and support of new immigrants whose testimony about Soviet crimes and atrocities was crucial. The hard-line anticommunist course that Rozmarek adopted on the Katyń issue was exactly the type of political involvement that many exiles considered a top priority for American Polonia.

According to historian Robert Szymczak, the Katyń case "became an inflammatory if short-lived Cold War issue and a potentially destructive weapon in the American propaganda arsenal against the Soviet Union in the early 1950s."[19] For American Polonia, the Katyń issue continued to signify the criminal methods and treachery of the Soviets, on the one hand, and the unwillingness of the American State Department to open and utilize the case, on the other. Despite some attempts to gain attention for the Katyń issue in the early 1940s, the massacre began to evoke public interest only in 1948, perhaps due to the publication of memoirs by Arthur Bliss Lane, Stanisław Mikołajczyk, and Jan Ciechanowski, as well as local and ethnic newspaper reports recounting the experiences of Poles who survived Soviet captivity and arrived in the United States under the DP Act. The veterans organizations, particularly the Polish Association of Former Soviet Political Prisoners, headquartered in London, contributed to the task by compiling records related to the war in Poland. The much-publicized visits of Polish military and political leaders, like generals Władysław Anders, Tadeusz Bór-Komorowski, and Kazimierz Sosnkowski, who toured major Polonia communities and received heroes' welcomes everywhere, also revived the Katyń issue and spurred Polonia into action.[20]

In 1949 the PAC obtained the support of some Congressional leaders, who spearheaded the campaign to renew interest in the Katyń affair. The efforts of the private American Committee for the Investigation of the Katyń Massacre (led by Arthur Bliss Lane), publications by *New York Herald-Tribune* journalist Julius Epstein, and, finally, congressional bills calling for the investigation of the crime at Katyń resulted in the formation of a congressional committee to conduct a full investigation in 1951. The committee's work included the collection of documents and the testimony of numerous witnesses, both within the United States and in Europe. An interim report, issued in July 1952, concluded beyond any doubt that the Soviet NKVD was responsible for the execution of fifteen thousand Polish officers and soldiers in the spring of 1940. The PAC, claiming victory for the Polish-American community in exposing the Soviets and vindicating Katyń victims, directed the matter further to the United Nations. As the political situation changed, however, both the petition and all the Katyń materials became stranded again and never received any serious consideration from the Eisenhower administration.[21]

The major beneficiary of Polish-American anticommunism—so visible in the Katyń massacre investigation—was the Republican party, which in early 1951 organized an Ethnic Origins Division and a Foreign Language Group Activities unit headed by Arthur Bliss Lane, former ambassador to Poland. Lane, convinced of the significance of the ethnic and especially Polish-American vote for Republican victory, was instrumental in placing the issue of Yalta at the center of the Republican foreign politics agenda. He pushed the "repudiate Yalta" slogan and promoted a liberation—as opposed to containment—policy for Eastern Europe. Republican propaganda found its way into the Polish-American press and was featured in speeches, leaflets, and political advertisements paid for by the Republican National Committee. Blaming Yalta and Katyń on the Democrats was easier, however, than selling General Eisenhower as a presidential candidate. Among the most serious objections to Eisenhower was his responsibility for the forced repatriation of Russian and Ukrainian prisoners of war and displaced persons to the Soviet Union during his service in Europe as Allied supreme commander. Nevertheless, swayed by Republican promises and propaganda, more than half of Polish-American voters supported Eisenhower in 1952, and the defection of Polonia from the Democratic fold that year might have been a significant factor in the Republican victory.[22]

The death of Stalin at the beginning of 1953 brought a great number of changes in the Soviet Union, spearheaded by the new prime minister, Georgi Malenkov, and by Party Secretary Nikita Khrushchev. An amnesty allowed hundreds of thousands of political prisoners to return home, and economic plans were restructured to incorporate the production of consumer goods. The Korean War came to an end, and the Kremlin renewed diplomatic relations with Yugoslavia's General Tito. The beginnings of the thaw could also be felt in other countries behind the Iron Curtain. In Poland, even though the Stalinist system remained intact until October 1956, some changes were still possible prior to that date. For example, the collectivization campaign in agriculture was slowed down, and in 1954 the ill-famed Ministry of Security was abolished and its director, Stanisław Radkiewicz, dismissed. Polish communist leader Władysław Gomułka was released from house arrest, and censorship was relaxed. While Nikita Khrushchev gradually solidified power in the Soviet Union, a similar liberalization took also place in Hungary and Czechoslovakia.[23]

Using this liberalization as a propaganda hook, in 1954 Moscow initiated an energetic campaign to persuade political émigrés from Central and Eastern Europe to return home. This action concentrated mostly on the intelligentsia and political leaders. In Poland, both radio and the press featured appeals for return dressed up in patriotic and national rhetoric. The Communist Party's authorities adopted an elaborate plan to encourage the returns. In early 1955 Towarzystwo Łączności z Wychodźstwem Polskim "Polonia" (Association for Cooperation with Polish Emigration "Polonia") was established to facilitate the development of cultural relationships with Polonia. A separate committee, also formed at that time, was to coordinate repatriation.[24] Beginning in July 1955, a special radio station, Kraj (Homeland), began broadcasting programs for Poles abroad.[25] Private contacts with the West lost the stigma of treason and Poles were allowed to reestablish relationships with their relatives abroad without fear of persecution. The liberalization of passport laws allowed many more Poles to travel to the West to visit their families there. Attractive offers of organized holiday tours to Poland were presented to the émigré communities.[26]

In the summer of 1955 the pressure to repatriate intensified. Kraj broadcasted an open letter inviting all émigrés to return to the homeland and to join in the work of rebuilding Poland. More than forty Polish intellectuals representing different ends of the political and cultural spectrum signed the letter, copies of which were subsequently widely distributed through Polish diplomatic institutions. The letter caused a stir in Polish émigré circles, whose members commented on its content and significance. They objected particularly strongly to a conciliatory quotation from a speech by the Communist Party first secretary, Bolesław Bierut—"We do not remember and do not want to remember committed faults and transgressions"—as no one felt that emigracja had been guilty of any.[27]

Repatriation pressure provoked a number of responses from the exiles. First, the Polish section of the KWE succeeded in persuading its American employers that in order to counteract potential defections by Polish intellectuals, a number of them needed to receive financial support that would allow them to survive in the West. The energetic communist repatriation propaganda was clearly proof that "Poles in the West are apparently an important card, which should not be downplayed." As a result, a quarter-million dollars was approved for stipends for artists and intellectuals in greatest need of funds.[28] Second, the KWE's Polish section successfully turned the tables on the repatriation issue and called for the return of Poles, who had been illegally imprisoned in the Soviet Union since the end of World War II. During a mass rally in Manchester, England, seven thousand Polish exiles who reaffirmed their loyalty to the exile mission also pledged never to forget their brethren in Russia. As a result of those actions and energetic diplomatic lobbying, in 1956 and 1957 more than one hundred thousand Poles were allowed to return to Poland from the Soviet Union.[29]

Kultura's editorial board responded to the invitation to return by publishing an open letter addressed to those who had signed the original appeal. In it, they invited their counterparts in Poland to an open discussion and a meeting at Maison Lafitte, the seat of *Kultura* in France. Predictably, neither a dialogue nor a meeting of any kind followed, exposing the communist scheme. More importantly, however, *Kultura*'s reaction foretold its future program of engaging Poland's intellectuals and probing opportunities for a gradual change, a stance differing from the inflexible position of London.[30]

Not all exiles rejected the communist overtures. Lured by propaganda, dissatisfied with the attitude of the West, or tormented by nostalgia, a small number of recognized Polish diaspora writers, intellectuals, and politicians took advantage of the political thaw and decided to return to Poland permanently. The group of returnees from the United States included politician-journalists Klaudiusz Hrabyk and Franciszek Szwajdler and writers Melchior Wańkowicz, Teodor Parnicki, and Zofia Kossak-Szczucka. The return of two former prime ministers of the government in exile, Hugon Hanke in 1955 and Stanisław Mackiewicz in 1956, had a particularly scandalous and discrediting character.[31]

The scale and rules of contact with Poland became a hotly debated topic. In the United States, tourist traffic to Poland increased significantly as Polonia traveled to visit their relatives. Although no one challenged the right of private persons to travel to Poland, tours organized with the cooperation of the Polish authorities drew much fire. According to some critics, these tours were propaganda ploys designed to dupe Polish Americans into believing in communist progress in Poland. On numerous occasions, different organizations of both Old and New Polonia repeated the warning against the tours first issued by the PAC convention in Philadelphia.³² The issue received so much attention and exposure that even during Rozmarek's 1956 visit to the White House, President Eisenhower reportedly showed concern about the popularity of organized tours to Poland and inquired about Polonia's increased contacts with the old country.³³

The year 1955 marked a noticeable warming trend in diplomatic relations between the East and the West as they entered a period of détente. After the 1955 Geneva summit between Eisenhower and Khrushchev, a number of other meetings followed: the foreign ministers' summit in the fall of 1955, and the visit of Khrushchev and Soviet prime minister Nikolai Bulganin in London in April 1956. The Cold War seemed to be getting warmer as old enemies were shaking hands and smiling for the photo opportunities of international press agencies. Polish government in exile and some of the political parties in exile did not fail to demand the inclusion of the Polish issue in these talks. Memoranda to this end found their way both to the White House and to the desks of other Western heads of state. Poles organized well-attended press conferences and cooperated with representatives of other nations from behind the Iron Curtain to gain publicity for their cause.³⁴ Despite the assurances of President Eisenhower and Secretary of State John Foster Dulles, however, the issue of freedom for captive nations was not placed on the agenda of the international negotiations.

In April 1956, during an official visit by Khrushchev and Bulganin in London, Polish exiles organized a large political demonstration. More than twenty thousand people participated in a silent march protesting Poland's subjugation and demanding freedom for Poland and other countries in Central and Eastern Europe, amnesty for Poles in Russia, the return of Poland's eastern territories, the release of Stefan Cardinal Wyszyński from house arrest, and an investigation of the Katyń Massacre. The demonstration received wide coverage in both the British and international press, including Polish-American newspapers, and strengthened the exiles' political resolve. Although most of their demands had no chance of realization, they succeeded in keeping the issue of Poland's independence alive. In the short run, however, two of these demands were met: Cardinal Wyszyński regained his freedom, and, as noted above, Poles in the Soviet Union were allowed to return home.³⁵

Communist repatriation pressures and the consequences of détente prompted some rethinking of the exile mission; both the émigrés and Polonia felt threatened and called for a closing of ranks. For example, the New York State division of the PAC announced: "We live in a period of a great offensive by all communist governments and regimes, which, following orders from Moscow, now have the goal of liquidating the political emigrations of all countries from behind the Iron Curtain." The unity within émigré and Polonia circles therefore was becoming "a moral obligation," as was the duty to warn the American government against the treachery of the Soviets, whose thaw was nothing but an illusion and manipulation of the West.[36] In September 1955 Klaudiusz Hrabyk published in New York's *Nowy Świat* a provocative article entitled "Sixteen Years after September [1939]." The article was one of the first comprehensive reevaluations of the achievements and goals of the exile mission during the period following the war. Since Yalta, Hrabyk reasoned, the exiles had been counting on a military conflict between the East and West, which could deprive Russia of its control over Poland. By 1955, however, any hopes for a third world war had disappeared, and the spirit of the Geneva summit between Eisenhower and Khrushchev brought the two superpowers into a period of closer cooperation. With each passing year, Hrabyk continued, the emigration's claim to speak for the homeland weakened. The émigrés needed to acknowledge that their political program had failed, to reexamine their mission, and to end the isolation between them and their compatriots in Poland. At this early date, however, Hrabyk's approach received neither popular support nor even much attention from other publicists, except for Zdzisław Stahl of London's *Orzeł Biały*, who harshly criticized Hrabyk's point of view.[37]

1956

Hrabyk's argument was just a prelude to a broader debate that erupted in 1956, prompted by political events in Poland and in the rest of the world. In February 1956 Khrushchev's secret speech to the Twentieth Party Congress denounced Stalinism. Although the *New York Times* published the speech only at the beginning of June, giving rise to an international sensation, the full text had been in unofficial circulation in Poland since almost immediately after the Polish delegation had returned from Moscow. In March news about Polish First Secretary Władysław Bierut's sudden death while in

Moscow shocked Poles, giving rise to speculation about the cause of his death. Edward Ochab replaced Bierut, and some of the most hated *apparatchiks* were pushed out of the party hierarchy. At the same time, internal conflicts within the party's leadership intensified as power-hungry factions vied for influence. The thaw continued with the release of about thirty thousand more political prisoners.[38] The amnesty, an official repudiation of Stalinism, and open frictions in the highest echelons of the party structure were viewed by the politically and economically repressed Polish nation as important and welcome changes.

American Polonia followed the situation in Poland with interest, but was unable fully to comprehend the changes seen through the Cold War lenses. Even the more sophisticated political analysts were both confused and distrustful of the real significance of the thaw. Changes in the party's leadership, the amnesty, greater openness, and especially increased contacts with families in Poland were, of course, greeted with gladness. But questions remained about the true intentions behind the limited improvements. Was the thaw just a foreign policy ploy from Moscow, designed to lull the vigilance of the West? Would the Kremlin recall the temporary achievements and return to full control of Polish society or perhaps allow the spread of Titoism? Or worse yet—was the thaw an "evil trick" to expose critics of the system and then get rid of them? In any case, the role of Emigracja and Polonia seemed to remain intact and focused on the increased political vigilance and work for Poland's full independence, because "even looser-fitting chains would always clank on the hands."[39]

In the early months of 1956, the Polish postwar diaspora celebrated the raising of the flag on a new ship, the SS *Wolna Polska* (Free Poland). The ship belonged to the Pulaski Transport Line, a shipping company owned by Polish-American entrepreneurs. Escapees from communist Poland made up nearly half of the crew. The ceremonies in New York Harbor attracted close to two thousand people and featured speeches by American officials, Polish-American congressmen and clergy, and numerous other representatives of Polonia. The symbolism of the SS *Wolna Polska* corresponded with the goals of the exile mission, and the connection was not lost on those present; for example, Congressman Tadeusz Machrowicz of Detroit concluded his speech with a call: "Prowadź Boże Wolną Polskę do wolnej Polski!" (God, lead *Wolna Polska* to a free Poland!). Other commentators saw the ship and her crew as emissaries carrying to the world a message about Poland's desire for freedom.⁴⁰ Throughout the entire year the press regularly reported on the itinerary of the SS *Wolna Polska,* and Captain Jan Ćwiklinski was an invited guest and speaker at many special occasions.

The Polish-language press in the United States also regularly informed American Polonia about new developments in the rest of the diaspora, particularly in London. When at the beginning of 1956 the Provisional Council of National Unity initiated the process of adopting the constitutional functions of the office of the president, the split in the government in exile and excessive political infighting drew even more criticism.⁴¹ PAC dignitaries struck a familiar note of renunciation and warning, cautioning against "cracks in the edifice of our Polonian society" resulting from "party conflicts among political exiles in London." They expressed disgust and shame, and sternly advised against transplanting political infighting onto American soil.⁴²

Although the PAC worked to distance itself from party politics, its official program closely resembled goals of the exile mission adhered to by the *niezłomni* from London. The best example was the May 3rd Polish Constitution Day celebration in Chicago in 1956. This annual gala, coming just weeks after the impressive April silent march in Great Britain, gathered an estimated one hundred thousand participants. A resolution adopted by the gathering listed familiar demands: the release of Poles in the Soviet Union, the freeing of Cardinal Wyszyński, and an investigation of the Katyń Massacre. Rozmarek's speech rang with Cold War rhetoric at its best when he called for the repudiation of Yalta and vowed to lead the fight against communism "as the worst enemy of humanity." Rozmarek also directly addressed Poles in Poland, assuring them that "American Polonia remembers Poland" and would continue to work for the cause of her freedom and safety. The exiles' presence in Chicago was noticeable. The delegation of the Polish section of Radio Free Europe recorded Rozmarek's address to broadcast it to the Polish nation. Representatives of the exiles' organizations marched in the parade, and General Anders, as one of the guests of honor, gave a rousing speech.⁴³

General Anders's presence in Chicago, as well as his visit to Washington, D.C., and meetings with President Eisenhower and a number of congressional leaders, did not pass without controversy.⁴⁴ American Polonia saw Anders in a dual role: as a decorated war hero on the one hand, and one of the leaders of the opposition Provisional Council of National Unity on the other. While acknowledging Anders's wartime exploits as commander in chief of the Polish Second Corps, pro-Zaleski Polish Americans could not accept his political views and considered him a symbol of the destructive discord within the government in exile.[45]

The issue of relationship between American Polonia and the politics of the government in exile came to a head again at the fourth national convention of the Polish American Congress, which took place in Philadelphia between May 30 and June 1, 1956. During preconvention preparations, numerous voices repeatedly called for a display of unity on the part of American Polonia and a rejection of political divisions characteristic of London.[46] The convention delegates abided by those sentiments. Despite some supporters' efforts to stage a speech by Adam Ciołkosz, a politician connected to Provisional Council of National Unity, the majority of delegates did not consent to any political speeches. General Anders, who had stayed in the United States to participate in the convention, was greeted with enthusiasm and allowed to speak, but only as "a soldier and hero of Monte Cassino," and not as a politician.[47]

By the end of the convention, close to a thousand PAC delegates had adopted two resolutions. The first one delineated the PAC's program for the future. Its major part focused on Poland and foreign politics. It included a call for freedom for captive nations, a guarantee of Poland's western border, the return of eastern lands to Poland, German reparations for wartime slave laborers, and the release of political prisoners. The convention obliged the PAC leadership to lobby both the Democratic and Republican parties to embrace the politics of liberation toward Russia's satellites in an opportune presidential election year. It also called on the American representatives to the United Nations to address the issues of Katyń, political prisoners, slave labor, free elections, and the persecution of the Roman Catholic Church in Poland. "Let's walk together," the declaration continued, "carrying high the banners of America and Poland." In its concluding section, the resolution returned to the issue of the split in the government in exile. It reaffirmed the resolution adopted at the PAC convention of 1952, in which the delegates had appealed "to the entire Polish political emigration" to make way for "harmonious cooperation and, overlooking insignificant differences, for the creation of a common front in the struggle for Poland's independence."[48] The domestic part of the PAC program was much more limited. It reminded Polonians of the need to support Polish "culture, language, and spirit" in America, to cooperate within the PAC, and to lobby for the overhaul of discriminatory immigration and naturalization laws. The resolution also warned American Polonia against participation in organized tours to Poland and cautioned the exiles against return to the communist-controlled country. The final warning was against "communist penetration, Titoism, or so-called national communism, and against the '*odwilż*.'"[49]

The second resolution spoke directly to the Polish nation. In it, the PAC clarified its opinion on the source of changes in Poland. "Despite the temporary thaw declared in Moscow, you are still separated from us by the Iron Curtain," read the resolution. "Hear us through the barriers of false propaganda set up by unwelcome protectors pretending to discard obedience to the Soviets!" The resolution also referred to "clever appeals" written under the control of the same "unwelcome protectors," a clear allusion to the repatriation letter by Polish intellectuals. The role of Polonia was to be the voice of the silenced nation, demanding justice and freedom in the international arena; the Polish nation was to continue its "spiritual resistance," refraining from "hasty actions"(*nieprzemyślane wystąpienia*), which might result in "great losses and casualties." "We believe," the resolution read further, "that . . . you will survive the period of odwilż, as you have survived the period of terror, and that you will not be provoked by the butchers now pretending to be lambs." Finally, rejecting the idea of the government in exile and the return of political parties to take over power in a communist-free Poland, the PAC resolution concluded: "We know that although you desire freedom, you do not want to return to the past with its many mistakes and faults. . . . Do not believe that the emigration [*emigracja*] intends to force upon you any specific political systems."[50]

In May 1956 Old Polonia and the New Emigration, represented by the PAC, formulated its own mission focused on the homeland. The PAC program adopted all the major elements of the larger exile mission, including the *imponderabilia:* the rejection of communism, a call for Poland's independence, guarantees of the western borders, and the return of the eastern territories lost to the Soviet Union after the war, as well as some related issues, such as Katyń, the persecution of the church, and the return of prisoners. There were, however, some important differences. Although the program did not explicitly challenge the symbolic role of constitutional legalism and historical continuity as represented by the government in exile, the PAC rejected its claim to leadership in the struggle for Poland. Open criticism of party squabbles, a call for unity, and, most importantly, the political choice presented to the Polish nation in the future strongly emphasized the PAC's detachment from London and suggested its own claims to leadership. This special position stemmed as much from tradition as from America's superpower status in the Cold War and Polonia's belief in its own potential to influence American foreign policy and to lobby the United Nations. The PAC's centrality in the struggle for Poland gained support and acknowledgment from the communities of the larger postwar diaspora: the convention received hundreds of telegrams from Polish organizations in Europe, Africa, South America, and Australia. Recognizing the Cold War political reality, émigré Poles scattered around the globe manifested their acceptance of the PAC's version of the exile mission.[51] In regard to Poland, the PAC's program did not stray from the universal belief that the thaw was to be distrusted. The PAC continued to cast itself as a spokesperson for the oppressed nation, a notion that within weeks would undergo a crucial test.

Even before the events in Poland captured Polonia's attention, the intellectual circles of the exiles had been disturbed by distressing news about the Congress of Free Polish Culture planned for June 1956 in Paris. PIASA, headed by Oskar Halecki and Stanisław Strzetelski, provided leadership for the organization of the congress, but the event was to be quietly sponsored and financed by the KWE—a solution hardly acceptable to some participants. The main goals of the congress were reevaluating the situation of Polish culture after a decade of emigration and charting plans for the future. Recognized intellectuals and artists from all the countries of the diaspora pledged their participation in this event, which promised to be an important display of the diaspora's intellectual strength.[52] Despite initial enthusiasm, support for the congress gradually waned amidst embarrassing quarrels and divisions. For example, Klaudiusz Hrabyk published an open letter resigning from participation in the congress and protesting its financing by American money, which, according to him, would prevent its full independence. Melchior Wańkowicz generated another scandal by accepting a ticket to Paris from congress organizers and then flying instead to Poland, ostensibly to collect materials for a new book and to negotiate publication of some of his earlier works there. The congress was postponed, first till September, but then the entire plan was quietly abandoned.[53]

On June 8, 1956, Jan Lechoń committed suicide in New York City, jumping from a hotel window. As grief-stricken crowds gathered at the poet's funeral, the leading Skamandryta's death seemed to acquire a broader, symbolic dimension. The thousands who filled the New York streets witnessed not only the personal tragedy of an individual, but also the passing of the brightest star in the Polish poetic pantheon. Lechoń's literary output as well as his cultural activities in exile represented a symbolic continuum between the culture of prewar Poland and that of the postwar diaspora. With his death, this intangible connection was irretrievably lost. Some Polish-language newspapers saw the poet's unfortunate death as a symbol of his ultimate patriotism, but also of his disappointment and despair. Commentaries pointed to Lechoń's letter, in which the poet allegedly criticized both the inactivity and divisions within the diaspora and the indifference of the West to the plight of Poland.[54]

Poznań

Events in Poland, however, stole the world's attention in the summer of 1956. At the end of June 1956, the city of Poznań in western Poland witnessed two days of riots, when the workers of the locomotive factory demonstrated in the streets under banners that read "Bread and Freedom" and "Russians Go Home." The riots were quickly overpowered by militia forces, which killed seventy-five people and injured about eight hundred others.

American Polonia did not find out about the revolution in Poznań from the Polish-language press until a few days after the events. The first reports were confusing and often inaccurate. The number of victims and the magnitude of the repression were usually exaggerated. Some American tourists and businesspeople in Poland (Poznań was hosting an international economic fair known as Targi Poznańskie) reported no knowledge about the riots. As more confirmed information flowed to the United States, the tragedy in Poznań became clearer.[55]

Polonia's first response to the Poznań revolution focused on a display of solidarity with the Polish nation. Rozmarek and the PAC, as well as many other organizations, immediately issued statements and resolutions and organized mass rallies and demonstrations. Most of the resolutions heralded the bravery of Poles and demanded that the U.S. government condemn the massacre and place it under UN investigation. The resolution adopted during the protest rally organized by the Illinois state division of the PAC on July 6, 1956, criticized détente and warned that, if America failed to react, the captive European nations would lose their trust in its power forever.[56] The Polish National Alliance's resolution called on all PNA groups to send letters and telegrams to their senators and congressmen, as well as to the president and Department of State, demanding action to "hasten [Poland's] release from the Bolshevik yoke."[57] The same appeal came from rank-and-file individuals, who saw intervention with local legislators as the most effective way of registering Polonia's voice.[58] A resolution passed at a rally in Milwaukee asked the American government and the United Nations to sponsor free elections in Poland and to "take all possible diplomatic measures to prevent mass reprisals."[59] President Rozmarek's office sent out a press release to about five hundred American newspapers cautioning that "[w]hat happened to Poland and other Iron Curtain countries will happen to the United States, unless our government organizes the anticommunist world for the rescue of liberty."[60]

Following the events in Poznań, Polish Americans and exiles spoke with one voice. Both Old Polonia and New Emigration participated in demonstrations all over the country. On June 30, 1956, about one thousand people showed up for a rally in front of the United Nations building and the seat of the Soviet delegation to the UN in New York. Several new exile organizations, as well as SWAP and other Old Polonia organizations, sponsored the rally, led by Bolesław Budzyń, a new arrival.[61] General Tadeusz Bór-Komorowski, on a visit from London, became the main speaker at the PAC rally in Chicago as well as one in Buffalo, New York.[62] Rallies continued throughout the summer, always attracting large crowds; according to press reports, more than a thousand people participated in each of the rallies in Jersey City, Elizabeth, and Perth Amboy in New Jersey; three thousand showed up in St. Michael's Cathedral in Springfield, Massachusetts; and close to fifteen hundred came to the rally held by the Polish Immigration Committee in Budd Lake, New York. The programs of such rallies were filled with patriotic speeches and artistic performances, which wove together Polish and American accents and built on the history of Polonia as well as on that of the exiles.[63] Representatives of both immigrant waves also came together at numerous church services for the victims of the Poznań massacre.[64]

While rallies, masses, and demonstrations still were taking place and the Cold War rhetoric ran strong, Rozmarek and the PAC were planning what was potentially the most effective campaign on behalf of Poland. In order to affect American foreign policy in a presidential election year, the task was to place the issue of Poland on both party platforms and to play the card of Polonia votes. The events in Poznań gave the PAC useful momentum and visibility. After the disappointment suffered by Polonia, mobilized to vote Republican in 1952 by promises of the repudiation of Yalta and the "rolling back of communism" went unmet by the GOP, both parties had to look for new ways of attracting the Polish vote. Rozmarek was invited to speak before both party platform committees. On August 7, 1956, he appeared before the Democratic committee, once again calling for the rejection of Yalta, Poland's independence, free elections, and the guarantee of Polish western borders. On August 15, 1956, Rozmarek stood before the Republican committee, asking for a return to the politics of liberation. The inclusion of the passage about the need for withdrawal of the Soviet Army from Central and Eastern Europe and for United Nations–sponsored free elections in the Democratic Party platform later that month was heralded as PAC's achievement.[65] Neither of the parties, however, seemed to be able fully to capitalize on Polonia's political mobilization during and immediately after the Poznań crisis.

Responding to the events in Poznań, exiled Poles and Polish Americans also concentrated on the need for economic aid to Poland. The press broadly commented on the slogan seen on the Poznań workers' signs: "We want bread" (*Chcemy chleba*). Although there was no doubt that the riots were not entirely economically motivated, financial help seemed a pragmatic and effective way of showing concern for and solidarity with the Polish people. Just a few days after the Poznań events, a reader wrote to *Kuryer Polski* in Milwaukee: "I read about the Poznań riots with tears in my eyes. ... We have here all we need, but still chase more wealth, a new house, a new car. ... In the meantime our brothers and sisters across the ocean call "WE WANT BREAD." Will we remain deaf? ... Let us deny ourselves some luxuries and bring material help to our families, friends, those whom we know and even those whom we do not."[66]

Some newspapers printed desperate pleas from needy Poles and appealed for increased giving, and organizers of patriotic celebrations conducted collections during the ceremonies. Private help could flow even more easily because Poland had reduced duty rates on parcels from abroad.[67] The dire straits of the Polish economy and everyday hardships of the Polish people found frequent confirmation in the reports of Polish Americans who traveled to the homeland to visit their relatives. Accounts of those trips brought the Polish reality closer to the average Polonian reader and reaffirmed negative opinions about the harshness of life under communism.[68] In the fall of 1956, and especially after the new communist government in Poland openly admitted the desperate state of the Polish economy, Rozmarek actively lobbied in Washington for an aid program for Poland, which could "strengthen Poland and render her less dependent on Moscow."[69] Rozmarek's actions were fully supported by the London émigré circles, which on their own lobbied for the same cause.[70] The program, once established, brought some $588 million in U.S. loans, aid, and credits, until it was terminated by Congress in 1964. Liberalization in Poland also allowed Rada Polonii to revive its activities there, which had dwindled in the early 1950s. As a result of a trip to Poland by Rada leadership in 1958, the organization launched a new appeal to collect funds for the purchase of equipment needed by Polish hospitals and orphanages. After 1963 Rada led a successful program for the distribution of surplus food products in Poland, sponsored by the American government as part of a program that was finally terminated in 1970.[71]

Poznań prompted displays of support and solidarity from representatives of other nations from behind the Iron Curtain. For example, a rally organized by the Russian-American Union in New York City to honor the victims of Poznań featured speeches by both Russian and Armenian activists and by representatives of Polish-American organizations. Representatives of the Latvian, Lithuanian, Hungarian, Bulgarian, Estonian, and Russian diasporas spoke during a rally at the Polish National Home in New York. Ukrainian, Lithuanian, Czech, Slovak, Hungarian, Romanian, Latvian, and Serbian delegations were also present during a memorial service for the workers slain in Poznań, celebrated by Bishop John Michael McNamara in St. Matthew's Cathedral in Washington, D.C.[72]

Response to the Poznań massacre in other countries of the diaspora differed little from that of American Polonia. From London to Chile and Argentina, massive rallies demonstrated the émigrés' concern for the homeland, churches filled with those praying for the victims, and funds were collected to aid the persecuted and their families. In London, political centers issued resolutions calling on Poles to remain calm and prudent and to avoid unnecessary bloodshed. The Council of National Unity pledged to the workers of Poznań that it would do "everything possible to make the free world realize the meaning of your actions."[73] President August Zaleski issued a statement to the Polish nation, calling for restraint and cautioning against communist provocation that could only weaken the nation. "I do not doubt," he wrote, "that a time will come when the liberation will be possible. At that moment, the legal and constitutional authorities of the Republic of Poland (Rzeczpospolita Polska), which carefully observe the world situation from abroad, will themselves appeal for action in the country. Until this time, conserve your strength."[74] The events in Poznań electrified and mobilized the exiles, who found a determination to fight for Poland from abroad. The recognition of anticommunist trends within the repressed nation made the émigrés feel much closer to their compatriots behind the Iron Curtain.[75] At the same time, however, the vexing question of the relevance of the government in exile and the role of émigré authorities in Poland's reality loomed large on the horizon. Polish workers in Poznań had demanded bread and justice and chanted anti-Soviet slogans, but had not called for the return of the legal government from London. Zygmunt Zaremba wrote in France: "The events [in Poznań] rendered false the belief—popular among the emigration, but naïve—that the homeland is some kind of soulless combination of human bodies, which could care only about 'biological survival' during hard times, while the thought and soul of the nation resides in the exile community. How much of the childish arrogance of this belief has the Poznań outburst exposed! Life, the real life of the nation, . . . is there. And only there."[76]

For the first time since the end of the war, the mission of the diaspora had been seriously challenged, but the exiles hardly had time to reflect on it, as the summer and fall brought new tensions in the international situation. Much attention focused on the Suez Canal and the crisis in the Middle East as the next place of potential East-West confrontation. In Poland the communists staged show trials of Poznań riot participants at the end of September, covered attentively by the Polonian press. In the United States, the pre-election campaign was in full swing. No one expected that the eventful year 1956 had still more in store.

Polish October and its Aftermath

On October 19, 1956, when the Central Committee of the Communist Party gathered for its eighth plenum in Warsaw, a plane from Moscow brought unexpected guests, including Khrushchev himself and a score of other high party officials and generals. At the same time, Soviet military forces stationed on Polish soil began moving toward Warsaw. The all-night conference between the Soviets and Polish party officials behind closed doors focused on impending changes in the Polish party leadership. As a result of frictions between competing factions, as well as pressure from the society, Władysław Gomułka, a Polish communist imprisoned during the Stalinist era, had gained power and support. Gomułka and his supporters were at the time perceived as "national communists" committed to finding Poland's "own road to Communism" and winning for Poland some degree of independence from the Kremlin. Reportedly, Gomułka stood up to Khrushchev on the matter of his upcoming election, while assuring the Soviet leadership of his loyalty to communist ideals. The Soviet delegation left Warsaw, and the eighth plenum elected Gomułka to the position of first secretary. A number of Stalinists were ousted from the political bureau of the party and removed from power. The threat of a major confrontation was averted. Gomułka strengthened his position amidst popular support and enthusiasm from Polish society. To the joy of Poland's Roman Catholics, Cardinal-Archbishop Stefan Wyszyński finally was released after three years of house arrest.[77]

The events of the Polish October were quickly overshadowed by the tragedy of the anti-Soviet movement in Hungary, which in the late fall of 1956 ended in Soviet military intervention and bloody suppression. Dissatisfied with the economic and political conditions in Hungary and encouraged by the Polish example, Hungarians began demonstrating against the repressive government of Stalinist leader Erö Gerö, demanding the return of the popular liberal Imre Nagy. Between October 23 and 26, after fighting off Soviet military units, revolutionary Hungarians took over Budapest and mobilized the rest of the country, responding to encouraging calls from the Hungarian section of Radio Free Europe. The demands of the people escalated, and on October 30 Nagy's government made a number of announcements, which, in practice, meant Hungary's independence from the Soviets and its withdrawal from the Warsaw Pact. The next day the Soviets began a full-fledged military intervention, which claimed the lives of three thousand Hungarians and left thousands more wounded. Harsh reprisals after the János Kádár regime restored peace but added to those numbers about two thousand executed and thousands more imprisoned and exiled.[78]

The Polish-American community in the United States rushed to show solidarity with the Hungarian nation. The Illinois division of the PAC, together with Niepodległość i Demokracja, organized the collection of money, medications, and warm clothing for the Hungarian freedom fighters and refugees. Referring to the traditional Polish-Hungarian friendship and historic ties, they appealed: "Polonia! The house of our Hungarian neighbor is on fire! We must help!"[79] *Nowy Świat* sponsored a collection of funds called *Serce Polonii* (Polonia's Heart); a check for one thousand dollars earmarked for aid to the Hungarians was then handed to the American Red Cross. The Polish Immigration Committee was involved in the resettlement of Hungarian freedom fighters, who arrived in the United States aboard the SS *Wolna Polska*. Their welcome in Philadelphia Harbor turned into a powerful demonstration attended by representatives of numerous Polish organizations and the public. The Polish-American press commented with approval on special immigration legislation that had allowed Hungarian refugees to enter the United States. And in London the Association of Polish Writers organized a meeting to show solidarity with Hungarian writers, which was well attended by both Polish and Hungarian exiles.[80]

The Polish October and the events in Hungary proved to be much more difficult for the diaspora to interpret than the Poznań uprising in June had been. Removed from the nuances of Polish politics, the émigrés found it hard to read the real meaning of the changes and the particular moods of the society. The Hungarian tragedy stunned and embittered them. Despite its assurances, the West had allowed Russia to drown the revolt in blood, proving the indifference of the West toward the struggle against communism. One commentator noted: "The three great crusaders of the free world watch Poland and Hungary in the same way that in the past England and France, both allied with Poland, watched Hitler take over Poland. . . . If today they could have brought themselves to some more energetic action, the communist 'imperium' would have fallen apart. But England has her Suez, France her Algeria, and the United States their elections. . . . It is doubtful that a chance like this would ever repeat itself."[81]

Against the background of the Hungarian bloodshed, the restraint of Poles was praised and greeted with relief. "The Polish Nation demonstrated a great political maturity," said Prime Minister Antoni Pająk during his speech in London, but compared the October changes to a revolt by prisoners who demand better living conditions, but who remain within the prison walls.[82] Despite widely expressed caution and suspicion about the significance and longevity of the changes, some positive outcomes of the Polish October were noticed, such as liberalization of economic, political, and cultural life in Poland.[83]

After the Polish October, the question of potential adjustments in the exile mission returned with full force; but opinions on the nature and degree of those adjustments varied as widely as did interpretations of those events. A more in-depth look into post-October attitudes reveals certain modifications in opinion and their impact on the exile mission. According to historian Anna Siwik, three basic attitudes dominated political thinking in the diaspora following October 1956.[84] The first approach assumed that nothing really had changed in Poland, which still remained under the communist yoke, and that the main goal of the exiles had to be an uncompromising struggle for Poland's full independence. This attitude was consistent with most pronouncements of the government in exile and the political parties and with their doctrinal stance of maximum demands (żądania maksymalne). Major London newspapers, like *Dziennik Polski i Dziennik Żołnierza*, *Orzeł Biały*, and *Wiadomości Literackie*, supported this point of view.[85] American Polonia, which had distrusted odwilż, now also generally distrusted Gomułka and *gomułkowszczyzna* (liberalization sponsored by Gomułka and his supporters). In an editorial entitled "Let's Not Be Deceived," the PNA weekly *Zgoda* wrote: "In the eyes of the uninformed, Władysław Gomułka could appear to be a national hero. That he is not. Gomułka is only a Polish communist. As Bierut was a communist, as Tito is one, too."[86]

But even the indomitable could not deny that the exile mission needed rethinking. After returning to Canada, in 1957 General Kazimierz Sosnkowski outlined a program for Polish political emigration. It emphasized the division of responsibilities between the Polish nation and the émigrés. "Our emigration—probably with the best of intentions, but in a completely improper manner— . . . tries to interfere in the Homeland's matters, to offer the Homeland advice, and to draw up directions for action," Sosnkowski declared. Émigrés did not have the right to instruct Poles in Poland without sharing in the suffering of the country, he added. At the same time, the exiles needed to guard themselves against the belief that the Polish question could be solved in Poland alone and that there was no real task left for political emigration abroad. Instead, Sosnkowski claimed, the exiles should concentrate on voicing an uncompromising demand for total independence for Poland (under the doctrine of maximum demands), and on fighting against the selfishness and political naiveté of the West.[87] Stanisław Gierat, the president of the U.S. branch of the SPK, expressed similar views. Poles in the West, he maintained, should support liberalization in Poland, but also make sure that it was just the first step on the road to complete freedom. The goals of Polonia should include, on the one hand, economic aid to the Polish nation and political pressure to ratify Polish western borders and, on the other, calls for independence more radical than what Poles in the country could afford in the present situation. In order to meet those goals, Gierat appealed for the concerted action of both "American Polonia and the war emigration."[88]

The second approach was consistent with Klaudiusz Hrabyk's early pronouncements about the need for drastic change to the existing exile mission to follow the political lead of the homeland and to support Gomułka because the nation supported him. In a series of articles published in the Polish-language press in both the United States and Great Britain in 1956 and 1957, Hrabyk developed his own vision of the new role for the diaspora. He spoke out against the exiles' attempts to lead the Polish nation and in favor of their auxiliary role as guardians of Polish interests in the West. The émigrés (Emigracja), he claimed, should abandon their isolation and establish programs for economic aid and cultural exchange with the Polish people. They also should lobby for foreign policy issues—such as the recognition of Poland's western borders—and sponsor promotion of the Polish image abroad. According to Hrabyk, the maximum demands concept could only endanger Poles (the events in Hungary provided an adequate warning), who had proved their own political maturity and whose lead should be followed, not negated, by the exiles.[89] Hrabyk's articles provoked a stir among the New Emigration. Leaders from the United States and London responded to his arguments in the press. Hrabyk was an invited speaker at gatherings of World War II veterans in New England and at a conference of Polonian journalists. He received letters from his readers and listeners, some supporting his argumentation, and others disputing it.[90] In 1957 Hrabyk made his first trip to Poland since the war, and in 1959 he and his wife returned to Poland permanently.

The third approach, represented by *Kultura* in Paris and the younger-generation exile circles, expressed a political middle ground. The political maturity and leadership of the opposition in Poland should be accepted, they claimed, and the exile mission revised. The changes in Poland should be viewed with skepticism, however, and support for Gomułka should be only conditional.[91] *Kultura*, mostly through columnist Juliusz Mieroszewski, opted for a gradual evolution of conditions in the homeland, with the émigré circles actively engaging Polish intellectuals in a constructive dialogue.[92]

In the larger diaspora, the debate within the Association of Polish Writers in Exile (Związek Pisarzy Polskich na Obczyźnie) best exemplified the main trends in the discussion about the range of contacts with the homeland. In 1947 the association had adopted a resolution forbidding its members to publish in Poland. However, during the liberalization of the early 1950s, and especially during the communist repatriation offensive directed toward the intelligentsia in exile, Polish writers saw new opportunities to have their works published in Poland. Because many of them had experienced serious economic hardships in their life abroad and had seen their audiences melt to a handful of émigré readers, such opportunities could seem rather tempting. A chance to speak directly to the Polish nation was also an attractive proposition. In April 1956 the association organized a symposium designed to look for a justification for remaining in exile. The meeting resulted in a book of essays written by some of the most accomplished Polish writers pondering their own exile mission.[93]

Responding to the issue of publishing in Poland, in August 1956 the leading journalist of *Kultura*, Juliusz Mieroszewski, formulated an opinion that immediately raised much controversy. According to Mieroszewski, no Polish writer in exile should give up on Polish readership. Only when émigré literature reached Polish readers directly and influenced them could one talk about the real fulfillment of the intellectual exile mission, he argued.[94] At the same time, Mieroszewski outlined the limits of cooperation: émigré writers should not accept payments in foreign currency and donate their earnings in Polish currency to their families or charities in Poland. They should not publish in the Polish press until Polish journalists were allowed to publish in the West. As far as visits in Poland were concerned, private persons should be able to go, but political and intellectual leaders and appointed officials should refrain from traveling, as it could be used for communist propaganda.[95]

Mieroszewski quickly was attacked in the émigré press, and the debate continued during the association's general assembly in October 1956. The assembly adopted a resolution confirming its 1947 ban on publication in Poland, stating that "[w]hile our country remains in political captivity and under Russian rule, Polish writers in exile ... should continue to refrain from any collaboration with institutions controlled by the totalitarian regime."[96] *Kultura* responded by sponsoring a questionnaire addressed to those who did not participate in the London meeting. Answers arrived from writers in many countries of the world, including the United States. Thirty-two of thirty-five respondents strongly condemned the association's October resolution.[97] Wiktor Weintraub, a professor of Polish literature at Harvard, rejected the resolution because of the instability of the situation in Poland. But Józef Wittlin, a writer and a poet, wrote from New York, making public his personal decision not to collaborate with publishers in Poland. "It is hard to be at the same time an 'exile' and a beneficiary of contracts with publishing institutions controlled by the government, whose existence is one of the main reasons for the 'exile,'" he reasoned.[98] Accepting the post-October changes in Poland and perhaps also criticism from the diaspora during its general assembly in December 1957, the Association of Polish Writers in Exile proclaimed that writers were free to make their own decisions whether to publish in Poland or not.[99]

| | |

The political elements of the exile mission had begun to take shape immediately after the outbreak of the war in 1939. All those who were outside of Poland during the war believed that the ultimate goal had always been Poland's independence. How one could fight for Poland depended on one's individual skills and opportunities. Soldiers participated in the struggle directly. Politicians engaged in international diplomacy. Rank-and-file refugees and prisoners created communities that ensured both physical survival and survival of the spirit.

The year 1945 brought bittersweet fruit: the war was over, the Allies had won, but Poland was to remain unfree. Yalta and the subsequent Western recognition of the communist regime in Poland meant that the struggle for independence had to continue. Poles abroad faced a conscious and difficult decision whether to remain in exile or to return to their homeland. These ultimately personal decisions were conditioned by individual situations and views, but were also highly influenced by the propaganda of politicians, whose concept of Little Poland in exile required that the largest numbers possible stay abroad. Some refugees reportedly did not want to have anything to do with any politics; others voiced their disappointment with Europe; and still others simply wanted to "search across the ocean for freedom from hunger, freedom from fear, and freedom to act according to one's own will and thought."[100] No doubt, some decisions were economically motivated. Most were complex, as all immigrant decisions usually are, combining various factors and influences. Eventually, the more politically conscious group became dominant and gave a special character to the entire immigrant wave of which it was a part. Consequently, most refugees framed their decisions in political terms and declared political motivations for their refusal to repatriate. As wartime experiences had become a common denominator providing collective bonds, so the Cold War defined their generational identity as political refugees and exiles.

The exile mission had to be strengthened and refined. The cornerstone of the political program was the refusal to accept communism and Yalta. The exiles denied communist authorities legitimacy and rejected any possibility of compromise. The only legal and constitutional authority was the government in exile; even if internal splits divided the exiles, the legitimacy of the government was beyond any doubt. The second tenet of the political program was a demand for the return of Poland's eastern territories lost at Yalta to the Soviet Union. At the same time, the mission required guarantees for Poland's safety and recognition of its western border on Oder and Neisse rivers.

The exile mission made the refugees look to the West for protection and leadership in the struggle against communism. The West was seen as a victorious ally, powerful enough to change the international situation, to repudiate Yalta, and to return Poland to the fold of democracy. The exiles aimed at presenting the Polish cause to the West, never letting it forget the Polish nation's plight, its contributions to the Allied victory, or its historic cultural achievements. The exiles focused strongly on international affairs. Individual attitudes and their impact on public opinion augmented the lobbying of diplomatic circles. These notions were often painfully challenged and contradicted by the fact that the West was coresponsible for Yalta and hardly responsive to Polish cries for justice. Thus, the very existence of the Polish exile diaspora was a symbolic protest against Yalta and against Western indifference.

The Polish nation occupied a central place in the exile mission. According to its early formulation, Poles in Poland were to conserve their biological forces and concentrate on physical survival in the harsh conditions. The nation was expected to rebuild its strength after the destruction of the war, to practice passive resistance, and to avoid unnecessary sacrifice. The image of a mute, subjugated Poland contrasted with the concept of an active and outspoken emigration, ready to represent the nation, to demand and to protest on its behalf.

Although purely political activity held the primary place in the exile mission, the refugees remembered the admonitions of their Romantic role models. One of the most quoted counsels from the times of the Great Emigration belonged to Tomasz Teodor Jeż: "[T]he trammel of an engineer, the chisel of a wood-carver, the paint brush of a painter, the pen of a writer, even the word of a poet . . . all can be turned into arms and used to defeat the enemy of Poland's independence."[101] Intellectual, cultural, and artistic activity was, therefore, also a patriotic and often politicized duty. Support for Polish culture in exile had added urgency and significance because of the great destruction suffered during the war and the perceived Sovietization of culture in Poland.

Last but not least, the exile mission called for *przetrwanie* or endurance—withstanding all adversities—and for unity. Emigration had to last and to survive in order to carry out the mission, to bear witness, and to act. Although the initial calls to create a full-fledged state in exile hardly could be carried out under conditions of dispersal on many continents, community life, complete with a variety of organizations and a press, created the best chance for the exiles to stay united on a local level. The younger generation, steeped in patriotism, was expected to carry on, if necessary. The unity of the entire diaspora could be achieved through personal and organizational ties, coordination of actions, and first and foremost loyalty to the mission.

The exile mission was idealistic, if not utopian, and set standards almost impossible to achieve. It was a yardstick by which to measure one's intentions and a compass to check one's direction; but the reality of the émigré experience often severely affected its implementation. The mission seemed broad enough to fit the particular conditions of Polish exile communities in different locations of the globe and flexible enough to bind them together.

As time passed, however, the mission kept changing, depending on the period and location. It had a chance to survive in its purer form only in very specific conditions: in communities that formed the earliest, that were numerous, condensed, and relatively homogenous, and that exerted enough social pressure to assure broad participation. Great Britain, and especially Polish London, fitted this model perfectly. For this reason, and because of the presence of a large number of politicians and intellectuals, Great Britain became a political and cultural center of the diaspora, one that influenced other communities.

But even there the mission could not remain unchanged. Within the first heroic period of the mission formulation, between 1945 and 1955, historians detect certain turning points. According to historian Rafał Habielski, 1947 was such a turning point, when the death of President Raczkiewicz began the split in the government, which in turn undermined the exiles' trust in the effectiveness of the political circles in London. The same year marked the end of mass repatriation to Poland, when the émigré community adopted its final shape. Simultaneously, the exiles began to distance themselves from Poland; the London press noticeably decreased the amount of information on developments in the country, and some émigrés expressed disappointment at the perceived acceptance of the communist rule by the Polish nation.[102]

The late 1940s and early 1950s brought an increase of political apathy, while Polish exiles in Great Britain strove to establish themselves economically and socially. The support for politicians among the rank and file waned, and even émigré publications had a harder time finding readers. The height of the Stalinist terror in Poland prevented contacts with relatives and the distance between homeland and Emigracja grew.[103] It took the political thaw in the communist bloc, the repatriation offensive, and the rapprochement between East and West to mobilize the British part of the diaspora once again. This mobilization continued throughout the eventful year 1956, as both leaders and the masses responded to the crises in Poland.

1956 was a turning point everywhere in the diaspora and initiated reexamination of the mission. Although the main tenets remained unchanged, some modification took place. First of all, the exiles altered their view of the Polish nation, recognizing the agency it demonstrated both in June and in

October. From that point on emigracja's role took into consideration the potential leadership of Polish opposition in the kraj. The debate over interpretations of the odwilż and the Polish October also revealed dissent in the dominant approaches toward Poland. As a result, a numerically negligible but highly visible group of individuals decided to return to Poland permanently. Both *Kultura* and Radio Free Europe showed readiness to engage Polish intellectuals in a dialogue, and *Kultura* offered a new concept of evolutionary changes in Poland, challenging the doctrine of maximum demands. Most importantly, in light of the East-West rapprochement, and especially after the Hungarian uprising, the exiles gave up their hope for a world war as a route toward Poland's independence. They realized that the West would not jeopardize its relations with the Soviet Union over the Polish issue. The myth of a speedy return remained in the sphere of dreams, and the exiles braced themselves to remain outside of Poland for the long haul. After 1956 they ceased to feel like sojourners. For example, many of those who treated America, to use a metaphor hammered out by Peter Yolles, "as a hotel" or "a rented apartment" were now forced to confront the political stability of the Yalta agreement.[104]

The American part of the refugee diaspora developed under specific conditions very different from those encountered by the community in London. First of all, the exiles were not the builders of Polonia in the United States, but joined already existing communities with impressive institutions and specific traditions. These traditions included an older version of the exile mission, one formulated and propagated by the nineteenth-century political refugees, who over the decades politicized masses of largely economic immigrants. The political elements of this mission were revived during World War II, as American Polonia again mobilized for the Polish cause and continued to strengthen when the United States entered the Cold War. After the exiles began arriving in the United States, the two groups clashed over a number of issues, but the most defining was negotiation of the mission and competition over leadership in its implementation.

Compared with Great Britain, the exile community in the United States formed late; the greatest influx of refugees came only after the DP Act of 1948. The numbers of newcomers were large, but due to their geographical dispersal and their melting into Old Polonia, their impact was reduced. Again, if compared with London, the American group was less socially homogenous and on average, less politicized. To the leadership group among them, it soon became obvious that only close cooperation with Old Polonia could guarantee the fullest implementation of the exile mission, as they could thereby utilize the resources of the established Polonia.

Their very location in itself carried a promise of heightened effectiveness, compared to their compatriots on other continents. The United States' leadership in the Cold War was undeniable and only increased with time. Exile in America meant potential access to centers of power unavailable to Polish émigré politicians elsewhere, and the perceived strength of the Polonia vote gave them leverage in the contest for political influence in American foreign politics. American anticommunism played well with the vehement anticommunism of the refugees, who responded positively to American Cold War propaganda.

In order to achieve this privileged position, cooperation with the established Polonia was necessary, although the cost of it was a compromise—something Tadeusz Wyrwa, for example, was not ready to accept. Through the blending of different elements of the exile mission, American Polonia as a whole (Polish Americans, as well as refugees) was able to construct its own version of the mission. While keeping all the basic Cold War tenets, this version differed from the diaspora's model in some important points. First, it challenged the leadership of the Polish government in exile and the political parties in the struggle for Poland. The government received support and loyalty, but only as a symbol of legitimacy and constitutional authority. Instead, American Polonia claimed leadership for itself, based on its traditions, numbers, and influence in the United States. Second, American Polonia was more inclined to rely almost solely on the United States' power and position in international politics, which could be influenced through the exercise of American citizenship rights by using the unified Polonia vote. Third, because of that privileged position, American Polonia felt less ready to cooperate with the diaspora. Finally, the cultural development required by the exile mission, which was generally understood as spreading Polish high culture, faced a specific challenge because of the advanced assimilation and working-class ethnicity prevalent in American Polonia.

Poznań brought to an end the period in which the émigrés were identified in the United States mostly with political squabbles of the London government. The uniform response to the Poznań massacre strengthened ties between the exiles and Polish Americans and brought them closer together. For example, in October 1956, a traditional Pułaski Day parade in New York City became a real display of unity. As in every year, this large event attracted Polonia from the East Coast and Mid Atlantic states. This time, for the first time, the SWAP and SPK contingents marched together. A group of more than one hundred newly arrived refugees from Europe sponsored by the Polish Immigration Committee emphasized a continued commitment to those left behind and to the most recent escapees from behind the Iron Curtain. They carried signs that read: "We escaped to be free," "God bless this country for our new life and liberty," and "We were there, we suffered there, we are witnesses and victims of Soviet terror." Other signs carried by marchers referred to the goals of the exile mission, calling for freedom and justice for Poland, declaring hatred of communism, and warning against rapprochement and the duplicity of the Soviet Union. References to the events at Poznań also abounded: "Poznań—mirror of all Poland," and "Bread and Freedom—Remember Poznań!" Both Old Polonia and the New Emigration reached to the past for symbols and meanings, bringing into the mix Pułaski and Kościuszko, the poetry of Mickiewicz and Lechoń, Polish folk costumes, and an enormous American flag made of fresh flowers.[105]

Both Old Polonia and the exiles, who felt threatened by the communist propaganda offensive, responded by closing ranks. Both also felt rather overwhelmed by the changes in Poland and initially were unsure how to interpret them. Gradually, a more pragmatic approach won out, and the PAC focused increasingly on the economic aspects of help for Poland, even though, as one scholar noted, "PAC rhetoric still rang militant."[106] In the late 1950s and 1960s, even as the thaw ended in Poland, the flow of tourists from the United States visiting Poland continued, and, due to the liberalization of Polish passport laws, more Poles were allowed to visit America. Exiles progressively accepted American citizenship and felt safer to travel with an American passport.[107] One of the most visible signs of change was the influx of new refugees from behind the Iron Curtain.

The exile mission endured, cultivated within the émigré communities of the diaspora, giving them identity, purpose, and motivation. Remaining loyal to its major tenets, the refugees in the United States still grew strong roots in their new home, cocreating the larger postwar experience of American Polonia.

EPILOGUE |||

ALTHOUGH THE POLITICAL THAW in Poland ended soon, liberalized passport laws allowed more emigration under the program for reunification of families. According to statistics from the Immigration and Naturalization Service, between 1953 and 1970, 130,576 quota and nonquota immigrants, as well as 20,755 refugees, arrived in the United States from Poland.[1] These so-called post-October immigrants were both fleeing increasing political oppression and searching for better economic opportunities, unavailable in communist Poland. The duality of their motivation for emigration and the fact that they had spent part of their lives under communist rule earned them a certain degree of suspicion on the part of earlier immigrants. For example, Feliks Gross, a Polish sociologist and himself an exile, characterized the refugees, escapees, and immigrants from the 1950s to the mid-1960s in a rather ambiguous way, as "a primarily political emigration, but of people who left a country which had been for more than a decade under Communist rule. They shared the traumatic experience of German occupation, of war, and then Soviet occupation. Their personalities, attitudes toward the world and man were shaped by this tragic past."[2]

Emigration from Poland continued throughout the 1960s and 1970s, bringing to American shores an immigration wave of an essentially economic character, one responding to the disastrous economic situation in Poland and pursuing mostly material gain. This characterization remained in conflict with the self-perception of some immigrants from that wave, who blamed the communist political system for a lack of economic opportunities and thus saw themselves, at least partially, as political refugees. The majority of these new arrivals, however, did not engage in any type of political action and focused exclusively on legal or illegal work and on sending remittances to cash-strapped relatives in Poland.³ According to some scholars, politically minded and politically active World War II–era émigrés distanced themselves from those who came in the 1960s and 1970s, perceiving them to be too materialistic.⁴

The birth of Solidarity in Poland in 1980 was a turning point in postwar Polonian history, and the subsequent wave of so-called post-Solidarity immigration to the United States in the early 1980s. The struggle of the Poles against communist control stimulated and mobilized American Polonia, heightening its visibility and providing it with a renewed political agenda.⁵ Between 1981 (the year that ended in the introduction of martial law in Poland) and 1988, close to sixty-two thousand Poles entered the United States. There were among them about two thousand Solidarity activists forced out of Poland on one-way passports. After a period of rather difficult adjustment to life in America, many post-Solidarity refugees involved themselves in vigorous political work on behalf of Poland. POMOST (Bridge), the Brotherhood of Dispersed Solidarity Members, Freedom for Poland, and other smaller organizations attracted those who vowed to continue their fight for Poland's independence from abroad.⁶

Largely unfamiliar with the experiences of their postwar predecessors, the new arrivals of the 1980s frequently criticized the leadership of American Polonia for excessive Americanization and inactivity and attempted to claim leadership for themselves. On the other hand, the established American Polonia too frequently failed to respond to the specific needs of the refugees. Conflict thus was born, often repeating the patterns of tension and the accusations that had pervaded the postwar years. The end of the decade, however, brought more cooperation between the two groups. Throughout the 1980s, links between the World War II émigrés and the post-Solidarity refugees became stronger, especially among those most actively involved in work for Poland. Both past experiences and a continuing focus on the homeland made the postwar émigrés recognize "that the Solidarity refugees shared 'a mission for Poland,'" which "made them eager to work together with this new political generation."⁷

These exiled Solidarity activists were not the only immigrants who reached the United States in the 1980s. Poland's collapsing economy pushed out mostly young people, who dispersed around the globe in search of a better life. The outflow of the most energetic and educated members of Poland's younger generation initiated a debate, during which the exodus drew criticism from both the communist government, the Roman Catholic hierarchy, and some democratic opposition leaders.[8] Nevertheless, traditionally Polish communities in large urban areas in the United States swelled with *wakacjusze* or *turyści* (vacationers or tourists), who came for "vacations" on tourist visas and worked—mostly illegally—in the American economy.[9] The trend continued in the early 1990s as Poland struggled through a period of difficult transition to a market economy, during which high unemployment rates and a lack of economic opportunities, especially in the most depressed areas of Poland, motivated people to emigrate. Along with these groups of economic immigrants, the United States admitted increasing numbers of Polish professionals and college students who were building their careers in a global market. Lack of specific studies on Polish immigration in this time period does not allow, however, for conclusive commentary on their experience.

Throughout the postwar decades, Polish refugees in the United States never lost contact with the rest of Polish postwar diaspora. From the moment of their resettlement, they made a conscious effort to create and to maintain strong bonds with the rest of the diaspora, animated with the exile mission. Communication among different communities of the diaspora was possible largely due to the Polish-language press, which became a forum to exchange information, ideas, and opinions. In the first phase of the resettlement, the Polish press in America frequently included news items about the experiences of DPs who had immigrated to different countries. The newspapers published correspondence from individuals and newly established organizations, depicting the local environment and living conditions. Many newspapers adopted regularly published sections devoted exclusively to the presentation of new Polish communities in the world.[10] The political activities of the London government also found a prominent place in the pages of the press, even when internal divisions and quarrels drew negative commentary and references to the details of party politics became more and more obscure to the average reader. Books by exiled authors appeared in serialized format, and newspapers customarily reprinted articles from the Polish-language press around the world.[11]

The individual level of involvement, although difficult to capture, was a significant part of the diaspora experience. Personal contacts and relationships, sometimes dating from the prewar period, strengthened during the war and continued despite resettlement in different parts of the world. Any conversation with a member of the diaspora always reveals examples of staying in touch through letter writing, occasional visits, exchanges of gifts, or extending help to others in need.[12] For example, in the late 1950s a Polish woman amused herself by planning a dream trip around the world. While mapping out the route, she discovered that she could complete her travels by staying with Polish friends scattered around the globe. In some countries she would even have to keep her visit a secret because there probably would have been too many volunteers to put her up.[13]

One unique example of creativity in individual contacts among people in the diaspora comes from Connecticut. The need to be in touch and to share thoughts and experiences prompted an exciting and long-lasting exchange under the name *Kulig*. The term *kulig* comes from an old Polish custom, when during Carnival people would visit neighbors by driving a horse-drawn sled and gathering more people from house to house. The ride usually ended with a large party with food, drink, and dancing in the last house visited. *Kulig* became a privately published magazine circulated among friends in many countries. The idea was born in 1956 as Ewa Karpińska-Gierat clipped interesting articles from both the American and Polish press, added carbon copies of personal letters and some photographs, and sent all of it out to a friend with a request to pass the materials on to others, after reading and enclosing new materials. Gradually, the circle of "editors" participating in *Kulig* grew to a few dozen addresses, and *Kulig* itself began to resemble a sizeable, colorful magazine. Close to two hundred full issues of *Kulig* circulated until 1966; afterwards, in a more limited form, it continued irregularly for more than a dozen years.[14]

Yet another example of keeping diaspora ties alive were reunions, for instance, of teachers and students from the Polish schools in DP camps in Germany and Austria. On an informal basis, former professors and pupils got together for a couple of days in the summer, always in a different location. The mailing list once included close to three hundred names from all the continents. The thirteenth reunion took place in Germany in July 2000.[15]

Ideas also were exchanged through the postwar diaspora's numerous publications and artistic accomplishments. One of the most important characteristics of the diaspora was its tremendous artistic and intellectual potential, because many prewar writers, painters, musicians, artists, scholars, and other intellectuals remained in exile. Even a brief look at the list of contributors to *Kultura* or of authors published in the *Biblioteka Kultury* book series reveals an astounding accumulation of talent and vision, represented, among others, by Gustaw Herling-Grudziński, Józef Wittlin, Kazimierz Wierzyński, Witold Gombrowicz, Melchior Wańkowicz, and Juliusz Mieroszewski.[16] Among the postwar arrivals in the United States were the 1980 winner of the Nobel Prize in literature, Czesław Miłosz (1960); Jerzy Kosiński, author of, among other works, *The Painted Bird* and *Being There* (1957); and Stanisław Skrowaczewski, the world-renowned conductor (1958).[17] Traditionally, Polish society expected intellectuals to lead and to inspire and assigned them an important and respected role, which gained even more significance in times of national need, such as war and exile. Polish writers, artists, and intellectuals provided the diaspora with its unique voice and expression, stimulating it and adding to its internal strength and unity.

Over the years, diaspora intellectuals presented their achievements during international meetings. The first such conferences took place in London in 1957 and in New York in 1966, but had a limited character. The 1970 Congress of Polish Science and Culture in Exile gathered a much larger representation of scholars from many countries. The Congress of Polish Culture in Exile of 1985 brought together participants from all over the world who participated in panel discussions, listened to papers, visited exhibitions, and enjoyed concerts and performances prepared especially for this occasion. The most recent congress took place in 1995 and attracted intellectuals from the émigré communities and from a free Poland.[18] Representatives of Polish exiles from the United States were present at all of the congresses. Many of them were active members of the professional institutions founded by the wartime group, PIASA and the Piłsudski Institute.

Because political activity remained the most important goal of the exile mission and because the effectiveness of the political involvement depended on the unity and cohesion of the diaspora, American émigrés contributed to the coordination of political, social, and cultural programs among the diaspora communities. Cooperation with the PAC was instrumental in these efforts, as the émigrés tried to utilize structures of established Polonia organizations over which they attempted to secure their leadership in political matters related to homeland. By 1978 eleven of the twenty-nine presidents of PAC state divisions came from the post–World War II immigration, and throughout the 1980s the committees on Polish affairs were dominated by postwar arrivals, who almost exclusively shaped and led the PAC's work for Poland. They were the authors of the memoranda and statements issued by the PAC, and they set the PAC's stance on U.S.-Poland relations.[19] Kazimierz Łukomski, a postwar émigré who was the PAC's vice-president since 1968 and the chair of the PAC Polish Affairs Committee, became a particularly influential architect of PAC policies. Aloysius A. Mazewski, PAC president since 1968 and himself a second-generation immigrant born and raised in Chicago, did not hesitate to surround himself with émigrés whose expertise in foreign politics and focus on the Polish question could bring support and weight to his decisions in this area. Next to Łukomski, one of Mazewski's closest advisors on foreign policy issues pertaining to Poland was Jan Krawiec, editor in chief of *Dziennik Związkowy*, who arrived in America with the DP wave from Germany.[20]

Increased cooperation, however, did not entirely erase the old patterns of tensions and suspicion, which often reopened old divisions. Conflicting views on the direction of political activities and cooperation with the rest of the diaspora spurred the renewal of friction, as in the 1970s, when the Polish American Congress became involved in initiatives to unite and coordinate efforts of the "Polonias in the Free World." A network of postwar activists was responsible for these ideas of unification, supported by Polish communities in many different countries. In 1969, during the celebration of the PAC's twenty-fifth anniversary in Washington, D.C., representatives of Polish communities in Canada, Great Britain, and Argentina discussed various possibilities for the coordination of their political activities. However, when Australian Polonia later prepared a project of unification, it was never put into effect.

In 1974 Canadian Polonia gathered around the Canadian Polish Congress attempted to win the assistance of the PAC on the unification issue. During a meeting between representatives of the two congresses in Detroit, Michigan, the Canadian and American delegations reached an agreement on the need for closer cooperation among Polonias in the world. Participants in the meeting issued a joint declaration that read:

> Polonia has a responsibility to inform public opinion in the Free World of the situation in Poland and to expose deceits of the official propaganda of

the regime [in Poland]. It has a responsibility to defend the Polish Nation's rights to full freedom, sovereignty, and self-determination.

The Polish government [in Poland] realizes the significance of the truth delivered by Polonia and has increased infiltration into Polonia in order to cause divisions, to weaken it, to control it, and to make it into its own tool.[21]

The declaration also identified topics for further discussion, such as the need to define the Polonias' roles in their respective countries, the maintenance and development of Polish culture, support for educational and youth organizations, coordination of antidefamation actions, as well as possibilities for cultural and scholarly exchanges.

Plans for an international congress of Polonia in 1975 aroused mixed emotions within the Polish-American community and exposed old divisions between established Polonia and the émigrés, especially the veterans organizations. In a letter to Aloysius Mazewski, Eugene Kusielewicz, president of the Kosciuszko Foundation, expressed his concerns that "the forthcoming congress of Poles would be under the influence of the S.P.K." He warned against the inflexibility of the veterans groups: "No one would doubt that such a meeting could have positive results, but a meeting in which S.P.K. plays a major role could be a disaster. I hope you take measures to protect yourself. The P.A.C. should not try to have Gierat [SPK president and New Emigration activist] try to tell you that a handful of his buddies from New Zealand are equal to the P.A.C." At the end of the letter, Kusielewicz concluded: "The more I work in Polonia, the more I am convinced that Gierat and his group have been a cancer in the side of the Polish American community."[22]

Kazimierz Łukomski, PAC vice-president and one of the main architects of the "Polonia of the Free World" congress, responded to such challenges by stressing the ties between Old Polonia and the émigrés. Łukomski denied that the meeting was to bring about a rigid organization, but rather was designed to coordinate certain actions and to promote the free exchange of ideas. Addressing the issue of divisions within Polonia, he wrote: "I was born a Pole (although in Lithuanian Samogitia), and I will remain a Pole. But there is something more than just citizenship that connects me to America and to the long-established Polonia here. It is an awareness of freedom, liberty, and a new beginning in life." During his years spent in the United States, Łukomski continued, his main objective always had been work for Poland, but at the same time work for the maintenance of Polishness, for increased significance, new vitality, and new values within the Polonia community. Thirty years after the end of the war, political emigration in its mass had been transformed to a large degree into Polonia, into a community for whom America had become a second homeland.... Through the integration process, postwar [soldier] emigration contributed to Polonia a new cultural potential and intensified its patriotic, national and independence-seeking [niepodległościowe] activities.... Similar processes took place in other countries in the world.[23]

In November 1975 the international congress "Polonia of the Free World" (also known as Polonia '75) took place in Washington, D.C., cosponsored by the Polish American Congress and the Canadian Polish Congress and led by the CPC's president, Władysław Gertler. In his opening speech, Mazewski emphasized that the conference was not a meeting of Polish political parties and political émigrés, nor a refugee parliament and competition for the Polish government in exile. "We gathered to analyze the international situation," he announced, "to inform each other about our strength, potential, and problems in our respective countries."[24] As a final result of the conference, the representatives of Polish communities in twelve different countries formulated an ideological resolution, declaring their intention to cooperate in the struggle for Poland's independence and to care for Polish communities abroad. The delegates decided to meet three years later in Canada to further the cause of unification. Any further unification initiatives, however, met resistance from Mazewski. "I was against the creation of any formal organizations with presidents and bureaucracy," he explained in his report, citing the lack of financial means for such organizations to develop any meaningful activity as a justification for his opposition. "Moreover," he continued, "Polonias in the majority of countries include primarily postwar immigrants engaged in Polish émigré politics. I was afraid that the newly created organization could become the grounds of political infighting, and in my opinion, we, as Americans, should not get involved in those quarrels."[25]

The 1978 conference, called Polonia 1978—Polonia Jutra (Polonia 1978—Polonia of Tomorrow) and organized by the Canadian Polish Congress in Toronto, brought together 175 delegates from eighteen countries, plus representatives of the largest world organizations, such as Polish scouting and veterans organizations, and numerous observers and press reporters. This time, the conference did establish a Coordinating Council of Polonia of the Free World responsible for overseeing the activities of Polish communities throughout the world. Mazewski declined the chairmanship of the council, and Władysław Gertler, president of the Canadian Polish Congress, accepted the position.[26] Nevertheless, in the 1970s and 1980s, Mazewski did participate in meetings of the council in Toronto, Rome, and London. The PAC, representing American Polonia, was irrevocably drawn into active involvement in the Polish diaspora animated by the postwar political exiles.[27]

The persistence of divisions between later-generation Polish Americans and the émigrés is an intriguing question, whose larger dimensions reach beyond the experience of Polonia in the United States.[28] Although few detailed studies exist on this topic, similar frictions reportedly took place between Polish refugees and the Polonia communities in Argentina and Brazil, where previous immigrant waves had arrived as a part of the great turn-of-the-century Atlantic migrations and had a predominantly peasant character. Unlike their predecessors, the postwar refugees in Brazil settled mostly in urban areas and encountered difficulties in integration with the second- and third-generation members of the older communities, who had moved up the social ladder. In Argentina, the mostly middle-class refugee Poles formed a number of new professional organizations, such as Stowarzyszenie Inżynierów Polskich w Argentynie (Association of Polish Engineers in Argentina), as well as several theater and artistic groups specializing in a national cultural repertoire.[29] Canada was another country where the refugees established separate organizations that better reflected their political and cultural mission and provided them with leaders from their own cohort, but at the cost of tensions between the newcomers and older Canadian Polonia.[30]

Polish postwar communities in European countries, such as Germany and Austria, which grew on the basis of the DP camps, took over elements of the organizational structure formed during the DP period. In Austria, refugees often entered the ranks of older organizations and cooperated with them, as it was the case with the oldest Austrian Polonia organization, Strzecha (Thatched Roof). The majority, however, joined a new association, Związek Polaków w Austrii (Association of Poles in Austria), which stressed political goals and closely adhered to the leadership of the London government. New Polonias in other European countries, including France, Switzerland, and the Scandinavian nations, also had their roots in the war years and grew in numbers as a result of the international resettlement effort.[31] Authors generally agree that in most cases communities of postwar and older Polish immigration waves developed largely separately, and their coexistence was not free of tensions. In Denmark, for example, the old Związek Polaków (Association of Poles) decided to develop relationships with the Polish communist authorities in Poland, while the exiles formed their own Związek Wolnych Polaków (Association of Free Poles), which was openly hostile to the communist regime and rejected any type of relationship with Poland.[32] On the other hand, in Great Britain, Australia, and New Zealand, the refugees quickly overwhelmed the small prewar Polonias and built their own communities from the bottom up.[33]

Other ethnic groups in the United States and elsewhere also gained considerable numbers of new immigrants after World War II. As in the case of Poles, the DPs of other ethnic backgrounds often clashed with earlier immigrants from the same group. For example, Lithuanian refugees, who formed the Supreme Committee for the Liberation of Lithuania and later the World Lithuanian Community, developed their own version of the exile mission, which imposed "the obligation on émigrés to preserve both the nation as a political entity and the nation as a cultural entity."[34] Staunchly anticommunist, the new Lithuanian community focused much of its attention on developments in the international arena and within their homeland.[35] Latvian émigrés adopted similar goals, creating a strong, united, and very active community determined to combine anticommunism with the preservation of the Latvian language and cultural heritage. The Latvian example is especially telling with regard to troubled relationships with earlier immigrants. In rural Wisconsin, for example, little interaction took place between the Latvian Americans and the DP newcomers, because "none of the colony's Latvians undertook to sponsor Latvian DP's, to associate with them, or to aid them in settlement," while many older Latvians who had emigrated before an independent Latvia was established in 1918 and who had never experienced life under Soviet rule, showed certain procommunist sympathies.[36]

The same focus and commitment to the political character of exile distinguishes Ukrainians, who entered older ethnic communities in the United States and Canada as a part of the DP wave.[37] The Ukrainian experience bears perhaps most resemblance to the Polish case because, as more recent studies demonstrate, the Ukrainian DP masses underwent a vigorous politicization by the nationalistic leaders already in the DP camps. After resettlement in Canada, they clung to the myth of a return to a free Ukraine and made Ukraine's independence their all-encompassing cause. "The political worldview of the refugees, particularly its militantly nationalistic pitch, reflecting an ideology which had been further cultivated within the DP camps and subsequently exported as part of the cultural baggage the refugees brought with them" became the main source of the deep rift and, at times, even a violent conflict between the DPs and Canadian Ukrainians.[38]

Hungarian and Slovene refugees also faced problems with integration into established ethnic communities. The postwar Hungarian refugees, for example, had to deal not only with class differences, but also with suspicion that Nazi sympathizers and supporters of the Hungarian extreme right might have been hiding among the refugees. Social and cultural differences between the postwar refugee wave and later-generation Hungarian Americans proved insurmountable and resulted in a permanent duality within the community.[39] The Slovene community split on the matter of cooperation with a communist regime in Slovenia. In the 1940s the DPs supported the political right wing, which included circles influenced by the Catholic Church, and opposed any contacts with the regime in the homeland. Many other Slovene-American organizations, however, were ready to cooperate with the Yugoslavian government from its inception.[40]

Some Jewish survivors of the Holocaust also had a troubled relationship with Jewish Americans, who distinguished themselves in an exceptional way in their lobbying efforts on behalf of the DP laws and resettlement in the United States. Jewish-American communities were, however, sometimes unable fully to facilitate the survivors' transition to life in America. In Pittsburgh, for example, although most of the newcomers felt welcomed and could count on social services developed in the Jewish community, some Jewish Americans lacked the understanding necessary to provide emotional support during the grieving process. For instance, despite special classes given in Yiddish, some hospital personnel had little patience with the survivors: "They complained that DPs were mourning too long, that they were not becoming Americans fast enough, that the war was over; 'enough already!'"[41] When some survivors were invited to join the Pittsburgh Friendship Club, they quickly dropped out, feeling out of place in a club composed predominantly of established German and Austrian Jews from previous migration waves. Others formed their own organizations, finding comfort and support among people who had similar experiences.⁴²

Even this brief and fragmentary review reveals certain similarities of experience for the entire postwar refugee wave. After the war, ethnic groups effectively lobbied to admit displaced persons and launched an impressive resettlement effort. But the influx of refugees brought conflict and tensions based on class differences, degree of assimilation, and refugee versus ethnic characteristics and needs. Most importantly, postwar refugees remained loyal to the exile mission elements of anticommunism, political work for the homeland, and maintenance of a national culture in a unified diaspora. This understanding of the mission and the demand to adhere strictly to it became another—and perhaps the most important—source of conflict. Further studies, no doubt, will shed additional light on this topic and elaborate on presently available evidence.

In 1989, amid a collapsing economy and growing social discontent, the Round Table talks among the representatives of the Polish democratic opposition, the communist government, and the Polish Roman Catholic Church resulted in a peaceful change in the political system in Poland. In the elections of June 1989, Poland became the first nation behind the Iron Curtain to oust the communists and formed a democratic government headed by Tadeusz Mazowiecki, a dissident and a Solidarity advisor. In the fall and winter of the same year, the Berlin Wall was brought down in Germany, and the Velvet Revolution in Czechoslovakia, a changing of the guard in Hungary, and a bloody coup in Romania ended communist rule in this part of Europe.

On December 22, 1990, president of the Polish government in exile Ryszard Kaczorowski, accompanied by an official delegation from London, handed over the insignia of state to the democratically elected president of the Republic of Poland, Lech Wałęsa. Poland was free again, and the exile governmental structures could disband. In his last official proclamation, dated one day before the ceremony in Warsaw, President Kaczorowski announced, "I will transfer to President Lech Wałęsa the authority over the *emigracja niepodległościowa* [independence emigration], which has fulfilled its mission, solicitously preserving the ideals of Independent Poland."⁴³

Forty-five years after the end of the war, the postwar Polish diaspora again faced the task of rethinking the exile mission and redefining its goals for the future. For example, reflecting on the significance of 1989, a Yale professor and student of Polish history, Piotr Wandycz, asked the question whether after the fall of communism, the Emigration (*Emigracja*) was still needed. His answer was affirmative. The exiles were still needed as a lasting symbol of Polish history and Poland's struggle for independence. They also provided a vital connection between the West and Poland, as well as between Polonia and Poland, and they could act as a catalyst for positive political, economic, and cultural change in the homeland.[44] Wandycz's attitude, although cautious at that early date, sounded an optimistic note. Other commentators were not so confident of the direction of changes in Poland, and some went as far as to claim that not much had changed at all: the same compromised group of communists simply had replaced political domination with the economic control. Tadeusz Wyrwa, now a retired university professor in Paris and an accomplished historian and writer, joined the ranks of the critics. His book, *Bezdroża dziejów Polski* (*The Crossroads of Polish History*), published in Poland in 1998, warned Polish society of those dangers. Wyrwa also reprimanded the émigré circles, especially the conflict-prone veterans organizations, calling for unity and collaboration within their thinning ranks. He paid special attention to the issues of caring for the historical legacy of the diaspora, and called for respect and recognition of the past.[45]

The debate over the future also attracted other voices. Jerzy Zubrzycki is one of the foremost students of the Polish postwar community in Great Britain, a sociology professor in Australia, and himself a member of the postwar diaspora. In 1993 Zubrzycki proposed the concept of *asymilacja bez wynarodowienia* (assimilation without loss of roots) as an acceptable way of the future of the exile diaspora. Careful to stress the distinction between old Polonias and the exiles, he argued that post-1939 emigration, which "has by and large succeeded in its political objectives" and "has achieved its goals," will be now transformed "into an ethnic group—an ethnic group conscious of its roots, necessarily assimilated and yet conscious of its cultural heritage. Its mission of constantly crossing and recrossing the cultural boundaries will be the daily experience of my generation still surviving, as well as the generation of our children.... In my judgment, *asymilacja bez wynarodowienia* is the motto, which we should all accept."[46] The question of the transformation of the exiles into Polonia has also attracted other scholars, such as Stanislaus Blejwas, a respected authority on American Polonia's history, who commented with irony:

The political emigration—the be-medaled officers, some who received several postwar promotions, the journalists, the artists, the professors, the politicians, the civil servants, the teachers, the musicians, the engineers—was now just like us! *Pani Hrabianka* from Berdyczów, *Pan Rotmistrz* from Lwów, *Pan Konsul* from Warsaw, *Pan Inżynier* from Tarnów were now just the same as Jacek from Chicago, Wanda from Pittsburgh, Edziu from Detroit, or Staszek from Brooklyn![47]

One of the most urgent problems on the postwar diaspora's agenda was securing a proper place in history, an issue confirming the significance of the exile mission's historical focus. Accepting the natural passing of the generation and prompted by the changes in Poland, diaspora exiles hurried to fulfill this remaining point of the mission. Since 1989 the number of publications dealing with the diaspora's past has noticeably increased, as a younger generation of Polish scholars has become attracted to this little-known part of Polish history and has gained access to its historical sources. Many memoirs authored by the exiles and often published in Poland sought to return the individual refugee experience to Polish historical memory. Concerned with the preservation of their records, some émigré organizations initiated controversial transfers of archives and library holdings to institutions in Poland, such as the rich archives of the *Wiadomości Literackie* to the newly created Archiwum Emigracji at the University of Toruń, Poland. In the meantime, some Polish archival institutions developed a specialization in materials related to diaspora history. For example, Archiwum Wschodnie of Ośrodek "Karta" (Eastern Archives of the "Charta" Center) in Warsaw continues to gather sources pertaining to the experiences of Polish deportees in Soviet Russia. In 1992 Polskie Towarzystwo Naukowe na Obczyźnie (Polish Society of Arts and Sciences Abroad), located in London, began publication of a seven-volume work on the history of the *emigracja niepodległościowa* (independence emigration), combining primary sources with scholarly commentary. In the United States, several New Emigration veterans associations founded separate rooms to deposit and display their records and artifacts in the Central Archives of American Polonia in Orchard Lake. As a result, individual museum, archive, and library collections were created for the Polish Army Second Corps, the First Polish Armored Division, the Polish Home Army, the Polish Air Force, the Association of Former Political Prisoners, as well as Polish Scouting.[48]

These are the grassroots interests and actions of individuals, however, that were particularly important for the preservation of the diaspora's history. This author was overwhelmed by the kind support from networks of exiles on many continents, ready to share their memories and materials for the sake of history. Some of the interviewees also were actively involved in the organization of local exhibits, talks at schools, and support for institutions such as the Holocaust Museum. Those who wanted to set the record straight wrote letters to the editor on historical issues, presented historical scholarship on Internet discussion lists, and shared information on new publications on the topics of common interest.[49] This historical interest is fully justified because the history of the Polish postwar diaspora since 1939 still contains a multitude of questions that need to be addressed, and the agenda for future research is long.[50]

The exile mission was a unique construction, born out of Polish history and reinforced by World War II and the Cold War. Jan Lechoń, a Polish poet and exile in New York, best captured the patriotic spirit of the exile mission in his poem-manifesto "Hymn of Poles in Exile," which began with a solemn declaration: "There is one Poland as one God in heaven." Lechoń saw himself and other exiles forever connected to Poland and to the Polish nation, attuned to their needs, and responsible for their future. Defining his exile obligation toward the homeland, Lechoń wrote

> I am like a soldier prepared for struggle,
> As in my country, in foreign lands, too,
> I guard and watch over the treasure of the Polish language,
> Polish spirit, and Polish tradition.[51]

Like many Pilgrims before them, Polish political refugees defined their immigrant experience within the framework of the mission. To follow the mission's objectives was a matter of honor and a patriotic duty. Bound by diaspora ties, Polish exile communities all over the world worked out their own ways to implement the mission's main goals. In the United States, the refugees joined the descendants of the previous immigrant waves, American Polonia, whose history also included a tradition of work and struggle for Poland. During the Cold War and the resettlement program, Polish Americans and refugees faced the challenge to negotiate both the mission and the leadership in its implementation. Between the outbreak of World War II and 1956, the exile mission in its most intense form remained at the core of relationships between these two groups.

Notes

Introduction

1. Norman Davies, *God's Playground: A History of Poland in Two Volumes*, vol. 2, *1795 to the Present* (New York: Columbia University Press, 1982), 275–76.

2. "The Books of the Polish Pilgrims," in *Poems by Adam Mickiewicz*, translated by various hands and edited by George Rapall Noyes (New York: Polish Institute of Arts and Sciences of America, 1944), 380–81.

3. In this book I accepted Merriam-Webster's definition of nationalism as "loyalty and devotion to a nation," while fully realizing that it is just the tip of the iceberg in the voluminous discussions on the many meanings, shades, and shapes of this phenomenon. The term "nationalism" (or "nationalistic") will be used here according to its English-language connotation and not its Polish-language meaning, which defines *nacjonalizm* as aggressive, extreme chauvinism, reserving the more positive term *narodowy* (national) for nation-oriented patriotism. For a useful discussion of Polish ethnic nationalism see Matthew Frye Jacobson, *Special Sorrows: The Diasporic Imagination of Irish, Polish, and Jewish Immigrants in the United States* (Cambridge, Mass.: Harvard University Press, 1995); and for the beginnings of Polish nationalism, see Brian Porter, *When Nationalism Began to Hate: Imagining Modern Politics in Nineteenth-Century Poland* (New York: Oxford University Press, 2000).

4. The term "Polonia" denotes all Poles and persons of Polish extraction living abroad.

5. Stanislaus A. Blejwas, "Stanisław Osada: Immigrant Nationalist," *Polish American Studies* 50, no. 1 (Spring 1993): 24.

6. Victor Greene, *For God and Country: The Rise of Polish and Lithuanian Ethnic Consciousness in America, 1860–1910* (Madison: State Historical Society of Wisconsin, 1975); Blejwas, "Stanisław Osada," 23–50; Andrzej Brożek, *Polish Americans, 1854–1939* (Warsaw: Interpress, 1985), 60–84; Helena Znaniecka Lopata, *Polish Americans*, 2nd ed. (New Brunswick, N.J.: Transaction Publishers, 1994), 96–100. According to Matthew Frye Jacobson, at the turn of the century the immigrant experience of the Poles, the Jews, and the Irish could be justifiably recast as an emigrant experience, as the nations "retained a central position in the migrants' ideological geographies." Jacobson, *Special Sorrows*, 2. See also Sucheng Chan, "European and Asian Immigration into the United States in Comparative Perspective, 1820s to 1920s," in *Immigration Reconsidered:*

History, Sociology, and Politics, ed. Virginia Yans-McLaughlin (New York: Oxford University Press, 1990), 37-75.

7. Joseph A. Wytrwal, *America's Polish Heritage: A Social History of Poles in America* (Detroit: Endurance Press, 1961), 36-76; Joseph Wieczerzak, "Pre- and Proto-Ethnics: Poles in the United States before the Immigration 'After Bread,'" *Polish Review* 21, no. 3 (1976): 7-38; Maria J. E. Copson-Niećko, "The Poles in America from the 1830s to 1870s: Some Reflections on the Possibilities of Research," in *Poles in America: Bicentennial Essays,* ed. Frank Mocha (Stevens Point, Wisc.: Worzalla Publishing, 1978), 45-302; James S. Pula, *Polish Americans: An Ethnic Community* (New York: Twayne, 1995), 2-13.

8. Brożek, *Polish Americans,* 36. After allowing for reemigration, which reached approximately 25 percent, 1.9 million is the net number of immigrants from Polish lands at the turn of the century.

9. Ibid., 39. Problems with estimation of the number of Polish immigrants to the United States are discussed in depth by Helena Znaniecki Lopata, "Polish Immigration to the United States of America: Problems of Estimation and Parameters," *Polish Review* 21, no. 4 (1976): 85-107. See also Pula, *Polish Americans,* 19-20.

10. Pula, *Polish Americans,* 30-38.

11. John J. Bukowczyk, *And My Children Did Not Know Me: A History of the Polish-Americans* (Bloomington: Indiana University Press, 1987), 30. More radical Poles founded their own organizations, such as the Alliance of Polish Socialists, established in New York in 1896, and their own newspapers, such as *Robotnik Polski* (Polish Worker) or *Dziennik Ludowy* (People's Daily). Some rose to prominence in the Industrial Workers of the World and other labor unions. Milwaukee socialist and union organizer Leo Krzycki became the vice-president of the Amalgamated Clothing Workers of America. Ibid., 26-31, 79-81; Pula, *Polish Americans,* 45-53.

12. Karol Wachtl, *Polonja w Ameryce: Dzieje i dorobek* (Philadelphia: published by the author, 1944), 286-358; Joseph A. Wytrwal, *Poles in American History and Tradition* (Detroit: Endurance Press, 1969), 318-47; Brożek, *Polish Americans,* 135-46; Pula, *Polish Americans,* 53-60.

13. Pula, *Polish Americans,* 60.

14. Wachtl, *Polonja w Ameryce,* 95-96.

15. Pula, *Polish Americans,* 67.

16. Brożek, *Polish Americans,* 182-89; Stanislaus A. Blejwas, "Old and New Polonias: Tensions within an Ethnic Community," *Polish American Studies* 38, no. 2 (Autumn 1981): 57-60; Bukowczyk, *And My Children,* 66-67.

17. Pula, *Polish Americans,* 74-75.

18. Davies, *God's Playground,* 2:406, 410; Jerzy Topolski, ed., *Dzieje Polski* (Warsaw: Państwowe Wydawnictwo Naukowe, 1981), 664-65, 746.

19. Davies, *God's Playground,* 2:406.

20. Ibid., 2:415–18.

21. Aleksander Gella, "An Introduction to the Sociology of the Intelligentsia," in *The Intelligentsia and the Intellectuals: Theory, Method, and Case Study*, ed. Aleksander Gella (London: SAGE Publications, 1976), 13.

22. Aleksander Gella, "The Life and Death of the Old Polish Intelligentsia," *Slavic Review* 30 (1971): 12–22.

23. One exception is Adam Bromke, *Polska diaspora* (Toronto: Polish Alliance Press, 1972).

24. The Polish experience is consistent with the findings of recent theoretical studies of diasporas, which define diasporas as

> [e]xpatriate minority communities whose members share several of the following characteristics: 1) they, or their ancestors, have been dispersed from a specific original 'center' to two or more 'peripheral,' or foreign, regions; 2) they retain a collective memory, vision or myth about their original homeland—its physical location, history, and achievements; 3) they believe that they are not—and perhaps cannot be—fully accepted by their host society and therefore feel partly alienated and insulated from it; 4) they regard their ancestral homeland as their true, ideal home and as the place to which they or their descendants would (or should) eventually return—when conditions are appropriate; 5) they believe that they should, collectively, be committed to the maintenance or restoration of their original homeland and to its safety and prosperity; and 6) they continue to relate, personally or vicariously, to that homeland in one way or another, and their ethnocommunal consciousness and solidarity are importantly defined by the existence of such a relationship.

William Safran, "Diasporas in Modern Societies: Myths of Homeland and Return," *Diaspora: A Journal of Transnational Studies* 1, no. 1 (1991): 83–84. Others have subsequently built upon Safran's definition, including Robin Cohen, who amended it with features that broadened the definition to fit in the categories of victim diasporas, labor and imperial diasporas, trade diasporas, and cultural diasporas. Robin Cohen, *Global Diasporas: An Introduction* (Seattle: University of Washington Press, 1997). For other definitions, see Nicholas van Hear, *New Diasporas: The Mass Exodus, Dispersal, and Regrouping of Migrant Communities* (Seattle: University of Washington Press, 1998), 5–6.

25. U.S. Department of Justice, Immigration and Naturalization Service, *Annual Report for the Fiscal Years Ended June 30, 1942–1953* (Washington, D.C.: U.S. Government Printing Office). Nationality quotas were set up as part of the National Origins Act of 1924 and functioned until 1965. Under this act the annual quota for Polish immigrants was 6,524.

26. According to some authors, between 16 and 19 percent of those who arrived under the Displaced Persons Act of 1948 were Polish Jews, for a total of about 37,500 Polish Jews admitted under the act. Barbara Stern Burstin, *After the Holocaust: The*

Migration of Polish Jews and Christians to Pittsburgh (Pittsburgh: University of Pittsburgh Press, 1989), 115–16. During the war, Nazi and Soviet policies segregated the two populations in occupied Poland. The end of the war found Polish Jews in more concentrated locations in Nazi death camps, as partisans in Poland, or as survivors in Soviet Russia, while Polish Christians formed a diaspora that spread across many continents. This segregation continued in the displaced persons camps, as the occupational authorities and international organizations provided separate camps for Jewish survivors. Separate Jewish organizations were in charge of their emigration (mostly to Palestine and the United States), as well as resettlement within older Jewish communities abroad. Polish Jews and Christians differed in their memories of prewar and wartime experiences and in their attitudes toward Poland in general. Burstin's studies indicate that most Polish Jews did not share the exile mission or the political concerns of Polish Christians. Ibid., 61.

27. According to the statistics of the International Refugee Organization (IRO), 45,044 Ukrainian DPs were resettled in the United States between July 1947 and December 1951. The IRO statistics divided refugees by "country of citizenship, last habitual residence, or ethnic group." Louise W. Holborn, *The International Refugee Organization, a Specialized Agency of the United Nations: Its History And Work, 1946–1952* (London: Oxford University Press, 1956), 439. Some scholars raise this number to 70,000 Ukrainians resettled under the DP Act. See, for example, Myron B. Kuropas, "Ukrainian-American Resettlement Efforts, 1944–1954," in *The Refugee Experience: Ukrainian Displaced Persons after World War II*, ed. Wsevolod W. Isajiw, Yury Boshyk, and Roman Senkus (Edmonton: Canadian Institute of Ukrainian Studies Press, University of Alberta, 1992), 399.

28. Pula, *Polish Americans*, 85.

29. About 37 percent claimed some professional status in their previous employment, although questions arise as to the accuracy of the study on this specific point. The study was conducted on a self-selected sample of more than two thousand questionnaires, and the author admitted that the formulation of the question about occupation before emigration was flawed. Danuta Mostwin, *The Transplanted Family: A Study of Social Adjustment of the Polish Immigrant Family to the United States after the Second World War* (New York: Arno Press, 1980), 146–52. See also Mostwin, "The Profile of a Transplanted Family," *Polish Review* 19, no. 1 (1974): 77–89; Mostwin, "Post-World War II Polish Immigrants in the United States," *Polish American Studies* 26, no. 2 (Autumn 1979): 5–14.

30. The PNA censor was an officer who presided at meetings of the organization's diet (*sejm*), which was the ultimate authority within the PNA structure. The office of a censor had nothing to do with censorship in the common meaning of this term. Pula, *Polish Americans*, 35.

31. Karol Wachtl, *Polonja w Ameryce*, 397. The quotation appears here as translated in Brożek, *Polish Americans*, 190.

32. Wachtl, *Polonja w Ameryce*, 396. Translation according to Brożek, *Polish Americans*, 191.

33. M. Haiman, *Dziennik Zjednoczenia*, September 25, 1934, cited in Brożek, *Polish Americans*, 190. See also Blejwas, "Old and New Polonias," 55–57; Pula, *Polish Americans*, 72–73.

34. Bukowczyk, *And My Children*, 75. He further concluded that "in reinforcing the bonds of mutual dependence and a reliance upon family and community ties," the Depression strengthened America's Polonia and, "paradoxically, it gave back their young." Ibid., 77.

35. Ibid., 79–80.

36. See for example, Lizabeth Cohen, *Making a New Deal: Industrial Workers in Chicago, 1919–1939* (Cambridge: Cambridge University Press, 1990).

37. Bukowczyk, *And My Children*, 83. For more on assimilation in the 1930s, see also David G. Januszewski, "Organizational Evolution in a Polish-American Community," *Polish American Studies* 42, no. 1 (Spring 1985): 54–58.

38. Bukowczyk, *And My Children*, 96.

39. Ibid., 96–97. See also Victor Greene, "Poles," in *Harvard Encyclopedia of American Ethnic Groups*, ed. Stephan Thernstrom (Cambridge, Mass.: Belknap Press of Harvard University Press, 1980), 799; Pula, *Polish Americans*, 124–32. Wytrwal further commented on changes within the community:

> If the automobile opened up America geographically for the members of the ethnic groups, and the movies introduced them to the mansions of the American "aristocracy," then radio and television have brought America into their own homes. The last stronghold of group separation—the home—has fallen. There is no longer a walled-off ethnic island. The war had enormous psychological effects on the Polish-American community. It enhanced the Polish-American status in American society, accelerated the already well advanced process of assimilation, and increased the confidence of the Polish-American people. Few, now, were prone to view themselves as Poles. In some quarters such designations were decidedly resented. They had become Polish Americans or Americans of Polish descent.

Joseph A. Wytrwal, *Behold! The Polish Americans* (Detroit: Endurance Press, 1977), 428–29.

40. Józef Wyrwa ("Furgalski," or "Stary"), *Pamiętniki Partyzanta* (London: Oficyna Poetów i Malarzy, 1991), 314.

41. The quotation comes from the poem "Polscy kombatanci" by Stanisław Kwaśniewski, published on page 4 of *Nowy Świat* on September 8, 1948 (my translation). General Stanisław Feliks Kwaśniewski (1886–1956) found himself in exile after September 1939. After immigrating to America, he engaged in political work and wrote articles and poetry.

42. The exiles defined Poland in terms of an "imagined community," to use Benedict

Anderson's concept. They drew a very clear and pronounced distinction between the Polish nation and the communist regime imposed illegally and forcibly from the outside. Benedict Anderson, *Imagined Communities: Reflections on the Origin and Spread of Nationalism* (London: Verso, 1989), 15-16.

43. In 1940 the Soviets executed about fifteen thousand Polish officers and soldiers. After the invading Germans discovered their mass grave in Katyń in 1943, the Soviets denied any responsibility for the massacre. Polish demands for an investigation became a leading cause for the breakup of relations between the Kremlin and the Polish government in exile in London.

44. Ukrainian exiles adopted a similar belief. Lubomyr Luciuk, *Searching for Place: Ukrainian Displaced Persons, Canada, and the Migration of Memory* (Toronto: University of Toronto Press, 2000), 217.

45. Stephane Dufoix, "The Coriolanus Complex: War, Politics, and Aliens," paper presented at the Social Science History Association Conference, Fort Worth, Texas, November 11-14, 1999. Irish immigrants to the United States in the nineteenth century adopted the interpretation of immigration as exile, which also politicized their relationship to the homeland. Kirby Miller, *Emigrants and Exiles: Ireland and the Irish Exodus to North America* (New York: Oxford University Press, 1985). Similar processes took place at the turn of the century in Polish and Jewish communities in the United States. See also Jacobson, *Special Sorrows*.

Chapter 1

The title of this chapter is taken from Stefan Themerson's "Fuga," written in Voiron, France, in November 1941. *Poezja* 22 (1987): 58-61.

1. Helena Podkopacz, *Smuga życia* (Kraków: ArsNova-Zjednoczeni Wydawcy, 1994), 46.

2. Norman Davies, *God's Playground: A History of Poland in Two Volumes*, vol. 2, *1795 to the Present* (New York: Columbia University Press, 1982), 435-39. Major Henryk Dobrzański ("Hubal") fought a guerrilla war in the Kielce region until his death in the spring of 1940. Ibid., 2:464.

3. Ibid., 2:443-44.

4. Ibid., 2:445; Józef Garliński, *Polska w drugiej wojnie światowej* (London: Odnowa, 1982), 50-51.

5. Garliński, *Polska w drugiej wojnie*, 51. Auschwitz was the largest, but not the only concentration camp that the Nazis located on Polish lands. In sum, more than two thousand camps and their branches functioned during the war, including camps in Birkenau (Brzezinka), Majdanek, Treblinka, Bełżec, and Sobibór. Józef Buszko, *Historia Polski, 1864-1948* (Warsaw: Państwowe Wydawnictwo Naukowe, 1982), 373.

6. Davies, *God's Playground*, 2:454-55. For details on life under the German oc-

cupation, see also Richard C. Lukas, *The Forgotten Holocaust: The Poles under German Occupation, 1939-1944* (Lexington: University of Kentucky Press, 1986).

7. Garliński, *Polska w drugiej wojnie*, 240-52.

8. Ibid., 61-69, 165-79, 217-39, 290-311, 464-65; Buszko, *Historia Polski*, 378-81.

9. Davies, *God's Playground*, 2:472-79; Garliński, *Polska w drugiej wojnie*, 387-412. British and American flyers from Italy undertook a courageous daylight air raid to drop supplies to the Polish fighters in September, but most of the containers landed in German-controlled areas. Some units of the Polish Army established within the Soviet Red Army managed to capture the river crossing in the Praga district of Warsaw, but after heavy losses were recalled. Diplomatic efforts of the Polish government in exile in London and American Polonia also fell on deaf ears of the West.

10. Historian Czesław Łuczak distinguished nine basic types of migration from the Polish territories:

1. Migration as a result of the war in September 1939;
2. Deportations from the territories annexed by the Soviet Union;
3. Deportations of labor force to the Reich and other German occupied countries;
4. Deportations of arrested people;
5. Deportations of population for the purpose of Germanization;
6. Movement of prisoners of war;
7. Illegal emigration from the occupied territories;
8. Service in the Nazi military forces and Waffen SS; and
9. Evacuation of the population during the last months of the German occupation.

Czesław Łuczak, "Przemieszczenia ludności z Polski podczas drugiej wojny światowej," in *Emigracja z ziem polskich w czasach nowożytnych i najnowszych (XVIII–XX w.)*, ed. Andrzej Pilch (Warsaw: Państwowe Wydawnictwo Naukowe, 1984), 453. Łuczak's article is the most systematic and comprehensive treatment of population movements within Poland during World War II. See also Malcolm Proudfoot, *European Refugees: 1939-1952; A Study in Forced Population Movement* (London: Faber and Faber, 1957), 35-37; Eugene M. Kulischer, *Europe on the Move: War and Population Changes, 1917-1947* (New York: Columbia University Press, 1948), 255-73.

11. Not all of the interned were evacuated to France. At the end of 1940 Romania agreed to extradite to Germany about twelve hundred interned Polish officers and more than forty thousand noncommissioned officers and privates, as well as more than four thousand civilians. Officers were then directed to *Oflagen* (German POW camps for officers) and the remaining group was used as a labor force in the German economy. In 1944 the Germans deported several thousand Polish refugees from Hungary who were later also employed as slave laborers. Łuczak, "Przemieszczenia," 453-54.

12. Jerzy Zubrzycki, *Polish Immigrants in Britain: A Study of Adjustment* (The Hague: Martinus Nijhoff, 1956), 54.

250 | *Notes to Pages 20-23*

13. Davies, *God's Playground*, 2:272.

14. Tadeusz Modelski, *The Polish Contribution to the Ultimate Allied Victory in the Second World War* (Worthing, England: published by the author, 1986), 151-60. For details of the story of the First Polish Armored Division, see also the memoirs of its commander, Stanisław Maczek, *Od podwody do czołga* (London: Orbis Books, 1984). On the history of the Polish Armed Forces under British command, see Keith Sword, Norman Davies, and Jan Ciechanowski, *The Formation of the Polish Community in Great Britain, 1939-1950* (London: School of Slavonic and East European Studies, University of London, 1989), 38-54.

15. Łuczak, "Przemieszczenia," 471-72.

16. Ibid., 473-75. Polish deserters from the *Wehrmacht* (German army) and *Organisation Todt* (a militarized German construction company run by the engineer Dr. Fritz Todt and then by Albert Speer, which oversaw construction of roads and military installations in occupied countries) who did not immediately return to Poland were formed into a reserve corps in Scotland in 1944 and 1945 that were "too late to go into action, and greatly helped to swell Polish unpopularity in this country." They were usually young peasants between the ages of seventeen and twenty-one. Their total number within the Polish forces was eighty-nine thousand. Zubrzycki, *Polish Immigrants*, 56. See also Sword, Davies, and Ciechanowski, *Formation of the Polish Community*, 464-66.

17. Wacław Jędrzejczak, *Love's Cadenza: A Migrant's Story, 1939-1956* (Adelaide, Australia: published by the author, 1999).

18. Those deported to work in the Reich included Polish citizens of various ethnic backgrounds as well as the population from territories annexed directly to Germany, often considered by the German Nazi officials as German. Moreover, the intensity of deportations fluctuated over time and differed in relation to different areas of Poland. All these considerations make any statistical estimates very difficult and liable to error. Łuczak, "Przemieszczenia," 458-66.

19. Victor Bik, "A Testimony of Victor Bik, Holocaust Survivor," April 9, 2000, typed manuscript in the author's possession, courtesy of Victor Bik.

20. Tadeusz Gubala, "Życiorys," n.p., n.d., typed manuscript in the author's possession, courtesy of Tadeusz Gubala.

21. Jerry T. Bigosiński, *The First Age: Memoirs of Jerry T. Bigosiński* (Bonita Springs, Fla.: published by the author, 1995), 29; Tadeusz G., interview by the author, St. Paul, Minn., August 16, 1996.

22. Łuczak, "Przemieszczenia," 466-69, 479-80.

23. Ibid., 469-71. Parents and families were able to find and claim only about 15 to 20 percent of those children after the end of the war. The rest either perished or were Germanized.

24. Czesław Łuczak, *Polska i Polacy w drugiej wojnie światowej* (Poznań: Uni-

wersytet im. Adama Mickiewicza, 1993), 556-57, 572-74, 621-25, 648-49. For individual experiences, see also Józef Kuropieska, *Obozowe refleksje: Oflag II C* (Kraków: Krajowa Agencja Wydawnicza, 1985).

25. Łuczak, *Polska i Polacy*, 543-46. For personal memories, see, for example, Tadeusz Piotrowski, *Vengeance of the Swallows: Memoirs of a Polish Family's Ordeal under Soviet Aggression, Ukrainian Ethnic Cleansing, and Nazi Enslavement, and Their Emigration to America* (Jefferson, N.C.: McFarland, 1995); Albert Tyde, unpublished manuscript of memoirs, chapters 3-6.

26. The largest Polish conspiratorial group existed in Buchenwald, with more than a hundred members in 1944. "Walking schools" existed in Buchenwald, Mauthausen-Gusen, and also in Ravensbrück, where it was organized by members of the underground girl scout organization *Mury* (Walls). Łuczak, *Polska i Polacy*, 582-84, 641, 649. For details of the ordeal of nearly eighteen hundred Polish Roman Catholic priests held in Dachau, see, for example, Henryk Maria Malak, *Klechy w obozach śmierci*, 2nd ed. (London: Veritas, [1960]); Stanisław Grabowski, *Follow Me: The Memoirs of a Polish Priest* (Roseville, Minn.: White Rose Press, 1997).

27. Łuczak estimates that tens of thousands of people left Poland through escapes and private channels. "Przemieszczenia," 472-73.

28. Irena Koprowska, *A Woman Wanders through Life and Science* (Albany: State University Press of New York, 1997), 85-95; Irena Lorentowicz, *Oczarowania* (Warsaw: Instytut Wydawniczy PAX, 1972), 167-210.

29. Łuczak, *Polska i Polacy*, 627-29, 631-37, 642-44. On the refugee camps in Hungary, Romania, the Baltic countries, and Switzerland, see Zbigniew Żaroń, *Wojenne losy ludności polskiej na obczyźnie w latach 1939-1947* (Warsaw: UNICORN, 1994), 9-31.

30. Łuczak, *Polska i Polacy*, 645-50.

31. Ibid., 481-82. Proudfoot's estimates remain within the same range. According to him, at the end of the war a minimum of 1,593,000 persons born in Poland were located in the SHAEF-controlled area of Germany, Austria, and Czechoslovakia, as well as the Soviet areas of occupation, France, Norway, the United Kingdom, Denmark, Italy, and Sweden. To these totals should be added about two million Poles deported to the USSR, and at least one hundred thousand others scattered around the world. Proudfoot, *European Refugees*, 220. About the conditions and the legal implications of slave labor in Germany, see ibid., 78-93.

32. Łuczak, *Polska i Polacy*, 560-61; Davies, *God's Playground*, 2:451-53.

33. Łuczak, *Polska i Polacy*, 562-64.

34. Elżbieta Wróbel and Janusz Wróbel, *Rozproszeni po świecie: Obozy i osiedla uchodźców polskich ze Związku Sowieckiego, 1942-1950* (Chicago: Panorama, 1992), 13-14.

35. Ibid., 20-21, 275. The experiences of Poles who went through "Soviet hell," constitute one of the grimmest and most moving chapters of World War II. Relatively

little known to the international public, they have received more attention in recent years as the changed political situation in Poland has allowed the creation of specialized archives collecting the papers and memoirs of Soviet camp survivors. Those who made it to the West often shared their stories with others within their own ethnic groups, revealing eyewitness testimony about the workings of the totalitarian regime. See also Keith Sword, *Deportation and Exile: Poles in the Soviet Union, 1939–1948* (New York: St. Martin's Press, 1994); Jan Tomasz Gross and Irena Grudzinska-Gross, *"W czterdziestym nas Matko na Sibir zesłali"* (Warsaw: Res Publica i Libra, 1989).

36. Olga Tubielewicz, interview by the author, tape recording, St. Paul, Minn., July 22, 1996.

37. Wróbel, *Rozproszeni po świecie*, 24–25.

38. Podkopacz, *Smuga*, 85–149; Tubielewicz, interview.

39. Wróbel, *Rozproszeni po świecie*, 38–64.

40. Ibid., 65–97; Łuczak, *Polska i Polacy*, 605, 642–43, 652. For detailed information on education in the Middle East, see Jan Draus, *Oświata i nauka polska na Bliskim i Środkowym Wschodzie, 1939–1950* (Lublin: Towarzystwo Naukowe Katolickiego Uniwersytetu Lubelskiego, 1993).

41. Wróbel, *Rozproszeni po świecie*, 99–141. For children's experiences in exile and in the refugee camps, see also Weronika Hort [Hanka Ordonówna], *Tułacze dzieci* (Beirut: Instytut Literacki, 1948). See also Żaroń, *Wojenne losy*, 57–119.

42. Wróbel, *Rozproszeni po świecie*, 142–204. Stefan Remiarz, interview by the author, tape recording, New Hope, Minn., July 15, 1996. See also Czesław Pławski, *Wydarci z ojczystej ziemi: Okres drugiej wojny światowej* (Łódź: RES POLONA, 2001), 153–70.

43. Tubielewicz, interview; Remiarz, interview; Helena Podkopacz, telephone interview by the author, August 10, 1996. On the Pahiatua camp in New Zealand, see Wróbel, *Rozproszeni po świecie*, 242–51. The research and publication of the Wróbels' book was financed by a Polish survivor who had immigrated to the United States from the Santa Rosa camp. The Santa Rosa group established its own association after settlement in the United States. Sabina Logisz, interview by the author, tape recording and notes, Chicago, Ill., January 4, 1995.

44. According to Modelski, the Carpathian Brigade was reorganized in October 1940. It was made up from

> soldiers of the Polish September 1939 campaign in Poland who had escaped in various ways to Rumania and Hungary; from individual Poles who had escaped to the Balkans from occupied Poland; from Poles of the French Foreign Legion; from soldiers of the Polish units organized in France who had escaped from France after her capitulation; from Poles from Russia who were able to escape from the communist paradise through India, China or even Japan, to reach the Brigade in Palestine; from a group of Poles who had arrived from South America; from Poles living in the Middle

East; and even from 14 young Poles from Manchuria who had come from the Balkans on Greek, Rumanian and French boats and then to Syria by the Polish "Warszawa" protected against German U-boats by the Polish destroyer "Gerland." Modelski, *Polish Contribution*, 131.

45. Davies, *God's Playground*, 2:271–72. See also Władysław Anders, *An Army in Exile: The Story of the Second Polish Corps* (London: Macmillan, 1949); Modelski, *Polish Contribution*. The most detailed treatment of the history of the Polish Armed Forces in the West can be found in Komisja Historyczna Polskiego Sztabu Głównego w Londynie, *Polskie siły zbrojne w drugiej wojnie światowej*, 3 vols., (London: Instytut Historyczny im. Gen. Sikorskiego, 1950-1962). See also Sword, Davies, and Ciechanowski, *Formation of the Polish Community*, 55–64.

46. Zubrzycki, *Polish Immigrants in Britain*, 56.

47. Łuczak, *Polska i Polacy*, 629–31; Kazimierz Krukowski, *Z Melpomeną na emigracji* (Warsaw: Czytelnik, 1987).

48. Tadeusz G., interview.

49. Zygmunt Wardziński, "General Władysław Anders as Educator: The Polish Gymnasium and Lyceum in Alessano, Italy, and Cawthorne, England," *Polish Review* 44, no. 1 (1999): 47-51; Roman Lewicki, ed., *Polscy studenci-żołnierze we Włoszech, 1945-1947* (Hove, England: Caldra House, 1996); Jan Kowalik, *"Kultura" 1947-1957: Bibliografia zawartości treści; Działalność wydawnicza (1946–maj 1959)* (Paris: Instytut Literacki, 1959).

50. On the history of Polonia in Great Britain, see Sheila Patterson, "The Poles: An Exile Community in Britain," in *Between Two Cultures: Migrants and Minorities in Britain*, ed. James L. Watson (Oxford: Basil Blackwell, 1977), 214–41; Tadeusz Radzik, "Polonia w Wielkiej Brytanii," in *Polacy w świecie: Polonia jako zjawisko społeczno-polityczne*, ed. Albin Koprukowniak and Władysław Kucharski (Lublin: Uniwersytet Marii Curie-Skłodowskiej, 1986), 2:111–46; Jacek Serwański, "Polacy w Wielkiej Brytanii w latach II wojny światowej," in *Polonia w Europie*, ed. Barbara Szydłowska-Cegłowa (Poznań: Polska Akademia Nauk, 1992), 423–36; Tadeusz Radzik, "Społeczność polska w Wielkiej Brytanii w latach 1945-1990," ibid., 437–68; Tadeusz Radzik, *Z dziejów społeczności polskiej w Wielkiej Brytanii po drugiej wojnie światowej (1945-1990)* (Lublin: Wydawnictwo UMCS, 1991).

51. *Pestki* comes from the similarity of the acronym PSK to the Polish word for "seed" (*pestka, pestki* pl.). Edward M. Car, *Kobiety w szeregach Polskich Sił Zbrojnych na Zachodzie, 1940-1948* (Warsaw: Oficyna Wydawnicza Audiutor, 1995); Lola Romańska and Andrzej Romański, eds., *W służbie dla Ojczyzny: Kobieta-żołnierz 2 Korpusu, 1941-1946* (Rome: Inspektorat PSK 2 Korpusu, 1946); Herminia Naglerowa, "W służbie dla Ojczyzny: Kobieta-żołnierz 2 Korpusu, 1941-1946," in *Polish Veterans of World War II, Inc., Post No. 19, Boston, Massachusetts, U.S.A., 1953-1978* [Boston: Polish Veterans of World War II, Inc.], 39–40.

52. For a review of wartime press publications, see Stanisława Lewandowska, *Prasa polskiej emigracji wojennej, 1939-1945* (Warsaw: Instytut Historii Polskiej Akademii Nauk, 1993).

53. For the fiscal years 1940 to 1945 the numbers were as follows:

1940	4,354
1941	4,406
1942	2,203
1943	1,533
1944	1,338
1945	1,122

U.S. Department of Justice, Immigration and Naturalization Service, *Annual Report for the Fiscal Year Ended June 30, 1945,* table 7; *Annual Report for the Fiscal Year Ended June 30, 1946,* table 6.

54. Kazimierz Wierzyński, *Moja prywatna Ameryka* (London: Polska Fundacja Kulturalna, 1966), 23.

55. Anna Węgrzyniakowa, "Pod znakiem Skamandra: Wprowadzenie," in *Literatura emigracyjna, 1939-1989,* ed. Marek Pytasz (Katowice: Śląsk, 1994), 1:25-29.

56. Ksawery Pruszyński, "Literatura emigracji walczącej," *Wiadomości Polskie,* no. 1 (1940), quoted in Joanna Dembińska-Pawelec, "'Emigracja walcząca' i jej poezja," in Pytasz, *Literatura emigracyna,* 101.

57. Ibid.

58. Kazimierz Wierzyński, "Współczesna literatura polska na emigracji," *Tygodnik Polski,* no. 22, June 6, 1943, 2. The paper was first presented as a PIASA lecture and subsequently was published in three parts in *Tygodnik Polski,* no. 22, June 6, 1943; ibid., no. 23, June 13, 1943; ibid., no. 24, June 20, 1943.

59. For a literary analysis of the output of émigré poets and writers, see the monumental Tymon Terlecki, ed., *Literatura polska na obczyźnie, 1940-1960,* vol. 1 (London: B. Świderski, 1964). According to Anna Węgrzyniakowa, many authors from the Skamander circle became increasingly Romantic in their writings. Węgrzyniakowa, "Pod znakiem," 88-91.

60. Czesław Miłosz, *The History of Polish Literature* (Berkeley: University of California Press, 1983), 387-89, 395-96, 397-98, 423-24, 521-32; Jerzy J. Maciuszko, "Polish Letters in America," in Mocha, *Poles in America,* 531-64.

61. *Tygodnik Polski,* no. 1, January 10, 1943.

62. *Tygodnik Polski,* no. 10, March 5, 1944, 6-7; no. 21, May 21, 1944, 6-7.

63. *Tygodnik Polski,* no. 2, January 17, 1943, 4. After her husband's death, Hanna Kister continued publishing by herself as a member of the American Women's Book Association. Lorentowicz, *Oczarowania,* 256-57.

64. *Tygodnik Polski,* February 20, 1944-May 7, 1944.

65. Michael Budny, "Józef Piłsudski Institute of America for Research in the Modern History of Poland," in Mocha, *Poles in America,* 687-708; Janusz Cisek, *In-*

stytut Józefa Piłsudskiego w Ameryce i jego zbiory (Warsaw: Biblioteka Narodowa, 1997), 7-45. A group of Polish-American supporters included, for example, a worker from Detroit, and one of the founding fathers Jan Zygmunt Dodatko; a baker from Philadelphia, Piotr Kulpiński; and a printer from New York, Jan Kowalski, who donated countless hours as a volunteer at the institute. Cisek, *Instytut*, 26.

66. Stanisław Strzetelski, *The Polish Institute of Arts and Sciences in America: Origin and Development* (New York: Polish Institute of Arts and Sciences in America, 1960); Damian S. Wandycz, *Polski Instytut Naukowy w Ameryce: W trzydziestą rocznicę, 1942-1972* (New York: Polski Instytut Naukowy, 1974); Thaddeus V. Gromada, *Polish Institute of Arts and Sciences of America: 50th Anniversary, 1942-1992* (New York: Polish Institute of Arts and Sciences of America, [1992]); Frank Mocha, "The Polish Institute of Arts and Sciences in America: Its Contributions to the Study of Polonia; The Origins of the Polish Historical Association (PAHA)," in Mocha, *Poles in America*, 709-24; John Bukowczyk, "'Harness for Posterity the Values of a Nation'—Fifty Years of the Polish American Historical Association and *Polish American Studies,*" *Polish American Studies* 50, no. 2 (Autumn 1993): 5-100; John Bukowczyk, "The Polish American Historical Association," in *The Polish Diaspora*, James S. Pula and M. B. Biskupski, eds., vol. 2, *Selected Essays from the Fiftieth Anniversary International Congress of the Polish Institute of Arts and Sciences of America* (Washington, D.C.: Columbia University Press, 1993), 99-102.

67. Emil Orzechowski, *Teatr polonijny w Stanach Zjednoczonych* (Wrocław: Zakład Narodowy im. Ossolińskich, 1989), 226-29.

68. Ibid., 229-33.

69. Ibid., 226-33; Lorentowicz, *Oczarowania*, 231-42.

70. Antoni Cwojdziński, "Za kulisami 'Pastorałki,'" *Tygodnik Polski*, no. 2, January 17, 1943, 3. See also Lorentowicz, *Oczarowania*, 231-39.

71. Lorentowicz, *Oczarowania*, 237. In addition to her work for the Polish theater, Lorentowicz supported herself over the years by restoring frescos, paintings, and altars for American churches; designing costumes for American ballet and stage for the Movietone Fox movie company in New York; illustrating books; and giving lectures on Polish and European art.

72. Jan Lechoń, "Premjera jak w Warszawie," *Tygodnik Polski*, no. 14, April 2, 1944, 6.

73. Lorentowicz, *Oczarowania*, 242.

74. Ibid., 219.

75. Aleksander Janta, *Nowe odkrycie Ameryki* (Paris: Libella, 1973), 75-76.

76. Lorentowicz, *Oczarowania*, 229-31.

77. Ibid., 249-54. The hotels also functioned after the war. See Klaudiusz Hrabyk, "Z drugiej strony barykady: Spowiedź z klęski; Lata 1902-1959; Wspomnienia i dzienniki," microfilm of an unpublished manuscript, Ossolineum, Wrocław, [1979], 667.

78. The declaration was published on September 1, 1939, in *Dziennik Chicagoski* and *Dziennik Zjednoczenia*, and on September 2, 1939, in *Nowy Świat* and *Kuryer Codzienny*. Wojciech Białasiewicz, *Pomiędzy lojalnością a serc porywem: Polonia amerykańska we wrześniu 1939 roku* (Chicago: Publishing Wici, 1989), 13.

79. The Rada Polonii Amerykańskiej (Polish American Council, or Rada, as it commonly was referred to) was first established in 1936 by the three leading Polish-American fraternal organizations: the Polish National Alliance (PNA), the Polish Roman Catholic Union (PRCU), and the Polish Women's Alliance (PWA). Its main goal was humanitarian assistance to members of Polonia. Donald E. Pienkos, *PNA: A Centennial History of the Polish National Alliance of the United States of North America* (New York: Columbia University Press, 1984), 31; Białasiewicz, *Pomiędzy lojalnością*, 73–74.

80. Franciszek X. Świetlik, *Sprawozdanie z Działalności Rady Polonii Amerykańskiej od października 1939 do Października 1948 na Zjazd Rady Polonii Amerykańskiej odbyty dnia 4go i 5go Grudnia, 1948 r. w hotelu Buffalo, N.Y.* (Chicago: Czas, 1948), 5–6. Rada succeeded in obtaining the State Department's backing to coordinate a fund drive on Poland's behalf, and any groups applying for permits to assist Poland were advised either to affiliate with Rada or to terminate further activities. Donald E. Pienkos, *For Your Freedom through Ours: Polish-American Efforts on Poland's Behalf, 1863–1991* (New York: Columbia University Press, 1991), 80–83; Białasiewicz, *Pomiędzy lojalnością*, 74–78.

81. Białasiewicz, *Pomiędzy lojalnością*, 44–45.

82. As Donald Pienkos indicates, "[D]espite the Polish government's hearty endorsement, only 772 men were eventually recruited for military duty during the two year interval between World War II's outbreak and America's entry into the struggle in December 1941 after Pearl Harbor." Pienkos, *For Your Freedom*, 77. See also Białasiewicz, *Pomiędzy lojalnością*, 118–28.

83. Białasiewicz, *Pomiędzy lojalnością*, 80–81.

84. Ibid., 102.

85. Ibid., 120–21.

86. Pienkos, *For your Freedom*, 85.

87. Rada Polonii Amerykańskiej, *Szczegółowy wykaz przychodów i rozchodów od 1-go maja, 1941 do 30-go września, 1942 roku, na Zjazd Rady Polonii Amerykańskiej, Buffalo, New York, w dniach 17-go i 18-go października, 1942* ([Chicago]: Rada Polonii Amerykańskiej, 1942).

88. Rada Polonii Amerykańskiej, *Protokół Zjazdu Rady Polonii Amerykańskiej: Buffalo, N.Y., 17go i 18go Października 1942* [Chicago: The Polish War Relief, 1942], 53.

89. Pienkos, *For Your Freedom*, 82–86.

90. Świetlik, *Sprawozdanie*, 84–87; The Polish War Relief of the USA, *The National War Fund and the Polish War Relief of the USA* (Chicago: The Polish War Re-

lief, 1947), [1–3]; John J. Olejniczak, *American Relief for Poland: Auditors' Report for the Period November 1, 1939, to September 30, 1948* (Buffalo, N.Y.: Everybody's Publishing Company, 1948), 5.

91. Pienkos, *For Your Freedom*, 86.

92. Świetlik, *Sprawozdanie*, 7. See also Pienkos, *For Your Freedom*, 83–90.

93. Rada Polonii Amerykańskiej, *Protokół Zjazdu 17go i 18go Października 1942 roku*, 50.

94. Ibid., 47–51. The publicity campaign included providing many different materials on Poland, Polish civilian refugees, and Polish military formations in the West. They encompassed photographs, informative brochures and publications containing pictures and illustrations, leaflets and posters, films, speeches, human interest stories for the press, radio scripts, and so on. Rada sent out also Polish flags and national emblems and organized rallies to support the Polish cause.

95. The Polish War Relief, *The Facts about the Polish War Relief* (Chicago: The Polish War Relief, [1945]).

96. The Polish War Relief, *Poland's Children* (Chicago: The Polish War Relief, [1945]).

97. See pictures in The Polish War Relief, *The National War Fund and the Polish War Relief* (Chicago: The Polish War Relief, [1947]).

98. Wróbel, *Rozproszeni po świecie*, 212–19.

99. The most comprehensive treatment of the Santa Rosa camp is by E. Wróbel, and J. Wróbel, who devoted a separate chapter to this topic in *Rozproszeni po świecie*, 205–41. Eileen Egan spent some time in Santa Rosa on behalf of Catholic Relief Services. Eileen Egan, *For Whom There Is No Room: Scenes from the Refugee World* (New York: Paulist Press, 1995), 11–88.

100. The complicated process of negotiation is reflected in detail in the John Locke collection, boxes 10 and 552, Harry S. Truman Library, Independence, Mo. See also Robert W. Kesting, "American Support of Polish Refugees and Their Santa Rosa Camp," *Polish American Studies* 48, no. 1 (Spring 1991): 79–90.

101. Wróbel, *Rozproszeni po świecie*, 237–38. Polish orphans placed in the Buffalo orphanage became the subject of a study by Sister Mary Gracille Rybij, Felician, O.S.F., "A Study of Twenty-three Polish Refugee Children at the Immaculate Heart of Mary Home in Care of the Felician Sisters, O.S.F., Buffalo, New York" (master's thesis, University of Buffalo, 1947). The author sets the number of children at 235. She does not mention the contribution of Rada in bringing the children to the United States. Instead, she points to the Committee on Refugees of the NCWC and Catholic Charities of Buffalo as the institutions responsible for the effort. Ibid., 5. A copy of the thesis is available in collection 024 (NCWC Department of Immigration, New York Office and Catholic Committee for Refugees), Center for Migration Studies, Staten Island, New York.

102. Wróbel, *Rozproszeni po świecie*, 137-39.

103. Female names dominated the lists of refugees recommended for financial aid. See the folder "Polish War Refugees, N.Y. Area" (PRNYA), vol. 1, American Relief for Poland Collection (ARP), Polish Museum of America (PMA), Chicago, Ill.

104. Dr. Karol Ripa, Council General, Chicago, to Rada Polonii, August 29, 1940, PRNYA, vol. 1, ARP.

105. Executive Committee for Aid to War Refugees from Poland in the U.S., "Spis imienny uchodźców wojennych chrześcijan, zarejestrowanych do dnia 15 sierpnia 1941 roku w 'Zrzeszeniu Uchodźców Wojennych z Polski w Stanach Zjedn.'" PRNYA, vol. 1, ARP.

106. Franciszek X. Świetlik, Chicago, to J. Ciechanowski, July 9, 1941, PRNYA, vol. 1, ARP.

107. Zygmunt Stefanowicz, executive secretary of Rada, to Jan Szewczyk, September 18, 1940; Zygmunt Stefanowicz to Koło Uchodźców Polskich, New York, September 18, 1940, folder "Polish Refugees, Chicago Area," ARP.

108. Rada Polonii Amerykańskiej, *Protokół Zjazdu 17go i 18go Października 1942 roku*, 41; Świetlik, *Sprawozdanie*, 30.

109. W. Korsak, "Informacje o akcji pomocy dla uchodźców wojennych z Polski w U.S.A. (na terenie New Yorku i okolic)," July 28, 1945, PRNYA, vol. 3, ARP.

110. Peter H. Irons, "'The Test Is Poland': Polish Americans and the Origins of the Cold War," *Polish American Studies* 30, no. 2 (Autumn 1973): 11. According to the author, the importance of the Polish vote was "not so much in its size but in the fact that it was highly concentrated in the urban areas swinging in an arc around the Great Lakes, from Buffalo to Milwaukee, as well as in the New Jersey-New York-Connecticut area, which together comprised the industrial heartland of the country and the northern bastion of the Democratic party." However, any political action by Polonia during the war was handicapped by the lack of Polish Americans in policy-making positions; there were no Poles in the White House, State Department, or Senate, and only a bloc of ten to twelve members of the House of Representatives. Ibid., 6-7, 9.

111. In March 1941 he met with Jan Ciechanowski, an ambassador of the Polish government, and a month later with General Władysław Sikorski, Polish prime minister. Roosevelt even persuaded Sikorski to undertake a speaking tour to several cities in the United States, hoping that the popular politician and soldier could influence Polish Americans and other Slavic workers, substantial numbers of whom had participated in strikes, such as the one organized by the Milwaukee United Auto Workers Union. Pula, *Polish Americans*, 86-87; Irons, "'Test Is Poland,'" 12. In addition to the Allis-Chalmers strike in Milwaukee, Wisconsin, which ended before Sikorski's tour began, the UAW-CIO organized a strike against the Ford Motor Company in River Rouge, Michigan. *Dziennik Polski*, April 2-12, 1941.

112. Wytrwal, *Poles in American History*, 390. According to some estimates, the

PNA—about 285,000 members strong in 1945—had 23,000 soldiers in the American army, about 900 of whom lost their lives. The PRCU contributed 5,377 of its 142,000 members, 453 of whom died. In addition, about 1,500 members of the Polish Women's Alliance served in the American army. Mieczysław Haiman, "The Polish American Contribution to World War II," *Polish American Studies* 3, no. 1-2 (Spring-Summer 1946): 36.

113. Jacobson, *Special Sorrows*, 229; Pula, *Polish Americans*, 87.

114. Charles Sadler, "'Pro-Soviet Polish-Americans': Oskar Lange and Russia's Friends in the Polonia, 1941-1945," *Polish Review* 22 (1977): 25-39; Irons, "'Test Is Poland,'" 17.

115. Wacław Jędrzejewicz, *Polonia amerykańska w polityce polskiej: Historia Komitetu Narodowego Amerykanów Polskiego Pochodzenia* (New York: National Committee of Americans of Polish Descent, 1954), 15-41; Tadeusz Paleczny, *Ewolucja ideologii i przemiany tożsamości narodowej Polonii w Stanach Zjednoczonych w latach 1870-1970* (Warsaw: Państwowe Wydawnictwo Naukowe, 1989), 195-96.

116. National Committee of Americans of Polish Descent, *Od apelu do Kongresu: Zbiór dokumentów Komitetu Narodowego Amerykanów Polskiego Pochodzenia (12 maja 1942-28 maja 1944)* (New York: Józef Piłsudski Institute of America for Research in the Modern History of Poland, 1944); Richard C. Lukas, *The Strange Allies: The United States and Poland, 1941-1945* (Knoxville: University of Tennessee Press, 1978), 107-16; Irons, "'Test Is Poland,'" 18-20; Bukowczyk, *And My Children*, 92-93; Blejwas, "Old and New Polonias," 62-70; Pula, *Polish Americans*, 88-89.

117. Irons, "'Test Is Poland,'" 23-24.

118. Ibid., 25-26.

119. David G. Januszewski, "The Case for the Exile Government in the American Press, 1939-1945," *Polish American Studies* 43, no. 1 (Spring 1986): 57-97.

120. Irons, "'Test Is Poland,'" 29; Pula, *Polish Americans*, 92-93.

121. As Robert Szymczak noted, Orlemański and Lange "had not only severely embarrassed Polonia, but their machinations had galvanized it into action" that soon bloomed in the creation of the Polish American Congress. Robert Szymczak, "A Matter of Honor: Polonia and the Congressional Investigation of the Katyń Forest Massacre," *Polish American Studies* 41, no. 1 (Spring 1984): 31. See also Sadler, "Pro-Soviet Polish-Americans," 31-35; Robert Szymczak, "Invitation to the Kremlin: The Adventures of Father Stanisław Orlemański, April-May 1944," *East European Quarterly* 25 (1992): 399-424.

122. Donald E. Pienkos, "The Polish American Congress: An Appraisal" *Polish American Studies* 36, no. 2 (Autumn 1979): 15-16. On the war and postwar politics, Polonia, and the PAC, see Lukas, *Strange Allies*; Irons, "'Test Is Poland,'" 5-63; Pienkos, "Polish American Congress," 5-33; Richard C. Lukas, "The Polish American Congress and the Polish Question, 1944-1947," *Polish American Studies* 38, no. 2 (Autumn

1981): 39–53; Stanislaus A. Blejwas, "The Local Ethnic Lobby: The Polish American Congress in Connecticut, 1944–1974," in *The Polish Presence in Canada and America*, ed. Frank Renkiewicz (Toronto: Multicultural History Society of Ontario, 1982), 305–25; M. B. Biskupski, "Poland in American Foreign Policy, 1918–1945: 'Sentimental' or 'Strategic' Friendship?—A Review Article," *Polish American Studies* 38, no. 2 (Autumn 1981): 5–15; George Janczewski, "The Significance of the Polish Vote in the American National Election Campaign of 1948," *Polish Review* 13 (1968): 101–9; Richard C. Lukas, *Bitter Legacy: Polish-American Relations in the Wake of World War II* (Louisville: University of Kentucky Press, 1982).

123. Pula, *Polish Americans*, 96–101.

124. Davies, *God's Playground*, 2:489.

125. Lukas, "Polish American Congress and the Polish Question," 43–44; Irons, "'Test Is Poland,'" 39–43.

126. Irons, "'Test Is Poland,'" 44.

127. Ibid., 45–51.

128. Sword, Davies, and Ciechanowski, *Formation of the Polish Community*, 189–90.

129. Ibid., 190, 193–96; Andrzej Friszke, *Życie polityczne emigracji*, vol. 1, *Druga Wielka Emigracja, 1945–1990* (Warsaw: Biblioteka WIĘZI, 1999), 29–31.

130. Friszke, *Życie polityczne*, 31.

131. Jędrzejewicz, *Polonia amerykańska*, 36. The author saw another source of the conflict in personality differences among the KNAPP leaders.

132. Ibid., 38.

133. "Od Redakcji," *Tygodnik Polski*, no. 1, January 10, 1943, 1.

134. Rev. S. A. Iciek, "Listy do redakcji," *Tygodnik Polski*, no. 2, January 17, 1943, 3.

135. See, for example, Władysław Gieysztor, "Na Majnach: U polskich i litewskich górników w Pennsylvanii," *Tygodnik Polski*, no. 13, April 4, 1943, 2; Marta Erdman-Wańkowicz, "Głos z 'Czykagowa,'" ibid., no. 50, December 17, 1944, 6–7; interview with General Barzyński, ibid., no. 7, February 21, 1943; and interview with Honorata Wolowska, ibid., no. 15, April 18, 1943, 3.

136. The cover of this issue, by Zdzisław Czermański, showed an oppressed Polish family gathered around the radio. Behind them, portraits of Kościuszko and President Wilson adorned the wall. The caption read: "Underground Poland listens to the congress in Buffalo."

137. Because of a lack of funds, *Tygodnik* did not appear for a few weeks in 1947. When publication resumed in March 1947, an editorial note proclaimed closer cooperation with American Polonia and broadened coverage of Polish-American issues. "Od Wydawnictwa," *Tygodnik Polski*, no. 1, March 9, 1947, 3–4. Around the same time, *Tygodnik* began publishing a page devoted to the Polish diaspora on other continents.

138. Jan Lechoń, "Wśród rodaków w Chicago," *Tygodnik Polski*, no. 12, March 24, 1946, 8-9.

139. Janta, *Nowe odkrycie*, 100.

140. *Tygodnik Polski*, no. 16, June 22, 1947, 8.

141. Tadeusz Nowakowski, *Aleja dobrych znajomych* (London: Polska Fundacja Kulturalna, 1968), 77-86.

142. Kazimierz Wierzyński, "Kasztan zwany Dewajtisem," in *Moja prywatna Ameryka* (London: Polska Fundacja Kulturalna, 1966), 11-22.

143. Lorentowicz, *Oczarowania*, 220-21.

144. Władysław Gieysztor, "Szare dni wygnańcze," *Tygodnik Polski*, no. 11, March 12, 1944, 11.

145. Lorentowicz, *Oczarowania*, 261-62.

146. Jerzy Paczkowski, "Do przyjaciela z tamtej strony Atlantyku," *Poezja*, no. 4-5 (1987): 47-48. Paczkowski was eventually captured and imprisoned by the Nazis and died in a concentration camp near Hamburg in February 1945. Bolesław Klimaszewski, Ewa R. Nowakowska, and Wojciech Wyskiel, *Mały słownik pisarzy polskich na obczyźnie, 1939-1980* (Warsaw: Wydawnictwo Interpress, 1992), 260-61.

147. *Tygodnik Polski*, no. 2, January 13, 1946, 2-3.

148. [Jan Lechoń], "Życzenia wolności," *Tygodnik Polski*, no. 50-51, December 23, 1945, 2-3; Władysław Konopczyński, "Siedem emigracji," ibid., no. 22, June 2, 1946, 4-7; Tymon Terlecki, "Do podstaw romantyzmu społecznego," ibid., no. 18, May 5, 1946, 2-4; Sergjusz Piasecki, "Czy wracać?" ibid., no. 35, September 8, 1946, 4-5; [Jan Lechoń], "Patrząc w przyszłość," ibid., no. 1, March 9, 1947, 2-3; [Jan Lechoń], "Codzienność i przyszłość emigracji," ibid., no. 10, May 11, 1947. See also Anna D. Jaroszyńska-Kirchmann, "An Elephant and the Polish Question: Politicization of American Polonia after World War II," *Spectrum* 6 (1994): 28-33.

Chapter 2

The title of this chapter is taken from the first stanza of an untitled poem by Wawrzyniec Czereśniewski (1911-1976):

    All that I have left
    Is my free song.
    Maybe it's a loaf of bread for the road
    And maybe a lonely brick,
    Which I carry in secret,
    To make it one day, one day,
    Into the cornerstone of a home?
            Poezja 22 (1987): 65-66.

Czereśniewski was an officer of the Polish Armed Forces in the West. After the war he settled in Great Britain, where he remained active in the Polish community and published in the Polish-language press. After retiring, he moved to Australia. Bolesław Klimaszewski, Ewa R. Nowakowska, and Wojciech Wyskiel, *Mały słownik pisarzy polskich na obczyźnie, 1939–1980* (Warsaw: Wydawnictwo Interpress, 1992), 70–71.

1. Leokadia Rowinski, *That the Nightingale Return: Memoir of the Polish Resistance, the Warsaw Uprising, and German P.O.W. Camps* (Jefferson, N.C.: McFarland and Company, 1999), 131–32.

2. Ibid., 137.

3. In September 1945 the number of refugees cared for or repatriated by the Supreme Headquarters Allied Expeditionary Force (SHAEF) was 6,795,000, and by the Soviet forces 6,869,660. In Italy, Denmark, and Norway, the Allied forces liberated about 200,000 additional displaced persons. Malcolm Proudfoot, *European Refugees, 1939–1952: A Study in Forced Population Movement* (London: Faber and Faber, 1957), 158–61; Mark Wyman, *DP: Europe's Displaced Persons, 1945–1951* (Philadelphia: Balch Institute Press, 1989), 15–37.

4. Proudfoot, *European Refugees*, 190–206, 131–33, 158–61. By July 2, 1945, 3.2 million refugees had found their way home, mostly to the USSR, France, Belgium, and the Netherlands. Wyman, *DP*, 19.

5. Proudfoot, *European Refugees*, 106–19, 147–52, 162–68. SHAEF superseded the Refugee and Displaced Persons Section of the Civil Affairs Division of the Headquarters of the Chief of Staff Supreme Allied Commander in January 1944.

6. Ibid., 98–106. For a detailed account of UNRRA's activities in different parts of the world, see George Woodbridge, *UNRRA: The History of the United Nations Relief and Rehabilitation Administration*, 3 vols., (New York: Columbia University Press, 1950). J. G. Stoessinger provides insight into the political debates surrounding UNRRA in *The Refugee and the World Community* (Minneapolis: University of Minnesota Press, 1956), 49–59.

7. Proudfoot, *European Refugees*, 189–228, 275–92, 415–18; Stoessinger, *Refugee*, 51–55; Leonard Dinnerstein and David M. Reimers, *Ethnic Americans: A History of Immigration and Assimilation* (New York: Harper and Row, 1975), 12.

8. A detailed history of the IRO can be found in Louise W. Holborn, *The International Refugee Organization, a Specialized Agency of the United Nations: Its History and Work, 1946–1952* (London: Oxford University Press, 1956). See also Stoessinger, *Refugee*, 60–82, 85–155; Proudfoot, *European Refugees*, 399–436; Gil Loescher and John A. Scanlan, *Calculated Kindness: Refugees and America's Half-Open Door, 1945 to the Present* (New York: Free Press, 1986), 15–18.

9. Stoessinger, *Refugee*, 163–69. Approximately half a million IRO refugees remained scattered throughout the camps in Germany, Austria, Italy, Greece, the Middle East, and Shanghai at the end of 1951. "The majority of these displaced persons were in

the so-called hard-core group, which implied that their opportunities of resettlement were limited for such diverse reasons as family composition, age, profession, and state of health. Only about thirty thousand of these were considered 'unresettleable'" by the Organization because of old age or ill health." Ibid., 161. New refugee crises in different parts of the world, however, generated new challenges. According to Stoessinger, "a conservative estimate would place the figure of refugees at the time of IRO's closure at fifteen million people.." Ibid., 163. For a detailed history of the UN High Commissioner for Refugees, see Louise W. Holborn, Philip Chartrand, and Rita Chartrand, *Refugees: A Problem of Our Time; The Work of the United Nations High Commissioner for Refugees, 1951-1972*, 2 vols. (Metuchen, N.J.: Scarecrow Press, 1975). 1959 was declared World Refugee Year and evoked renewed interest in the fate of displaced persons left behind in European camps. See, for example, Edgar H. S. Chandler, *The High Tower of Refuge: An Inspiring Story of Refugee Relief throughout the World* (New York: Frederick A. Praeger, 1959); Yul Brynner, *Bring Forth the Children: A Journey to the Forgotten People of Europe and the Middle East* (New York: McGraw-Hill, 1960).

10. Czesław Łuczak, *Polacy w okupowanych Niemczech, 1945-1949* (Poznań: Pracownia Serwisu Oprogramowania, 1993), 13.

11. Ibid., 21–23.

12. Statistics concerning the number of Polish DPs in any specific locale present multiple difficulties in assessment. The DP population remained in constant movement, mostly initiated by the UNRRA and IRO, but also resulting from individual choices. Combining small camps and dividing larger ones were frequent occurrences, especially during the UNRRA period. The population of the camps also changed because of individual movements. DPs transferred from camp to camp in search of better living conditions or moved out of camps to live privately. Some looked for lost members of their families; others were recruited to different camps as teachers, actors, or organizers. In the initial period of the DP camps' existence, there were also cases of reporting "dead souls" to obtain extra rations for the camp inhabitants. In time the DP population swelled with returnees from Poland (that is, those who were repatriated and escaped back to the West through the green border) and newcomers fleeing the communist regime. Finally, the DP baby boom quickly became a factor, when after long years of war people could start new families and go on with their lives. The departures of DPs on various international immigration schemes additionally complicated any attempts to capture the size of the Polish DP population in a precise manner. In order to keep up with the changes and to have control over the statistical data pertaining to the Polish population, Polish organizations compiled their own statistics. A report prepared by the Main Resettlement Department of the Polish Union in the American zone of Germany in 1948 pointed to the three sources of available statistical data on Polish DPs: the American military

government, basing its statistics on the German administration's sources; the IRO; and Polish organizations. According to the authors of the report, data provided by the German administration showed a strong tendency to overstate the figures, in order to stress the proportion of the DP burden that fell on the German economy. On the other hand, the IRO statistics, in the opinion of the report's authors, demonstrated numbers below the actual Polish refugee population, in order to decrease the volume of aid to the DPs. The IRO statistics, naturally, excluded all refugees who returned from Poland after repatriation, those who escaped from Poland after the war ended, and any others without legitimate refugee status. The Polish organizations in the areas of Würtenberg and Baden obtained lists of Poles registered by the German administration and mailed questionnaires to all thirty-five hundred of them. The results of the questionnaire demonstrated that substantial numbers of registered Polish DPs either had emigrated by that time, had moved to different locations, or had died. "Główny referat osiedleńczy Zjednoczenia Polskiego amerykańskiej okupacji Niemiec," report, [1948], 2, F. #162, Józef Piłsudski Institute (JPI), New York. A comparison of the totals for November 1948 in the American zone indicated 46,987 Polish DPs, according to the IRO estimates and 71,000 according to the Polish sources. Ibid., 4-6.

13. Woodbridge, *UNRRA*, 3:502.

14. Ibid., 3:426-27, 3:498.

15. Łuczak, *Polacy w okupowanych Niemczech*, 43.

16. "Główny referat osiedleńczy," 8. The Polish Union's report of 1948 illuminated the potential bias of the IRO data. The report blamed difficulties in the precise quantification of the DP occupations on several interrelated factors. First, DPs tended to claim occupations that seemed to them especially desirable for immigration screening purposes, for example, an agricultural background for immigration to the United States or the South American countries. Second, many DPs graduated from one or more of the numerous courses organized in the DP camps and often claimed occupations that corresponded not to their prewar work experience but to their recently obtained knowledge. Lastly, forced laborers often gained new skills while working in German factories and agriculture during the war and decided that those qualifications could help them meet labor market demands in the countries of resettlement.

17. "Ludność polska w strefie amerykańskiej Niemiec," report, [1949], 1, F. #153, JPI.

18. Łuczak, *Polacy w okupowanych Niemczech*, 43-44. Compare Wiesław Hładkiewicz, *Polacy w zachodnich strefach okupacyjnych Niemiec, 1945-1949* (Zielona Góra: Wyższa Szkoła Pedagogiczna, 1982), 12-31. The only data for postwar Polish immigrants that came to the United States derive from studies by Danuta Mostwin, based on a self-selective sample of 2,049 questionnaire respondents from thirty-five states. The majority of Mostwin's respondents arrived in the United States between

January 1948 and December 31, 1952 (the closing date for resettlement under the DP Act and its amendments), mostly from Great Britain. The next largest group, about 16.5 percent of the sample, arrived between 1957 and 1962, mostly from Poland. Danuta Mostwin, "The Profile of a Transplanted Family," *Polish Review* 19, no. 1 (1974): 77–81; idem., "Post–World War II Polish Immigrants in the United States," *Polish American Studies* 26, no. 2 (Autumn 1979): 6–9.

19. Alarmed by information about the conditions of Jews in DP camps and the conduct of the American military, President Truman appointed the dean of the University of Pennsylvania Law School, Earl G. Harrison, to investigate conditions in Europe. Harrison, who also served as the American representative on the Inter-Governmental Committee on Refugees, went to Europe on a fact-finding mission and returned with a report, which he presented to Truman in August 1945. Harrison's report contained a devastating criticism of conditions in DP camps in general and particularly of the situation and treatment of Jewish DPs. Wyman, *DP*, 44–45, 57, 131–37; Marta Dyczok, *The Grand Alliance and Ukrainian Refugees* (New York: St. Martin's Press, 2000), 66–67.

20. Smaller camps housing DPs of various backgrounds did not avoid conflict. For examples of tensions between Polish and Ukrainian DPs, see the interpretations of the incident in the Polish DP camp in Bockhorn, F. #154, JPI. The records abound also in complaints about preferential treatment of Baltic DPs by UNRRA employees.

21. For example, among the students attending the Polish Technical College in Esslingen in 1947 there were nine Jews, two Bulgarians, and one Belorussian. Bolesław Budzyń, *The Polish Technical College in Esslingen/Germany, 1945–1949* (Kraków: Jagiellonian Foundation Press, 1996), 51–52. On the users of the Ingolstadt library, see F. #168, JPI.

22. See, for example, detailed reports from the bureau's meetings in July 1946 and December 1947 in F. #154, 160, JPI; and a diploma commemorating a Polish-Ukrainian journalists' meeting, June 14–15, 1947, F. #154, JPI. On the peculiar legal situation of Ukrainian DPs, whom international agencies denied a separate national identity, see Dyczok, *Grand Alliance*. Many Ukrainians were classified as Polish citizens and placed in DP camps together with ethnic Poles. Some Ukrainians, trying to avoid repatriation to the Soviet Union, assumed new identities as Poles, Romanians, or Czechoslovaks; others claimed stateless status, and many demanded to be classified as Ukrainians. Dyczok, *Grand Alliance*, 124–25, 140, 159–60.

23. Wacław Sterner, *Gefengeni i Dipisi* (Warsaw: Książka i Wiedza, 1979), 171–72.

24. Jan Michalski, *Obóz przy Sandstrasse* (Warsaw: Czytelnik, 1975), 57–59; Sterner, *Gefengeni*, 306. About the difficulties in organizing the camp in Marienthal, see also Klaudiusz Hrabyk, "Z drugiej strony barykady: Spowiedź z klęski; Lata 1902–1959; Wspomnienia i dzienniki," microfilm of an unpublished manuscript, Ossolineum, Wrocław, [1979], 240–51.

25. Sterner, *Gefengeni*, 219–20. Spackenberg became the site of frequent visitations by UNRRA dignitaries. In April 1946 the British zone authorities demanded that the entire camp population move to the camp in Lauenberg, which was located in old German military buildings with large rooms and primitive living conditions. The inhabitants of Spackenberg went on strike and hung a black flag as a sign of rebellion against the move. The British Army broke the revolt with a mass show of soldiers and weapons. The camp population was transferred to Lauenberg, and Lithuanian and Latvian DPs were moved into Spackenberg. Ibid., 307–10.

26. The best description of life in Wildflecken (the author never mentions the camp's Polish name, Durzyń) can be found in Kathryn Hulme, *The Wild Place* (Boston: Little, Brown, 1953). However, the author presents her story from the specific point of view of a UNRRA/IRO team worker and does not spend much time on explorations of the intricacies of the DP life and activities.

27. Stefan Nienaski-Koper, "Z życia Polaków w Niemczech," *Nowy Świat*, March 17, 1946, 10. The authorities of the Polish Union accepted an initiative to discontinue usage of the term "DP camp" as reminiscent of labor or—worse yet—concentration camps and replaced it with the term "DP center." "Sprawozdanie z działalności Zrzeszenia Ośrodków Polskich Bawarii Północnej za czas od 1.2. do 31.7.46," 3; "Tezy w sprawie organizacji ośrodków polskich," [1946], 1, F. #171, JPI. Colloquial usage of the term "camp" was retained, however, throughout the entire period of their existence.

28. Hulme, *Wild Place*, 9.

29. Ibid., 90–91. See also Eileen Egan, *For Whom There Is No Room: Scenes from the Refugee World* (New York: Paulist Press, 1995), 152–58.

30. Łuczak, *Polacy w okupowanych Niemczech*, 45; Stefan Nienaski-Koper, "Miasto Maczków"; Andrzej Pilch, *Losy Polaków w Austrii po drugiej wojnie światowej* (Wrocław: Ossolineum, 1994), 94.

31. Łuczak, *Polacy w okupowanych Niemczech*, 69–70; Czesław Brzoza, "Zapomniana armia: Polskie oddziały wartownicze w Europie (1945–1951)," *Zeszyty Historyczne* 494 (1996): 3–21.

32. After the American military initiated the demobilization of the Guards at the end of 1947, their Polish members created the Association of Former Guards Units in the American zone, admitting both the demobilized Guards and those still on active duty. At the time of its establishment, the association numbered more than seven thousand members. "Ludność polska"; Centralny Komitet Organizacyjny organizacji b. polskich wartowników w strefie amerykańskiej, *Okólnik*, July 22, 1947; "Instrukcja Nr. 1," F. #109, JPI.

33. Zrzeszenie Ośrodków Polskich Bawarii Północnej, report, November 4, 1947, F. #172, JPI.

34. Ibid., 4–6. Camp transfers also frequently resulted in the loss of privately owned property such as furniture.

35. Painful memories of frequent moves from camp to camp haunted DP children for decades after their successful resettlement in the United States. For example, John Guzłowski in a book of poems dedicated to his parents remembered:

>And then the British came,
>And put them in another camp,
>Where the corpses still had not been buried,
>Where the water was bad, where my mother
>Got sick, where her stool was as red
>As the beets she had to dig everyday....
>... And it was cold in the new place, and some
>Of the babies died, and my sister was very sick,
>Maybe from drinking the dirty water.
>We were always being moved around.

John Guzlowski, "My Mother Talks about the Slave Labor Camps," in *Language of Mules* (Charleston, Ill.: DP Press, 1999), 27 (by permission of the author).

36. Wyman, *DP*, 52. The theoretical UNRRA goal for the normal consumer was 2,650 calories per day. Woodbridge, *UNRRA*, vol. 1, 503. See also Łuczak, *Polacy w okupowanych Niemczech*, 77–80. According to some opinions, the food situation in Austria was the worst, especially in camps dependent on the Austrian authorities for supplies. During the harsh winter of 1946 and 1947, the DP camps in the French zone received only 1,550 calories a day per person. Pilch, *Losy Polaków w Austrii*, 115–16.

37. Zrzeszenie Ośrodków Polskich Bawarii Północnej, 10; Michalski, *Obóz*, 71–72; Hulme, *Wild Place*, 52–53.

38. Hulme describes Durzyń rising up in a riot and a sit-down strike over the division of products from Red Cross parcels, *Wild Place*, 55–69. She also depicts cases of infant death from malnutrition, 78–79. Michalski reminisces about full parcels or single items serving as a kind of barter currency. See for example Michalski, *Obóz*, 231. The same author recounts how the camp council included about two hundred "dead souls" on the food list, in order to create an emergency supply of Red Cross parcels for the camp. The survival tactics learned and practiced during the war were continued after the war had ended. Michalski, *Obóz*, 144–53.

39. Hulme, *Wild Place*, 93–98; Sterner, *Gefengeni*, 229–31.

40. "Protokół zebrania Polskiego Obozu Nr. 28 odbytego w dniu 8 sierpnia 1945 r. przy obecności 195 osób, na ogólny stan 280 osób," August 8, 1945, F. #92, JPI.

41. Hrabyk, "Z drugiej strony barykady," 240–41. One report from the Polish DP camps in Northern Bavaria complained that the DPs received shoes sized either for little children or for full-grown adults, a situation that left teenagers clad in clogs or canvas in the late fall and winter months. Zrzeszenie Ośrodków Polskich Bawarii Północnej, 5. See also Łuczak, *Polacy w okupowanych Niemczech*, 86–87. Pilch, *Losy Polaków w Austrii*, 117.

42. Letter of March 23, 1952, IHRC 84, Box 35, Fol. 260, PAC, also quoted in Anna D. Jaroszyńska-Kirchmann, "'Nowa Emigracja' and 'Stara Polonia': The Transformation of Social Relations and the Displaced Persons Resettlement Program in the United States," in *The Polish Diaspora*, ed. James S. Pula and M. B. Biskupski, vol. 2, *Selected Essays from the Fiftieth Anniversary International Congress of the Polish Institute of Arts and Sciences of America* (Columbia University Press, 1993), 67.

43. Łuczak, *Polacy w okupowanych Niemczech*, 91-95, Pilch, *Losy Polaków w Austrii*, 129-35.

44. H. B. Murphy, "The Camps," in *Flight and Resettlement*, ed. H. B. Murphy (Lucerne: United Nations Educational, Scientific, and Cultural Organization, 1955), 58-63.

45. Eduard Bakis, "'D.P. Apathy,'" in Murphy, *Flight and Resettlement*, 76-77.

46. Tadeusz Nowakowski, a writer, a journalist, and a political prisoner throughout the war, saw the camps as the epitome of brutality, cruelty, violence, and moral as well as physical abuse. Tadeusz Nowakowski, *Obóz Wszystkich Świętych* (Warsaw: Czytelnik, 1990).

47. Łuczak, *Polacy w okupowanych Niemczech*, 47-50.

48. Michalski, *Obóz*, 286-93, 307-32; Wyman, *DP*, 108-9; Łuczak, *Polacy w okupowanych Niemczech*, 50-52; Pilch, *Losy Polaków w Austrii*, 121-22; "Ludność polska"; *Okólnik* Nr. 8, November 22, 1947, F. #167, JPI, informed readers about incidents of demobilized Polish Guard members behaving in an "improper way in public places" and appealed to them not to bring shame on the good name of the Polish community in Germany.

49. Wyman, *DP*, 178-85.

50. The good reputation of the committee members must have been unchallenged. In Ludwigsburg the camp chaplain opposed appointment to the disciplinary committee of a man who lived with a woman without the sacrament of marriage. Rev. M. B. to the Camp Council in Ludwigsburg, July 2, 1949, F. # 170, JPI.

51. *Okólnik*, no. 11, December 13, 1947, F. #167, JPI.

52. See, for example, the pronouncement of July 15, 1949, by the Ludwigsburg Disciplinary Committee, F. #170, JPI.

53. The institution of liaison officers was liquidated in the American zone of Germany on August 6, 1946. *Nowy Świat*, September 22, 1946, 18. UNRRA authorities, not without reason, commonly considered them as hampering repatriation efforts. Proudfoot, *European Refugees*, 280-82; Łuczak, *Polacy w okupowanych Niemczech*, 17-18.

54. Andrzej Friszke, *Życie polityczne emigracji*, vol. 1, *Druga Wielka Emigracja, 1945-1990* (Warsaw: Biblioteka WIĘZI, 1999), 41-45; Grzegorz Janusz, "Stowarzyszenie Naczelne Polskich Ośrodków Wysiedleńczych w Niemczech Zachodnich w latach 1945-1980," in *Organizacje Polonijne w Europie Zachodniej: Współczesność i*

tradycje; Materiały z konferencji naukowej w dniach 2 i 3 kwietnia 1987 r. w Poznaniu, ed. Barbara Szydłowska-Cegłowa and Jerzy Kozłowski (Poznań: PAN, Zakład Badań nad Polonią Zagraniczną, 1991), 152.

55. Michalski, *Obóz*, 36-49.

56. Pilch, *Losy Polaków w Austrii*, 97, 101.

57. According to the official history of UNRRA, "camp self-government in the fullest sense was one of the goals of UNRRA camp administration; it is, indeed, no exaggeration to say that it was the goal toward which all activities were pointed." Woodbridge, *UNRRA*, 522. As Woodbridge explains, the progress of the displaced persons in learning self-government was slow and uneven, but once "they had learned to govern themselves; they had been rehabilitated." Ibid., 525. The history of UNRRA is full of equally patronizing statements. The beginnings of camp governments in Austria were similar; see Pilch, *Losy Polaków w Austrii*, 96-99.

58. "Protokół 6 posiedzenia Zarządu Zrzeszenia Ośrodków Polskich Bawarii Północnej odbytego w Regensburgu w dniu 9.5.1947 r.," May 9, 1947, F. #172 JPI.

59. Ibid., 9-10. Hulme's recollections from her work in Durzyń do include instances of conflict with the DP City Council but many more examples of cooperation and good working relations between the UNRRA/IRO teams and the camp's representatives. However, the author's attitude toward the Durzyń government, although filled with sympathy and compassion for the difficult situation of the Polish DPs, often seems to be rather patronizing and lacks true understanding of the role and significance of the Durzyń City Council.

60. "Sprawozdanie z działalności Komitetu Ośrodka za czas od 16 XI 48 do 3 VIII 49," F. #170, JPI.

61. Roman M. to the Committee of the Center in Ludwigsburg, June 17, 1949, F. #170, JPI; Stanisław K. to the Camp Council in Ludwigsburg, August 7, 1949, F. #170, JPI; "Protokół, IV-te Nadzwyczajne Posiedzenie Komitetu Ośrodka [Ludwigsburg] zwołane przez Przewodniczącego na dzień 12 Października 1949 r. na godz. 19:45," October 12, 1949, F. #170, JPI.

62. By-Laws, January 12, 1946, Durzyń, F. #172, JPI; "Protokół 6 posiedzenia Zarządu Zrzeszenia Ośrodków Polskich Bawarii Północnej odbytego w Regensburgu w dniu 9.5.1947 r.," 3-4, F. #172, JPI.

63. Hulme, *Wild Place*, 93-98, 101-2, 124-26, 129-30; Sterner, *Gefengeni*, 229-31; Michalski, *Obóz*, 131-40, 307-32.

64. See examples of persecution and suffering in the concentration camps, especially Dachau, in Henryk Maria Malak, *Klechy w obozach śmierci* (London: Veritas, [1960]), and Monsignor Stanisław Grabowski, *Follow Me: The Memoirs of a Polish Priest* (Roseville, Minn.: White Rose Press, 1997).

65. Between 1945 and 1949 about six hundred priests returned to Poland. Łuczak, *Polacy w okupowanych Niemczech*, 211-15; Wyman, *DP*, 110-11. Father Henryk Maria

Malak provides an excellent insight into the work of the Polish clergy in the DP camps in his book richly illustrated with photographs. The book-album was designed to be a memento to the DPs, in order to remind them and their children about the special times in the DP camps. Henryk Maria Malak, *Na Wychodźczym Szlaku: Album, naświetlający: Przyczyny powstania, historyczny przebieg, prace, zadania i osiągnięcia—Polskiego Wychodźstwa Powojennego z drugiej wojny światowej na ziemi niemieckiej* (Chicago: Wydawnictwo im. św. Jadwigi, 1952).

66. "126 Księży Polskich w Okupacji Angielskiej w Niemczech," *Naród Polski*, June 5, 1947, 5. According to Łuczak, between 1945 and 1948, Polish priests in Germany performed 55,848 weddings, more than 60,000 baptisms, 15,000 funerals, and prepared 8,000 children for First Communion. Łuczak, *Polacy w okupowanych Niemczech*, 217.

67. Wyman, *DP*, 111–12. About the legal problems of marriage procedures in the DP camps, see Michalski, *Obóz*, 154–64.

68. M. Lawrentiuk to K. Hrabyk, report, March 8 1949, the Hohenfels-Lechów camp, F. #109, JPI. At the beginning of its existence, the camp had about thirteen thousand people. About the large number of weddings, see also Hrabyk, "Z drugiej strony barykady," 244–45, 260–61.

69. Ibid.; Report from Ingolstadt, March 9, 1949, F. #168, JPI; Report from Altenstadt, March 7, 1949, F. #168, JPI; Łuczak, *Polacy w okupowanych Niemczech*, 217.

70. See Rev. Anastazy Nadolny, *Opieka duszpasterska nad dziećmi i młodzieżą polską na terenie Niemiec zachodnich w latach 1945–1965* (Lublin: Katolicki Uniwersytet Lubelski, 1980); Łuczak, *Polacy w okupowanych Niemczech*, 225–28.

71. In Tadeusz Nowakowski's novel *Camp of All Saints*, the priest is the only positive character among corrupted and demoralized DPs, as he tries to watch over the spiritual needs of the community and to re-build the DPs' deeply damaged moral structure. Nowakowski, *Obóz Wszystkich Świętych*.

72. Łuczak, *Polacy w okupowanych Niemczech*, 220–21.

73. Janusz, "Stowarzyszenie Naczelne," 148–52; "Ludność polska."

74. Janusz, "Stowarzyszenie," 152–54; "Pismo Okólne Nr. 5/49 Zjednoczenia Polskiego na terenie okupacji amerykańskiej Niemiec, Regensburg, 8.4.49," F. #162, JPI; "Statut organizacji pod nazwą Zjednoczenie Polskie na terenie okupacji amerykańskiej Niemiec," F. #162, JPI.

75. "Statut organizacji pod nazwą Zjednoczenie Polskie."

76. "Sprawozdanie z działalności Zjednoczenia Polskiego na terenie okupacji amerykańskiej Niemiec za rok 1948," 8–11, F. #162, JPI.

77. "Odezwa prezydium Zjednoczenia Polskiego na terenie okupacji amerykańskiej Niemiec," Regensburg, July 1948, F. #162, JPI.

78. "Sprawozdanie . . . za rok 1948," 9–12. The report indicates numerous problems with the maintenance of the PU headquarters in Regensburg, payments to office personnel, and trips taken by PU representatives for meetings with the local

authorities. In 1948 the PU's finances took an additional blow in connection with the publicized cigarette scandal, when cigarette donations for the PU were confiscated by the American authorities and the leaders of the PU were imprisoned and sentenced for black market activities. Polish Guards came to the financial rescue of the organization by voluntarily taxing all their members for the benefit of the PU.

79. Janusz, "Stowarzyszenie naczelne," 160. The author points to the internal power struggle within the PU leadership, conflicts, and dissensions in the late 1940s. He emphasizes, however, that although the conflicts within the PU could suggest deep internal divisions among Polish DPs in Germany, "in reality, only a narrow group of people participated in those confrontations.... The conflicts, having their source mostly in hurt ambitions of individuals, did not interest an average DP." Ibid., 159.

80. The PU leaders had worked with the zone and IRO authorities toward the legalization of the PU since 1947. In August 1948 General Lucius D. Clay, the American military governor in Germany, stated that the PU did not require any formal recognition from the American occupational authorities to continue its activities. On the basis of that statement, the IRO established liaison officers from the ranks of the PU in each of its resettlement centers. "Sprawozdanie ... za rok 1948," 4–5.

81. *Kronika,* December 21 1946, 2; ibid., January 5, 1947, 1. According to its by-laws, the ZPUW's goals included:

a. organization of the Polish war emigration's communal life, b. care over the maintenance and development of the Polish culture and education, c. strengthening of the basis of democracy and social justice in public life, and the basis of Christian morality as the source of the nation's power in both public and personal lives, d. representation of the war emigration in front of the international organizations designed to care for the refugees, and if needed, the state authorities in countries of resettlement, e. cooperation with the social organizations of emigrations from other ethnic groups, f. cooperation with organizations of older [Polish] emigrations, g. organization of the basis for the economic well being and self-help of Polish war emigrants and conducting of the resettlement action in cooperation with proper authorities, h. winning of the world opinion for the Polish question.

Ibid., 1.

82. Ibid., 14–17.

83. Ibid., 13; "Ludność polska."

84. "Sprawozdanie ... za rok 1948," 17.

85. "Komitet pomocy uchodźcom," report, [1948], F. #162, JPI.

86. Ryszard Jachowicz, "W sprawie opieki społecznej nad polskimi wysiedleńcami. (Częściowy materiał do memoriału, mającego być przedłożonym w I.R.O.)," 2, Hohenfels, October 28, 1947, F. #172, JPI.

87. Welfare Office, DP Camp Hohenfels, "Sprawozdanie ogólne, 27.10.1947," F. #172, JPI.

88. "Sprawozdanie . . . za rok 1948," 12–13, F. # 162, JPI.
89. "Z uchwał Rady Strefowej Zjednoczenia, 1949," F. # 162, JPI.
90. "Pismo okólne Nr. 6/50," Ludwigsburg, June 28, 1950, 7–10.
91. In Austria, too, Polish DPs united within the Związek Polaków w Austrii (ZPA, Association of Poles in Austria) established in 1945 in the American zone and the Związek Polaków w Tyrolu (ZPT, Association of Poles in Tyrol) in the French zone. Their goals and initiatives resembled closely those of the PU. Pilch, *Losy Polaków w Austrii*, 103–8, 111–15.
92. "Statut organizacji pod nazwą Zjednoczenie Polskie," F. #162, JPI.
93. The records of the PU indicate that throughout its existence the court was busy with numerous cases, many of which dragged on for a long time, causing the costs of the courts to rise tremendously. In an effort to curtail inefficiency and to cut down the expenses, appeals were made to the court to accept only cases with valid import and to reduce the number of trials on slander and personal offenses.
94. Janusz, "Stowarzyszenie naczelne," 152.
95. *Załoga: Biuletyn Organizacji Zawodowych Zjednoczenia Polskiego na Terenie Okupacji Amerykańskiej Niemiec*, no. 11, August 25, 1947, 19–22, F. #188, JPI. "Ludność polska"; "Polska Rada Zawodowa," report [1948], F. #162, JPI.
96. "Polska Rada Zawodowa," 1.
97. The first agency created to carry out the organization of vocational training for Polish DPs in the American and French zones was the Division for Vocational Training (Sekcja Szkolenia Zawodowego) established in 1945 as a part of the Polish Military Mission (USFET-Frankfurt/M), headed by engineer Jerzy Skiba. The organization of a network of vocational training courses by the IRO was a blow to the Polish vocational education system, which began to liquidate its structure in June 1948. According to statistics for 1947, in that year the division sponsored 193 courses taught by 419 lecturers and instructors and attended by 6,567 students. In October 1948 the number of courses decreased to 24, staffed by 52 instructors and attended by 676 students. Ibid., 162.
98. For example, the Syndicate of Polish Journalists gave loans (both repayable and nonrepayable) to its members in difficult financial situations. "The goals of the Syndicate of Polish Journalists in the Former Reich," F. #154, JPI.
99. *Załoga*, no. 11, August 25, 1947, 1–5; "Ludność polska."
100. *Załoga*, no. 11, August 25, 1947, 10–11; "Ludność polska."
101. According to a report from 1949, Belgium, France, the Netherlands, Great Britain, Canada, Bolivia, Venezuela, and Morocco accepted the documents. "Ludność polska."
102. *Załoga*, no. 11, August 25, 1947, 13–16; "Ludność polska."
103. *Załoga*, no. 11, August 25, 1947, 17–18.
104. Ibid., 8–10. About the beginnings of the Syndykat and personalities involved

in its establishment, see Hrabyk, "Z drugiej strony barykady," 271-86. Klaudiusz Hrabyk was the first president of the Syndykat, replaced in 1947 by Józef Białasiewicz.

105. The UNRRA-sponsored university in Munich was established in late 1945. Most of the faculty were DPs. Classes were conducted in German. In 1946 the enrollment reached fourteen hundred students of various nationalities. The UNRRA closed the university in early 1947, justifying its decision by its unwillingness to provide DPs with any incentives to remain in Germany and force them to repatriate. Wyman, *DP*, 123-25. The Circle of Polish Professors and Teaching Assistants was initially formed at the UNRRA University in Munich in 1946 and included twenty-one members. It published its own journal, *Przekroje* (Reviews), and participated in verification commissions of other unions and Polish school systems. In 1948, the circle organized the Polish Scholarly Conference in Munich. *Załoga*, no. 11, August 25, 1947, 5-7; "Ludność polska." On the activities of the union of Polish artists see *Załoga*, no. 11, August 25, 1947, 7; on the writers' union, see ibid., 11-12; and on the union of stage artists, see ibid., 12-13.

106. For a more detailed treatment of Polish DP schools in Germany, see Anna D. Jaroszyńska-Kirchmann, "Patriotism, Responsibility, and the Cold War: Polish Schools in DP Camps in Germany, 1945-1951," *Polish Review* 47, no. 1 (2002): 35-66.

107. Michalski, *Obóz*, 190.

108. Ibid., 202.

109. Łuczak, *Polacy w okupowanych Niemczech*, 189, 191, 203.

110. *Dziennik Zarządzeń i Informacji Centralnego Komitetu dla Spraw Szkolnych i Oświatowych*, (Blomberg, 1948), 3-5, F. "Uchodźcy-Prasa-Dublety II," JPI.

111. "Instrukcja w sprawie organizacji szkolnictwa i oświaty polskiej w Niemczech, Londyn, Ministerstwo W.R.I.O.P., 1945," F. #1, JPI.

112. Ibid., 2.

113. Ibid., 26.

114. Władysław Kowalczyk, *Szkolnictwo polskie w Niemczech, 1945-1948* (Warsaw: Państwowe Zakłady Wydawnictw Szkolnych, 1961), 115-19.

115. The decision of the UNRRA to close Polish schools in the American zone resonated in the international press. On behalf of the Polish DPs, the PAC president Charles Rozmarek and the American Polonia delegation visiting Europe intervened with the American secretary of state. Interventions were made also in the British Parliament, and UNRRA was finally forced to withdraw its decision. *Dziennik Zarządzeń i Informacji*, 13-15.

116. Ibid., 7-46.

117. "Pismo okólne Nr. 4/50," April 19, 1950, F. #166, JPI. The school closing was a result of the completion of the emigration program and transfer of the remaining DP population into the German economy. On Polish DP schools in Germany, see

also Łuczak, *Polacy w okupowanych Niemczech,* 179–209; and on the schools in Austria, see Pilch, *Losy Polaków w Austrii,* 146–52.

118. *Dziennik Zarządzeń i Informacji,* 47–48; Rev. Roman Nir, *Szkice z dziejów Polonii* (Orchard Lake, Mich.: Archiwum, 1990), 90–95.

119. *Dziennik Zarządzeń i Informacji,* 48–49. In Austria, Polish students enrolled in the universities at Graz, Innsbruck, Leoben, Salzburg, and Vienna. The highest number of students estimated for 1947 and 1948 reached close to five hundred, the majority studying in Graz and Innsbruck. The Związek Studentów Polskich (Association of Polish Students) was established in Graz in January 1946 and developed extensive self-help and cultural programs. Similar organizations formed in Innsbruck in 1945. The Związek Akademików Polskich (ZAP, Association of Polish Academicians) had a library of more than fifteen hundred volumes and directed its own choir and performance group. It established ties with Polish students in Belgium, Switzerland, and Italy. Both student organizations benefited from the support of the Polish Second Corps stationed in Italy. Pilch, *Losy Polaków w Austrii,* 154–62.

120. For the story of the Esslingen college, see Budzyń, *Polish Technical College in Esslingen.*

121. In 1946 the Council for Youth was created by the representatives of the PU, clergy, teachers' union, students' union, Polish scouting, and the Gymnastic Association Sokół. However, because this central organization did not demonstrate much activity, in 1948 the PU disbanded it, justifying the decision by the fact that "the education of the youth is taken care of sufficiently by the church, school, and scouting." "Sprawozdanie . . . za rok 1948," 19–20.

122. "Ludność polska."

123. Łuczak, *Polacy w okupowanych Niemczech,* 114–15.

124. Ibid.

125. *Okólnik,* no. 11, December 13, 1947.

126. Pilch, *Losy Polaków w Austrii,* 152–54.

127. *Polish Daily-Biuletyn Informacyjny Dziennik Polski,* no. 11, April 24, 1945, F. Uchodźcy-Prasa-Dublety II, JPI.

128. Jerzy Grot-Kwaśniewski, "Prasa polskiego wychodźstwa przymusowego na terenie b. Rzeszy," 5, report, August 16, 1946, F. # 160, JPI.

129. John Krawiec (junior member of the *Polska* editorial group), interview by the author, tape recording, Chicago, Ill., January 5, 1995. Krawiec, a political prisoner who spent two years in Auschwitz and Buchenwald, had previous experience with control of the DP press by occupation authorities in the British zone. In April 1945 he began publishing a weekly *Biuletyn Polski.* In one issue, Krawiec criticized Churchill and Roosevelt for dealing with Stalin, who, in Krawiec's opinion, was "no better than Hitler." The next day he was arrested by the British and imprisoned together with

German common criminals. The intervention of Polish DPs protesting Krawiec's imprisonment helped to secure his release.

130. Grot-Kwaśniewski, "Prasa polskiego wychodźstwa," 2–4; Łuczak, *Polacy w okupowanych Niemczech*, 142. About the closing of *Polska*, see Hrabyk, "Z drugiej strony barykady," 280–81.

131. Łuczak, *Polacy w okupowanych Niemczech*, 142–43.

132. Grot-Kwaśniewski, "Prasa polskiego wychodźstwa," 4–7. In 1946 in Austria's American zone the main Polish press center was Salzburg, with two weeklies: *Głos Polski* and *Biuletyn Informacyjny*. Polish DPs in the French zone of Germany published many local bulletins and two newspapers with general circulation: *Wiadomości Polskie* and *Przegląd Dwutygodniowy*. Ibid., 1–2. The press in all zones of occupation experienced serious problems in obtaining paper for printing. According to a 1946 report, 40 percent of publishing houses did not have any extra supplies of paper, buying it for each printing; 30 percent had supplies for one month; 20 percent, for two weeks; 7 percent for more than 3 months; and 3 percent for three months. Ibid., 7.

133. Grot-Kwaśniewski, "Prasa polskiego wychodźstwa," 5–7.

134. The YMCA and YWCA published *Szlak* for the Guards. F. Uchodźcy-Prasa-Dublety, JPI.

135. Selected issues of the journals are available in the file Uchodźcy-Prasa-Dublety, located in the holdings of the JPI.

136. The best available study of the Polish press in the DP camps is Jan Kowalik, *Prasa polska w Niemczech, 1945–1971* (Toronto: Kanadyjsko-Polski Instytut Badawczy, 1976). See also Łuczak, *Polacy w okupowanych Niemczech*, 143–59.

137. Hrabyk, "Z drugiej strony barykady," 368–69.

138. The Polish Union in the American zone, appeal, July 1948, F. #162, JPI.

139. Stanisław Mikiciuk, president of the Polish Union, to the Syndicate of Polish Journalists in Eppstein, December 1, 1948, F. #162, JPI.

140. "Pismo Okólne Nr. 5/49," April 8, 1949, 2–3; "Ludność polska." About the history of *Kronika*, see Hrabyk, "Z drugiej strony barykady," 306–17, 368–69, 373.

141. Łuczak, *Polacy w okupowanych Niemczech*, 157. The story of the Polish press in Austria runs parallel to its development in Germany. The American zone distinguished itself in its exceptionally intensive press activities. It was mostly due to the fact that the greatest numbers of Polish DPs resided on that territory, including many members of intelligentsia liberated from the concentration camps and Oflags. The key difference between the DP press in Austria and that in Germany was the support, financial and organizational, that the Polish press in Austria received from the Second Corps stationed in Italy. Some titles published in Italy were also available in the DP camps in Austria, and Second Corps press agencies supplied local bulletins with current news. As in Germany, the Polish press in Austria shrank to a handful of titles in the late 1940s, led by *Wiadomości Polskie*, and published through the cooperation of

the DPs and the older Polish immigrant population in Austria. Pilch, *Losy Polaków w Austrii,* 259–64.

142. "Ludność polska w strefie amerykańskiej," JPI, F.# 153; Wyman, *DP,* 161.

143. Polish authors active in exile published their works also in the Polish and, to some extent, Polish-American press. Several collections of short fiction, memoirs, and poems, as well as larger novels appeared separately, many of them sponsored by the Literary Club or the Association of the Polish Writers in Germany led by Jerzy Jur-Sten. *Załoga,* no. 11, August 25, 1947, 12, 17; "Ludność polska."

144. *Załoga,* no. 11, August 25, 1947, 12.

145. The Ingolstadt library traced its origin back to the POW camp library in camp "F" in Ingolstadt. The library did not include any books published after 1939. In 1949 the library had 281 active readers of various ethnic backgrounds. Feliks Robakiewicz, report, February 22, 1949, F. #168, JPI. Libraries in the Polish Guard unit training centers also contained larger numbers of books. A brochure, *Świetlica Kompanii Wartowniczych,* no. 4, August 15, 1946, features an article on the proper organization of the library, and strategies to encourage readership. "Wskazówki dla prowadzenia biblioteki w kompaniach wartowniczych," F. Uchodźcy-Prasa-Dublety VI, JPI.

146. Exhibition guest book, F. #134, JPI.

147. Grot-Kwaśniewski, "Prasa polskiego wychodźstwa," 1.

148. Łuczak, *Polacy w okupowanych Niemczech,* 160–61.

149. Wyman, *DP,* 158–60.

150. Other dates remembered by the DPs related to recent events and had a rather mournful character, for example, September 1, 1939, the beginning of the war; September 17, 1939, the entry of Soviet forces into Poland's eastern territories; August 1, 1944, outbreak of the Warsaw Uprising. Polski Komitet Kulturalno-Oświatowy w Ingolstadt, report, February 22, 1949, F. #168, JPI. See also Wyman, *DP,* 159–60.

151. Zjednoczenie Polskie w Niemczech, Zarząd Główny, "Odezwa do wszystkich Polaków na terenie trzech zachodnich stref okupacyjnych w Niemczech," F. #188, JPI.

152. Wyman, *DP,* 161.

153. Ibid., 159; Michalski, *Obóz,* 244–57.

154. Wyman, *DP,* 160.

155. "Sprawozdanie . . . za rok 1948," 20.

156. Wyman, *DP,* 164.

157. Polski Komitet Kulturalno-Oświatowy w Ingolstadt, report, February 22, 1949, F. #168, JPI.

158. Introduction to the exhibition catalog, 4, F. # 133, JPI.

159. The catalog introduction described the Polish DPs' difficult decision to emigrate, as well as their faith in the future: "In this new life they want only to stand next to men of the West and show that they can work well with them, and therefore

deserve the same rights. The reward for all the hardship endured will be the inexpressibly high feeling of freedom of a man living in a democratic society.... Let us hope that well-disposed hands will open for those people the gate toward this life." Catalog, 4–5. See also *Okólnik*, Nr. 5, November 1, 1947, 1–2, F. #167, JPI.

160. To coordinate the work of several smaller camps in the same area, Polish DPs from Ingolstadt initiated an intercamp committee with several different sections, such as theater, sports, celebrations, education, and public lectures. Michał Poczynek, report, March 9, 1949, F. #168, JPI.

161. *Polak w Waldeck*, no. 1, May 8, 1946, F. #161, JPI.

162. M. Lawreniuk, report, March 8, 1949, F. #109, JPI.

163. Władysław Mikosz, report on the Altenstadt camp, March 7, 1949, F. #168, JPI. For Austria, see Pilch, *Losy Polaków w Austrii*, 141–45.

164. Michalski, *Obóz*, 265–85.

165. Poczynek, report, March 9, 1949.

166. *Polak w Waldeck*, no. 2, May 8, 1946, F. #161, JPI.

167. *Okólnik*, no. 8, November 22, 1947.

168. "Ludność polska."

169. "Przed olimpiadą DP's," *Kronika*, June 13, 1948. About sports and other ethnic groups, see Wyman, *DP*, 118–19.

170. In 1947 the International Women's League in Munich requested that the Polish Union assist in compiling statistical data on Polish women in DP camps. Data provided by six camps (Bamberg, Flossenburg, Auerbach, Aschafenburg, Weiden, Coburg) indicated that the number of women under forty-five years of age significantly exceeded the number of older women and that women with families were much more numerous than single women. The number of women engaged in physical labor was greater than the number of female white-collar workers in all the camps. The most frequently mentioned professions included farmer, factory worker, housekeeper, and secretarial staff. Wł. Jaroszewski, Wiesbaden, to PU, Northern Bavaria, June 18, 1947, F. #172, JPI. According to Czesław Łuczak, in the first years of the war German authorities mostly targeted men as slave laborers from the territory of Poland, but during the last two years of the war the number of women deported to Germany substantially increased. For example, in January 1941 women constituted 23.2 percent of the Polish slave labor force in the Reich, while in September 1944 the number was already 34.5 percent. Łuczak, *Polacy w okupowanych Niemczech*, 9.

171. Róża Nowotarska, "Kobiety ... kobiety ... ," *Kronika*, May 16, 1948, 5. Nowotarska also noticed that women lacked representation in the Polish DP press. According to her, there were just a few women journalists, and other women were not interested in publishing their creative works or participating in discussions on DP issues in the newspapers. She used Polish-American women as an example and called for an active women's organization in DP Germany. Hrabyk mentions several

women involved in the publication of *Kronika*, many of them as typists, graphic designers, and secretaries. "Z drugiej strony barykady," 309–12.

172. "Ludność polska"; "Sprawozdanie . . . za rok 1948," 20; "Polska Rada Zawodowa," 4.

173. "Sprawy kobiece," *Echo polskie: Pismo tygodniowe Polaków w Niemczech,* no. 18, May 3, 1946.

174. "Odezwa," F. #172, JPI.

175. The election of Julia Krzemińska to head the camp council in Fallingsbostel, (and of two other women to lead special council committees) was noted in *Kronika* as the first example of a woman in charge of a large (more than fifteen hundred inhabitants) camp. *Kronika,* January 5, 1947, 6.

176. Teresa R. to the Ludwigsburg Camp Council, July 12, 1949; Ludwigsburg Camp Council to Teresa R., August 1, 1949, F. #170, JPI. In Austria, a group of Polish DP women contributed to the revival in 1948 of the prewar Koło Kobiet (Women's Circle), active within Strzecha (Thatched Roof), an ethnic organization of older Austrian Polonia. Through the cooperation of refugee and prewar immigrant women, Koło Kobiet organized several sewing, cooking, and foreign language classes. It also secured legal advice and self-help aid, invited speakers, and sent close to thirty women to participate in a special course for social activists. By mid-1949, Koło Kobiet boasted 114 members. Pilch, *Losy Polaków w Austrii,* 209–10.

177. "Ludność polska."

178. Łuczak, *Polacy w okupowanych Niemczech,* 107; Hrabyk, "Z drugiej strony barykady," 340–44.

179. Łuczak, *Polacy w okupowanych Niemczech,* 104–5; "Ludność polska."

180. "Ludność polska"; Łuczak, *Polacy w okupowanych Niemczech,* 112–13. According to Klaudiusz Hrabyk, a journalist and Piłsudskiite who actively participated in the political life of the DP camps, the political parties' following was largely fictitious. Hrabyk recalled meetings of up to a hundred representatives who met periodically, proposed policies, wrote statements, and discussed issues without the knowledge of or contribution from the DP masses, and eventually created a "classic caricature of political life." Hrabyk concluded that the need for political activity was born from the years of war and deprivation of normal forms of political expression. Hrabyk, "Z drugiej strony barykady," 318–23.

181. Stefan Nienaski-Koper, "Miasto Maczków leży nad rzeką Ems," *Nowy Świat,* January 27, 1946.

182. For example, Polish DPs from the Hohenfels camp erected a cross commemorating the Warsaw Uprising and a cross for the unity of all the nations; they also cleaned and organized a cemetery. Report from Hohenfels, March 8, 1949, F. #109, JPI. In 1946 Polish DPs initiated an action to build the Great International Cemetery in Bergen-Belsen, the site of the Nazi concentration camp. F. #111, JPI.

183. See the correspondence between the Józef Piłsudski Institute in New York and the Syndicate of Polish Journalists in the British zone in Germany, 1946–1950, F. #209, JPI.

184. Michalski, *Obóz*, 416.

185. Ihor V. Zielyk, "The DP Camp as a Social System," in *The Refugee Experience: Ukrainian Displaced Persons after World War II*, ed. Wsevolod W. Isajiw, Yury Boshyk, and Roman Senkus (Edmonton: Canadian Institute of Ukrainian Studies Press, University of Alberta, 1992), 461.

Chapter 3

The title of this chapter is taken from the poem "Dipisi," by Broni-Sława Wiktor, in *Pamiętasz?* (Detroit: Glow Press, 1967), 57.

1. Helena Podkopacz, *Smuga życia* (Kraków: ArsNova-Zjednoczeni Wydawcy, 1994), 173.

2. Louise W. Holborn, *The International Refugee Organization, a Specialized Agency of the United Nations: Its History And Work, 1946-1952* (London: Oxford University Press, 1956), 438.

3. Kathryn Hulme, *The Wild Place* (Boston: Little, Brown, 1953) 199.

4. Mark Wyman, *DP: Europe's Displaced Persons, 1945-1951* (Philadelphia: Balch Institute Press, 1989), 192–94.

5. Hulme, *Wild Place*, 187.

6. Ibid., 178.

7. Holborn, *IRO*, 377–82.

8. Ibid., 393–96; Egon F. Kunz, *Calwell's New Australians* (Sydney: Australian National University Press, 1988), 257–59. On Polish and other DP communities in Australia, see Jerzy Zubrzycki, *Immigrants in Australia: A Demographic Survey Based upon the 1954 Census* (Melbourne: Melbourne University Press, 1960); idem., *Settlers of the Latrobe Valley: A Sociological Study of Immigrants in the Brown Coal Industry in Australia* (Canberra: Australian National University Press, 1964); idem., "The Immigrant Family: Some Sociological Aspects," in *New Faces*, ed. A. Stoller (Melbourne: Melbourne Cheshire, 1966), 60–74.

9. Holborn, *IRO*, annex 41, 438.

10. Keith Sword, Norman Davies, and Jan Ciechanowski, *The Formation of the Polish Community in Great Britain, 1939-1950* (London: School of Slavonic and East European Studies, University of London, 1989), 248–49.

11. Ibid., 246.

12. Ibid., 265, 446.

13. Holborn, *IRO*, 389–93.

14. Norman Davies, *God's Playground: A History of Poland in Two Volumes*, vol. 2, *1795 to the Present* (New York: Columbia University Press, 1982), 559–72; Piotr S. Wandycz, *The Price of Freedom: A History of East Central Europe from the Middle Ages to the Present* (London: Routledge, 1992), 244–50.

15. Andrzej Friszke, *Życie polityczne emigracji*, vol. 1, *Druga Wielka Emigracja, 1945–1990* (Warsaw: Biblioteka WIĘZI, 1999), 75–105.

16. Ibid., 130–41.

17. Ibid., 156–214, 368–80. For a more systematic account of political and social life in Polish London, see B. Czaykowski and B. Sulik, *Polacy w W. Brytanii* (Paris: Instytut Literacki, 1961), 251–374, 397–542. See also Sword, Davies, and Ciechanowski, *Formation of the Polish Community*, 199. The history of the London government and émigré politics became the focus of new studies by Polish scholars. See, for example, Arkadiusz Urban, *Emigracyjny dramat* (Warsaw: Dom Wydawniczy Bellona, 1998); and Paweł Ziętara, *Misja ostatniej szansy: Próba zjednoczenia polskiej emigracji politycznej przez gen. Kazimierza Sosnkowskiego w latach 1952–1956* (Warsaw: Instytut Historyczny Uniwersytetu Warszawskiego, 1995).

18. Rafał Habielski, *Niezłomni i nieprzejednani: Emigracyjne "Wiadomości" i ich krąg, 1940–1981* (Warsaw: Państwowy Instytut Wydawniczy, 1991).

19. The report from the trip was included in Francis X. Świetlik, *The Polish Displaced Persons* (Chicago: American Relief for Poland, [1945]). For a detailed history of Polonia's lobbying action, see Anna D. Jaroszyńska-Kirchmann, "The Mobilization of American Polonia for the Displaced Persons' Cause," *Polish American Studies* 58, no.1 (Spring 2001): 29–62.

20. *Chicago Herald-American*, September 23, 1945. Many press releases from American newspapers are quoted in *Story of the Polish American Congress and Poland's Case in Press Clippings*, 3 vols. (Chicago: Polish American Congress, 1948–1954). See also *Chicago Sun*, August 23, 1945; *Chicago Tribune*, September 27, 1945; *Detroit News*, October 13, 1945.

21. About twenty-eight thousand of the issued visas were granted to Jews, despite the fact that only about 20 percent of the DP population was Jewish. Although the estimates vary as to the precise number of Jewish refugees admitted under the directive, authors generally agree on the reasons for that situation. Barbara Stern Burstin indicates that although both Christian and Jewish resettlement agencies were already accredited and active at that time, "there clearly was a difference in the effectiveness of the various organizations; the bulk of the agency assurances issued under the Truman directive were from Jewish agencies. It is reported that between March 31, 1946, and June 30, 1948, 25,594 out of 35,515 new arrivals were Jewish. . . . This poor showing on the part of the Catholic agency was viewed with considerable consternation by Catholics and other interested parties." Barbara Stern Burstin, *After the Holocaust: The Migration of Polish Jews and Christians to Pittsburgh* (Pittsburgh: University of

Pittsburgh Press, 1989), 67–68. See also Leonard Dinnerstein, *America and the Survivors of the Holocaust* (New York: Columbia University Press, 1982), 163–64, 263; Gil Loescher and John A. Scanlan, *Calculated Kindness: Refugees and America's Half-Open Door, 1945 to the Present* (New York: The Free Press, 1986), 5–6.

22. Robert A. Divine, *American Immigration Policy, 1924–1952* (New Haven: Yale University Press, 1957), 115; Jaroszyńska-Kirchmann, "Mobilization," 42–52.

23. Divine, *American Immigration Policy*, 126–27. Mortgaging against quotas meant subtracting the number of admitted DPs from the annual quota set for a given nationality under the National Origins Act of 1924. For Polonia's reaction to mortgaging against quotas, see Jaroszyńska-Kirchmann, "Mobilization," 59.

24. Loescher and Scanlan, *Calculated Kindness*, 22. After more lobbying, the DP law was extended in 1951. The PAC was also involved in lobbying for other issues in connection with the immigration laws. Jaroszyńska-Kirchmann, "Mobilization," 52–59.

25. Displaced Persons Commission, *Memo to America: The DP Story; The Final Report of the United States Displaced Persons Commission* (Washington, D.C.: U.S. Government Printing Office, 1952). 42–45, 336.

26. Ibid., 48–50.

27. Ibid., 271.

28. According to the Immigration and Naturalization Service, between June 25, 1948, and June 30, 1953, a total of 132,851 of immigrant aliens born in Poland were admitted to the United States under the DP Act of 1948, as amended. That included 126,459 DPs, 214 nonquota DP orphans, 12 other nonquota DPs, and 6,392 so-called ethnic Germans—which in practice meant DP children born in DP camps in Germany, as well as German spouses of Polish DPs. U.S. Department of Justice, Immigration and Naturalization Service, *Annual Report for the Fiscal Year Ended June 30, 1953*, table 6B. The INS statistics for fiscal year 1948 show 12,117 persons born in Poland admitted to the United States under the Truman Directive between May 20, 1946 (arrival of the first ship), and June 30, 1948. U.S. Department of Justice, Immigration and Naturalization Service, *Annual Report for the Fiscal Year Ended June 30, 1948*, 13–14. The total number of refugees born in Poland who were admitted to the United States between 1946 and 1953 was 144,968. See also Helena Znaniecki Lopata, "Polish Immigration to the United States of America: Problems of Estimation and Parameters," *Polish Review* 21, no. 4 (1976): 97 (table 7).

Holborn indicates 110,566 as the number of DPs from Poland resettled in the United States between July 1, 1947, and December 31, 1951. Holborn, *IRO*, 438. Although the precise number is hard to establish, the statistics of the Displaced Persons Commission demonstrate that 34 percent of immigrants admitted under the DP Act, as of May 31, 1952, indicated Poland as their country of birth, which sets the total at a little below 134,000. See *Memo*, tables 2 and 3, 366. DP Commission statistics give 154,556 as the total number of visas issued to DPs from Poland by December 31, 1951.

The same number for Polish veterans is 10,472. Ibid., 376. See also Anna D. Jaroszyńska-Kirchmann, "Communications," *Polish American Studies* 46, no. 2 (Autumn 1989): 90; Burstin, *After the Holocaust*, 115–16. Burstin accepts 120,000 as the number of Polish Christians admitted to the United States under the DP Act.

29. Hieronim Kubiak, *The Polish National Catholic Church in the United States of America from 1897 to 1980: Its Social Conditioning and Social Functions* (Warsaw: Państwowe Wydawnictwo Naukowe, 1982), 173.

30. Haim Genizi, *America's Fair Share: The Admission and Resettlement of Displaced Persons, 1945–1952* (Detroit: Wayne State University Press, 1993), 170.

31. Ibid., 170–75; Burstin, *After the Holocaust*, 67–71.

32. Burstin, *After the Holocaust*, 78. The NRC was composed of representatives from the War Relief Services of the NCWC in Europe, the NCWC Bureau of Immigration, the Catholic Committee for Refugees, local dioceses, and eleven nationality groups involved in work for the DPs. On the NCWC and its participation in the admission and resettlement of DPs, see Genizi, *America's Fair Share*, 174–86. Catholic organizations sponsored 34.5 percent of the DPs admitted under the DP Act. According to Genizi, despite a late start the NCWC's resettlement program became a real success.

33. Halina Korsak, "America 'Land of Promise,'" *Nowy Świat*, September 8, 1946, 11; "Żołnierz polski nie potrzebuje dolarów," *Nowy Świat*, September 11, 1946, 4; Stanisław Strzetelski, "O los wysiedleńców," *Nowy Świat*, October 5, 1946, 4; P. P. Yolles, "Wyspa łez," *Nowy Świat*, October 7, 1946, 4; "Potrzeba nacisku," *Nowy Świat*, October 14, 1946, 4; Andrzej Pleszczyński, "Jak zlikwidować problem wysiedleńców," *Nowy Świat*, October 26, 1946, 4.

34. "O zwołanie walnego zjazdu Rady Polonii Amerykańskiej," *Nowy Świat*, January 7, 1948, 4; Kazimierz Dąbski, "Rada Polonii, jej prace i program," *Nowy Świat*, March 2, 1948, 3. See also "Prezes Zjednoczenia Józef Kania na czele nowego departamentu dla wysiedleńców," *Naród Polski*, March 4, 1948, 14.

35. Kazimierz Dąbski, "Trzeba wyjść z błędnego koła," *Nowy Świat*, May 24, 1948, 4; May 25, 1948, 4; May 26, 1948, 4; May 27, 1948, 4. The articles were reprinted in *Dziennik Związkowy*, between May 27 and June 1, 1948.

36. With the establishment of the ACRPDP, the Polish-American community had three separate agencies devoted to the resettlement program. Such fragmentation raised concerns about the effectiveness of the effort. The press appealed for cooperation and unity. "Rada Polonii przeciw Kongresowi Pol.," *Dziennik Związkowy*, July 15, 1948, 4 (reprinted from *Pittsburczanin*); "Szerzenie zamętu," ibid., July 17, 1948, 4; "Dalszy ciąg tragicznego widowiska," ibid., September 21, 1948, 4; "Na drodze do zgody," *Nowy Świat*, November 17, 1948, 4. One of the participants in the discussion wrote: "No one has a monopoly on good deeds." "Dość już dyskusji nad sprawą wysiedleńców," *Nowy Świat*, November 17, 18, 19, 20, 1948, 4. Others concluded: "Let

there now be a race between Rada and Congress, who can get more affidavits and assurances.... We want such competition!" *Nowy Świat*, December 10, 1948, 4.

37. Franciszek X. Świetlik, *Sprawozdanie z działalności Rady Polonii Amerykańskiej od października 1939 do października 1948 na zjazd Rady Polonii Amerykańskiej odbyty dnia 4go i 5go grudnia, 1948 r. w hotelu Buffalo, N.Y.* (Chicago: Czas Publishing Co., 1948), 61.

38. Donald E. Pienkos, *For Your Freedom through Ours: Polish-American Efforts on Poland's Behalf, 1863–1991* (New York: Columbia University Press, 1991), 98. The records of Rada's districts from many different states, however, do contain numerous expressions of frustration with the headquarters' lack of direction, failure or delays in responding to their correspondence, and, in general, insufficient communication with the local organizations. In one letter, the president of Rada's District 28 in Milwaukee, Wisconsin, wrote: "We came to the conclusion that Rada does not respond to any actions of our committee.... Rada Polonii does not have any program itself, the work is limping, and this discourages that small group of people who since the inception of the committee selflessly work for the cause." Leon M. Gurda to Rada Polonii, May 21, 1949, Wisconsin, vol. 3: 1947-1953, American Relief for Poland Collection (ARP), Polish Museum of America (PMA), Chicago, Ill.. The Detroit districts, having to cope with an especially difficult economic situation, repeatedly appealed to Rada for help and direction. Angry members threatened that in the event of a continued lack of response by Rada, a special delegation would be sent directly to Chicago, and resignations and press publicity would follow. W. Kędzierski to J. Olejniczak, May 30, 1949; J. Tyrka to Świetlik, October 12, 1951, District 34 Detroit, vol. 1: 1948-1951, ARP.

39. Jan J. Olejniczak, "Sprawozdanie działu wysiedleńców przy Radzie Polonii Amerykańskiej w Chicago, Illinois, za okres od 15 sierpnia 1948 do 30 kwietnia 1950 r.," 9, fol. District 34 Detroit, vol. 1: 1948-1951, ARP.

41. Ibid.

41. Correspondence between Father Burant and Casimir E. Midowicz, vice-president of Rada, August 22, 1946–March 12, 1947, Immigration Committee, vol. 1: 1947, ARP.

42. "Polski Komitet Imigracyjny," *Nowy Świat*, February 6, 1947, 3.

43. "Immigration Committee Objectives," November 1947; "Sprawozdanie Polskiego Komitetu Imigracyjnego American Relief for Poland za m-ce luty i marzec 1947," Immigration Committee, vol. 1: 1947, ARP.

44. "15,000 Amerykanów polskiego pochodzenia przybywa do St. Zjednoczonych," *Nowy Świat*, April 5, 1947, 3.

45. Jan S. Pargiełło to F. X. Świetlik, December 5, 1947, Immigration Committee, vol. 1: 1947, ARP.

46. "Transport żołnierzy polskich," *Nowy Świat*, April 15, 1947, 3; "Sprowadzanie

narzeczonych," *Nowy Świat*, September 26, 1947, 3; "150 żołnierzy polskich," *Nowy Świat*, September 11, 1948, 7.

47. "Polski Komitet Imigracyjny został włączony do dyrektoriatu N.C.R.C.," *Dziennik Związkowy*, December 3, 1948, 1; "Po zjeździe Rady Polonji Amerykańskiej w Buffalo, N.Y.," *Nowy Świat*, December 11, 1948, 1, 8.

48. "Z działalności Polskiego Komitetu Imigracyjnego w New Yorku," *Nowy Świat*, March 5, 1949, 6.

49. Thaddeus Theodore Krysiewicz, *The Polish Immigration Committee in the United States: A Historical Study of the American Committee for the Relief of Polish Immigrants, 1947-1952* (New York: Roman Catholic Church of St. Stanislaus, [1953]), 18.

50. "Censor Gunther's Report at the Polish American Congress Convention on the Activities of the American Committee for the Resettlement of Polish D.P.s," *Zgoda*, July 15, 1952, 5. For a more detailed history of the ACRPDP, see Anna Dorota Jaroszyńska, "The American Committee for the Resettlement of Polish Displaced Persons (1948-1968) in the Manuscript Collection of the Immigration History Research Center," *Polish American Studies* 46, no.1 (Spring 1987): 67-73.

51. The composition of officers soon changed. The new executive body was formed as follows: chairman, B. F. Gunther; vice-chairman, J. Stanek; secretary, E. E. Plusdrak; treasurer, W. Karcz; directors, A. Lagodzinska, K. Rozmarek, J. Pawłowski, F. Dymek, and T. Adesko. In 1957 Rev. Karcz was elected as the new chairman of the ACRPDP.

52. Adam Olszewski, *Historia Związku Narodowego Polskiego*, (Chicago: Zakłady Graficzne Dziennika Związkowego, 1967), 6:354.

53. B. Wichrowski, "The Overseas Branch Operation of ACRPDP," report, *Sprawozdania Zarządu Wykonawczego Poszczególnych Komisji i Komitetów oraz Biur w Chicago i Washingtonie na Trzecią Krajową Konwencję Kongresu Polonii Amerykańskiej w Atlantic City, N.J. w Dniach 30-31 Maja i 1 Czerwca 1952* (Chicago: Polish American Congress, 1952), 78-81; "Wice-Prez. Dymek po powrocie z Niemiec wzywa do zwiększenia pomocy Dipisom," *Dziennik Związkowy*, April 17, 1950, 8; "W. prezeska Dymek otrzymała odznakę Oddz. Wartowniczych w Niemczech," *Dziennik Związkowy*, April 20, 1950, 2. Dymek also visited Polish communities in France, the Netherlands, Belgium, Great Britain, and Italy.

54. *Sprawozdania zarządu*, 72. The same report points to the fact that, for many different reasons, "not all the assurances were taken advantage of," which suggests that a lower number of people actually came to the United States. Ibid., 73. The number was mistakenly printed as 85,000 in Jaroszyńska, "American Committee," 70. See also Jaroszyńska-Kirchmann, "Communications," 90.

55. "Censor Gunther's Report," *Zgoda*, August 15, 1952, 5; September 1, 1952, 5. See also Pienkos, *For Your Freedom*, 127.

56. Displaced Persons Commission, *Second Semiannual Report to the President and the Congress*, August 1, 1949, 20–21.
57. "Już nie wysiedleńcy, ale wolni obywatele—Witajcie!" *Dziennik Związkowy*, November 3, 1948, 1–2.
58. "Tylko 20 Polaków," *Dziennik Związkowy*, January 31, 1949, 4.
59. "Polakowi przypadł zaszczyt być 50,000 wysiedleńcem przybyłym do St. Zjedn.," *Dziennik Związkowy*, July 27, 1949, 1–2.
60. "Inicjatywa Kongresu Polonii dokonała wielkiego dzieła," *Dziennik Związkowy*, April 8, 1952, 1; "Cenzor ZNP., B. F. Gunther powitał w New Yorku ostatniego wysiedleńca z Niemiec," *Dziennik Związkowy*, April 16, 1952, 1, 8.
61. "Report of the Massachusetts Displaced Persons Commission, October 23, 1948–May 23, 1952, Boston, 1952," 5, American Council for Nationalities Service, Shipment 6, Box 35, F.: DPs-General, IHRC. "Filia wydziału kobiet na wschodnią część stanu New York zajmuje się sprawami wysiedleńców polskich," *Naród Polski*, May 19, 1949, 8.
62. "Tłumy witały przybyłych tu wysiedleńców," *Dziennik Związkowy*, March 16, 1949, 1–6; "Kongres Polonii Amerykańskiej witał w Chicago wysiedleńców 2-go transportu," *Dziennik Związkowy*, March 22, 1949, 10.
63. "Wydział kongresu ma pełne ręce pracy nad rozmieszczeniem wysiedleńców," *Dziennik Związkowy*, January 18, 1951, 8. The first house, at 4246 N. Kedvale Avenue, was entirely remodeled and furnished by volunteers. On October 23, 1949, the official opening and blessing of the house gathered crowds of Polonia activists. The house and its residents stayed at the center of attention; traditional Christmas parties for DP children took place there, and press reported on the first baby born on the hospitable premises. "Stow. Dobroczynności umebluje jeden pokój w Domu dla Wysiedleńców," *Dziennik Związkowy*, September 14, 1949, 7; "Szereg nowych spraw przed Wydziałem Kongresu Polonii na Stan Illinois," *Dziennik Związkowy*, September 22, 1949, 8; "Otwarcie Domu dla Wysiedleńców połączone z bogatym programem," *Dziennik Związkowy*, October 5, 1949, 8; "Tłumy osób zwiedziły wczoraj Dom dla Wysiedleńców w Chicago," *Dziennik Związkowy*, October 24, 1949, 8; "Pierwsze dziecko urodzone w Domu Wysiedleńców," *Dziennik Związkowy*, December 14, 1949; "Jutro gwiazdka w Domu Wysiedleńców zgromadzi licznie Polonię," *Dziennik Związkowy*, December 31, 1949, 16.
64. *American Relief for Poland—District 5—State of New Jersey: Tenth Anniversary Souvenir Journal, 1939–1949* (New Jersey, 1949), 21; "Wyniki pracy wysiedleńczej okręgu piątego Rady Polonii Amerykańskiej na stan New Jersey: Za czas od 1-go lipca, 1948 do 31-go grudnia 1952 roku," report, District 5, New Jersey, ARP; Stanisław E. Czaster to F. X. Świetlik, November 16, 1950, District 8, Buffalo, New York, vol. 2, 1947–1956, ARP; American Relief for Poland, District 34, Detroit, to headquarters, n.d., District 34 Resettlement Commission, Detroit, Michigan, vol. 1, 1948–1951, ARP.

65. "Wiceprezeska Fr. Dymek wzywa do podpisywania 'Assurances,'" *Dziennik Związkowy,* March 23, 1951, 6; Edward Różański, interview by the author, tape recording, Chicago, Ill., January 4, 1995.

66. "Find Joy in Making Home for Displaced Persons Family," *Dziennik Związkowy,* February 21, 1950, 2.

67. "Przestajemy być Dipisami," *Nowy Świat,* September 11, 1949, 6–7.

68. "Farmerzy Polscy na Long Island sprowadzają rodaków z obozów dla 'DP' w Europie," *Nowy Świat,* April 20, 1949, 1; "Ponad 400 wysiedleńców wezmą farmerzy na Long Island," *Nowy Świat,* April 21, 1949, 1; "Farmy na Long Island czekają na wysiedleńców polskich," *Nowy Świat,* May 25, 1949, 8; "Ksiądz Pułk. Burant przemawiał w sprawie wysiedleńców," *Nowy Świat,* June 9, 1949, 4; "Polski Komitet Imigracyjny ustanawia ważny precedens," *Nowy Świat,* June 18, 1949, 1.

69. "Przybyli z Niemiec polscy wartownicy witani serdecznie przez Polonię na L.I.," *Nowy Świat,* July 10, 1949, 1; "Dalsze grupy byłych wartowników przybywają z Niemiec na Long Island," *Nowy Świat,* July 19, 1949, 1; "Pierwsze dwa transporty powietrzne polskich wartowników przybyły na lotnisko Idlewild," *Nowy Świat,* July 28, 1949, 1; "Gorączkowa robota Polskiego Komitetu Imigracyjnego w dni strasznych upałów lipcowych," *Nowy Świat,* July 30, 1949, 1; "Przeszło 15,000 wysiedleńców przybędzie w ciągu sierpnia," *Nowy Świat,* August 2, 1949, 1; "Dalszy ciąg 'Operation Long Island' 2 grupy wartowników," *Nowy Świat,* September 2, 1949, 1; P. P. Yolles, "Jeden dzień," *Nowy Świat,* September 12, 1949, 6.

70. "Wśród polskich farm powiatu Suffolk," *Nowy Świat,* November 1, 1949, 4.

71. See the column "Wśród polskich farm powiatu Suffolk, L.I.," *Nowy Świat,* September 13, 1949, 2; September 20, 1949, 5; September 27, 1949, 3; October 11, 1949, 2; October 18, 1949, 4; November 1, 1949, 4; November 3, 1949, 7; November 8, 1949, 4. Not all guards adjusted well to life on the farms. One of the Polish workers commented that the barracks the guards were housed in on a potato farm reminded him of a concentration camp. After four months there, he moved to New Jersey to work in a bakery with a friend. See Burstin, *After the Holocaust,* 126–27.

72. "31 chłopców z Kompanii Wartowniczych odleciało do Texasu," *Nowy Świat,* October 17, 1949, 2; "NCRC skierowało już 90 polskich wysiedleńców do stanu Texas," *Nowy Świat,* November 2, 1949, 1. The resettlement in Texas began in 1948, when the PAC, acting on an invitation from the Texas Chamber of Commerce, directed a group of Polish veterans and their families there from Great Britain. See "Żołnierze polscy z Anglii na amerykańskich farmach," *Dziennik Związkowy,* October 2, 1948, 1.

73. Krysiewicz, *Polish Immigration Committee,* 17.

74. "Wysiedleńcy polscy skarżą się w Montana na trudne warunki życia," *Dziennik Związkowy,* January 31, 1950, 2.

75. "Red. Dąbski wyjeżdża na południe badać możliwości osiedlenia tam DP," *Dziennik Związkowy,* January 26, 1949, 4.

76. "Zrobiono dobry początek zbiórki funduszu na pomoc wysiedleńcom," *Dziennik Związkowy*, April 19, 1949, 9. The impressions of one family brought over from Louisiana to Chicago appeared in *Dziennik Związkowy*, July 6, 1949, 7.

77. "The Louisiana Story," report, n.d., Papers of Harry N. Rosenfield (Rosenfield Papers), Box 18, F. DPC—Louisiana Resettlement Problem, Harry S. Truman Library, Independence, Missouri.

78. Ibid., 2.

79. Ibid., 2, 4.

80. Rev. Joseph B. Koncius to Harry S. Truman, May 20, 1949, Rosenfield Papers. Box 18, F. DPC—Louisiana Resettlement Problem.

81. Ibid., 5.

82. Ugo Carusi to Dr. Steelman, June 29, 1949, Rosenfield Papers, Box 18, F. DPC—Louisiana Resettlement Problem. In 1950 the Institute of Population Research in the department of sociology at Louisiana State University sponsored a study on 2,039 displaced persons in Louisiana and Mississippi. Poles constituted 44 percent of that number, and their settlements concentrated mostly (70 percent) in the sugar cane country around New Orleans. According to the authors of the study, both the material conditions and social adjustment of the DP population were fully satisfactory and proved that "the resettlement of eastern Europeans in the Deep South is by no means a failure." As to the reasons for the initial dissatisfaction, the study put the blame on the DPs themselves and their excessive expectations, culture shock, and susceptibility to adverse propaganda. Rudolf Heberle, and Dudley S. Hall, *Displaced Persons in Louisiana and Mississippi* (Baton Rouge: Louisiana State University, 1950), 45-47.

83. Jan Śliwowski, "O pomoc dla wysiedleńców," *Nowy Świat*, September 7, 1948, 4, 6. About Rev. Śliwowski's work in Africa, see Czesław Pławski, *Wydarci z ojczystej ziemi: Okres drugiej wojny światowej* (Łódź: RES POLONA, 2001), 165.

84. Letter dated July 8, 1952, IHRC 84, Box 37, Fol. 272, PAC.

85. Władysław Kędzierski to Jan J. Olejniczak, November 5, 1949, District 34 Resettlement Committee, Detroit, vol. 1: 1948-1951, ARP.

86. Letter dated May, 1952, IHRC 84, Box 26, Fol. 199, PAC.

87. Letters dated September 22, 1948 and November 1, 1948, IHRC 84, Box 41, Fol. 289, PAC.

88. In one author's words, with the coming of "the fresh wave of refugees, exiles, and immigrants ... new matrimonial frontiers were opened up for some of the second generation girls." Joseph A. Wytrwal, *Behold! The Polish Americans* (Detroit: Endurance Press, 1977), 429.

89. Displaced Persons Commission, *Second Semiannual Report*, 25; *Memo*, 257-58. See also John J. Bukowczyk, *And My Children Did Not Know Me: A History of the Polish-Americans* (Bloomington: Indiana University Press, 1987), 94-95.

90. Jan Olejniczak, "Sprawozdanie Działu Wysiedleńców," 12-13.

91. "700 rodzin nowoprzybyłych Polaków w Detroit zagrożonych głodem," *Dziennik Związkowy*, January 21, 1952, 1; Tadeusz K. Czechowski, vice-president of District 34, to Jan Olejniczak, February 15, 1952, Detroit Resettlement Committee, vol. 2: 1952, ARP; Jan Olejniczak, "Sprawozdanie Działu Wysiedleńców," 8.

92. Letters dated 1952 and September 22, 1953, IHRC 84, Box 35, Fol. 263, PAC; letter dated November 8, 1952, Box 28, Fol. 216, ibid.; letter dated August 10, 1952, Box 37, Fol. 272, ibid..

93. "Report of the Massachusetts Displaced Persons Commission, October 23, 1948—May 23, 1952, Boston, 1952," 29, American Council for Nationalities Service, Shipment 6, Box 35, F. DPs—General, IHRC. See also Holborn, *IRO*, 426-28; Edward B. Rooney, S.J., "Professors in the DP Camps," reprinted from *College and University* (April 1949): 329-38, in Coll. # 24, CMS, Staten Island.

94. According to John J. Bukowczyk, "heavily middle-class in background those refugee Poles who did make their way into better paying factory jobs, the only employment for which many were suited because they lacked English-language skills, now felt déclassé." Bukowczyk, *And My Children*, 95. Letter dated September 3, 1949, IHRC 84, Box 33, Fol. 251, PAC; letter dated February 22, 1952, IHRC 84, Box 35, Fol. 260, PAC. The resettlement of intellectuals remained one of the unsolved problems of the IRO, J. G. Stoessinger, *The Refugee and the World Community*, (Minneapolis: University of Minnesota Press, 1956), 139.

95. Pennsylvania Commission on Displaced Persons, *Third Annual Report*, 1951 (Commonwealth of Pennsylvania, [1952]), 26.

96. "Report of the Massachusetts Displaced Persons Commission, October 23, 1948—May 23, 1952, Boston, 1952," 16, American Council for Nationality Service, Shipment 6, Box 35, F. DPs—General, IHRC.

97. *Memo*, 228.

98. Olejniczak, "Sprawozdanie Działu Wysiedleńców," 18.

99. Rev. William D. Larkin, diocesan director of resettlement, Duluth, Minnesota, to John W. Poor, administrative secretary, Minnesota Commission on Resettlement, June 15, 1950; Francis J. Nahurski to Bureau of Catholic Charities, Duluth, June 21, 1950; Francis J. Nahurski to American Relief for Poland, June 24, 1950, District 10, Minnesota, vol. 2, 1942-1944, ARP.

100. Olejniczak, "Sprawozdanie Działu Wysiedleńców," 7-8.

101. John W. Poor, administrative secretary, Minnesota DP Commission, to Francis J. Nahurski, July 14, 1950, District 10, Minnesota, vol. 2, 1942-1944, ARP. Some health problems were handled by professional social workers; see Rev. Stanislaus T. Sypek, "The Displaced Polish Persons in the Greater Boston Community" (Ph.D. diss., Fordham University, 1955), 190-96, 199-202, 206-8.

102. "Cenzor Gunther uratował polskiego wysiedleńca od deportacji do Niemiec,"

Dziennik Związkowy, September 22, 1951. See also the records of the ACRPDP, IHRC 48, Box 6, Fol. 33.

103. Stoessinger, *Refugee,* 188–96; Liucija Baskauskas, "The Lithuanian Refugee Experience and Grief," *International Migration Review* 15 (Spring-Summer 1981): 276–91; Burstin, *After the Holocaust,* 120–21.

104. IHRC 84, Box 27, Fol. 207; Box 28, Fol. 218, PAC.

105. Letters to the ACRPDP, IHRC 84, Box 36, Fol. 270; Box 29, Fol. 225; Box 27, Fol. 208, PAC. See also a case described by Sypek, "Displaced Polish Persons," 197–99. One report of the ACRPDP includes a brief mention of the problem: "We also had several persons who, after arriving in this country, broke down and became mentally ill. Due to our efforts, those people were placed in psychiatric hospitals. After adequate treatment, some of them regained their health and now work and live a normal life." "Sprawozdanie ACRPDP" [1955?], IHRC 48, Box 6, Fol. 32. See also P. P. Yolles, "Głos serca," *Nowy Świat,* July 24, 1956, 3.

106. "Winna cała Polonja amerykańska," *Nowy Świat,* March 7, 1949, 4.

107. "Podpisywanie deklaracji na sprowadzanie wysiedleńców nie nakłada obowiązków," *Dziennik Związkowy,* February 10, 1949, 5.

108. "Przybyli tutaj wysiedleńcy mogą podpisywać zapewnienia dla D.P.," *Dziennik Związkowy,* January 26, 1950, 6; "Prezes K. Rozmarek witał wczoraj transport wysiedleńców na dworcu," *Dziennik Związkowy,* May 25, 1951.

109. "ZNP sprowadzi 10,000 DPs," *Dziennik Związkowy,* July 24, 1948; "2,000 aplikacji wręczonych zostało komisji federalnej," *Dziennik Związkowy,* November 13, 1948, 1; "Związkowczynie z Stow. Dobroczynności spieszą z pomocą wysiedleńcom," *Dziennik Związkowy,* April 13, 1949, 10.

110. "Wiceprezeska Fr. Dymek wzywa do podpisywania Assurances," *Dziennik Związkowy,* March 23, 1951, 6.

111. Correspondence between Joseph Onka and F. X. Świetlik, February 14–26, 1951, District 5, New Jersey, ARP. The same district was later warned by Rada headquarters against providing fictitious sponsors in an effort to collect large numbers of assurances. J. J. Olejniczak to Józef Onka, November 9, 1951, District 5, New Jersey, ARP.

112. P. P. Yolles, "Polonja," *Nowy Świat,* April 25, 1949, 4.

113. "Wydział Kongresu wyasygnował $20,000 na sprowadzanie 100 wysiedleńców," *Dziennik Związkowy,* March 18, 1948, 8; "Ratujmy polskich wysiedleńców," *Dziennik Związkowy,* April 17, 1948, 8; "Sukces Dnia Polonii zależy od zainteresowania Polonii losem wysiedleńców," *Dziennik Związkowy,* July 8, 1949, 8. "Dzień Polonii," organized every year, became a steady source of extra money for the DP Fund. In 1950 the Third of May collection brought to the DP Fund close to $11,000, and in 1951 close to $12,000. "Z.N.P. całą sumę ze zbiórek na obchodach oddał na wysiedleńców," *Dziennik Związkowy,* February 22, 1952.

114. "Co myślą i mówią liderzy Polonii o drajwie i bankiecie dla wysiedleńców," *Dziennik Związkowy*, February 22, 1950, 8; "Prezes Rozmarek ostrzega U.S. przed niebezpieczeństwem utraty wolności," *Dziennik Związkowy*, March 9, 1950, 8; "Starajmy się o zapewnienia...," *Dziennik Związkowy*, February 22, 1951, 6.

115. "Obóz letni dla dzieci imigrantów," *Nowy Świat*, July 29, 1948, 2; "Gdy się ma serce...," *Nowy Świat*, August 7, 1948, 4.

116. Lagodzinska was the president of the Polish Women's Alliance and vice-president of the PAC. About her resettlement effort, see Myrna Lenard, "Remembering Adela Lagodzinska: Polonia Leader and President of P.W.A., 1947–1971," paper presented during the 56th Annual Meeting of the Polish Institute of Arts and Sciences of America, Georgetown University, Washington, D.C., June 12–13, 1998.

117. *Opłatek* is a wafer. Sharing of the wafer is one of the most important parts of the Polish Christmas tradition. "Z uroczystości tradycyjnego opłatka Stow. Nowych Amerykanów," *Kuryer Polski*, January 20, 1951, 5.

118. "Cała Polonia zapraszana jest na piknik 'Młodej Emigracji,'" *Kuryer Polski*, August 29, 1951, 4; "Wielki piknik Stowarzyszenia Nowych Amerykanów," *Kuryer Polski*, June 22, 1954, 6.

119. *Dziennik Związkowy* published announcements from Samopomoc free of charge; most of them appeared in "Dział Nowej Emigracji." See, for example, reports on Samopomoc activities in *Dziennik Związkowy*, November 9, 1950, 6; February 8, 1951, 7; *Pamiętnik Jubileuszu 25-lecia Stowarzyszenia Samopomocy Nowej Emigracji Polskiej w Chicago* ([Chicago:] 1975). Similar self-help organizations were formed in practically all larger Polish-American communities.

120. *100-Lecie wystawienia Polskiej Opery Narodowej Halka Stanisława Moniuszki: Pamiętnik koncertu wydany przez Chór im. M. K. Ogińskiego* (New York: 1958); Wacław Grygorcewicz (choir president), telephone interview by the author, August 31, 1995; "Chór byłych wysiedleńców przystąpił do Związku Śpiewaków Polskich w Ameryce," *Nowy Świat*, March 3, 1951, 6. Choirs were also established in many other locations. For example, in 1952 the Polonia Paderewski Choir, consisting mainly of refugees, came into being in Connecticut. According to Mr. Grygorcewicz, the Paderewski Choir is still active, performing in the Connecticut, New York, and New Jersey areas.

121. Emil Orzechowski, *Teatr Polonijny w Stanach Zjednoczonych* (Wrocław: Zakład Narodowy im. Ossolińskich, 1989), 238–39. Czesław Rawski wrote about his theater experience in such a way: "We never went to the theater of Lucjan Krzemieński to 'save the culture,' or to rattle off a hard civic duty. We were going there for what millions of people all over the world go to theaters: to spend a nice evening. And the Polish culture in that theater 'saved itself,' without being pushed by us and without unnecessary praise." Quoted in Orzechowski, *Teatr*, 238.

122. "Z życia Polaków w Ameryce," *Ameryka-Echo*, August 9, 1953, 4; "Dział Nowej Emigracji," *Dziennik Związkowy*, August 20, 1953, 3; November 12, 1953, 6.

123. Orzechowski explicitly credits the revitalization of the Polonia theater in the period from 1950 to 1970 to the influx of postwar immigrants. Orzechowski, *Teatr*, 256–71.

124. Rev. Roman Nir, *Szkice z dziejów Polonii* (Orchard Lake, Mich.: Wydawnictwo Centralnego Archiwum Polonii Amerykańskiej w Orchard Lake, 1990), 186–91.

125. Asked how the instructors could incorporate such intense activity into their busy schedules as immigrants trying to establish themselves in a foreign land, Mr. Kuncewicz responded: "Once a harcerz, always a harcerz." Jerzy Kuncewicz, telephone interview by the author, August 29, 2002. See also Ewa Gieratowa, *Powojenna historia Harcerstwa w Stanach Zjednoczonych* (Detroit: Nakł. Zarzadu Okregu ZHP w Stanach Zjednoczonych, 1990), 187–88.

126. In 1932 the PNA—and a year later the PRCUA—set up scout troops for Polonia youth. Both organizations remained integral part of the fraternal organization. Andrzej Brożek, *Polish Americans, 1854–1939* (Warsaw: Interpress, 1985), 230.

127. Walter Zachariasiewicz, "Organizational Structure of Polonia," in *Poles in America: Bicentennial Essays*, ed. Frank Mocha (Stevens Point, Wisc.: Worzalla Publishing, 1978), 657–58. For a more detailed account of the history of the organization see Gieratowa, *Powojenna historia*.

128. "Kronika I Drużyny Harcerek im. Królowej Jadwigi w Chicago," Edward C. and Loda Różański, IHRC 144, Box 74, Fol. 1.

129. Gieratowa, *Powojenna historia*, 126–27; Maryann Wojciechowski (in consultation with Marian Wojciechowski), e-mail interview by the author, February 22, 2000.

130. Zachariasiewicz, "Organizational Structure of Polonia," 667–68; "Kącik Nowej Emigracji," *Dziennik Związkowy*, September 7, 1950, 6; November 29, 1951, 7; November 13, 1952; April 2, 1953, 3; May 6, 19554, 3; July 24, 1954, 7; "Polonia w Los Angeles," *Nowy Świat*, April 19, 1952, 2. On the jurists' and physicians' organizations see, for example, "Dział Nowej Emigracji," *Dziennik Związkowy*, November 5, 1953; "Z życia towarzyskiego Polonii," *Dziennik Związkowy*, July 17, 1951, 3. Some members of Old Polonia appreciated the fact that when DPs or their children achieved professional status, they did not hesitate to fund scholarships for others. Sabina Logisz, interview by the author, tape recording and notes, Chicago, Ill., January 4, 1995.

131. Jan Wawrzkiewicz, ed., *Dwadzieścia pięć lat Stowarzyszenia Polskich Kombatantów* (London: P.C.A. Publications, Ltd., 1971), 6. See also Bolesław T. Łaszewski, *Z wojskowych szeregów do życia cywilnego: Historia powstania i pierwszych pięciu lat działalności Stowarzyszenia Polskich Kombatantów, 1945–1950* (New York: Bicentennial Publishing Corporation of New York, 1984). See also Sword, Davies, and Ciechanowski, *Formation of the Polish Community*, 191.

132. By 1971 American SPK numbered about thirty-five hundred members. Wawrzkiewicz, *Dwadzieścia pięć lat Stowarzyszenia*, 186–97.

133. Bohdan Pawłowicz, "Droga życia," *Ameryka-Echo*, September 20, 1959, part 2, 2.

134. Zachariasiewicz, "Organizational Structure of Polonia," 655-56.

135. "Kącik Nowej Emigracji," *Dziennik Związkowy*, March 13, 1952, 6; "Stow. Byłych Więźniów Politycznych w sprawie Billu Cellera," *Dziennik Związkowy*, July 21, 1952, 2.

136. "Odezwa do Polaków emigrantów z Ingolstadtu w Bawarii," *Dziennik Związkowy*, December 24, 1952, 5; "Dział Nowej Emigracji," *Dziennik Związkowy*, July 16, 1953, 3; August 6, 1953, 3; December 3, 1953, 3; April 1, 1954, 7.

137. See, for example, "Pomost," *Nowy Świat*, January 3, 26, 1956, 3; "Szesnastu Polaków przybyło z Niemiec," *Nowy Świat*, January 10, 1956, 1.

138. "Dział Nowej Emigracji," *Dziennik Związkowy*, December 13, 1951, 7.

139. See announcements in "Pomost," *Nowy Świat*, for 1953-1954.

140. See, for example, "Kącik Nowej Emigracji," *Dziennik Związkowy*, December 18, 1952, 2. The organizations included Koło Nowa Polonia [the New Polonia Circle], the Home Army, the Polish Scouting organization, and the Polish American Academic Association.

141. "Dział Nowej Emigracji," *Dziennik Związkowy*, January 29, 1953, 3.

142. "Dział Nowej Emigracji," *Dziennik Związkowy*, August 27, 1953, 3; September 23, 1954, 7; October 28, 1954, 9.

143. Both Helena Podkopacz and Olga Tubielewicz joined historically Polish parishes and became active in their structures. Olga Tubielewicz, interview by the author, tape recording, St. Paul, Minn., July 22, 1996; Helena Podkopacz, telephone interview by the author, August 10, 1996.

144. "Rolny [roczny?] dorobek nowej Polonii w Bayonne, New Jersey," *Dziennik Związkowy*, July 3, 1952, 6.

145. Danuta Mostwin, "Post-World War II Polish Immigrants in the United States," *Polish American Studies* 26, no. 2 (Autumn 1979): 11. The significance of these statistics is clear when they are compared to other results of the questionnaire related to rates of the home ownership and residential patterns. Sixty-six percent of respondents owned their homes but lived away from primarily Polish neighborhoods: 50 percent in the city, 40 percent in the suburbs, and 7 percent in the country. Mostwin further discovered that "[a]mong persons who belong to a parish, those who are members of a Polish parish tend to be less satisfied with their living arrangements. Membership in a Polish parish also is associated partially with the respondent's satisfaction from employment. More persons (29.48%) within the group of Polish parish members have low employment satisfaction than those (22.57%) who have high employment satisfaction."

146. Although the altered patterns of religious life among Polish postwar refugees are readily observable, the question of religion and church organization among

this immigrant wave deserves much more systematic study. For the role of the Roman Catholic Church in Polish communities in Great Britain, see Archbishop Szczepan Wesoły, *Fifty Years of the Church in the Polish Diaspora, 1945–1995* (London: School of Slavonic and East European Studies, University of London, 1996).

147. "Kącik Nowej Emigracji," *Dziennik Związkowy*, September 28, 1950, 6; October 6, 1950, 6.

Chapter 4

The title of this chapter is taken from the poem "Rhymes of a Refugee," published in *Ameryka-Echo* on October 30, 1949, and signed "One of Them."

1. Historians of Polish America are increasingly aware of the often troubled relationships among different groups within the same ethnic community. For an overview of Polonia's relationships and construction of "otherness," see John J. Bukowczyk, "Polish Americans, Ethnicity, and Otherness," *Polish Review* 43, no. 3 (1998): 299–313. Mary Patrice Erdmans, who focused on Polonia in the 1980s, pointed to the acute differences between the needs of immigrants (especially immediately after their arrival)—finding housing, jobs, and social services, and becoming familiar with the language and culture of the host society—and the needs of "ethnics" (second, third, and later immigrant generations), whose primary goal was the maintenance of ethnic heritage and support for the established ethnic cultural institutions. Mary P. Erdmans, "Immigrants and Ethnics: Conflict and Identity in Polish Chicago," *Sociological Quarterly* 36, no. 1 (1995): 175–95. See also Mary Patrice Erdmans, *Opposite Poles: Immigrants and Ethnics in Polish Chicago, 1976–1990* (University Park: Pennsylvania State University Press, 1998), 215.

2. William S. Bernard, "Refugee Asylum in the United States: How the Law was Changed to Admit Displaced Persons," *International Migration* 13, no. 1-2 (1975): 9. The Polish-American community utilized radio, too. In the summer of 1946, Franciszek J. Wazeter, president of the New York PAC state division, began a series of talks on station WHOM. The DP situation, UNRRA, or the humanitarian activities of Rada Polonii were often the topics of those weekly presentations. Wazeter's speeches were reprinted in *Tygodnik Polski*.

3. Bernard, "Refugee Asylum," 10.

4. Ibid., 11–14.

5. Donald E. Pienkos, *For Your Freedom through Ours: Polish American Efforts on Poland's Behalf, 1863–1991* (New York: Columbia University Press, 1991), 94.

6. Francis X. Świetlik, *The Polish Displaced Persons* (American Relief for Poland: Chicago, [1945]), n.p.

7. Anna D. Jaroszyńska-Kirchmann, "The Mobilization of American Polonia for

the Cause of the Displaced Persons," *Polish American Studies* 58, no.1 (Spring 2001): 42–46.

8. "Program wiecu manifestacyjnego," *Dziennik Związkowy*, November 30, 1946, 12; "Doniosłe oświadczenie prezesa Kongresu Polonii Amerykańskiej," *Dziennik Związkowy*, December 2, 1946, 1–2; "Rezolucja przyjęta na masowym wiecu Polonii," ibid., 3; "Imponująca manifestacja Polonii," ibid., 8. Shortened versions of Rozmarek's and Nurkiewicz's reports from the European trip found their way into the official protocols of the PAC Supreme Council meeting in February, 1947. *Protokół Drugiego Zjazdu Rady Naczelnej Kongresu Polonii Amerykańskiej odbytego w dniach 13–14 lutego 1947 w Hotelu Statler, Washington, D.C.* (Dziennik Związkowy: Chicago, [1947]), 6–15, 30–37. For the full text of the speech, see IHRC 144, E. C. and Loda Różański collection, Box 37, Fol. 6.

9. *Nowy Świat*, October 6, 1946, 4.

10. *Nowy Świat*, October 17, 1946, 5.

11. *Nowy Świat*, January 21, 1948, 4.

12. Tadeusz Nowakowski, "Religia wysiedleńców," *Nowy Świat*, November 11, 1946. See also another poem, by Jan Klyczka, "The Prayer of the Refugees," *Nowy Świat*, January 6, 1948, 4.

13. See, for example, *Nowy Świat*, February 13, 1946, 1; March 2, 1946, 4, 7; September 17, 1946, 5; *Dziennik Związkowy*, September 10, 1947, 1, 2; September 12, 1947, 1, 2; February 2, 1948, 1.

14. "Obrazek z dna nędzy polskich ludzi bezdomnych w Austrii," *Nowy Świat*, October 16, 1946, 4. The phrase "homeless people" (*ludzie bezdomni*) is a direct link to Stefan Żeromski's novel of the same title. According to the article, in the early morning hours on June 15, 1946, more than eighty American MPs descended upon camp number two of the Ebensee DP center and began searching the camp. After they left, terrified DPs found doors broken and their personal belongings scattered and damaged. Some DPs reported items missing after the search.

15. *Nowy Świat*, February 19, 1947, 4; February 24, 1947, 4; March 8, 1947, 4; March 25, 1947, 5. See also *Tygodnik Polski*, no. 24, June 23, 1946, 10–11; no. 25, June 30, 1946, 6–7; no. 27, July 14, 1946, 6.

16. *Nowy Świat*, February 13, 1947, 4. The uniforms were dyed dark navy blue. The author of the article noted: "The navy blue of the uniforms is the same shade as the color of German police uniforms. And we are not police—we were and we are an army! They do not recruit us from the civilian population; we come from the POW camps!" In one report from the PAC delegation's visit to the DP camps, the author remarked that there were cases of skin diseases among the Polish Guards caused by the bad dye on their uniforms. *Nowy Świat*, October 17, 1946, 5.

17. See for example, *Dziennik Związkowy*, September 12, 1947, 1, 2; March 5, 1948, 6; *Nowy Świat*, October 4, 1946, 1.

18. *Nowy Świat,* May 5, 1946, 1 (section 3). See also ibid., October 16, 1946, 4; August 12, 1946, 4.

19. "The Dangers of Mixed Marriages," *Nowy Świat,* April 16, 1948, 4.

20. Ibid. Concern over single mothers and children born out of wedlock returned to the pages of Polish American press. In the spring of 1948, a heartbreaking story appeared in *Nowy Świat* about a fourteen-month-old Polish boy thrown into a stream by his mother and left there to die. The boy survived, and the mother was sentenced to prison. The child found his way to the orphanage of the Polish Felician sisters in Lodi, New Jersey. "Janek Does Not Know That His Mother Wanted to Kill Him," *Nowy Świat,* April 30, 1948, 4. See also "Need to Approach a Difficult Problem with Heart," *Nowy Świat,* September 16, 1948, 4.

21. *Dziennik Związkowy,* December 31, 1947, 1.

22. *Nowy Świat,* September 4, 1947, 4.

23. "Letters from the Abyss" began appearing on September 16, 1948. For letters from soldiers, see, for example, *Nowy Świat,* September 8, 1946, 4; October 6, 1946, 4.

24. *Nowy Świat,* February 6, 1947, 4, 8; February 9, 1947, 4; *Dziennik Związkowy,* January 28, 1947, 1; February 1, 1947, 1, 2.

25. One report of the camp transfers carried out by the IRO was accompanied by a plea: "We ask all the Polonia newspapers to include a mention [about the incident]. Old officers of UNRRA, now in IRO, are afraid of just one thing: press publicity!" "S.O.S. of Poles in Germany," *Nowy Świat,* June 14, 1948, 4, 6. See also for example an article "Evidence Collected of German Greed for Revenge and Retaliation toward Polish DPs," *Dziennik Związkowy,* March 5, 1948, 6.

26. *Dziennik Związkowy,* May 12, 1947, 1; *Nowy Świat,* May 14, 1947, 1. Polish DPs in Altenstadt lowered the American flag and raised a black flag signifying rebellion. They were protesting UNRRA's decision to replace their elected government officials with UNRRA appointees. American military police entered the camp grounds, threw three tear gas bombs among the protesters and fired machine guns above their heads. Regarding incidents in Neustadt (British zone), where Polish DPs threw stones and used water hydrants against German police, see *Dziennik Związkowy,* February 2, 1948, 1. The reason for the hunger strike among the DP patients of the tuberculosis hospital in Goisern, Austria, was UNRRA's decision to release a hundred patients to the DP camps and to transfer the remaining two hundred to the camp in Reit, known for its poor conditions and damp living quarters. The strike lasted ten days. *Nowy Świat,* October 18, 1946, 4.

27. K. Dąbski to Zjednoczenie Polskie w Niemczech, March 9, 1948, F. #166, Józef Piłsudski Institute (JPI), New York.

28. See for example, *Dziennik Związkowy,* January 9, 1947; June 23, 1947, 2; June 25, 1947, 2; September 6, 1947, 4; September 25, 1947, 2; October 15, 1947, 2; December 11, 1947, 2; December 31, 1947, 1; January 9, 1948, 4; March 26, 1948, 1; April 6, 1948, 1; May 29, 1948, 2; June 2, 1948, 1.

29. *Nowy Świat*, October 4, 1946, 1.

30. *Nowy Świat*, October 17, 1946, 5.

31. On life in Germany, see *Nowy Świat*, January 27, 1946, 15; February 3, 1946, 11, 13; and March 17, 1946, 10. On Maczków, see *Nowy Świat*, January 27, 1946.

32. *Nowy Świat*, "Voice of a DP," May 7, 1948, 4.

33. Ryszard Kiersnowski, "Lord, Look at Our Barracks!" *Nowy Świat*, March 2, 1946, 4.

34. *Dziennik Związkowy*, January 7, 1947, 2.

35. Jan Kowalik, "D.P.," *Nowy Świat*, January 21, 1948, 4.

36. On January 12, 1948, *Nowy Świat* reported that about forty thousand Polish escapees entered illegally Germany. Their situation was by far the worst in the American zone, where they were imprisoned for illegal border crossing and received sentences ranging from a few weeks to a year. In January 1948 more than a thousand new Polish refugees were serving jail terms. *Nowy Świat*, January 12, 1948, 4. For Barzyński's report see Gen. Józef E. Barzyński, "What I Saw in Germany," *Nowy Świat*, May 11, 1948, 4.

37. Zbigniew Łukaczyński, "General Clay Will Secure DP Rights," *Nowy Świat*, August 12, 1948, 4.

38. "Brutal Search in Köl-Mülheim Camp," *Nowy Świat*, September 17, 1947, 5.

39. *Nowy Świat*, June 1, 1948, 1; ibid., September 16, 1948, 4.

40. "We Have to Make the Selection Ourselves," *Nowy Świat*, October 27, 1948, 4.

41. "Without Home and Homeland," *Nowy Świat*, October 24, 1946, 4. See also P. P. Yolles, "Polish American Congress," *Nowy Świat*, November 20, 1946, 5.

42. *Nowy Świat*, September 20, 1946, 4; May 22, 1948, 4; ibid., April 23, 1948, 4.

43. *Nowy Świat*, May 14, 1948, 4; ibid., May 28, 1948, 4.

44. *Nowy Świat*, April 2, 1948, 4. The letter appeared as a part of a section entitled "DP Matters: News on Life, Work, Deceptions, and Hopes of the Displaced Persons."

45. See for example, Stanisław Zybała, "Weryfikacja 'dipisa' Wojciecha," *Nowy Świat*, August 21, 1948, 3; Jan Obrębski, "Troski obracajmy w śmiech," ibid., July 10, 1948, 4; Jan Zandler (Sowizdrzał), "Listy polecone z Niemiec," *Dziennik Związkowy*, October 9, 1948, 2; October 16, 1948, 2.

46. *Nowy Świat*, September 24, 1947, 4.

47. Displaced Persons Commission, *Memo to America: The DP Story; The Final Report of the United States Displaced Persons Commission* (Washington, D.C.: U.S. Government Printing Office, 1952), 203; see also Holborn, *The IRO*, 302-3.

48. "Sprawozdanie z działalności Zjednoczenia Polskiego," 7, F. #162, JPI.

49. See, for example, Z. M. Rakowski, "Słowa uznania i podzięki," *Nowy Świat*, May 4, 1948.

50. *Świat i Kraj*, Norymberga, May-June, 1946, 2, Fol. Uchodźcy-Prasa-Dublety, VI, JPI.

51. Fol. #111, Kompanie Wartownicze, JPI.
52. Janina Muklewicz, "Pierwsze miesiące w USA," *Kronika*, January 25, 1948, 4.
53. *Kronika*, March 3, 1948.
54. Aleksander Hertz, *Refleksje amerykańskie* (Paris: Instytut Literacki, 1966), 83.
55. Ibid., 85–86.
56. See also my earlier attempt to explore this problem, Anna D. Jaroszyńska-Kirchmann, "'Nowa Emigracja' and 'Stara Polonia': Transformations of Social Relations and the DP Resettlement Program in the United States," in *The Polish Diaspora*, ed. James S. Pula and M. B. Biskupski, vol. 2, *Selected Essays from the Fiftieth Anniversary International Congress of the Polish Institute of Arts and Sciences of America* (Washington, D.C.: Columbia University Press, 1993), 69–84.
57. Correspondence of December 10–17, 1951, IHRC 84, Box 26, Fol. 199, PAC.
58. Correspondence of August 7–November 6, 1952, IHRC 84, Box 37, Fol. 272 and Box 35, Fol. 260, PAC.
59. T. Stapiński, "Sprawa żołnierzy i wysiedleńców," *Ameryka-Echo*, November 27, 1949, 9. See also Rev. Stanislaus T. Sypek, "The Displaced Polish Persons in the Greater Boston Community" (Ph.D. diss., Fordham University, 1955), 61–62.
60. *Ameryka-Echo*, July 22, 1951, 14.
61. *Dziennik Związkowy*, January 11, 1951, 3.
62. Sypek, "Displaced Polish Persons," 62–66.
63. Letter of November 17, 1949, IHRC 48, Box 33, Fol. 248.
64. Letter of May 8, 1952, IHRC 84, Box 35, Fol. 260, PAC.
65. Letter of May 8, 1952, IHRC 84, Box 35, Fol. 260, PAC; letter of October 20, 1952, IHRC 84, Box 28, Fol. 218, PAC; letter of August 27, 1955, IHRC 84, Box 27, Fol. 209, PAC.
66. Letter of October 20, 1952, IHRC 84, Box 28, Fol. 218, PAC. Hrabyk remarked that the social mobility and resourcefulness of many younger DPs were the outcome of their wartime and postwar experiences, which developed in them traits that allowed them to survive in adverse conditions. The United States did not intimidate these most energetic individuals; during their exile, they already had visited several other foreign countries on different continents, and culture shock was not an issue for them. Klaudiusz Hrabyk, "Z drugiej strony barykady: Spowiedź z klęski; Lata 1902–1959; Wspomnienia i dzienniki," microfilm of an unpublished manuscript, Ossolineum, Wrocław, [1979], 454.
67. Letter of October 4, 1949, IHRC 84, Box 33, Fol. 247, PAC. The majority of letters quoted here was written in Polish; my translations.
68. Letter of March 10, 1955, IHRC 84, Box 37, Fol. 273, PAC; letter of August 1949, IHRC 84, Box 33, Fol. 251, PAC; letter of May 20, 1952, IHRC 84, Box 37, Fol. 272, PAC.
69. Undated letter to the ACRPDP, IHRC 84, Box 33, Fol. 249, PAC.

70. J. Donald Cohon, Jr., "Psychological Adaptation and Dysfunction among Refugees," *International Migration Review* 15, no. 1-2 (1981): 255.

71. Cohon, "Psychological Adaptation," 259.

72. Miriam L. Gaertner, "A Comparison of Refugee and Non-refugee Immigrants to New York City," in *Flight and Resettlement*, ed. H. B. Murphy (Lucerne: United Nations Educational, Scientific, and Cultural Organization, 1955), 101-4.

73. Barry N. Stein, "The Refugee Experience: Defining the Parameters of a Field of Study," *International Migration Review* 15 (Spring-Summer 1981): 325-26.

74. Henry P. David, "Involuntary International Migration: Adaptation of Refugees," *International Migration* [Netherlands] 7, no. 3-4 (1969): 71.

75. William S. Bernard, "Immigrants and Refugees: Their Similarities, Differences, and Needs," *International Migration* [Netherlands] 14, no. 4 (1976): 271. See also Richard Kolm, "The Change of Cultural Identity: An Analysis of Factors Conditioning the Cultural Integration of Immigrants" (Ph.D. diss., Wayne State University, 1966), 146-48. Some examples of studies on psychopathology among displaced persons can be found in Murphy, *Flight and Resettlement*, 147-213. See, for example, Maria Pfister-Ammende, "The Symptomatology, Treatment, and Prognosis in Mentally Ill Refugees and Repatriates in Switzerland," 147-72; H .B. M. Murphy, "Refugee Psychoses in Great Britain: Admissions to Mental Hospitals," 173-94; F. F. Kino, "Refugee Psychoses in Great Britain: Aliens' Paranoid Reaction," 195-201; Libuse Tyhurst, "Psychosomatic and Allied Disorders," 202-14.

76. David, "Involuntary International Migration," 72.

77. See also E. F. Kunz, "The Refugee in Flight: Kinetic Models and Forms of Displacement," *International Migration Review* 7, no. 22 (Summer 1973): 130.

78. *Dziennik Związkowy*, June 5, 1948; June 23, 1948; October 29, 1948; November 17, 1948.

79. *Dziennik Związkowy*, October 15, 1949, 1.

80. John J. Bukowczyk, *And My Children Did Not Know Me: A History of the Polish-Americans* (Bloomington: Indiana University Press, 1987), 95.

81. John Krawiec, interview by the author, tape recording, Chicago, Ill., January 5, 1995.

82. Serafin Dobczyński, "Wrażenia, wspomnienia, 'polka' i Polonja," *Nowy Świat*, February 14, 1948, 4.

83. Hrabyk recalled some exceptionally painful cases. For example General Władysław Bortnowski, commander in chief of the Polish Army Pomorze and a hero of the war in September 1939, worked as a waiter in the hotel in the Catskills frequented by many Polish exiles, while his wife was employed there as a cook. In later years, Bortnowski tried his luck as a grocer and a factory worker. Hrabyk, "Z drugiej strony barykady," 563c-563d. Hrabyk also emphasized the resourcefulness of Polish women who had belonged to the higher echelons of prewar Polish society, but who

worked as domestics, sold greeting cards door-to-door, and established tailoring and alteration shops in the United States. Ibid., 946–47. Sociologist Alicja Iwańska, who studied the adjustment of intelligentsia in Chicago in the 1950s, gives several examples of efforts to preserve traditional values under conditions of exile. Alicja Iwańska, *Polish Intelligentsia in Nazi Concentration Camps and American Exile: A Study of Values in Crisis Situations* (Lewiston, N.Y.: Edwin Mellen Press, [1998]).

84. Bukowczyk, *And My Children*, 95. Rev. S. T. Sypek recorded some telling examples of professionals struggling to regain their prewar position in America in selected case histories, "Displaced Polish Persons," 176–90.

85. Ignacy Matuszewski, "Paląca sprawa," *Nowy Świat*, March 26, 1947. The series appeared between March 24 and March 29, 1947.

86. P. P. Yolles, "'D.P.,'" *Nowy Świat*, January 21, 1948, 4.

87. P. P. Yolles, "Jubileusz poety," *Nowy Świat*, February 17, 1948, 4.

88. S. Kania, "Pod uwagę organizacjom polskim," *Ameryka-Echo*, February 5, 1950, 14.

89. Feliks Tontarski, "Do komitetów wysiedleńczych i do niektórych wysiedleńców," *Ameryka-Echo*, November 20, 1949, 14.

90. Leonidas Dudarew Ossetyński, "Nie ośmieszajmy się . . . ," *Nowy Świat*, July 29, 1950, 4; July 31, 1950, 4; August 1, 1950, 4.

91. P. P. Yolles, "Gość w dom," *Nowy Świat*, May 10, 1948.

92. "Z. Nagórski odpowiada," *Nowy Świat*, July 7, 1948, 4.

93. "Znów szkodliwy i błazeński wyskok," *Nowy Świat*, July 16, 1948.

94. P. P. Yolles, "O wysiedleńcach," part 3, *Nowy Świat*, July 28, 1948, 4.

95. P. P. Yolles, "O wysiedleńcach," part 4, *Nowy Świat*, July 29, 1948, 4.

96. Maria Plater-Zyberk, "O zrozumienie dla nowych imigrantów," *Nowy Świat*, August 17, 1948, 4–5.

97. Magdalena Roszkowska, "Jeszcze o wysiedleńcach," *Nowy Świat*, August 28, 1948, 4. See also a letter from a refugee in Norway responding to Yolles's articles, August 26, 1948, 4.

98. *Nowy Świat*, June 6, 1949, 8.

99. "Rozmowy z Wujem Samem," *Nowy Świat*, March 8, 1950, 4.

100. "Listy do Wuja Sama," *Nowy Świat*, March 22, 1950, 4.

101. See "Pomost," *Nowy Świat*, February 22, 1950; March 1, 1950; March 8, 1950; March 15, 1950; March 22, 1950; May 6, 1950; May 9, 1950; June 1, 1950; and June 6, 1950.

102. "List polskiego wysiedleńca z Ameryki do Niemiec," *Dziennik Związkowy*, September 1, 1951, 8.

103. "List dipisa z Ameryki do kolegi w Niemczech," *Dziennik Związkowy*, September 8, 1951, 2. See also "Nie przeszkadzaj mi," a humorous description of confusion resulting from the unfamiliarity of the newcomers with the Polonian language, *Ameryka-Echo*, March 18, 1951, 14.

104. Aleksander Janta, *Nowe odkrycie Ameryki* (Paris: Libella, 1973), 142–45, 150–63.

105. "Yolles pisze o naszym Majku i o spaczaniu języka polskiego," *Kuryer Polski*, July 15, 1953, 3. For a description of the DP journalist's experience at *Gwiazda Polarna*, a popular weekly in Stevens Point, Wisconsin, see Alfons Hering, *So, You Wanted America... One DP's Story*, comp. Helen D. Hering (Wausau, Wisc.: Evergreen Press, 1996), 122–29, 140–47. Exiled Poles were employed also in some radio programs. Jerzy Lerski, "Symbioza," *Kultura* 12/50 (1951): 55.

106. "Gdzie są Polacy?" *Ameryka-Echo*, February 20, 1949, 14; "O czystość mowy polskiej," *Nowy Świat*, January 8, 1950, 8; "List dipisa z Ameryki do kolegi w Niemczech," *Dziennik Związkowy*, September 8, 1950, 2.

107. Janta, *Nowe odkrycie*, 171. Elsewhere Janta wrote: "The notion of Polish language and Polish 'culture' are made synonymous. Among Americans of Polish origin most efforts, many of them with the best intention, are directed towards maintaining some semblance of the ability to speak Polish. These sponsors are satisfied that this is the way to serve, 'maintain,' or 'preserve' Polish culture on American soil. The majority of those attached to the Polish tradition speak, as a consequence, some Polish; few, if any, are able to utter in English anything that might contribute to a knowledge or understanding of Polish problems." Alexander Janta, "Barriers into Bridges: Notes on the Problem of Polish Culture in America," *Polish Review* 2, no. 2–3 (Spring-Summer 1957): 83.

108. Janta, *Nowe odkrycie*, 308. On the story of theater performances in Buffalo presenting Polish classic drama in English, 195–203, 307–15. See also "Listy do Redakcji," *Kultura* 1/63 (1953): 145–47.

109. "Gdzie są Polacy?" *Ameryka-Echo*, February 20, 1949, 14. The same problem was addressed in correspondence "Uwagi o 'wygnańcu,'" *Nowy Świat*, November 2, 1951, 8.

110. "Najważniejsza sprawa," *Nowy Świat*, March 8, 1950, 4.

111. "Polskość w polskich osiedlach," *Ameryka-Echo*, October 15, 1950, 14.

112. Leonidas Dudarew Ossetyński, "Nie ośmieszajmy się" *Nowy Świat*, July 31, 1950, 4; August 1, 1950, 6; "Obojętność uchodźców w Kalifornii," November 15, 1949, 6.

113. P. P. Yolles, "Amerykanizacja," *Nowy Świat*, May 19, 1947; May 20, 1947; May 21, 1947; May 22, 1947, 4.

114. P. P. Yolles, "Obrona," *Nowy Świat*, April 2, 1948, 4.

115. Feliks Czarnowski, "Dowód amerykanizacji, czy braku charakteru," *Nowy Świat*, April 7, 1948, 4. For the opposite view on the names of Polish organizations, see a reader's letter "Po co ten 'Polish' pyta 'Gwiazda,'" *Nowy Świat*, September 1, 1947, 4.

116. Dr. J. P. Zajączkowski, "Polak czy Amerykanin?" *Nowy Świat*, August 3, 1950, 4.

117. Janta, "Barriers," 81.

118. Ibid., 91; Janta, *Nowe odkrycie*, 170–71. Danuta Mostwin presents an image of this kind of celebration in her novel *Ameryko! Ameryko!* (Paris: Instytut Literacki, 1961), 128–32.

119. Janta, *Nowe odkrycie*, 307–29.

120. Janta, "Barriers," 95–97.

121. "'Awantura o Józię' była wspaniałą zabawą, choć publika nie dopisała," *Kuryer Polski*, May 29, 1950, 5. "Publiczność świetnie się bawiła na przedstawieniu 'Polska Parada,'" *Kuryer Polski*, May 8, 1950, 5.

122. T. G. . . . . . ki, "Nie przeszkadzaj mi," *Ameryka-Echo*, March 18, 1951, 14. See also Rev. S. T. Sypek, "Displaced Polish Persons," 75–84.

123. Joseph Wittlin, "Sorrow and Grandeur of Exile," *Polish Review* 2, no. 2–3 (1957): 106.

124. Ibid., 109.

125. Ibid., 111.

126. Wacław Lednicki, "The Role of the Polish Intellectual in America," *Polish Review* 12, no. 2 (1967): 7–8.

127. Hertz, *Refleksje*, 69.

128. See, for example, the 1987 issue of the literary magazine *Poezja*, devoted in full to post–World War II émigré poetry in the Polish diaspora. See also Paul Tabori, *The Pen in Exile: An Anthology of Exiled Writers* (London: International P.E.N. Club Centre For Writers in Exile, 1954); idem, *The Pen in Exile: A Second Anthology* (London: International P.E.N. Club Centre For Writers in Exile, 1956); Marek Pytasz, ed., *Literatura emigracyjna, 1939–1989*, vol. 1 (Katowice: Śląsk, 1994); Wojciech Ligęza, "Commonplaces: Polish Émigré Poetry, 1945–1980," *Polish Review* 34, no. 1 (1989): 17–27.

129. Melchior Wańkowicz, *Polacy i Ameryka* (London: Oficyna Poetów i Malarzy na Emigracji w Anglii, [1952]), 146–60. Jerzy Zubrzycki attempted to bridge the gap between the concept of political-military soldier immigration represented in the national "great" tradition, and economic-peasant immigration expressed in the family-based "small" tradition. According to Zubrzycki, throughout the ages Polish immigrants of peasant background actively participated as soldiers in the struggle for independence, contributing in this way to the political and national traditions of Polish emigration. He concluded: "Peasants and soldiers, peasants or soldiers are inseparable in the sociology of Polish migration—both in its structural and social organizational aspects." Jerzy Zubrzycki, "Żołnierze i chłopi: Socjologia emigracji polskiej," *Przegląd Polonijny* 15, no. 4 (1989): 21.

130. Jan Obrębski, "'Przyjechaliśmy nie po dolary . . . ,'" *Nowy Świat*, November 28, 1949, 6.

131. "Polonia, uchodźcy, i wysiedleńcy zjednoczeni pod hasłem wspólnej sprawy," *Nowy Świat*, November 13, 1948, 1, 8.

132. B. Czaykowski and B. Sulik, *Polacy w W. Brytanii* (Paris: Instytut Literacki, 1961), 452.

133. Melchior Wańkowicz, *Klub Trzeciego Miejsca* (Paris: Instytut Literacki, 1949), 45-80. On Wańkowicz's attitudes and opinions, see also Bogusław Włodawiec, "Melchior Wańkowicz wobec rzeczywistości lat 1939-1956," *Przegląd Polonijny* 21, no. 3 (1995): 55-62.

134. See for example, "Co życie niesie," *Dziennik Związkowy,* January 13, 1950, 4; "Oświadczenie Kongresu Polonii Amerykańskiej," ibid., January 18, 1950, 5; "W jedności siła," ibid., February 3, 1950, 7; "Co życie niesie," ibid., March 2, 1950, 4; "Emigracja polityczna a Polonja," *Nowy Świat,* September 5, 1950; September 6, 1950; September 7, 1950; September 8, 1950; and September 9, 1950, 6; "Co życie niesie," *Dziennik Związkowy,* September 4, 1951, 4; ibid., February 6, 1952, 4.

135. Tadeusz Paleczny, *Ewolucja ideologii i przemiany tożsamości narodowej Polonii w Stanach Zjednoczonych w latach 1870-1970* (Warsaw: Państwowe Wydawnictwo Naukowe, 1989), 236; Richard C. Lukas, *Bitter Legacy: Polish-American Relations in the Wake of World War II* (Louisville: University of Kentucky Press, 1982) 132; George Janczewski, "The Significance of the Polish Vote in the American National Election Campaign of 1948," *Polish Review* 13, no. 4 (1968): 104-6; Richard C. Lukas, "The Polish American Congress and the Polish Question, 1944-1947," *Polish American Studies* 38, no. 2 (Autumn 1981), 52.

136. Paleczny, *Ewolucja ideologii,* 237.

137. Janta, *Nowe odkrycie,* 176.

138. According to Klaudiusz Hrabyk, active in New York and New England political life in the 1950s, their effectiveness in the larger refugee community was as limited as it had been during the DP camp period. Hrabyk wrote later that in comparison with the powerful Polish American Congress, the political parties of the new emigration wielded virtually no influence over American Polonia as a whole. Hrabyk, "Z drugiej strony barykady," 480-82, 604. The influence of party politics among refugees settled in the United States never reached the level or intensity of those in Great Britain, but involved some newcomers directly and others incidentally. Danuta Mostwin's description of a party meeting in her novel *Ameryko! Ameryko!* conveys the atmosphere of party politics. See pages 87–91. On general characteristics of the European émigré circles and their politics, see Robert C. Williams, "European Political Emigrations: A Lost Subject," *Comparative Studies in Society and History* 12, no. 2 (April 1970): 140-48.

139. The intellectual output of these political writers in exile is impressive. See, for example, Zygmunt Tkocz, ed., *Chrześcijańska myśl społeczna na emigracji,* vol. 1 of *Myśl społeczna i polityczna na emigracji,* ed. Feliks Gross (London: Odnowa, 1991); Zygmunt Tkocz and Teofil Roll, eds., *Wybór pism emigracji politycznej Niepodległej PPS (WRN) 1940-1970,* vol. 2 of *Myśl społeczna i polityczna na emigracji,*

ed. Feliks Gross (Londyn: Odnowa, 1994); Feliks Gross, ed., *Rowmund Piłsudski: Pisma wybrane, 1972–1982* (Warsaw: Instytut Studiów Politycznych Polskiej Akademii Nauk, 1998); Anna Siwik, *Polska Partia Socjalistyczna na emigracji w latach 1945–1956* (Krakow: Księgarnia Akademicka, 1998); Andrzej Friszke, ed., *Warszawa nad Tamizą: Z dziejów polskiej emigracji politycznej po drugiej wojnie światowej* (Warsaw: Instytut Studiów Politycznych Polskiej Akademii Nauk, 1994); Andrzej Friszke, ed., *Myśl polityczna na wygnaniu: Publicyści i politycy polskiej emigracji powojennej* (Warsaw: Instytut Studiów Politycznych Polskiej Akademii Nauk, 1995).

140. "Polsko-Amerykańska Rada Pracy w Chicago do nowoprzybyłych," *Nowy Świat*, March 13, 1952, 6.

141. "O pozyskanie przybyszów, którzy od nas stronią," *Nowy Świat*, October 6, 1947, 4; John H. Grzywa, "Co boli Polonię w Chicago," *Ameryka-Echo*, October 18, 1953, 14; "O współpracy wysiedleńców z Polonią," *Ameryka-Echo*, July 19, 1953, 6.

142. *Ameryka-Echo*, January 7, 1951, 4.

143. Władysław Zachariasiewicz, "Wstępujmy w szeregi istniejących organizacji," *Nowy Świat*, February 15, 1950, 4; idem, "Polonia amerykańska liczy na przybywających tu wysiedleńców," *Nowy Świat*, November 2, 1950, 6. "Uchodźcy i wysiedleńcy w Kaliforni," *Nowy Świat*, October 24, 1949, 3; October 26, 1949, 6–7; "Obojętność uchodźców w Kalifornji," *Nowy Świat*, November 14, 1949, 4; November 15, 1949, 6; November 16, 1949, 4.

144. Jan Szeklicki, "Wielkie trudności nowych imigrantów," *Nowy Świat*, December 6, 1946, 4.

145. Zygmunt Nagórski, "Stara i nowa emigracja," *Nowy Świat*, August 25, 1951, 6; August 28, 1951, 6; August 30, 1951, 6. See also September 1, 1951, 6.

146. Janta, *Nowe odkrycie*, 331–54.

147. Stanislaus A. Blejwas, "Old and New Polonias: Tensions within an Ethnic Community," *Polish American Studies* 38, no. 2 (Autumn 1981): 70.

148. Stanisław Gierat, "List do kolegów członków Stowarzyszenia Polskich Kombatantów, osiedlających się w Ameryce," *Nowy Świat*, January 19, 1952, 6; "Debaty w Londynie nad harmonią dawnej i nowej imigracji w Stanach Zjednoczonych," *Dziennik Związkowy*, April 3, 1952, 2. Suggestions for changes included decreasing the waiting period for full membership rights to six months or accepting the period of membership in the SPK toward the required five-year membership in the SWAP; the formation of a separate unit representing World War II veterans' interests within the supreme council. Later, the demand to elect three World War II veterans to the supreme council was also added. "Troska o harmonijne współżycie między SPK i SWAP na zjeździe w Londynie," *Dziennik Związkowy*, August 8, 1952, 2. See also Bolesław Łaszewski, "Emigracja żołnierska," *Nowy Świat*, May 15, 1952, 6; May 17, 1952, 6; May 20, 1952, 6; and May 22, 1952, 6. The beginnings of the SPK are also recalled in Bolesław T. Łaszewski, *Z wojskowych szeregów do życia cywilnego: Historia powstania i*

pierwszych pięciu lat działalności Stowarzyszenia Polskich Kombatantów, 1945-1950 (New York: Bicentennial Publishing Corporation of New York, 1984).

149. "Po jedenastym walnym zjeździe Stow. Weteranów Armii Polskiej," *Weteran*, June 1952, 6-9; "Protokół z XI-go walnego zjazdu Stowarzyszenia Weteranów Armii Polskiej, odbytego w dniach 30-go, 31-go maja i 1-go czerwca 1952 w Utica, N.Y.," *Weteran*, July 1952, 10-20; "Troska o harmonijne współżycie między SPK i SWAP na zjeździe w Londynie," *Dziennik Związkowy*, August 8, 1952, 2.

150. K. J. Zielecki, "Weterani nie każą wyrzekać się obywatelstwa, przysięgi czy munduru," *Weteran*, July 1952, 1-2; "Mylne tłumaczenie kwestii umundurowania," ibid., 3; Jan Dec, "Od komendanta SWAP," *Weteran*, September 1952, 1; "Oświadczenie zarządu głównego SWAP w Ameryce," *Nowy Świat*, October 21, 1952, 4.

151. "Komunikat uchwała nadzwyczajnego walnego zebrania Pl. 201 o odłączeniu się od SWAP zapadła 14 września," *Nowy Świat*, October 14, 1952, 4; "Łączy nas jeden cel—wolna Polska," "Odpowiedź żołnierza na emigracji," letters to the editor, ibid.; "W sprawie rozłamu w SWAP—odezwa," *Ameryka-Echo*, October 26, 1952, 14; "Rezolucja zjazdu okr. VIII SWAP w Worcester, Mass.," *Nowy Świat*, September 29, 1952, 6; "Rozłam wśród weteranów," *Ameryka-Echo*, October 5, 1952, 4; "Młodzi weterani armii polskiej proszeni do placówki 3-ej SWAP," *Kuryer Polski*, March 13, 1953, 6; "'Burza w szklance wody,'" *Weteran*, October 1952, 4-6; "Oświadczenia kolegów, weteranów drugiej wojny światowej," ibid., 6-7; "Widzi mi się...," *Weteran*, November 1952, 4; Bolesław T. Łaszewski, "O wspaniałomyślność i dobrą wolę," *Nowy Świat*, November 7, 1952, 4. See also Blejwas, "Old and New," 71.

152. Jan Wawrzkiewicz, ed., *Dwadzieścia pięć lat Stowarzyszenia Polskich Kombatantów* (Londyn: P.C.A. Publications Limited, 1971), 186.

153. For a shorter account of the affair, see Tadeusz Wyrwa, "'Private war' with the U.S. Government," chap. 9 in *Bezdroża dziejów Polski* (Lublin: Norbertinum, 1998), 172-88.

154. Major Henryk Dobrzański (pseudonym "Hubal"), who had refused to surrender to the Germans from the outbreak of the war in September 1939, was the leader of a group of Polish partisans fighting against German occupiers in the Kielce region. Hubal died in a battle in April 1940. Norman Davies, *God's Playground: A History of Poland in Two Volumes*, vol. 2, *1795 to the Present* (New York: Columbia University Press, 1982), 464.

155. Józef Wyrwa ("Furgalski," or "Stary"), *Pamiętniki Partyzanta* (London: Oficyna Poetów i Malarzy, 1991), 301.

156. *Dziennik Związkowy*, August 4, 1950, 8.

157. *Kuryer Codzienny* (Boston), August 10, 1950, 4.

158. *Dziennik Chicagoski*, August 9, 1950, 4.

159. *Nowy Świat*, August 22, 1950, 8. Yolles returned to the issue in three more editorials entitled "Character," published between September 19 and 21, 1950.

160. *Dziennik Polski,* September 7, 1950, 4. The entire series was published between August 30 and September 7, 1950.
161. *Dziennik Polski,* August 25, 1950, 4.
162. *Dziennik Polski,* September 9, 1950, 1–4.
163. *Dziennik Związkowy,* August 30, 1950, 2.
164. Letter quoted in Wyrwa, *Pamiętniki,* 356.
165. *Nowy Świat,* August 30, 1950, 8.
166. Letter quoted in Wyrwa, *Pamiętniki,* 353.
167. Ibid., 353.
168. Ibid., 355.
169. Ibid., 341. Hrabyk commented also on the Wyrwa affair in his official presentation given at the convention. Defining the responsibilities of political emigrants versus Old Polonia, he said: "We can neither let ourselves be drawn into the atmosphere of 'bara' [a bar serving alcoholic beverages, as an inseparable element of any Polonian celebration or entertainment] and table parties as ideals of social life, nor can we surrender in the name of peace in our everyday life. We can't accept opportunism for our program or get ensnared by the syrupy sweet phraseology of empty words and noisy patriotism in which the real political sense of the Polish question is lost." Ibid., 344 (my translation).
170. Ibid., 369–72.
171. Ibid., 340, 374–425.
172. *Dziennik Chicagoski,* August 14, 1950, 4.
173. *Dziennik Chicagoski,* August 21, 1950, 5. Later on, General Anders talked to both Wyrwas personally during his sojourn in Chicago and again expressed his full support. Wyrwa, *Pamiętniki,* 482.
174. The belief that political refugees could play a part in international politics was not merely wishful thinking on the part of Polish government circles in London. According to Paweł Machcewicz, after the outbreak of war in Korea, American diplomats showed an increased interest in the situation of Polish local émigré communities, seeking to establish contacts, which they had previously avoided. In 1951, the Department of State requested detailed reports about numbers, organizations, and opinions prevalent in the Polish diaspora. In unofficial talks, some American politicians probed the possibility of the formation of Polish armed forces in the event of expansion in the war in Korea and pressured Polish leaders to step up efforts for the unification of the diaspora. In 1951 Congress debated the appropriation of $100 million to form military units of refugees from behind the Iron Curtain that could be used within the defense system of Western Europe. Machcewicz, *Emigracja,* 69–89. Limited numbers of escapees from behind the Iron Curtain were also recruited and trained secretly by the American army stationed in Germany, with the goal of preparing operatives for the Polish arena in case of an American-Soviet war. Czesław

Pławski, *Wydarci z ojczystej ziemi: Okres drugiej wojny światowej* (Łódź: RES POLONA, 2001), 262-70.

175. *Kuryer Codzienny*, August 30, 1950, 4.

176. The law was the Universal Military Training and Service Act, approved by the Congress and signed by Truman in mid-June 1951. It read: "Every male citizen and every male alien admitted for permanent residence between ages 18 (and) ½ and 26 shall be liable for training and service in the armed forces." *Congressional Quarterly Almanac, 82nd Congress, First Session-1951*, Vol. VII, 247. See also the reaction of the Polonia press, which interpreted the law as a response to the Wyrwa scandal. "Kongres zaostrza prawo o poborze," *Dziennik Związkowy*, April 21, 1951, 1; "Wszyscy przybyli D.P. w wieku od 18 do 26 lat podlegają służbie wojskowej," ibid., May 1, 1951, 1; "Prawo o służbie w armii U.S.—obywateli oraz cudzoziemców—podpisał prezydent," ibid., July 12, 1951, 2.

177. Wyrwa, *Pamiętniki*, 451-56.

178. Ibid., 463-64.

179. Ibid., 467-70.

180. Ibid., 495.

181. Józef Wyrwa devotes the entire second part of his book to his son's story. Ibid., 301-551. The book contains rich and detailed primary documentation relating to the case and abundant quotations from the Polish-language press in the United States. I would like to thank Dr. Tadeusz Wyrwa for providing me with a copy of his father's book and for his friendly correspondence on the subject.

182. Stanisław Michalski, "Nie ośmieszajmy . . . ," *Nowy Świat*, August 19, 1950, 6; August 22, 1950, 6.

183. See for example "Manifestacja współpracy Polonii ameryk. i polskiej emigracji politycznej," *Dziennik Związkowy*, March 7, 1953, 15; Halina Trzensioch, "Urojone zasługi i bezsensowne żale," *Nowy Świat*, January 12, 1952, 6; Zygmunt Polkowski, "My i wy," *Nowy Świat*, November 7, 1952, 6; November 8, 1952, 4, 5; Ignacy Matuszewski, "Paląca sprawa," *Nowy Świat*, March 26, 1947, 4; Zygmunt Polkowski, "My i wy," *Nowy Świat*, November 8, 1952, 4.

Chapter 5

The title of this chapter is taken from the essay "Nie łatwo być ambasadorem," by Zbigniew Chałko, published in *Kultura* 12, no. 38, in 1950.

1. Rafał Habielski, *Niezłomni nieprzejednani: Emigracyjne "Wiadomości" i ich krąg, 1940-1981* (Warsaw: Państwowy Instytut Wydawniczy, 1991), 78.

2. Zbigniew Chałko, "Nie łatwo być ambasadorem," *Kultura* 12/38 (1950): 127.

3. Andrzej Friszke, *Życie polityczne emigracji*, vol. 1, *Druga Wielka Emigracja, 1945-1990* (Warsaw: Biblioteka WIĘZI, 1999), 215-31.

4. Ibid., 156–61.
5. Ibid., 161–63.
6. Paweł Machcewicz, *Emigracja w polityce międzynarodowej*, vol. 2, *Druga Wielka Emigracja, 1945–1990* (Warsaw: Biblioteka WIĘZI, 1999), 48; J. F. Leich, "Great Expectations: The National Councils in Exile 1950–1960," *Polish Review* 35, no. 3 (1990): 183–96.
7. Friszke, *Życie polityczne*, 162, 165–66.
8. Ibid., 169–96.
9. The Berg affair (named for its base of operation in Berg, Germany) referred to the cooperation of one section of the Political Council with the CIA to create a spy ring in Poland and to obtain information critical to the American intelligence. Operation Spotlight (*akcja balonikowa*) was an effort to release over Poland's territory small balloons containing Western propaganda information. See Machcewicz, *Emigracja*, 89–90, 112–22.
10. Ibid., 98–100; Leich, "Great Expectations," 193–94; "Narody ujarzmione," *Nowy Świat*, January 20, 1956, 3.
11. Machcewicz, *Emigracja*, 56–64; Jan Nowak-Jeziorański, *Wojna w eterze: Wspomnienia*, vol. 1, *1948–1956* (London: Odnowa, 1986).
12. Scholarship on the influence of *Kultura* has grown considerably during recent years. See for example *O "Kulturze": Wspomnienia i opinie* (Warsaw: POMOST, 1988); Jerzy Giedroyć, *Listy, 1950–1987* (Warsaw: Czytelnik, 1995); Jerzy Giedroyć, *Listy, 1946–1961* (Warsaw: Czytelnik, 1997); Jerzy Giedroyć, *Listy, 1946–1969* (Warsaw: Czytelnik, 1998); Jerzy Giedroyć, *Listy, 1949–1956* (Warsaw: Czytelnik, 1999); Jerzy Giedroyć, *Autobiografia na cztery ręce* (Warsaw: Czytelnik, 1996); Renata Gorczyńska, *Portrety paryskie* (Kraków: Wydawnictwo Literackie, 1999); Andrzej Stanisław Kowalczyk, *Giedroyć i "Kultura"* (Wrocław: Wydawnictwo Dolnośląskie, 1999).
13. *Protokół Trzeciej Krajowej Konwencji Kongresu*, 69–73.
14. T. Aleksandrowicz, "W pochodzie ku wolnej Polsce," *Nowy Świat*, March 21, 1950, 6; ibid., March 22, 1950, 3; "Pierwszy zjazd NID'u odbył się w stolicy Polonii amerykańskiej," *Dziennik Związkowy*, December 10, 1951, 8.
15. *Dziennik Związkowy*, April–May, 1953 (Jarecki's escape); ibid., July 1953 (Jaźwiński's escape).
16. Richard Polenberg, *One Nation Divisible: Class, Race, and Ethnicity in the United States since 1938* (New York: Viking Press, 1980), 120.
17. Ibid., 121.
18. Ibid., 126. For the impact of McCarthyism on the destruction of the Slavic Left, see, for example, Stanislaus A. Blejwas, "A Polish American Fellow Traveler," *Polish Review* 36, no. 2 (1991): 169–77; Stanislaus A. Blejwas, "Polonia and Politics," in *Polish Americans and Their History: Community, Culture, and Politics*, ed. John

J. Bukowczyk (Pittsburgh: University of Pittsburgh Press, 1996), 146. On the basis of the still limited studies in this area it is now believed that not many Polish Americans succumbed to McCarthyism in its most aggressive form.

19. Robert Szymczak, "A Matter of Honor: Polonia and the Congressional Investigation of the Katyń Forest Massacre," *Polish American Studies* 41, no. 1 (Spring 1984): 25-26.

20. Ibid., 39-40.

21. Ibid., 40-65.

22. Robert Szymczak, "Hopes and Promises: Arthur Bliss Lane, the Republican Party, and the Slavic-American Vote," *Polish American Studies* 45, no. 1 (Spring 1988): 12-28; Pula, *Polish Americans*, 113-14. Polish Americans voted Republican twice more, in 1972 for Nixon, after Edmund Muskie's campaign folded, and in 1984 for Reagan. Blejwas, "Polonia and Politics," 140; James S. Pula, *Polish Americans: An Ethnic Community* (New York: Twayne Publishers, 1995), 134-36.

23. Norman Davies, *God's Playground: A History of Poland in Two Volumes*, vol. 2, *1795 to the Present* (New York: Columbia University Press, 1982), 582-83; Piotr S. Wandycz, *The Price of Freedom: A History of East Central Europe from the Middle Ages to the Present* (London: Routledge, 1992), 250-51.

24. For details on Towarzystwo "Polonia," see Jan Lencznarowicz, "Rola Towarzystwa 'Polonia' w polityce PRL wobec Polonii w krajach zachodnich," *Przegląd Polonijny* 22, no. 1 (1996): 43-60.

25. Nowak-Jeziorański, *Wojna*, 174.

26. Friszke, *Życie polityczne*, 232-36; Machcewicz, *Emigracja*, 128-29.

27. Nowak, *Wojna*, 179-80.

28. Ibid., 176-77.

29. The issue of Poles in Russia was also publicized during the silent march organized in London in April 1956. Friszke, *Życie polityczne*, 237-41; Machcewicz, *Emigracja*, 131-41. The Polish-American press also featured articles on the subject. See, for example, "Gdzie są Polacy wywiezieni do Rosji?," *Nowy Świat*, January 3, 1956, 3; "O Polakach przebywajacych w sowieckich łagrach," *Nowy Świat*, January 14, 1956, 3.

30. Rafał Habielski, *Niezłomni i nieprzejednani: Emigracyjne "Wiadomości" i ich krąg, 1940-1981* (Warsaw: Państwowy Instytut Wydawniczy, 1991), 113-14.

31. Hanke turned out to be a communist spy, having collaborated with the authorities in Poland since 1952. The group of returnees numbered about one hundred. Marian M. Drozdowski, ed., *1956: Polska Emigracja a Kraj* (Warsaw: Oficyna Wydawnicza Typografika, 1998), 11; Nowak-Jeziorański, *Wojna*, 177-78; Friszke, *Życie polityczne*, 239. For examples of the press debate on the safety and rationale for returns, see "Stanowisko b. żołnierzy w sprawie reżymowej akiji powrotu," *Ameryka-Echo*, November 13, 1955, 4; "Reemigracja i reemigranci," *Nowy Świat*, January 9, 1956, 3;

"Smutna karjera generałów repatrjantów z Anglji," *Nowy Świat*, February 14, 1956, 3; "Dlaczego pisarze nie wracają do Kraju?" *Nowy Świat*, May 29, 1956, 3.

32. "Oświadczenie Polskiego Komitetu Międzyorganizacyjnego w Chicago," *Ameryka-Echo*, November 4, 1956. See also the exchange of letters to the editor in *Kuryer Polski* (Milwaukee), August 13–14, 1956, 2–3; "Arcybiskup Gawlina ostrzega przed reżymowymi zjazdami i pielgrzymkami," *Nowy Świat*, May 18, 1956, 1; "Sprawa wyjazdów do Polski," *Nowy Świat*, October 20, 1956, 3; "O wycieczkach do Polski i o ich organizatorach," *Nowy Świat*, October 22, 1956, 3.

33. *Zgoda*, October 15, 1956, 1.

34. Machcewicz, *Emigracja*, 122–27.

35. Different estimates indicate the total number of participants to be between twenty and forty thousand. Machcewicz, *Emigracja*, 138–40; Friszke, *Życie polityczne*, 247–48. For examples of coverage in the Polish-American press, see "Demonstracja Polaków w Londynie," *Nowy Świat*, April 25, 1; "Polacy przygotowują manifestacje protestacyjne na przyjazd Bułganina i Chruszczowa," *Nowy Świat*, April 9, 1956, 1; "Potężna manifestacja protestacyjna Polaków," *Nowy Świat*, April 24, 1956, 1; "Depesza b. więźniów politycznych do premjera W. Brytanii Edena," *Nowy Świat*, April 24, 1956, 1.

36. "Rezolucja rocznego zjazdu wydziału stanowego Kongresu Polonji w New Yorku, 8 kwietnia, 1956," *Nowy Świat*, April 14, 1956, 7. See also "W Gwatemali i u nas," *Nowy Świat*, January 9, 1956, 3.

37. Klaudiusz Hrabyk, "Szesnaście lat po wrześniu," in *Kraj i Emigracja* (New York: published by the author, 1957), especially 15–25.

38. Nowak, *Wojna*, 226–29.

39. F. Olszowy, "'Odwilż' w Polsce," *Ameryka-Echo*, May 20, 1956; "Po sowieckiej odwilży," *Nowy Świat*, January 9, 1956, 3; "Co się dzieje w Polsce?," *Nowy Świat*, March 16, 1956, 3.

40. "Blisko 2,000 przedstawicieli Polonii," *Nowy Świat*, January 16, 1956, 1; "S.S. Wolna Polska," *Nowy Świat*, January 11, 1956, 3.

41. Drozdowski, *1956*, 11.

42. "Rozbicie czy siła?," *Ameryka-Echo*, February 19, 1956.

43. *Zgoda*, May 15, 1956, 1; *Ameryka-Echo*, May 20, 1956, 4; *Nowy Świat*, May 8, 1956, 1.

44. *Ameryka-Echo*, May 20, 1956, 4.

45. See, for example, numerous articles, including letters to the editor, in the openly pro-Zaleski *Ameryka-Echo*, May, 20, 1956; May 27, 1956; and June 10, 1956. For contrasting views, see articles in the pro-Provisional Council *Nowy Świat*, for example, on May 2, 1956, 1; May 26, 1956, 1; and June 12, 1956, 1.

46. *Ameryka-Echo*, May 13, 1956; May 20, 1956; and May 27, 1956; *Nowy Świat*, May 4, 1956, 3.

47. *Ameryka-Echo*, June 10, 1956, 1; and July 22, 1956, 14; *Nowy Świat*, June 2, 1956, 1. An attack on Ciołkosz in *Ameryka-Echo* prompted him to respond to his critics in a letter to the editor. It initiated a longer exchange between Ciołkosz and the readers on the pages of the newspaper. See for example *Ameryka-Echo*, June 10, 1956; September 2, 1956.

48. "Rezolucja czwartej krajowej konwencji Kongresu Polonii Amerykańskiej," *Ameryka-Echo*, June 17, 1956, 1.

49. Ibid.

50. *Zgoda*, July 1, 1956, 1.

51. "Konwencja Kongresu," *Nowy Świat*, June 30, 1956, 3; "Echa konwencji K.P.A.," *Nowy Świat*, June 11, 1956, 2; "Przywrócenie wolności Polsce," *Nowy Świat*, May 31, 1956, 1; "Z całego świata," *Nowy Świat*, May 25, 1956, 7.

52. The American delegation included scholars Oskar Halecki, Władysław Lednicki, Marian Korowicz, Zygmunt Nagórski, Sr., Wiktor Weintraub, Józef Krzywicki, and Stanisław Skrzypek. The writers' group included Kazimierz Wierzyński, Maria Kuncewiczowa, Józef Wittlin, Zygmunt Chałko, Wiktor Londzin (Jan Leszcza), and Melchior Wańkowicz. Journalists included Stanisław Strzetelski, Bolesław Wierzbiański, Antoni Korczyński, Ryszard Mossin, and Ewa Mieroszewska. Artists and painters included Ziemowit Karpiński and Zdzisław Czermański. "Przygotowania do Kongresu Wolnej Kultury," in "Kącik dla Wszystkich," *Ameryka-Echo*, September 2, 1956, 14.

53. See correspondence on the congress in PIASA, 1–7, 8. Klaudiusz Hrabyk commented on the failure of the congress in "Z drugiej strony barykady: Spowiedź z klęski; Lata 1902–1959; Wspomnienia i dzienniki," microfilm of an unpublished manuscript, Ossolineum, Wrocław, [1979], 685–702.

54. Tadeusz Stapiński, "Mackiewicz i Lechoń," *Ameryka-Echo*, July 1, 1956, 12; "Dziś pogrzeb," *Nowy Świat*, June 12, 1956, 1.

55. See, for example, *Kuryer Polski* (Milwaukee), June 29 and July 2, 1956; *Zgoda*, July 15, 1956.

56. *Zgoda*, July 15, 1956, 1–4.

57. Ibid., 1. SWAP and the Polish Immigration Committee also sent telegrams to President Eisenhower, "Telegram Pol. Kom. Imigracyjnego do Prezydenta Eisenhowera," *Nowy Świat*, July 6, 1956, 4; "Apel SWAP do prezydenta w obronie Polski," *Nowy Świat*, July 5, 1956, 1.

58. A letter from Stefan Fuszara, "Kącik dla Wszystkich," *Ameryka-Echo*, July 29, 1956, 14.

59. *Kuryer Polski* (Milwaukee), July 28, 1956, 1.

60. *Zgoda*, August 1, 1956, 1.

61. *Ameryka-Echo*, July 15, 1956, 2.

62. *Ameryka-Echo*, August 19, 1956; *Dziennik Dla Wszystkich*, July 17, 18, 1956.

63. "Msza Św. i akademja...," *Nowy Świat*, July 6, 1956, 4; "Trzy potężne manifestacje Polonji w Jersey City, Elizabeth, i Perth Amboy," *Nowy Świat*, July 16, 1956, 1; "Oby tak było wszędzie," *Nowy Świat*, October 20, 1956, 3; "W niedzielę 29 lipca wielka manifestacja Polonii stanu N.J.," *Nowy Świat*, July 27, 1956, 2.

64. See, for example, *Dziennik Dla Wszystkich*, July 11, 1956, and July 17, 1956.

65. *Zgoda*, September 1, 1956, 2.

66. Irena U. Zugehoer, "Sytemu.(Polakowi w Ameryce) trudno zrozumieć głodnego (Polaka w Polsce)," *Kuryer Polski* (Milwaukee), July 3, 1956.

67. See, for example, *Dziennik Dla Wszystkich*, July 18, 1956, 1; *Kuryer Polski* (Milwaukee), October 23, 1956, 3; *Ameryka-Echo*, August 19, 1956, 12.

68. See, for example, A. Łażewski "Wśrod szarego tłumu," *Dziennik Dla Wszystkich*, September 20, 1956, 1; F. Wardyński, "Po sześćdzięsieciu dniach pobytu w Polsce," *Dziennik Dla Wszystkich*, October 24, 1956, 14; "Czerwony raj," *Kuryer Polski* (Milwaukee), July 3, 1956, 6.

69. *Kuryer Polski* (Milwaukee), October 23, 1956; *Zgoda*, November 1, 1956, 1; "Delegacja Polonji amerykańskiej przedstawia Dullesowi swe postulaty," *Nowy Świat*, October 24, 1956, 1; "Gomułka mówi o pomocy amerykańskiej dla Polski," *Nowy Świat*, December 3, 1956, 1.

70. *Kuryer Polski* (Milwaukee), December 20, 1956, 8.

71. Donald E. Pienkos, *For Your Freedom through Ours: Polish American Efforts on Poland's Behalf, 1863-1991* (New York: Columbia University Press, 1991), 141, 99-100.

72. "Podniosła akademia Organizacji Wolnych Rosjan," *Nowy Świat*, July 7, 1956, 2; "Polonja nowojorska robotnikom Poznania," *Nowy Świat*, July 9, 1956, 1; "Msza żałobna w Waszyngtonie za poległych w Poznaniu," *Nowy Świat*, July 18, 1956, 2.

73. Proclamation of the Council of National Unity, June 29, 1956, in Drozdowski, *1956*, 165; "Polacy w Chile wobec masakry robotników w Poznaniu," *Nowy Świat*, July 7, 1956, 2.

74. President's proclamation to the homeland, June 30, 1956, in Drozdowski, *1956*, 167-68.

75. Wojciech Wasiutyński, "Powstanie poznańskie," in Drozdowski, *1956*, 188.

76. Zygmunt Zaremba, "Znaczenie i konsekwencje manifestacji poznańskiej," in Drozdowski, *1956*, 176.

77. Davies, *God's Playground*, 2:583-86; Wandycz, *Price of Freedom*, 250-52; Nowak-Jeziorański, *Wojna*, 249-51.

78. Wandycz, *Price of Freedom*, 252-54; Davies, *God's Playground*, 2:582-88; Anna Radziwiłł and Wojciech Roszkowski, *Historia, 1945-1990* (Warsaw: Wydawnictwo Naukowe PWN, 1994), 98-107, 177-93; Nowak-Jeziorański, *Wojna*, 265-71.

79. "Wydział stanowy Kongresu Polonji Amer. w Chicago idzie z pomocą Węgrom," *Nowy Świat*, December 3, 1956, 3.

80. "Czytelnicy 'Nowego Świata' dla bohaterskiej ludności Węgier," *Nowy Świat*, December 11, 1956, 1; "Uroczyste powitanie Węgrów przybywajacych na statku Wolna Polska," *Nowy Świat*, December 15, 1956, 1; "Manifestacja przyjaźni i solidarności polsko-węgierskiej w porcie w Filadelfii," *Nowy Świat*, December 20, 1956, 1; "Prezydent otworzył bramy Ameryki dla 21,500 uchodźców węgierskich," *Nowy Świat*, December 26, 1956, 3; "Odpowiedź na apel pisarzy węgierskich," *Nowy Świat*, December 27, 1956, 3.

81. Tadeusz Stapiński, "Krucjata i ukrzyżowani," *Ameryka-Echo*, November 11, 1956, 12.

82. *Ameryka-Echo*, November 18, 1956, 10.

83. F. Olszowy, "Przewrót-powrót i rozsądek," *Ameryka-Echo*, December 9, 1956, 12; *Zgoda*, December 1, 1956, 2.

84. For reactions among the Australian diaspora, see Jan Lencznarowicz, *Prasa i społeczność polska w Australii, 1928-1980* (Kraków: Księgarnia Akademicka, 1994), 137-44.

85. Anna Siwik, "Polski Październik a emigracja," *Przegląd Polonijny* 20, no. 1 (1994): 87; Habielski, *Niezłomni*, 129-33.

86. *Zgoda*, December 1, 1956, 2. See also "Rewolucja wsród komunistów a nie przeciw komunizmowi," *Nowy Świat*, October 20, 1956, 1; "Wypowiedzi znanych Amerykanów polskiego pochodzenia o ostatnich wydarzeniach w Polsce," *Nowy Świat*, October 26, 1956, 3; "Gomułka i ja," *Nowy Świat*, October 30, 1956, 3; "Adam Ciołkosz o sprawie polskiej na nowym etapie," *Nowy Świat*, December 7, 1956, 2; "Sprawdzian wolności słowa," *Nowy Świat*, December 10, 1956, 3.

87. "List Gen. Kazimierza Sosnkowskiego o sytuacji międzynarodowej i zadaniach uchodźstwa," *Kombatant w Ameryce*, March 1957, 2-6.

88. Stanisław Gierat, "Kraj i Emigracja po Październiku," and "Prezes Stanisław Gierat do Polonii w Ameryce," *Kombatant w Ameryce*, March 1957, 6-10.

89. The articles were later privately published by Hrabyk in book form under the title *Kraj i Emigracja* (New York: published by the author, 1957).

90. Hrabyk, "Z drugiej strony barykady," 767-824.

91. Siwik, "Polski Październik," 87.

92. Drozdowski, *1956*, 133-36.

93. Habielski, *Niezłomni*, 114-15.

94. Ibid., 116-17.

95. Juliusz Mieroszeski, "Dialog," in Drozdowski, *1956*, 311-13.

96. Habielski, *Niezłomni*, 117.

97. Ibid., 118. See also ibid., 328-48.

98. Drozdowski, *1956*, 335-36.

99. Ibid., 348.

100. Stanisław Klinga, *Polskie wychodźstwo wojenne* (London: [n.p.], 1947), 11

(quoted in Dariusz Stola, "Uwagi o powojennej emigracji politycznej (1945–1947)," in *Warszawa nad Tamizą: Z dziejów polskiej emigracji politycznej po drugiej wojnie światowej*, ed. Andrzej Friszke (Warsaw: Instytut Studiów Politycznych Polskiej Akademii Nauk, 1994), 17.

101. Quoted in Habielski, *Niezłomni*, 79.
102. Ibid., 72–83.
103. Ibid., 84–86.
104. P. P. Yolles, "Hotel, mieszkanie—dom," *Nowy Świat*, January 4, 1950, 4. Egon F. Kunz observed the remarkable increase in the number of naturalizations among Polish and Hungarian displaced persons in Australia following the events of the Polish thaw and the Hungarian revolution. This "catharsis naturalization" points to the homeland as the source of the "second push," stronger than the "pull" of the country of settlement, to acquire citizenship. Egon F. Kunz, "Political Events 'At Home' and the Concept of Catharsis Naturalization among Refugees," *International Migration* 9, no. 1/2 (1971): 55–67.
105. "Podsumowanie chlubnych osiągnięć Polonji w tegorocznej Paradzie Pułaskiego w New Yorku," *Nowy Świat*, October 30, 1956, 2.
106. Pienkos, *For Your Freedom*, 141.
107. Opinions on this matter were sometimes divided within the same family. For example, Ewa Karpińska-Gierat became an American citizen in 1960 and visited Poland in 1961. Her husband, Stanisław Gierat of the SPK, refused to become naturalized or ever to travel to communist Poland. Ewa Karpińska-Gierat, *Korzenie i owoce: Wspomnienia i listy* (Bethlehem, Conn.: published by the author, 1998), 346–50, 366.

Epilogue

1. Helena Znaniecki Lopata, "Polish Immigration to the United States of America: Problems of Estimation and Parameters," *Polish Review* 21, no. 4 (1976): 97, table 7, based on Commissioner of the Bureau of Immigration, *Annual Report* (Washington, D.C.: U.S. Government Printing Office, 1947–1972).
2. Feliks Gross, "Notes on the Ethnic Revolution and the Polish Immigration in the U.S.A.," *Polish Review* 21, no. 1–2 (1976): 162–63.
3. See, for example, Ryszard Kantor, *Między Zaborowem a Chicago: Kulturowe konsekwencje istnienia zbiorowości imigrantów z parafii zaborowskiej w Chicago i jej kontaktów z rodzinnymi wsiami* (Wrocław: Zakład Narodowy im. Ossolińskich, 1990); Danuta Mostwin, *Emigranci polscy w USA* (Lublin: Redakcja Wydawnictw Katolickiego Uniwersytetu Lubelskiego, 1991).
4. Mary Patrice Erdmans, *Opposite Poles: Immigrants and Ethnics in Polish Chicago, 1976–1990* (University Park: Pennsylvania State University Press, 1998), 226–

32; John Krawiec, interview by the author, tape recording, Chicago, Ill., January 5, 1995.

5. See Anna D. Jaroszyńska-Kirchmann, "Displaced Persons, Émigrés, Refugees, and Other Polish Immigrants: World War II through the Solidarity Era," in *Polish Americans and Their History, Community, Culture, and Politics*, ed. John J. Bukowczyk (Pittsburgh: University of Pittsburgh Press, 1996), 152–79; Erdmans, *Opposite Poles*.

6. Jaroszyńska-Kirchmann, "Displaced Persons," 170–72.

7. Erdmans, *Opposite Poles*, 228. See also idem, "Immigrants and Ethnics: Conflict and Identity in Chicago Polonia," *Sociological Quarterly* 36, no. 1 (1955): 175–95. Joseph Wardzala, telephone interview by the author, July 24, 2002.

8. Jaroszyńska-Kirchmann, "Displaced Persons," 169.

9. Ibid., 172–74.

10. Such sections existed, for example, in *Dziennik Związkowy*, *Nowy Świat*, *Kuryer Codzienny* (Boston), *Dziennik Dla Wszystkich*, and others.

11. Jan Lencznarowicz, *Prasa i społeczność polska w Australii, 1928–1980* (Kraków: Księgarnia Akademicka, 1994), 111–13. The weekend edition of 1956 *Nowy Świat* included a separate section entitled "Książka polska na Emigracji" (Polish book in Emigration) and published serialized versions of books by exiled authors, which had appeared in the publishing houses of France and Great Britain. If individuals could not afford a subscription to some titles, they often shared them, passing newspapers from one to another. For example, Tadeusz G. both subscribed to and published in *Kultura*; Victor Bik borrowed *Kultura* issues to read from a friend. Bik also read *Zgoda* and *Dziennik Chicagoski*, and followed news about Poland in the American press, for example, *Time* and *U.S. News and World Report*. Tadeusz G., telephone interview by the author, St. Paul, Minn., July 25, 2002; Victor Bik, telephone interview by the author, July 25, 2002; Wardzala, interview.

12. Mrs. Olga Tubielewicz named families resettled in Argentina and Australia among her closest friends. Friends from Argentina (whom she and her family visited after resettlement) sent her a book published in London on the experiences of Poles, who, like themselves, had gone through the work camps of Siberia. She considered the book a most precious gift. "My whole life is here," she said, pointing to it. Olga Tubielewicz, interview by the author, tape recording, St. Paul, Minn., July 22, 1996; Tadeusz G., interview by the author, August 16, 1996, St. Paul, Minn.; Ewa Budek-Bielski, telephone interviews by the author, January 17, 2001, and July 24, 2002; Zofia L. Zatyrka-Bugno, telephone interviews by the author, January 18, 2001, and July 24, 2002; Victor Bik, telephone interviews by the author, January 19, 2001, and July 25, 2002.

13. Karpińska-Gierat, *Korzenie*, 232.

14. Ibid., 230–32.

15. Budek-Bielski, interviews, January 17, 2001, and July 24, 2002; Bik, interviews,

January 19, 2001, and July 25, 2002; Albert Tyde, telephone interview by the author, January 18, 2001; Zatyrka-Bugno, interviews, January 18, 2001, and July 24, 2002; Ola, telephone interviews by the author, January 18, 2001, and July 25, 2002.

16. Recent studies on the diaspora's literary output strongly indicate the value of its intellectual and artistic legacy. See Tymon Terlecki, ed., *Literatura polska na obczyźnie, 1940–1960*, vol. 1 (London: B. Świderski, 1964); Marek Pytasz, ed., *Literatura emigracyjna, 1939–1989*, 2 vols. (Katowice: Śląsk, 1994); Marta Fik, ed., *Między Polską a światem: Kultura emigracyjna po 1939 roku* (Warsaw: Wydawnictwo KRĄG, 1992); Dobrochna Ratajczak, ed., *Polski dramat emigracyjny, 1939–1969: Antologia* (Poznań: LEKTOR, 1993); Izolda Kiec, Dobrochna Ratajczak, and Jacek Wachowski, eds., *Teatr i dramat polskiej emigracji* (Poznań: Wydawnictwo ACARUS, 1994); Elżbieta Kalemba-Kasprzak and Dobrochna Ratajczak, eds., *Dramat i teatr emigracyjny po roku 1939* (Wrocław: Wiedza o kulturze, 1998). See also the comprehensive Bolesław Klimaszewski, Ewa R. Nowakowska, and Wojciech Wyskiel eds., *Mały słownik pisarzy polskich na obczyźnie, 1939–1980* (Warsaw: Wydawnictwo Interpress, 1992).

17. Jaroszyńska-Kirchmann, "Displaced Persons," 166. See also others mentioned, for example, in W. S. Kuniczak, *My Name Is Million: An Illustrated History of the Poles in America* (New York: Doubleday, 1978), 172–76.

18. The 1970, 1985, and 1995 Congresses of Polish Culture in Exile illustrate the level of involvement and achievement of Polish scholars, scientists, and artists. See *Kongres Współczesnej Nauki i Kultury Polskiej na obczyźnie, Londyn, 9–12 września 1970* (London: Komitet Organizacyjny Kongresu, 1970); *Prace Kongresu Kultury Polskiej na obczyźnie, Londyn, 14–20 września 1985*, 10 vols. (London: Polskie Towarzystwo Naukowe na Obczyźnie, 1986); *Prace III Kongresu Kultury Polskiej na Obczyźnie* (London: Polskie Towarzystwo Naukowe na Obczyźnie, 1998).

19. Donald Pienkos, "The Polish American Congress—An Appraisal," *Polish American Studies* 36, no. 2 (Autumn 1979): 21; Mary Patrice Erdmans, "Recent Political Action on Behalf of Poland: The Interrelationship among Polonia's Cohorts, 1978–1990," in *Polish Americans*, ed. Helena Znaniecka Lopata, 2nd ed. (New Brunswick, N.J.: Transaction Publishers, 1994), 219. On the state level of the PAC structure, see also Stanislaus A. Blejwas, "The Local Ethnic Lobby: The Polish American Congress in Connecticut, 1944–1974," in *The Polish Presence in Canada and America*, ed. Frank Renkiewicz (Toronto: Multicultural History Society of Ontario, 1982), 318.

20. Krawiec, interview.

21. "Oświadczenie," September 28, 1974, Detroit, Michigan, IHRC 127, Box 144, Fol. 1.

22. Eugene Kusielewicz to Aloysius Mazewski, April 21, 1975, IHRC 127, Box 144, Fol. 3. Kusielewicz developed the same theme in his controversial editorial "The Cancer in Our Side." Frustrated by the opposition of the exile organizations to his efforts to expand cultural and scholarly exchanges with Poland, Kusielewicz focused his

anger on the "reactionaries" from the SPK. *Kosciuszko Foundation Newsletter* 31 (1976-1977): 1-4.

23. Kazimierz Łukomski, "Polonia '75—Perspektywy," press release, IHRC 127, Box 144, Fol. 5.

24. Aloysius A. Mazewski, speech for Polonia '75, November 7, 1975, Washington, D.C. IHRC 127, Box 144, Fol. 5.

25. *Sprawozdania Prezesa Kongresu Polonii Amerykańskiej Alojzego A. Mazewskiego na Dziesiątą Krajową Konwencję w Filadelfii, Pennsylvania, w dniach 24, 25 i 26 września, 1976 r.* (Chicago, Ill.: Polish American Congress, 1976), 88. The 1948 national convention of the PAC in Philadelphia created a special commission for the cooperation with Polonias in other countries, headed by Wiktor L. Alski. Alski's reports to the consecutive conventions voiced a great deal of frustration, pointing to the chronic lack of financial and administrative support for the commission's work, limited to establishing archives with information on other Polonias and sending off some PAC publications to Polish communities abroad. See, for example, Wiktor Alski's reports in *Protokół Trzeciego Zjazdu Rady Naczelnej Kongresu Polonii Amerykańskiej odbytego w dn. 17-18 listopada 1950 w Hotelu Raleigh, Washington, D.C.*, 35-39; *Protokół Czwartej Konwencji Kongresu Polonii Amerykańskiej odbytej w dniach 30 i 31 maja i 1-go czerwca 1956 w Hotelu Benjamin Franklin, Philadelphia, Pennsylvania*, 31-34.

26. Jarosław Żaba, *"Polonia 1978—Polonia Jutra": Przegląd Uchwał Konferencji Polonii Wolnego Świata w Toronto, 25 - 28 maja 1978* (London: Polska Fundacja Kulturalna, 1978), 16.

27. See A. A. Mazewski's papers in IHRC 127, Boxes 144-49. Kazimierz Łukomski was a *spiritus movens* behind the PAC's involvement in diaspora unification efforts. On local responses and initiatives to the Polonia of the World's ideas, see Ewa Karpińska-Gierat, *Korzenie*, 580.

28. For an overview of the scholarship, see Anna D. Jaroszyńska-Kirchmann, "The Polish Post-World II Diaspora: An Agenda for a New Millennium," *Polish American Studies* 57, no. 2 (Autumn 2000): 45-66.

29. Jan Sęk, "Polonia w Ameryce Łacińskiej," in *Polacy w świecie: Polonia jako zjawisko społeczno-polityczne*, ed. Albin Koprukowniak and Władysław Kucharski (Lublin: Uniwersytet Marii Curie-Skłodowskiej, 1986), 3:73-77, 3:80-81; Kazimierz Krukowski, *Z Melpomeną na emigracji* (Warsaw: Czytelnik, 1987), 99-142.

30. Henry Radecki and Benedykt Heydenkorn, *A Member of a Distinguished Family: The Polish Group in Canada* (Toronto: McClelland and Stewart, 1976), 72-74.

31. Grzegorz Janusz, "Polonia w Niemczech Zachodnich po II wojnie światowej," in Koprukowniak and Kucharski, *Polacy w świecie*, 2:81-110; Władysław Stanisław Kucharski, *Polacy i Polonia w rdzennej Austrii w XIX i XX wieku* (Lublin: Uniwersytet Marii Curie-Skłodowskiej w Lublinie, Forum Polonii w Austrii, 1994); Wiesław Śladkowski, "Polonii Francuskiej przeszłość i teraźniejszość," in Ko-

prukowniak and Kucharski, *Polacy w świecie*, 2:7-54; Jan Lewandowski, "Polacy w Szwajcarii," in Koprukowniak and Kucharski, *Polacy w świecie*, 2:213-36; Ryszard Kucha, "Z zagadnień Polonii skandynawskiej," in Koprukowniak and Kucharski, *Polacy w świecie*, 2:237-60.

32. Kucha, "Z zagadnień Polonii Skandynawskiej," 247; Kucharski, *Polacy i Polonia*, 294-98. In the 1980s Związek Polaków i Strzecha made closer cooperation their priority, and in 1991 in the face of political changes in Poland, they formally united into one organization.

33. Egon F. Kunz, *Calwell's New Australians* (Sydney: Australian National University Press, 1988). On Polish and other DP communities in Australia, see studies by Jerzy Zubrzycki: *Immigrants in Australia: A Demographic Survey Based upon the 1954 Census* (Melbourne: Melbourne University Press, 1960); *Settlers of the Latrobe Valley: A Sociological Study of Immigrants in the Brown Coal Industry in Australia* (Canberra: Australian National University Press, 1964); "The Immigrant Family: Some Sociological Aspects," in A. Stoller, *New Faces* (Melbourne: Melbourne Cheshire, 1966), 60-74. See also Jan Sęk, "Polonia w Australii i Nowej Zelandii," in Koprukowniak and Kucharski, *Polacy w świecie*, 3:85-110; "Poles," in James S. Jupp, ed., *The Australian People: An Encyclopedia of the Nation, Its People, and Their Origins* (North Ryde, NSW, Australia: Angus and Robertson Publishers, 1988), 734-47, 999. For details of the beginning of the Polish community in Great Britain, see Keith Sword, Norman Davies, and Jan Ciechanowski, *The Formation of the Polish Community in Great Britain, 1939-1950* (London: School of Slavonic and East European Studies, University of London, 1989). See also Jerzy Zubrzycki, *Polish Immigrants in Britain: A Study of Adjustment* (The Hague: Martinus Nijhoff, 1956); Sheila Patterson, "The Poles: An Exile Community in Britain," in James L. Watson, ed., *Between Two Cultures: Migrants and Minorities in Britain* (Oxford: Basil Blackwell, 1977), 214-41; Tadeusz Radzik, "Polonia w Wielkiej Brytanii," in Koprukowniak and Kucharski, *Polacy w świecie*, 2:111-46; B. Czaykowski and B. Sulik, *Polacy w W. Brytanii* (Paris: Instytut Literacki, 1961).

34. Alfred Erich Senn, "Émigrés and Immigrants: Problems of National Consciousness," *Spectrum* 6 (1994): 6.

35. Milda Danys, *DP: Lithuanian Immigration to Canada after the Second World War* (Toronto: Multicultural History Society of Ontario, 1986), 224-32. See also Antanas J. Van Reenan, *Lithuanian Diaspora: Königsberg to Chicago* (Lanham, Md.: University Press of America, 1990); Liucija Baskauskas, "Planned Incorporation of Refugees: the Baltic Clause," *International Migration* [Netherlands] 14, no. 3 (1976): 219-28.

36. Juris Veidemanis, "A Twentieth-Century Pioneer Settlement: Latvians in Lincoln County, Wisconsin," *Midcontinent American Studies Journal* 4 (1963): 22-23. For example, the author recalled a confrontation during which "visiting DP's were

accused by some old 'socialists' of being 'fascists' for having fled 'the workers' paradise.' In response, the DP's wrote a letter offering to buy a one-way ticket to this 'paradise' for anyone wishing to go." I would like to thank Andris Straumanis of the University of Minnesota for helping me obtain the publications on the Latvian community and alerting me to the problems of the conflict within it. See also Juris Veidemanis, "Latvian Settlers in Wisconsin: A Comparative View," *Wisconsin Magazine of History* 45 (1962): 251–55.

37. Yury Boshyk and Boris Balan, *Political Refugees and "Displaced Persons," 1945-1954: A Selected Bibliography and Guide to Research with Special Reference to Ukrainians* (Edmonton: Canadian Institute of Ukrainian Studies, University of Alberta, 1982); Yury Boshyk and Wlodzimierz Kiebalo, eds., *Publications by Ukrainian "Displaced Persons" and Political Refugees, 1945-1954 in the John Luczkiw Collection, Thomas Fisher Rare Books Library, University of Toronto: A Bibliography* (Edmonton: Canadian Institute of Ukrainian Studies, University of Alberta, 1988); Wsewolod W. Isajiw, Yury Boshyk, and Roman Senkus, eds., *The Refugee Experience: Ukrainian Displaced Persons after World War II* (Edmonton: Canadian Institute of Ukrainian Studies, University of Alberta, 1992); Myron B. Kuropas, *The Ukrainian Americans: Roots and Aspirations, 1884-1954* (Toronto: University of Toronto Press, 1991).

38. Lubomyr Luciuk, *Searching for Place: Ukrainian Displaced Persons, Canada, and the Migration of Memory* (Toronto: University of Toronto Press, 2000), 222.

39. Julianna Puskás, *Ties that Bind, Ties that Divide: One Hundred Years of Hungarian Experience in the United States* (New York: Holmes and Meier, 2000), 279–83.

40. Matjas Klemencic, *Slovenes of Cleveland: The Creation of the New Nation and a New World Community Slovenia and the Slovenes of Cleveland, Ohio* (Novo Mesto: Dolenjska Zaloba, 1995), 374–75.

41. Barbara Stern Burstin, *After the Holocaust: The Migration of Polish Jews and Christians to Pittsburgh* (Pittsburgh: University of Pittsburgh Press, 1989), 112. See also reviews by Frederick B. Lindstrom, *Annals of the American Academy of Political and Social Science* 511 (1990): 191–92; Thomas Szendrey, *International Migration Review* 25 (1991): 416–17.

42. Burstin, *After the Holocaust*, 90–93. See also the autobiographical Jacob Biber, *Risen from the Ashes: A Story of the Jewish Displaced Persons in the Aftermath of World War II; Being a Sequel to Survivors* (San Bernardino, Calif.: Borgo Press, 1990).

43. Andrzej Suchcitz, Ludwik Maik, Wojciech Rojek, eds., *Wybór dokumentów do dziejów polskiego uchodźstwa niepodległościowego, 1939-1991* (London: Polskie Towarzystwo Naukowe na Obczyźnie, 1997), 678; Anna D. Jaroszyńska-Kirchmann, "The Exile Mission: Polish Post War Diaspora in the United States, 1939–1956," in *The Fiedorczyk Lecture in Polish American Studies, Occasional Papers in Polish and Polish*

American Studies, no. 11 (New Britain, Conn.: Polish Studies Program, Central Connecticut State University, 2001), 9.

44. Piotr Wandycz, "Czy emigracja jest jeszcze potrzebna?" *Kultura* 10/505 (1989): 3–15.

45. Tadeusz Wyrwa, *Bezdroża dziejów Polski* (Lublin: Norbertinum, 1998). For other opinions on the future of the postwar political emigration see Jerzy Zubrzycki, "Whither Emigracja? The Future of the Polish Community in Great Britain," *Polish Review* 38, no. 4 (1993): 391–406.

46. Zubrzycki, "Whither Emigracja?" 405.

47. Stanislaus Blejwas, "Czesiu! Jak się mamy!?" *Sarmatian Review* (1999): 1.

48. Rev. Roman Nir, "The Archives, Libraries and Museums of Polonia at Orchard Lake," *Polish American Studies* 40, no. 1 (Spring 2003), 72–75.

49. Zofia L. Zatyrka-Bugno, interviews, January 18, 2001, and July 24, 2002; Budek-Bielski, interviews, January 17, 2001, and July 24, 2002; Wardzala, interview; Tadeusz G., interviews, August 16, 1996, and July 25, 2002; Bik, interviews, January 19, 2001, and July 25, 2002.

50. For a more detailed discussion of a research agenda, see Jaroszyńska-Kirchmann, "The Polish Post-World II Diaspora," 45–66; idem., "Displaced Persons," 152–79.

51. Jan Lechoń, "Hymn Polaków na obczyźnie," in *Poezje* (Lublin: Wydawnictwo Lubelskie, 1989), 197 (my translation).

Bibliography

Primary Sources

Newspapers and Journals

    Ameryka-Echo
    Dziennik Chicagoski
    Dziennik Dla Wszystkich
    Dziennik Polski
    Dziennik Związkowy
    Głos Ludowy
    Głos Polek
    Gwiazda Polarna
    Kombatant w Ameryce
    Kosciuszko Foundation Newsletter
    Kronika
    Kultura (Paris)
    Kuryer Codzienny (Boston)
    Kuryer Polski (Milwaukee)
    Naród Polski
    Nowy Świat
    Poezja
    Straż
    Tygodnik Polski
    Weteran
    Zgoda

Archival Collections

Immigration History Research Center, University of Minnesota, St. Paul, Minnesota

    American Committee for the Resettlement of Polish DP's
    American Council for Émigrés in Professions
    American Council for Nationalities Service
    American Relief for Poland, District 33
    Polish American Congress

Aloysius A. Mazewski
Edward C. and Loda Różański
Wilhelm A. Wolny

Polish Museum of America, Polish Roman Catholic Union of America, Chicago, Illinois

American Relief for Poland

Józef Piłsudski Institute for Research in the Modern History of Poland, New York, New York

Stanisław Gierat (1903–1977)
Klaudiusz Hrabyk (1902–1989)
Polski Ruch Wolnościowy "Niepodległość i Demokracja" (1945–1991)
Stowarzyszenie Polskich Kombatantów
Wysiedleńcy polscy po 1945 roku w Niemczech [Polish Displaced Persons in Germany after 1945]

Polish Institute of Arts and Sciences of America, New York, New York

Feliks Gross
Jan Lechoń
Polish Institute of Arts and Sciences of America
Karol Popiel
Jerzy Ptakowski
Edmund Urbański

Harry S. Truman Library, Independence, Missouri

John W. Gibson
Edwin A. Locke Jr.
John Locke
Howard J. McGrath
Presidential Papers—Official File; Confidential File
Harry N. Rosenfield

Center for Migration Studies, Staten Island, New York

National Catholic Welfare Conference, Department of Immigration—General Correspondence
National Catholic Welfare Conference, Department of Immigration New York Office and Catholic Committee for Refugees
National Catholic Welfare Conference, War Relief Services

Central Connecticut State University, New Britain, Connecticut

Polish Library and Archives

Interviews

Bik, Victor. January 19, 2001, and July 25, 2002. Telephone interview by the author.

Budek-Bielski, Ewa. January 17, 2001, and July 24, 2002. Telephone interview by the author.

Grygorcewicz, Wacław. August 31, 1995. Telephone interview by the author.

Kehne, Roma. July 22, 1996. Tape recording. Interview by the author. St. Paul, Minn.

Krawiec, Jan. January 5, 1995. Tape recording. Interview by the author. Chicago, Ill.; July 31, 2002. Telephone interview by the author.

Kuncewicz, Jerzy. August 29, 2002. Telephone interview by the author.

Logisz, Sabina. January 4, 1995. Tape recording and notes. Interview by the author. Chicago, Ill.

Ola. January 18, 2001, and July 25, 2002. Telephone interview by the author.

Podkopacz, Helena. August 10, 1996. Telephone interview by the author.

Remiarz, Helena. July 15, 1996. Tape recording. Interview by the author. New Hope, Minn.

Remiarz, Stefan. July 15, 1996. Tape recording. Interview by the author. New Hope, Minn.

Różański, Edward C. January 4, 1995. Tape recording. Interview by the author. Chicago, Ill.

Tadeusz G. August 16, 1996. Notes. Interview by the author. St. Paul, Minn.; July 25, 2002. Telephone interview by the author.

Tubielewicz, Olga. July 22, 1996. Tape recording. Interview by the author. St. Paul, Minn.

Tyde, Albert. January 18, 2001. Telephone interview by the author.

Wardzala, Joseph. July 24, 2002. Telephone interview by the author.

Wojciechowski, Maryann. February 22, 2000. E-mail. Interview by the author.

Zatyrka-Bugno, Zofia L. January 18, 2001, and July 24, 2002. Telephone interview by the author.

Unpublished Sources

Bik, Victor. "A Testimony of Victor Bik, Holocaust Survivor." Typed manuscript in the possession of the author, courtesy of Victor Bik.

Dufoix, Stephane. "The Coriolanus Complex: War, Politics, and Aliens." Unpublished paper presented at the Social Science History Association Conference, Fort Worth, Texas, November 11–14, 1999.

Gubala, Tadeusz. "Życiorys." Typed manuscript in the possession of the author, courtesy of Tadeusz Gubala.

Hrabyk, Klaudiusz. "Z drugiej strony barykady: Spowiedź z klęski; Lata 1902–1959; Wspomnienia i dzienniki." Manuscript. Ossolineum, Wrocław.

Lenard, Myra. "Remembering Adela Lagodzinska: Polonia Leader and President of P.W.A., 1947–1971." Paper presented at PIASA's 56th Annual Meeting, Georgetown University, Washington, D.C., June 12–13, 1998.

Secondary Sources

100-Lecie wystawienia Polskiej Opery Narodowej Halka Stanisława Moniuszki. Pamiętnik koncertu wydany przez Chór im. M. K. Ogińskiego. New York: [Chór im. M. K. Ogińskiego], 1958.

American Relief for Poland—District 5—State of New Jersey: Tenth Anniversary Souvenir Journal, 1939–1949. New Jersey: [American Relief for Poland], 1949.

Anders, Władysław. *An Army in Exile: The Story of the Second Polish Corps.* London: Macmillan, 1949.

———. *Bez ostatniego rozdziału.* London: Gryf, 1981.

Anderson, Benedict. *Imagined Communities: Reflections on the Origin and Spread of Nationalism.* London: Verso, 1989.

Auerbach, Frank L. *The Admission and Resettlement of Displaced Persons in the United States: A Handbook of Legal and Technical Information for the Use of Local Social and Civic Agencies.* New York: Common Council for American Unity, 1949.

Baker, Richard P. "Eastern Refugees: Implications for Social Work." *Journal of Sociology and Social Welfare* 16, no. 3 (1989): 81–94.

Bakis, Eduard. "'D.P. Apathy.'" In *Flight and Resettlement*, ed. H. B. Murphy, 76–88. Lucerne, Switzerland: United Nations Educational, Scientific, and Cultural Organization, 1955.

Baskauskas, Liucija. "The Lithuanian Refugee Experience and Grief." *International Migration Review* 15 (Spring-Summer 1981): 276–91.

———. "Planned Incorporation of Refugees: The Baltic Clause." *International Migration* [Netherlands] 14, no. 3 (1976): 219–28.

Bennett, Marion T. *American Immigration Policies: A History.* Washington, D.C.: Public Affairs Press, 1963.

Bernard, William S. "Immigrants and Refugees: Their Similarities, Differences, and Needs." *International Migration* [Netherlands] 14, no. 4 (1976): 267–81.

---. "Refugee Asylum in the United States: How the Law Was Changed to Admit Displaced Persons." *International Migration* 13, no. 1-2 (1975): 3-20.

Białasiewicz, Wojciech. *Pomiędzy lojalnością a serc porywem: Polonia amerykańska we wrześniu 1939 roku.* Chicago: Publishing Wici, 1989.

Biber, Jacob. *Risen from the Ashes: A Story of the Jewish Displaced Persons in the Aftermath of World War II; Being a Sequel to Survivors.* San Bernardino, Calif.: Borgo Press, 1990.

Bigosiński, Jerry T. *The First Age: Memoirs of Jerry T. Bigosiński.* Bonita Springs, Fla.: published by the author, 1995.

Biskupski, M. B. "Poland in American Foreign Policy, 1918-1945: 'Sentimental' or 'Strategic' Friendship?—A Review Article." *Polish American Studies* 38, no. 2 (Autumn 1981): 5-15.

Blejwas, Stanislaus A. "American Polonia: The Next Generation." *Polish American Studies* 49, no. 1 (Spring 1992): 81-86.

---. "The Local Ethnic Lobby: The Polish American Congress in Connecticut, 1944-1974." In *The Polish Presence in Canada and America,* ed. Frank Renkiewicz, 305-25. Toronto: Multicultural History Society of Ontario, 1982.

---. "Old and New Polonias: Tensions within an Ethnic Community." *Polish American Studies* 38, no. 2 (Autumn 1981): 57-60.

---. "People's Poland and American Polonia (1944-1956)." *Przegląd Polonijny* 22, no. 1 (1996): 9-42.

---. "A Polish American Fellow Traveler." *Polish Review* 36, no. 2 (1991): 169-77.

---. "Polonia and Politics." In *Polish Americans and Their History: Community, Culture, and Politics,* ed. John J. Bukowczyk, 121-51. Pittsburgh: University of Pittsburgh Press, 1996.

---. "Stanisław Osada: Immigrant Nationalist." *Polish American Studies* 50, no. 1 (Spring 1993): 23-50.

Boshyk, Yury. *Political Refugees and "Displaced Persons," 1945-1954: A Selected Bibliography and Guide to Research with Special Reference to Ukrainians.* Edmonton: Canadian Institute of Ukrainian Studies, University of Alberta, 1982.

Boshyk, Yury, and Wlodzimierz Kiebalo, eds. *Publications by Ukrainian "Displaced Persons" and Political Refugees, 1945-1954 in the John Luczkiw Collection, Thomas Fisher Rare Books Library, University of Toronto: A Bibliography.* Edmonton: Canadian Institute of Ukrainian Studies, University of Alberta, 1988.

Bromke, Adam. *Polska diaspora.* Toronto: Polish Alliance Press, 1972.

Brożek, Andrzej. *Polish Americans, 1854-1939.* Warsaw: Interpress, 1985.

Brynner, Yul. *Bring Forth the Children: A Journey to the Forgotten People of Europe and the Middle East.* New York: McGraw-Hill, 1960.

Brzoza, Czesław. "Zapomniana armia: Polskie oddziały wartownicze w Europie (1945-1951)." *Zeszyty historyczne* 494, no. 116 (1996): 3-21.

Budny, Michael. "Józef Piłsudski Institute of America for Research in the Modern History of Poland." In *Poles in America: Bicentennial Essays*, ed. Frank Mocha, 687-708. Stevens Point, Wisc.: Worzalla Publishing, 1978.

Budzyń, Boleslaw. *The Polish Technical College in Esslingen/Germany, 1945-1949.* Kraków: Jagiellonian Foundation Press, 1996.

Bukowczyk, John J. *And My Children Did Not Know Me: A History of the Polish-Americans.* Bloomington: Indiana University Press, 1987.

———. "'Harness for Posterity the Values of a Nation'—Fifty Years of the Polish American Historical Association and Polish American Studies." *Polish American Studies* 50, no.2 (Autumn 1993): 5-100.

———. "The Polish American Historical Association." In *Selected Essays from the Fiftieth Anniversary International Congress of the Polish Institute of Arts and Sciences of America.* Vol. 2 of *The Polish Diaspora*, ed. James S. Pula and M. B. Biskupski, 99-102. Washington, D.C.: Columbia University Press, 1993.

———. "Polish Americans, Ethnicity, and Otherness." *Polish Review* 43 (1998): 299-313.

Burstin, Barbara Stern. *After the Holocaust: The Migration of Polish Jews and Christians to Pittsburgh.* Pittsburgh: University of Pittsburgh Press, 1989.

Buszko, Józef. *Historia Polski, 1864-1948.* Warsaw: Państwowe Wydawnictwo Naukowe, 1982.

Car, Edward M. *Kobiety w szeregach Polskich Sił Zbrojnych na Zachodzie, 1940-1948.* Warsaw: Oficyna Wydawnicza Audiutor, 1995. 127-33.

Chałko, Zbigniew. "Nie łatwo być ambasadorem." *Kultura* 12/38 (1950): 127.

Chan, Sucheng. "European and Asian Immigration into the United States in Comparative Perspective, 1820s to 1920s." In *Immigration Reconsidered: History, Sociology, and Politics*, ed. Virginia Yans-McLaughlin, 37-75. New York: Oxford University Press, 1990.

Chandler, Edgar H. S. *The High Tower of Refuge: An Inspiring Story of Refugee Relief throughout the World.* New York: Frederick A. Praeger, 1959.

Chojnacki, Wojciech. "Bibliografia publikacji prasowych o najnowszej emigracji z lat 1980-1987." *Przegląd Polonijny* 4 (1989): 129-43.

Cisek, Janusz. *Instytut Józefa Piłsudskiego w Ameryce i jego zbiory.* Warsaw: Biblioteka Narodowa, 1997.

Cohen, Lizabeth. *Making a New Deal: Industrial Workers in Chicago, 1919-1939.* Cambridge: Cambridge University Press, 1990.

Cohen, Robin. *Global Diasporas: An Introduction.* Seattle: University of Washington Press, 1997.

Cohon, J. Donald, Jr. "Psychological Adaptation and Dysfunction among Refugees." *International Migration Review* 15 (1981): 255-75.
Copson-Niećko, Maria J. E. "The Poles in America from the 1830s to 1870s: Some Reflections on the Possibilities of Research." In *Poles in America: Bicentennial Essays*, ed. Frank Mocha, 45-302. Stevens Point, Wisc.: Worzalla Publishing, 1978.
Czaykowski, B., and B. Sulik. *Polacy w W. Brytanii.* Paris: Instytut Literacki, 1961.
Danys, Milda. *DP: Lithuanian Immigration to Canada after the Second World War.* Toronto: Multicultural History Society of Ontario, 1986.
David, Henry P. "Involuntary International Migration: Adaptation of Refugees." *International Migration* [Netherlands] 7, no. 3-4 (1969): 67-105.
Davie, Maurice R. *Refugees in America: Report of the Committee for the Study of Recent Immigration from Europe.* New York: Harper and Brothers, 1947.
Davies, Norman. *God's Playground: A History of Poland in Two Volumes.* Vol. 2, *1795 to the Present.* New York: Columbia University Press, 1982.
Dembińska-Pawelec, Joanna. "'Emigracja walcząca' i jej poezja." In *Literatura emigracyjna, 1939-1989*, ed. Marek Pytasz, vol. 1, 95-120. Katowice: Śląsk, 1994.
Dinnerstein, Leonard. *America and the Survivors of the Holocaust.* New York: Columbia University Press, 1982.
Dinnerstein, Leonard, and David M. Reimers. *Ethnic Americans: A History of Immigration and Assimilation.* New York: Harper and Row, 1975.
Displaced Persons Commission. *Memo to America: The DP Story; The Final Report of the United States Displaced Persons Commission.* Washington, D.C.: U.S. Government Printing Office, 1952.
———. *Second Semiannual Report to the President and the Congress, August 1, 1949.* Washington, D.C.: U.S. Government Printing Office, [1949].
Divine, Robert A. *American Immigration Policy, 1924-1952.* New Haven: Yale University Press, 1957.
———. "The Cold War and the Election of 1948." *Journal of American History* 59, no. 1 (1972): 90-110.
Draus, Jan. *Oświata i nauka polska na Bliskim i Środkowym Wschodzie, 1939-1950.* Lublin: Towarzystwo Naukowe Katolickiego Uniwersytetu Lubelskiego, 1993.
Drozdowski, Marian M., ed. *1956: Polska Emigracja a Kraj.* Warsaw: Oficyna Wydawnicza Typografika, 1998.
Dyczok, Marta. *The Grand Alliance and Ukrainian Refugees.* New York: St. Martin's Press, 2000.
Egan, Eileen. *For Whom There Is No Room: Scenes from the Refugee World.* New York: Paulist Press, 1995.
Englert, Juliusz L., and Jerzy Witting. *W harcerskiej służbie: ZHP na obczyźnie,*

1946–1996. London: Naczelnictwo Związku Harcerstwa Polskiego poza Granicami Kraju, 1997.

Erdmans, Mary Patrice. "Immigrants and Ethnics: Conflict and Identity in Chicago Polonia." *Sociological Quarterly* 36, no. 1 (1995): 175–95.

———. *Opposite Poles: Immigrants and Ethnics in Polish Chicago, 1976–1990.* University Park: Pennsylvania State University Press, 1998.

———. "Recent Political Action on Behalf of Poland: The Interrelationships among Polonia's Cohorts, 1978–1990." In *Polish Americans,* ed. Helena Znaniecka Lopata, 213–42. 2nd ed. New Brunswick, N.J.: Transaction Publishers, 1994.

———. "The Social Construction of Emigration as a Moral Issue." *Polish American Studies* 49, no. 1 (Spring 1992): 7–25.

Friszke, Andrzej. *Życie polityczne emigracji.* Vol. 1 of *Druga Wielka Emigracja, 1945–1990.* Warsaw: Biblioteka WIĘZI, 1999.

Friszke, Andrzej, ed. *Myśl polityczna na wygnaniu: Publicyści i politycy polskiej emigracji powojennej.* Warsaw: Instytut Studiów Politycznych Polskiej Akademii Nauk, 1995.

———. *Warszawa nad Tamizą: Z dziejów polskiej emigracji politycznej po drugiej wojnie światowej.* Warsaw: Instytut Studiów Politycznych Polskiej Akademii Nauk, 1994.

Gach, Piotr. "Refleksja o współczesnej emigracji polskiej." *Biuletyn Ruchu Apostolatu Emigracyjnego* 2, no. 6 (1989): 25–28.

Gaertner, Miriam L. "A Comparison of Refugee and Non-Refugee Immigrants to New York City." In *Flight and Resettlement,* ed. H. B. Murphy, 99–112. Lucerne, Switzerland: United Nations Educational, Scientific, and Cultural Organization, 1955.

Garliński, Józef. *Polska w drugiej wojnie światowej.* London: Odnowa, 1982.

Gella, Aleksander. "An Introduction to the Sociology of the Intelligentsia." In *The Intelligentsia and the Intellectuals: Theory, Method, and Case Study,* ed. Aleksander Gella, 9–34. London: SAGE Publications, 1976.

———. "The Life and Death of the Old Polish Intelligentsia." *Slavic Review* 30 (1971): 1–27.

Genizi, Haim. *America's Fair Share: The Admission and Resettlement of Displaced Persons, 1945–1952.* Detroit: Wayne State University Press, 1993.

Gieratowa, Ewa. *Powojenna historia Harcerstwa w Stanach Zjednoczonych.* Detroit: Nakł. Zarządu Okręgu ZHP w Stanach Zjednoczonych, 1990.

Grabowski, Stanisław. *Follow Me: The Memoirs of a Polish Priest.* Roseville, Minn.: White Rose Press, 1997.

Greene, Victor. *For God and Country: The Rise of Polish and Lithuanian Ethnic Consciousness in America, 1860–1910.* Madison: State Historical Society of Wisconsin, 1975.

———. "Poles." In *Harvard Encyclopedia of American Ethnic Groups*, ed. Stephan Thernstrom, 787–803. Cambridge, Mass.: Belknap Press of Harvard University Press, 1980.

Gromada, Thaddeus V. *Polish Institute of Arts and Sciences of America: 50th Anniversary, 1942–1992.* New York: Polish Institute of Arts and Sciences of America, [1992].

Gross, Feliks. "Notes on the Ethnic Revolution and the Polish Immigration in the U.S.A.." *Polish Review* 21, no. 1–2 (1976): 149–73.

Gross, Jan Tomasz and Irena Grudzinska-Gross. *"W czterdziestym nas Matko na Sibir zesłali."* Warsaw: Res Publica i Libra, 1989.

Guzlowski, John. *Language of Mules.* Charleston, Ill.: DP Press, 1999.

Habielski, Rafał. *Życie społeczne i kulturalne emigracji.* Vol. 3 of *Druga Wielka Emigracja, 1945–1990.* Warsaw: Biblioteka WIĘZI, 1999.

Haiman, Mieczysław. "The Polish American Contribution to World War II." *Polish American Studies* 3, no. 1–2 (Spring-Summer 1946): 35–39.

Hartman, Susan M. *Truman and the 80th Congress.* Columbia: University of Missouri Press, 1971.

Hayes, Florence. *Joe-Pole, New American.* Boston: Riverside Press, 1952.

Heberle, Rudolf, and Dudley S. Hall. *Displaced Persons in Louisiana and Mississippi.* Baton Rouge: Louisiana State University, 1950.

Hering, Alfons. *So, You Wanted America... One DP's Story.* Comp. Helen D. Hering. Wausau, Wisc.: Evergreen Press, 1996.

Hertz, Aleksander. *Refleksje amerykańskie.* Paris: Instytut Literacki, 1966.

Heydenkorn, Benedykt. *A Member of a Distinguished Family: The Polish Group in Canada.* Toronto: McClelland and Stewart, 1976.

Higham, John. "The Mobilization of Immigrants in Urban America." In *Scandinavians and Other Immigrants in Urban America: The Proceedings of a Research Conference, October 26–27, 1984,* ed. Odd S. Lovoll, 1–28. Northfield, Minn.: Saint Olaf College Press, 1985.

Hładkiewicz, Wiesław. *Polacy w zachodnich strefach okupacyjnych Niemiec, 1945–1949.* Zielona Góra: Wyższa Szkoła Pedagogiczna, 1982.

Holborn, Louise W. *The International Refugee Organization, a Specialized Agency of the United Nations: Its History And Work, 1946–1952.* London: Oxford University Press, 1956.

Holborn, Louise W., with the assistance of Philip and Rita Chartrand. *Refugees: A Problem of Our Time: The Work of the United Nations High Commissioner for Refugees, 1951–1972.* 2 vols. Metuchen, N.J.: Scarecrow Press, 1975.

Hort, Weronika [Hanka Ordonówna]. *Tułacze dzieci.* Beirut: Instytut Literacki, 1948.

Hrabyk, Klaudiusz. *Kraj i Emigracja.* New York: published by the author, 1957.
Hulme, Kathryn. *The Wild Place.* Boston: Little, Brown, 1953.
Irons, Peter H. "'The Test Is Poland': Polish Americans and the Origins of the Cold War." *Polish American Studies* 30, no. 2 (Autumn 1973): 5-63.
Isajiw, Wsewolod W., Yury Boshyk, and Roman Senkus, eds. *The Refugee Experience: Ukrainian Displaced Persons after World War II.* Edmonton: Canadian Institute of Ukrainian Studies, University of Alberta, 1992.
Iwańska, Alicja. *Polish Intelligentsia in Nazi Concentration Camps and American Exile: A Study of Values in Crisis Situations.* Lewiston, N.Y.: Edwin Mellen Press, [1998].
———. "Values in Crisis Situations." Ph.D. diss., Columbia University, 1957.
Jacobson, Matthew Frye. *Special Sorrows: The Diasporic Imagination of Irish, Polish, and Jewish Immigrants in the United States.* Cambridge, Mass.: Harvard University Press, 1995.
Janczewski, George. "The Significance of the Polish Vote in the American National Election Campaign of 1948." *Polish Review* 13, no. 4 (1968): 101-9.
Janta, Alexander [Janta, Aleksander]. "Barriers into Bridges: Notes on the Problem of Polish Culture in America." *Polish Review* 2, no. 2-3 (Spring-Summer 1957): 79-97.
———. "Listy do Redakcji." *Kultura,* 1/63 (1953): 145-47.
———. *Nowe odkrycie Ameryki.* Paris: Libella, 1973.
Janusz, Grzegorz. "Polonia w Niemczech Zachodnich po II wojnie światowej." In *Polacy w świecie: Polonia jako zjawisko społeczno-polityczne,* ed. Albin Koprukowniak and Władysław Kucharski, 81-110. Lublin: Uniwersytet Marii Curie-Skłodowskiej, 1986.
———. "Stowarzyszenie Naczelne Polskich Ośrodków Wysiedleńczych w Niemczech Zachodnich w latach 1945-1980." In *Organizacje Polonijne w Europie Zachodniej: Współczesność i tradycje; Materiały z konferencji naukowej w dniach 2 i 3 kwietnia 1987 r. w Poznaniu,* ed. Barbara Szydłowska-Cegłowa and Jerzy Kozłowski, 149-69. Poznań: PAN, Zakład Badań nad Polonią Zagraniczną, 1991.
Januszewski, David G. "The Case for the Exile Government in the American Press, 1939-1945." *Polish American Studies* 43, no.1 (1986): 57-97.
———. "Organizational Evolution in a Polish-American Community," *Polish American Studies* 42, no. 1 (Spring 1985): 43-58.
Jaroszyńska, Anna Dorota. "The American Committee for the Resettlement of Polish Displaced Persons (1948-1968) in the Manuscript Collection of the Immigration History Research Center." *Polish American Studies* 46, no. 1 (Spring 1987): 67-73.
Jaroszyńska-Kirchmann, Anna D. "Communications." *Polish American Studies* 46, no. 2 (Autumn 1989): 87-93.

———. "Displaced Persons, Émigrés, Refugees, and Other Polish Immigrants: World War II through the Solidarity Era." In *Polish Americans and Their History, Community, Culture, and Politics*, ed. John J. Bukowczyk, 152–79. Pittsburgh: University of Pittsburgh Press, 1996.

———. "An Elephant and the Polish Question: Politicization of American Polonia after World War II." *Spectrum* 6 (1994): 28–33.

———. "The Exile Mission: Polish Post War Diaspora in the United States, 1939–1956." In *The Fiedorczyk Lecture in Polish American Studies, Occasional Papers in Polish and Polish American Studies*, no. 11. New Britain, Conn.: Polish Studies Program, Central Connecticut State University, 2001.

———. "The Mobilization of American Polonia for the Cause of the Displaced Persons." *Polish American Studies* 58, no. 1 (Spring 2001): 29–62.

———. "'Nowa Emigracja' and 'Stara Polonia': Transformations of Social Relations and the DP Resettlement Program in the United States." In *Selected Essays From the Fiftieth Anniversary International Congress of the Polish Institute of Arts and Sciences of America*. Vol. 2 of *The Polish Diaspora*, ed. James S. Pula and M. B. Biskupski, 69–84. Washington, D.C.: Columbia University Press, 1993.

———. "Patriotism, Responsibility, and the Cold War: Polish Schools in DP Camps in Germany, 1945–1951," *Polish Review* 47, no. 1 (2002): 35–66.

———. "The Polish Post-World II Diaspora: An Agenda for a New Millennium." *Polish American Studies* 57, no. 2 (Autumn 2000): 45–66.

Jędrzejczak, Wacław. *Love's Cadenza: A Migrant's Story, 1939–1956.* Adelaide, Australia: published by the author, 1999).

Jędrzejewicz, Wacław. *Polonia amerykańska w polityce polskiej: Historia Komitetu Narodowego Amerykanów Polskiego Pochodzenia.* New York: National Committee of Americans of Polish Descent, 1954.

Jupp, James S., ed. *The Australian People: An Encyclopedia of the Nation, Its People, and Their Origins.* North Ryde, Australia: Angus and Robertson Publishers, 1988.

Kantor, Ryszard. "Kluby parafii Zaborów w Chicago: Geneza, dzieje i stan obecny." In *Studia nad organizacjami polonijnymi w Ameryce Północnej*, ed. Grzegorz Babiński, 141–45. Wrocław: Zakład Narodowy im. Ossolińskich, 1988.

———. "Kluby parafii Zaborów w Chicago w okresie międzywojennym i w latach II wojny światowej." *Przegląd Polonijny* 15 (1989): 35–60.

———. "Miejsce Chicago we współczesnych migracjach zarobkowych ludności parafii Zaborów (woj. Tarnów)." *Przegląd Polonijny* 10, no. 3 (1984): 57–72.

———. *Między Zaborowem a Chicago: Kulturowe konsekwencje istnienia zbiorowości imigrantów z parafii zaborowskiej w Chicago i jej kontaktów z rodzinnymi wsiami.* Wrocław: Zakład Narodowy im. Ossolińskich, 1990.

———. Review of *Wakacjuszka*, by Zofia Mierzyńska. *Przegląd Polonijny* 13, no. 3 (1987): 119–20.

———. "Współczesne migracje zarobkowe mieszkańców Podhala do USA: Raport z badań terenowych w latach 1987-1988." *Przegląd Polonijny* 27, no. 1 (1991): 13-32.

Karpinska-Gierat, Ewa. *Korzenie i owoce: Wspomnienia i listy.* Bethlehem, Conn.: published by the author, 1998.

Kesting, Robert W. "American Support of Polish Refugees and Their Santa Rosa Camp." *Polish American Studies* 48, no. 1 (Spring 1991): 79-90.

Klimaszewski, Bolesław, Ewa R. Nowakowska, and Wojciech Wyskiel. *Mały słownik pisarzy polskich na obczyźnie, 1939-1980.* Warsaw: Wydawnictwo Interpress, 1992.

Kłoczowski, Jerzy. "Chrześcijaństwo polskie i jego tysiącletnia historia." In *Naród-Kościół-Kultura: Szkice z historii Polski,* 243-58. Lublin: Redakcja Wydawnictw KUL, 1986.

Kolm, Richard. "The Change of Cultural Identity: An Analysis of Factors Conditioning the Cultural Integration of Immigrants." Ph.D. diss., Wayne State University, 1966.

Komisja Historyczna Polskiego Sztabu Głównego w Londynie. *Polskie siły zbrojne w drugiej wojnie światowej.* 3 vols. London: Instytut Historyczny im. Gen. Sikorskiego, 1950-1962.

Koprowska, Irena. *A Woman Wanders through Life and Science.* Albany: State University Press of New York, 1997.

Korewa, Maria Barbara. "Casework Treatment of Refugees: A Survey of Selected Professional Periodicals for the Period from January 1, 1939, to January 1, 1956. Master's thesis, Wayne State University, 1957.

Kowalczyk, Władysław. *Szkolnictwo polskie w Niemczech, 1945-1948.* Warsaw: Państwowe Zakłady Wydawnictw Szkolnych, 1961.

Kowalik, Jan. *"Kultura," 1947-1957: Bibliografia zawartości treści; Działalność wydawnicza (1946-maj 1959).* Paris: Instytut Literacki, 1959.

———. *Prasa polska w Niemczech w latach 1945-1971.* Toronto: Kanadyjsko-Polski Instytut Badawczy, 1976.

Krukowski, Kazimierz. *Z Melpomeną na emigracji.* Warsaw: Czytelnik, 1987.

Krysiewicz, Thaddeus Theodore. *The Polish Immigration Committee in the United States: A Historical Study of the American Committee for the Relief of Polish Immigrants, 1947-1952.* New York: Roman Catholic Church of St. Stanislaus, [1953].

Kubiak, Hieronim. *The Polish National Catholic Church in the United States of America from 1897 to 1980: Its Social Conditioning and Social Functions.* Warsaw: PWN, 1982.

Kucha, Ryszard. "Z zagadnień Polonii skandynawskiej." In *Polacy w świecie: Polonia jako zjawisko społeczno-polityczne,* ed. Albin Koprukowniak and Władysław Kucharski, vol. 2, 237-60. Lublin: Uniwersytet Marii Curie-Skłodowskiej, 1986.

Kucharski, Władysław Stanisław. *Polacy i Polonia w rdzennej Austrii w XIX i XX wieku*. Lublin: Uniwersytet Marii Curie-Skłodowskiej w Lublinie, Forum Polonii w Austrii, 1994.

Kulischer, Eugene M. *Europe on the Move: War and Population Changes, 1917-1947*. New York: Columbia University Press, 1948.

Kuniczak, Wiesław S. *Milcząca Emigracja*. Chicago: Polski Klub Artystyczny, 1968.

———. *My Name Is Million: An Illustrated History of the Poles in America*. New York: Doubleday, 1978.

Kunz, Egon F. *Calwell's New Australians*. Sydney: Australian National University Press, 1988.

———. "Political Events 'At Home' and the Concept of Catharsis Naturalization among Refugees." *International Migration* 9, no.1/2 (1971): 55-67.

———. "The Refugee in Flight: Kinetic Models and Forms of Displacement," *International Migration Review* 7, no. 22 (Summer 1973): 125-46.

Kuropas, Myron B. *The Ukrainian Americans: Roots and Aspirations, 1884-1954*. Toronto: University of Toronto Press, 1991.

———. "Ukrainian-American Resettlement Efforts, 1944-1954," in *The Refugee Experience: Ukrainian Displaced Persons after World War II*, ed. Wsevolod W. Isajiw, Yury Boshyk, and Roman Senkus (Edmonton: Canadian Institute of Ukrainian Studies Press, University of Alberta, 1992).

Kuropieska, Józef. *Obozowe refleksje: Oflag II C*. Kraków: Krajowa Agencja Wydawnicza, 1985.

Lechoń, Jan. *Poezje*. Lublin: Wydawnictwo Lubelskie, 1989.

Lednicki, Wacław. "The Role of the Polish Intellectual in America." *Polish Review* 12, no. 2 (1967): 3-10.

Leich, J. F. "Great Expectations: The National Councils in Exile, 1950-1960." *Polish Review* 35, no. 3 (1990), 183-96.

LeMay, Michael C. *From Open Door to Dutch Door: An Analysis of U.S. Immigration Policy Since 1820*. New York: Praeger, 1987.

Lencznarowicz, Jan. *Prasa i społeczność polska w Australii, 1928-1980*. Kraków: Księgarnia Akademicka, 1994.

———. "Rola Towarzystwa "Polonia" w polityce PRL wobec Polonii w krajach zachodnich." *Przegląd Polonijny* 22, no. 1 (1996): 43-60.

Lerski, Jerzy. "Symbioza." *Kultura* 12/50 (1951): 57-58.

Lewandowska, Stanisława. *Prasa polskiej emigracji wojennej, 1939-1945*. Warsaw: Instytut Historii Polskiej Akademii Nauk, 1993.

Lewandowski, Jan. "Polacy w Szwajcarii." In *Polacy w świecie: Polonia jako zjawisko społeczno-polityczne*, ed. Albin Koprukowniak and Władysław Kucharski, vol. 2, 213-36. Lublin: Uniwersytet Marii Curie-Skłodowskiej, 1986.

Lewicki, Roman, ed. *Polscy studenci-żołnierze we Włoszech, 1945-1947.* Hove, England: Caldra House, 1996.

Ligęza, Wojciech. "Commonplaces: Polish Émigré Poetry, 1945-1980." *Polish Review* 34, no. 1 (1989): 17-27.

Loescher, Gil, and John A. Scanlan. *Calculated Kindness: Refugees and America's Half-Open Door, 1945 to the Present.* New York: Free Press, 1986.

Lorentowicz, Irena. *Oczarowania.* Warsaw: Instytut Wydawniczy PAX, 1972.

Lowenstein, Sharon R. *Token Refugee: The Story of the Jewish Shelter at Oswego, 1944-1946.* Bloomington: Indiana University Press, 1986.

Luciuk, Lubomyr Y. *Searching for Place: Ukrainian Displaced Persons, Canada, and the Migration of Memory.* Toronto: University of Toronto Press, 2000.

Lukas, Richard C. *Bitter Legacy: Polish-American Relations in the Wake of World War II.* Louisville, Kentucky, University of Kentucky Press, 1982.

———. *The Forgotten Holocaust: The Poles under German Occupation, 1939-1944.* Lexington: University of Kentucky Press, 1986.

———. "The Polish American Congress and the Polish Question, 1944-1947." *Polish American Studies* 38, no. 2 (Autumn 1981): 39-53.

———. *The Strange Allies: The United States and Poland, 1941-1945.* Knoxville: University of Tennessee Press, 1978.

Łaszewski, Bolesław T. *Z wojskowych szeregów do życia cywilnego: Historia powstania i pierwszych pięciu lat działalności Stowarzyszenia Polskich Kombatantów, 1945-1950.* New York: Bicentennial Publishing Corporation of New York, 1984.

Łuczak, Czesław. *Polacy w okupowanych Niemczech, 1945-1949.* Poznań: Pracownia Serwisu Oprogramowania, 1993.

———. *Polska i Polacy w drugiej wojnie światowej.* Poznań: Uniwersytet im. Adama Mickiewicza, 1993.

———. "Przemieszczenia ludności z Polski podczas drugiej wojny światowej." In *Emigracja z ziem polskich w czasach nowożytnych i najnowszych (XVIII-XX w.),* ed. Andrzej Pilch, 451-83. Warsaw: Państwowe Wydawnictwo Naukowe, 1984.

Machcewicz, Paweł. *Emigracja w polityce międzynarodowej.* Vol. 2 of *Druga Wielka Emigracja, 1945-1990.* Warsaw: Biblioteka WIĘZI, 1999.

Maciuszko, Jerzy J. "Polish Letters in America." In *Poles in America: Bicentennial Essays,* ed. Frank Mocha, 531-64. Stevens Point, Wisc.: Worzalla Publishing, 1978.

Maczek, Stanisław. *Od podwody do czołga.* London: Orbis Books, 1984.

Malak, Henryk Maria. *Klechy w obozach śmierci.* 2nd ed. London: Veritas, [1960].

———. *Na Wychodźczym Szlaku: Album, naświetlający: Przyczyny powstania, historyczny przebieg, prace, zadania i osiągnięcia—Polskiego Wychodźtwa Powojen-*

nego z drugiej wojny światowej na ziemi niemieckiej. Chicago: Wydawnictwo im. Św. Jadwigi, 1952.

Marrus, Michael R. *The Unwanted: European Refugees in the Twentieth Century.* New York: Oxford University Press, 1985).

Michalski, Jan. *Obóz przy Sandstrasse.* Warsaw: Czytelnik, 1975.

Michnik, Adam. *Letters from Prison and Other Essays.* Berkeley: University of California Press, 1985.

Mickiewicz, Adam. *Poems by Adam Mickiewicz.* Ed. George Rapall Noyes. New York: PIASA, 1944.

Mierzyńska, Zofia. *Wakacjuszka.* Chicago: Z and L Song and Publishing, 1983.

Miller, Kirby. *Emigrants and Exiles: Ireland and the Irish Exodus to North America.* New York: Oxford University Press, 1985.

Miłosz, Czesław. *The History of Polish Literature.* Berkeley: University of California Press, 1983.

Mocha, Frank "The Polish Institute of Arts and Sciences in America: Its Contributions to the Study of Polonia; The Origins of the Polish Historical Association (PAHA)." In *Poles in America: Bicentennial Essays,* ed. Frank Mocha, 709-24. Stevens Point, Wisc.: Worzalla Publishing, 1978.

Modelski, Tadeusz. *The Polish Contribution to the Ultimate Allied Victory in the Second World War.* Worthing, England: published by the author, 1986.

Mostwin, Danuta. *Ameryko! Ameryko!* Paris: Instytut Literacki, 1961.

———. "Córki." In *Asteroidy,* 89-114. London: Nakł. Polska Fundacja Kulturalna, 1965.

———. *Emigranci polscy w USA.* Lublin: Redakcja Wydawnictw Katolickiego Uniwersytetu Lubelskiego, 1991.

———. *Ja za Wodą, Ty za Wodą.* Paris: Instytut Literacki, 1972.

———. "Post-World War II Polish Immigrants in the United States." *Polish American Studies* 26, no. 2 (Autumn 1979): 5-14.

———. "The Profile of a Transplanted Family." *Polish Review* 19, no. 1 (1974): 77-89.

———. *The Transplanted Family: A Study of Social Adjustment of the Polish Immigrant Family to the United States after the Second World War.* New York: Arno Press, 1980.

———. *Trzecia wartość: Formowanie się nowej tożsamości polskiego emigranta w Ameryce.* Lublin: Instytut Badań nad Polonią i Duszpasterstwem Polonijnym, Katolicki Uniwersytet Lubelski, 1985.

Murphy, H. B. "The Camps." In *Flight and Resettlement,* ed. H. B. Murphy, 58-63. Lucerne, Switzerland: United Nations Educational, Scientific, and Cultural Organization, 1955.

Nadolny, Anastazy. *Opieka duszpasterska nad dziećmi i młodzieżą polską na terenie*

Niemiec zachodnich w latach 1945-1965. Lublin: Katolicki Uniwersytet Lubelski, 1980.

———. *Polskie duszpasterstwo w Austrii, 1801-1945.* Lublin: Instytut Badań nad Polonią i Duszpasterstwem Polonijnym KUL, 1994.

Naglerowa, Herminia. "W służbie dla Ojczyzny: Kobieta-żołnierz 2 Korpusu, 1941-1946." In *Polish Veterans of World War II, Inc., Post No. 19, Boston, Massachusetts, U.S.A., 1953-1978.* [Boston: Polish Veterans of World War II, Inc., 1978].

National Committee of Americans of Polish Descent. *Od apelu do Kongresu: Zbiór dokumentów Komitetu Narodowego Amerykanów Polskiego Pochodzenia (12 maja 1942-28 maja 1944).* New York: Józef Piłsudski Institute of America for Research in the Modern History of Poland, 1944.

Nir, Roman. "The Archives, Libraries and Museums of Polonia at Orchard Lake." *Polish American Studies* 40, no. 1 (Spring 2003): 51-80.

———. *Szkice z Dziejów Polonii.* Orchard Lake, Mich.: Wydawnictwo Centralnego Archiwum Polonii Amerykańskiej w Orchard Lake, 1990.

Nowak-Jeziorański, Jan. *Wojna w eterze: Wspomnienia.* Vol. 1, *1948-1956.* London: Odnowa, 1986.

Nowakowski, Tadeusz. *Aleja dobrych znajomych.* London: Polska Fundacja Kulturalna, 1968.

———. "Hard Core." In *Niestworzone rzeczy: Zbiór opowiadań,* 133-60. London: Polska Fundacja Kulturalna, 1968.

———. *Obóz Wszystkich Świętych.* Warsaw: Czytelnik, 1990.

Olejniczak, John J. *American Relief for Poland: Auditors' Report for the Period November 1, 1939, to September 30, 1948.* Buffalo, N.Y.: Everybody's Publishing Company, 1948.

Olszewski, Adam. *Historia Związku Narodowego Polskiego.* Vol. 6. Chicago: Zakłady Graficzne Dziennika Związkowego, 1967.

Orzechowski, Emil. *Teatr polonijny w Stanach Zjednoczonych.* Wrocław: Zakład Narodowy im. Ossolińskich, 1989.

Paleczny, Tadeusz. *Ewolucja ideologii i przemiany tożsamości narodowej Polonii w Stanach Zjednoczonych w latach 1870-1970.* Warsaw: Państwowe Wydawnictwo Naukowe, 1989.

Pamiętnik Jubileuszu 25-lecia Stowarzyszenia Samopomocy Nowej Emigracji Polskiej w Chicago, 1975. [Chicago: Stowarzyszenie Samopomocy Nowej Emigracji, 1975].

Patterson, Sheila. "The Poles: An Exile Community in Britain." In *Between Two Cultures: Migrants and Minorities in Britain,* ed. James L. Watson, 214-41. Oxford: Basil Blackwell, 1977.

Patyna, Józef, and Krystyna Patyna. "Solidarity: Józef and Krystyna Patyna; Refugees from Trzebinia, Poland; Factory Workers, Providence, Rhode Island." Interview by Al Santoli. In *New Americans: An Oral History; Immigrants and Refugees in the U.S. Today*, ed. Al Santoli, 56-84. New York: Viking, 1988.

Pennsylvania Commission on Displaced Persons. *Third Annual Report, 1951.* Commonwealth of Pennsylvania, [1952].

Pienkos, Donald E. *For Your Freedom through Ours: Polish American Efforts on Poland's Behalf, 1863-1991.* New York: Columbia University Press, 1991.

———. *PNA: A Centennial History of the Polish National Alliance of the United States of North America.* New York: Columbia University Press, 1984.

———. "The Polish American Congress. An Appraisal." *Polish American Studies* 36 (Autumn 1979): 5-19.

Pilch, Andrzej. *Losy Polaków w Austrii po drugiej wojnie światowej, 1945-1955.* Wrocław: Ossolineum, 1994.

Piłsudski, Rowmund. *Pisma wybrane, 1972-1982.* Vol. 3 of *Myśl społeczna i polityczna na emigracji*, ed. Feliks Gross. Warsaw: Instytut Studiów Politycznych Polskiej Akademii Nauk, 1998.

Piotrowski, Tadeusz. *Vengeance of the Swallows: Memoir of a Polish Family's Ordeal under Soviet Aggression, Ukrainian Ethnic Cleansing, and Nazi Enslavement, and Their Emigration to America.* Jefferson, N.C.: McFarland, 1995.

Pławski, Czesław. *Wydarci z ojczystej ziemi: Okres drugiej wojny światowej.* Łódź: RES POLONA, 2001.

Podkopacz, Helena. *Smuga życia.* Kraków: ArsNova-Zjednoczeni Wydawcy, 1994.

Polenberg, Richard. *One Nation Divisible: Class, Race, and Ethnicity in the United States Since 1938.* New York: Viking, 1980.

Polish American Congress. *Story of the Polish American Congress and Poland's Case in Press Clippings.* 3 vols. Chicago: Polish American Congress, 1948, 1952, 1954.

Polish Veterans of World War II. *Polish Veterans of World War II, Inc., Post No. 19, Boston, Massachusetts, U.S.A., 1953-1978.* [Boston, Mass.: Polish Veterans of World War II, 1978].

Polish War Relief. *The Facts About the Polish War Relief.* Chicago: The Polish War Relief, [1945].

———. *The National War Fund and the Polish War Relief of the USA.* Chicago: The Polish War Relief, 1947.

———. *Poland's Children.* Chicago: The Polish War Relief, [1945].

Polzin, Theresita. *The Polish Americans: Whence and Whither.* Pulaski, Wisc.: Franciscan Press, 1973.

Porter, Brian. *When Nationalism Began to Hate: Imagining Modern Politics in Nineteenth-Century Poland.* New York: Oxford University Press, 2000.

Protokół Czwartej Konwencji Kongresu Polonii Amerykańskiej odbytej w dniach 30 i 31 maja i 1-go czerwca 1956 w hotelu Benjamin Franklin, Philadelphia, Pennsylvania. [Chicago: Polish American Congress, 1956].

Protokół Drugiego Zjazdu Rady Naczelnej Kongresu Polonii Amerykańskiej odbytego w dniach 13-14 lutego 1947 w Hotelu Statler, Washington, D.C. Chicago: Dziennik Związkowy, [1947].

Protokół Trzeciego Zjazdu Rady Naczelnej Kongresu Polonii Amerykańskiej odbytego w dn. 17-18 listopada 1950 w Hotelu Raleigh, Washington, D.C. [Chicago: Polish American Congress, 1950].

Protokół Zjazdu Rady Polonii Amerykańskiej, Buffalo, N.Y., 17go i 18go Października 1942. [Chicago: The Polish War Relief, 1942].

Proudfoot, Malcolm J. *European Refugees: 1939-52; A Study in Forced Population Movement.* London: Faber and Faber, 1957.

Pula, James S. *Polish Americans: An Ethnic Community.* New York: Twayne, 1995.

Puskás, Julianna. *Ties that Bind, Ties that Divide: One Hundred Years of Hungarian Experience in the United States.* New York: Holmes and Meier, 2000.

Rada Polonii Amerykańskiej. *Szczegółowy wykaz przychodów i rozchodów od 1-go maja, 1941 do 30-go września, 1942 roku, na Zjazd Rady Polonii Amerykańskiej, Buffalo, New York, w dniach 17-go i 18-go października, 1942.* [Chicago]: Rada Polonii Amerykańskiej, 1942.

Radzik, Tadeusz. "Polonia w Wielkiej Brytanii." In *Polacy w świecie: Polonia jako zjawisko społeczno-polityczne,* ed. Albin Koprukowniak and Władysław Kucharski, vol. 2, 111-46. Lublin: Uniwersytet Marii Curie-Skłodowskiej, 1986.

———. "Społeczność polska w Wielkiej Brytanii w latach 1945-1990." In *Polonia w Europie,* ed. Barbara Szydłowska-Cegłowa, 437-68. Poznań: Polska Akademia Nauk, 1992.

———. *Z dziejów społeczności polskiej w Wielkiej Brytanii po drugiej wojnie światowej (1945-1990).* Lublin: Wydawnictwo UMCS, 1991.

Radziwiłł, Anna, and Wojciech Roszkowski. *Historia, 1945-1990.* Warsaw: Wydawnictwo Naukowe PWN, 1994.

Ristelhueber, Rene. "The International Refugee Organization," *International Conciliation* 470 (April 1951): 167-228.

Rokicki, Jarosław. "'Wakacjusze' na Jackowie i inni: Szkic o sytuacji współczesnych polskich emigrantów zarobkowych w Chicago." *Przegląd Polonijny* 15, no. 3 (1989): 105-18.

Romańska, Loda, and Andrzej Romański. *W służbie dla Ojczyzny: Kobieta-żołnierz 2 Korpusu, 1941-1946.* Rome: Inspektorat PSK 2 Korpusu, 1946.

Rowinski, Leokadia. *That the Nightingale Return: Memoir of the Polish Resistance, the Warsaw Uprising, and German P.O.W. Camps.* Jefferson, N.C.: McFarland, 1999.

Sadler, Charles. "'Pro-Soviet Polish-Americans': Oskar Lange and Russia's Friends in the Polonia, 1941-1945." *Polish Review* 22 (1977): 25-39.

Safran, William. "Diasporas in Modern Societies: Myths of Homeland and Return," *Diaspora: A Journal of Transnational Studies* 1, no. 1 (1991): 83-99.

Seller, Maxine Schwartz. *To Seek America: A History of Ethnic Life in the United States*. Englewood, N.J.: J. S. Ozer, 1988.

Senn, Alfred Erich. "Émigrés and Immigrants: Problem of National Consciousness." *Spectrum* 6 (1994): 5-10.

Serwański, Jacek. "Polacy w Wielkiej Brytanii w latach II wojny światowej." In *Polonia w Europie*, ed. Barbara Szydłowska-Cegłowa, 423-36. Poznań: Polska Akademia Nauk, 1992.

Sęk, Jan. "Poles." In *The Australian People: An Encyclopedia of the Nation, Its People, and Their Origins*, ed. James Jupp. North Ryde, NSW, Australia: Angus and Robertson Publishers, 1988.

———. "Polonia w Ameryce Łacińskiej." In *Polacy w świecie: Polonia jako zjawisko społeczno-polityczne*, ed. Albin Koprukowniak and Władysław Kucharski, vol. 3, 49-84. Lublin: Uniwersytet Marii Curie-Skłodowskiej, 1986.

———. "Polonia w Australii i Nowej Zelandii." In *Polacy w świecie: Polonia jako zjawisko społeczno-polityczne*, ed. Albin Koprukowniak and Władysław Kucharski, vol. 3, 85-110. Lublin: Uniwersytet Marii Curie-Skłodowskiej, 1986.

Simon, Rita J. *Public Opinion and the Immigrant: Print Media Coverage, 1880-1980*. Lexington, Mass.: D. C. Heath, 1985.

Siwik, Anna. *Polska Partia Socjalistyczna na emigracji w latach 1945-1956*. Kraków: Księgarnia Akademicka, 1998.

———. "Polski Październik a emigracja." *Przegląd Polonijny* 20, no. 1 (1994): 79-94.

Sprawozdania Prezesa Kongresu Polonii Amerykańskiej Alozjego A. Mazewskiego na Dziesiątą Krajową Konwencję w Filadelfii, Pennsylwania, w dniach 24, 25 i 26 września, 1976 r. Chicago: Polish American Congress, 1976.

Sprawozdania Prezesa Zarządu Wykonawczego, poszczególnych komisji i komitetów Wydziałów Stanowych i Biur Kongresu P.A. w Chicago i w Washingtonie na drugą konwencję Kongresu Polonii Amerykańskiej w Philadelphia, PA., 29-30-31 maja 1948. Chicago: Dziennik Związkowy i Zgoda, [1948].

Sprawozdania Zarządu Wykonawczego Poszczególnych Komisji i komitetów oraz Biur w Chicago i Washingtonie na Trzecią Krajową Konwencję Kongresu Polonii Amerykańskiej w Atlantic City, N.J. w dniach 30-31 Maja i 1 Czerwca 1952. [Chicago]: Polish American Congress, 1952.

Stein, Barry N. "The Refugee Experience: Defining the Parameters of a Field of Study." *International Migration Review* 15 (Spring-Summer 1981): 320-33.

Sterner, Wacław. *Gefengeni i Dipisi*. Warsaw: Książka i Wiedza, 1979.

Stoessinger, John George. *The Refugee and the World Community*. Minneapolis: University of Minnesota Press, 1956.

Stola, Dariusz. "Forced Migrations in Central European History." *International Migration Review* 26, no.2 (1992): 324–41.

Stowarzyszenie Polskich Kombatantów. *Piąty Zjazd Krajowy, 31 Sierpień, 1 i 2 Wrzesień, 1963*. Chicago: Stowarzyszenie Polskich Kombatantów, 1963.

Strzetelski, Stanisław. *The Polish Institute of Arts and Sciences in America: Origin and Development*. New York: Polish Institute of Arts and Sciences in America, 1960.

Sword, Keith. *Deportation and Exile: Poles in the Soviet Union, 1939–1948*. New York: St. Martin's Press, 1994).

Sword, Keith, Norman Davies and Jan Ciechanowski. *The Formation of the Polish Community in Great Britain, 1939–1950*. London: School of Slavonic and East European Studies, University of London, 1989.

Sypek, Stanislaus T. "The Displaced Person in the Greater Boston Community." Ph.D. diss., Fordham University, 1955.

Szydłowska-Cegłowa, Barbara, ed. *Polonia w Europie*. Poznań: PAN, 1992.

Szymczak, Robert. "Hopes and Promises: Arthur Bliss Lane, the Republican Party, and the Slavic-American Vote." *Polish American Studies* 45, no. 1 (Spring 1988): 12–28.

———. "Invitation to the Kremlin: The Adventures of Father Stanisław Orlemański, April–May 1944." *East European Quarterly* 25 (1992): 399–424.

———. "A Matter of Honor: Polonia and the Congressional Investigation of the Katyń Forest Massacre." *Polish American Studies* 41, no. 1 (Spring 1984): 25–65.

Śladkowski, Wiesław. "Polonii Francuskiej przeszłość i teraźniejszość." In *Polacy w świecie: Polonia jako zjawisko społeczno-polityczne*, ed. Albin Koprukowniak and Władysław Kucharski, vol. 2, 7–54. Lublin: Uniwersytet Marii Curie-Skłodowskiej, 1986.

Świetlik, Francis X. *The Polish Displaced Persons*. Chicago: The American Relief for Poland, [1945].

Świetlik, Franciszek X. *Sprawozdanie z Działalności Rady Polonii Amerykańskiej od Października 1939 do Października 1948 na Zjazd Rady Polonii Amerykańskiej odbyty dnia 4go i 5go Grudnia, 1948 r. w hotelu Buffalo, N.Y.* Chicago: Czas, 1948.

Tabori, Paul. *The Pen in Exile: An Anthology of Exiled Writers*. London: International P.E.N. Club Centre for Writers in Exile, 1954.

———. *The Pen in Exile: A Second Anthology*. London: International P.E.N. Club Centre for Writers in Exile, 1956.

Terlecki, Tymon, ed. *Literatura polska na obczyźnie, 1940–1960*. Vol. 1. London: B. Świderski, 1964.

Tkocz, Zygmunt, ed. *Myśl społeczna na emigracji*. Vol. 1 of *Myśl społeczna i polityczna na emigracji*, ed. Feliks Gross. London: Odnowa, 1991.

Tkocz, Zygmunt, and Teofil Roll, eds. *Wybór pism emigracji politycznej Niepodległej PPS (WRN), 1940-1970.* Vol. 2 of *Myśl społeczna i polityczna na emigracji*, ed. Feliks Gross. London: Odnowa, 1994.

Topolski, Jerzy, ed. *Dzieje Polski.* Warsaw: Państwowe Wydawnictwo Naukowe, 1981.

Ubriaco, Robert D., Jr. "Bread and Butter Politics or Foreign Policy Concerns? Class Versus Ethnicity in the Midwestern Polish American Community During the 1946 Congressional Elections." *Polish American Studies* 51 (1994): 5-32.

United States, Bureau of the Census, *Statistical Abstract of the United States: 1991 (111th edition).* Washington, D.C.: U.S. Government Printing Office, 1991.

———, Committee on the Judiciary. *Displaced Persons: Hearing before the Subcommittee on Amendments to the Displaced Persons Act of the Committee on the Judiciary, United States Senate.* Washington, D.C.: U.S. Government Printing Office, 1950.

———, Department of Justice, Immigration and Naturalization Service. *The Annual Report for the Fiscal Year Ended June 30, 1945-1956.* Washington, D.C.: U.S. Government Printing Office.

———, House of Representatives. *Hearings before the President's Commission on Immigration and Naturalization, September-October, 1952.* Washington, D.C.: U.S. Government Printing Office, 1952.

———, President. *Economic Report of the President Transmitted to the Congress: January 1989, Together with the Annual Report of the Council of Economic Advisers.* Washington D.C.: U.S. Government Printing Office, 1989.

———. *Whom Shall We Welcome: Report of the President's Commission on Immigration and Naturalization.* Washington, D.C.: U.S. Government Printing Office, 1953.

Urban, Arkadiusz. *Emigracyjny dramat.* Warsaw: Dom Wydawniczy Bellona, 1998.

Van Atken-Rutkowski, Sarah. "Integration and Acculturation of the Polish Veteran of World War II to Canadian Society." Master's thesis, University of Windsor, 1982.

Van Hear, Nicholas. *New Diasporas: The Mass Exodus, Dispersal, and Regrouping of Migrant Communities.* Seattle: University of Washington Press, 1998.

Van Reenan, Antanas J. *Lithuanian Diaspora: Königsberg to Chicago.* Lanham, Md.: University Press of America, 1990.

Veidemanis, Juris. "Latvian Settlers in Wisconsin: A Comparative View." *Wisconsin Magazine of History* 45, no. 4 (1962): 251-55.

———. "A Twentieth-Century Pioneer Settlement: Latvians in Lincoln County, Wisconsin." *Midcontinent American Studies Journal* 4 (1963): 13-26.

Vernant, Jacques. *The Refugee in the Post-War World.* London: Allen and Unwin, 1953.

———. *The Refugee in the Post-War World. Preliminary Report of a Survey.* Geneva: n.p., 1951.
Wachtl, Karol. *Polonja w Ameryce: Dzieje i dorobek.* Philadelphia: published by the author, 1944.
Wandycz, Damian S. *Polski Instytut Naukowy w Ameryce: W trzydziestą rocznicę, 1942-1972.* New York: Polski Instytut Naukowy, 1974.
Wandycz, Piotr. "Czy emigracja jest jeszcze potrzebna?" *Kultura* 10/505 (1989): 3-15.
———. *The Price of Freedom: A History of East Central Europe from the Middle Ages to the Present.* London: Routledge, 1992.
Wańkowicz, Melchior. *Klub Trzeciego Miejsca.* Paris: Instytut Literacki, 1949.
———. *Polacy i Ameryka.* London: Oficyna Poetów i Malarzy na Emigracji w Anglii, [1952].
Wardziński, Zygmunt. "General Władysław Anders as Educator: The Polish Gymnasium and Lyceum in Alessano, Italy, and Cawthorne, England." *Polish Review* 44, no. 1 (1999): 47-51.
Wawrzkiewicz, Jan, ed. *Dwadzieścia pięć lat Stowarzyszenia Polskich Kombatantów.* London: P.C.A. Publications, 1971.
Wesoły, Archbishop Szczepan. *Fifty Years of the Church in the Polish Diaspora, 1945-1995.* London: School of Slavonic and East European Studies, University of London, 1996.
Węgrzyniakowa, Anna. "Pod znakiem Skamandra: Wprowadzenie." In *Literatura emigracyjna, 1939-1989,* ed. Marek Pytasz, vol. 1, 25-29. Katowice: Śląsk, 1994.
Wieczerzak, Joseph. "Pre- and Proto-Ethnics: Poles in the United States before the Immigration 'After Bread.'" *Polish Review* 21, no. 3 (1976): 7-38.
Wierzyński, Kazimierz. "Kasztan zwany Dewajtisem." In *Moja prywatna Ameryka,* 11-22. London: Polska Fundacja Kulturalna, 1966.
———. *Wybór poezji.* Ed. Krzysztof Dybciak. Wrocław: Zakład Narodowy im. Ossolińskich, 1991.
Wiktor, Broni-Sława. *Pamiętasz?* Detroit, Michigan: Glow Press, 1967.
Williams, Robert C. "European Political Emigrations: A Lost Subject." *Comparative Studies in Society and History* 12, no. 2 (April 1970): 140-48.
Witkowska, Alina. *Cześć i skandale: O emigracyjnym doświadczeniu Polaków.* Gdańsk: Słowo/Obraz Terytoria, 1997.
Wittlin, Joseph. "Sorrow and Grandeur of Exile." *Polish Review* 2, no. 2-3 (1957): 99-111.
Włodawiec, Bogusław. "Melchior Wańkowicz wobec rzeczywistości lat 1939-1956." *Przegląd Polonijny* 21, no. 3 (1995): 55-62.
Woodbridge, George. *UNRRA: The History of the United Nations Relief and Rehabilitation Administration.* 3 vols. New York: Columbia University Press, 1950.

Wróbel, Elżbieta, and Janusz Wróbel, *Rozproszeni po świecie: Obozy i osiedla uchodźców polskich ze Związku Sowieckiego, 1942-1950.* Chicago: Panorama, 1992.
Wyman, David S. *The Abandonment of the Jews.* New York: Pantheon, 1984.
———. *Paper Walls.* Boston: University of Massachusetts Press, 1968.
Wyman, Mark. *DP: Europe's Displaced Persons, 1945-1951.* Philadelphia: Balch Institute Press, 1989.
Wyrwa, Józef ["Furgalski," or "Stary"]. *Pamiętniki Partyzanta.* London: Oficyna Poetów i Malarzy, 1991.
Wyrwa, Tadeusz. *Bezdroża dziejów Polski.* Lublin: Norbertinum, 1998.
Wytrwal, Joseph A. *America's Polish Heritage: A Social History of Poles in America.* Detroit: Endurance Press, 1961.
———. *Behold! The Polish Americans.* Detroit: Endurance Press, 1977.
———. *Poles in American History and Tradition.* Detroit: Endurance Press, 1969.
Zachariasiewicz, Walter. "Organizational Structure of Polonia." In *Poles in America: Bicentennial Essays,* ed. Frank Mocha, 627-70. Stevens Point, Wisc.: Worzalla Publishing, 1978.
Zawistowska-Gorzela, Severina. "Problems of Recent Polish Immigrants." *PNCC Studies* 4 (1983): 61-66.
Zieliński, Henryk. *Historia Polski, 1914-1939.* Wrocław: Zakład Narodowy im. Ossolińskich, 1983.
Zielyk, Ihor V. "The DP Camp as a Social System." In *The Refugee Experience: Ukrainian Displaced Persons after World War II,* ed. Wsevolod W. Isajiw, Yury Boshyk, and Roman Senkus, 461-70. Edmonton: Canadian Institute of Ukrainian Studies Press, University of Alberta, 1992.
Ziętara, Paweł. *Misja ostatniej szansy: Próba zjednoczenia polskiej emigracji politycznej przez gen. Kazimierza Sosnkowskiego w latach 1952-1956.* Warsaw: Instytut Historyczny Uniwersytetu Warszawskiego, 1995.
Znaniecka Lopata, Helena. *Polish Americans.* New Brunswick, N.J.: Transaction Publishers, 1994.
Znaniecki Lopata, Helena. *Polish Americans: Status Competition in an Ethnic Community.* Englewood Cliffs, N.J.: Prentice-Hall, 1976.
———. "Polish Immigration to the United States of America: Problems of Estimation and Parameters." *Polish Review* 21, no. 4 (1976): 85-107.
Zubrzycki, Jerzy. "The Immigrant Family: Some Sociological Aspects." In *New Faces,* ed. A. Stoller, 60-74. Melbourne: Melbourne Cheshire, 1966.
———. *Immigrants in Australia: A Demographic Survey Based upon the 1954 Census.* Melbourne: Melbourne University Press, 1960.

———. *Polish Immigrants in Britain: A Study of Adjustment.* The Hague: Martinus Nijhoff, 1956.

———. *Settlers of the Latrobe Valley: A Sociological Study of Immigrants in the Brown Coal Industry in Australia.* Canberra: Australian National University Press, 1964.

———. "Whither Emigracja? The Future of the Polish Community in Great Britain," *Polish Review* 38, no. 4 (1993): 391–406.

———. "Żołnierze i chłopi: Socjologia emigracji polskiej." *Przegląd Polonijny* 15, no. 4 (1989): 5–23.

Żaba, Jarosław. *"Polonia 1978—Polonia Jutra": Przegląd Uchwał Konferencji Polonii Wolnego Świata w Toronto, 25-28 maja 1978.* London: Polska Fundacja Kulturalna, 1978.

Żaroń, Zbigniew. *Wojenne losy ludności polskiej na obczyźnie w latach 1939-1947.* Warsaw: UNICORN, 1994.

Index

ACRPDP. *See* American Committee for the Resettlement of Polish DP's
actors, Polish, 36-38
Adesko, Tadeusz (Thaddeus), 118
Advisory Committee on Voluntary Foreign Aid, 117
AK. *See* Armia Krajowa
Akt Zjednoczenia (Act of Unification), 197
Alliance of Polish Socialists, 244n11
Alski, Wiktor L., 316n25
Altenhagen DP camp (Germany), 68
Altenstadt DP camp (Germany), 76, 152, 295n26
Amalgamated Clothing Workers of America, 244n11
Amberg DP camp (Germany), 67
American Commission for Relief of Polish Immigrants, 117
American Committee for the Investigation of the Katyń Massacre, 200
American Committee for the Resettlement of Polish DP's (ACRPDP): and DP resettlement, 113, 116, 117-18, 126-27, 130-31, 161, 162-63, 289n105; founding of, 115, 117; and organizational separation, 282-83n36
Americanization. *See* assimilation
American Polish Labor Council (APLC), 50
American Red Cross, 40-41, 68, 217, 267n38
American Relief for Poland. *See* Rada Polonii Amerykańskiej
American Slav Congress, 46-47, 48
Ameryka-Echo, 140, 310n47; and resettlement-related conflict, 161-62, 168, 175; and Wyrwa affair, 188
Anders Army, 42
Anderson, Benedict, 247-48n42
Anders, Władysław (Gen.): American Polonia view of, 207-8; and government in exile, 196, 197; and Katyń Massacre investigation, 200; and Poles in Korean War, 189-90; and state in exile concept, 51; during WWII, 26, 28-29
anticommunism: American Polonia and, 199-201; and anti-immigrant prejudice, 199; exile mission and, 179-80, 221-23; perceived Western indifference toward, 217; of Polish DPs, 156-57, 274-75n129; as source of collaboration, 179-80, 193-94, 239; and WWII diaspora, 226, 247-48n42
Archiwum Emigracji (University of Toruń, Poland), 241
Archiwum Wschodnie of Ośrodek "Karta" (Eastern Archives of the "Charta" Center), 241
Arciszewski, Tomasz, 109, 197
Argentina, 24, 106, 236, 314n12
Armia Krajowa (Home Army; AK): historical records of, 241; oath sworn in, and Wyrwa affair, 188-89, 191-92; origins of, 18-19; resistance movement of, 23; soldiers' circles, 101; veterans' organization of, 141; and Warsaw Uprising, 49; women in, 31; Wyrwas in, 185
Arolsen DP camp (Germany), 97, 98
Assembly of Captive European Nations (ACEN), 198
assimilation: Great Depression and, 11; as source of conflict, 5, 172-76, 226, 229, 239; without loss of roots (*asymilacja bez wynarodowienia*), 240; WWII and, 247n39
Association for Cooperation with Polish Emigration "Polonia," 202
Association of Circles of Polish Technicians, 83

Association of Former Guards Units, 266n32
Association of Friends of the Polish Soldier, 152
Association of Iranian Studies, 27
Association of New Americans, 135-36, 177
Association of Polish Academicians, 274n119
Association of Polish Artists, 85
Association of Polish Engineers in Argentina, 236
Association of Polish ex-Combatants (SPK). *See* Stowarzyszenie Polskich Kombatantów
Association of Polish Jurists in the United States, 140
Association of Polish Lawyers, 84, 92
Association of Polish Performing Artists, 85
Association of Polish Physicians in Exile, 140
Association of Polish Pilots, 141
Association of Polish Teachers in Emigration in Germany, 86
Association of Polish War Refugees, 189
Association of Polish Women in Durzyń, 99-100
Association of Polish Writers in Exile, 220, 221
Association of Polish Writers in Germany, 276n143
Association of Polish Youth, 138-39
Association of Publishers and Booksellers, 84, 93
asymilacja bez wynarodowienia (assimilation without loss of roots), 240
Auerbach DP camp (Germany), 67
Auschwitz Nazi concentration camp (Poland), 18, 248n5
Australia, 105-6, 313n104, 314n12
Austria: concentration camps in, 23; DP camps in, 58, 59, 267n36; organizational separation in, 236; Polish press in, 275-76n141; Polish students in, 274n119

Bagiński, Kazimierz, 109-10

Baliński, Stanisław, 32
Balt Cygnet, 107
Bank Polski (Bank of Poland), 6
Bardowik-bei-Lüneberg (Germany), 77
Barzyński, Józef (Gen.), 154
Bataliony Chłopskie (Peasant Battalions), 19
Bayer, Walter, 44
Belgium, 105
Benda, W. T., 43
Berg affair, 197, 307n9
Bergen-Belsen concentration camp (Germany), 22, 23
Bezdroża dziejów Polski (Wyrwa), 240
Białous, Ryszard, 95
Biblioteka Kultury, 232
Bierut, Bolesław, 202, 205-6
Bigosiński, Jerzy, 22
Bik, Victor, 21-22, 314n11
Biuletyn Informacyjny (Ingolstadt, Germany), 91, 275n132
Biuletyn Informacyjny Dziennik Polski (Brunswick, Germany), 89-90
Biuletyn Organizacyjno-Informacyjny, 92
Biuletyn Polski, 274-75n129
black market, in DP camps, 68, 154-55
Blejwas, Stanislaus, 240-41
Bohdanowiczowa, Zofia, 34
Borowski, Tadeusz, 95
Bortnowski, Władysław, 298n83
Boston, 119-20, 138, 162
Bór-Komorowski, Tadeusz (Gen.), 181, 200, 212
Bratnie Pomoce Studentów Polaków, 88
Brazil, 24, 106, 236
Bremenhaven (Germany), 119
Bridgeport (Conn.), 138-39
Britain, Battle of (1940), 20
British Air Force of Occupation, 61
Broniewski, Władysław, 57
Bronowicz, Józef, 174-75
Brotherhood of Dispersed Solidarity Members, 229
Brygada Świętokrzyska, 60-61
Buchenwald concentration camp (Germany), 18, 23, 251n26

Buchhorst DP camp (Germany), 65
Budzyń, Bolesław, 212
Buffalo (N.Y.), 138, 176, 257n94
Bujak, Józef, 120
Bukowczyk, John J., 247n34, 288n94
Bulganin, Nikolai, 204
Burant, Felix (Feliks) F. (Msgr.), 115-16, 117, 123
Burke, Charles (Karol), 120
Burstin, Barbara Stern, 245-46n26, 280-81n21
Buszko, Józef, 248n5
Byrnes, James, 111

Cambridge Springs (Penn.), 44
Canada, 24, 106, 174, 236
Canadian Polish Congress, 233-34, 235-36
CARE, 68
Caritas, 76, 79
Carpathian Brigade, 28, 252-53n44
Carusi, Ugo, 119-20
catharsis naturalization, 313n104
Catholic Charities, 257n94
Catholic Committee for Refugees, 114, 282n32
CCDP (Citizens Committee on Displaced Persons), 111-12, 148
Central Archives of American Polonia, 241
Centrala Szkolnictwa Polskiego w Niemczech (Head Office for Polish Schools in Germany), 86, 87
Central Committee for Schools and Education, 86
Central Intelligence Agency (CIA), 307n9
Centralny Okręg Przemysłowy (Central Industrial Region), 6
Centraly Komitet dla Spraw Szkolnych i Oświatowych (Central Committee for Schools and Education), 86
Chałko, Zbigniew, 195
Charitable Association (Chicago), 132
Chicago: aid to refugees in, 45, 285n63; New Emigration/Old Polonia relations in, 145; New Emigration theater in, 138; Polish scouting in, 139; Polish women's organizations in, 41; refugee associations in, 44-45; WWII exile community in, 9-10
Chicago Sun-Times, 186
Chicago Tribune, 186
choirs, 136-37, 290n120
Chorągiew Jagiellonów (Jagiellonian Troop), 89
Chorągiew Wisła (Vistula Troop), 89
Christian Social Movement, 101
Churchill, Winston, 49-50, 274n129
Church World Service, 114
Ciechanowski, Jan, 45, 200, 258n111
Ciejko, Feliks, 137
Ciołkosz, Adam, 208, 310n47
Circle of Former Teachers and Pupils of the Polish High Schools from Germany, 140
Circle of Polish Professors and Teaching Assistants, 85, 273n105
Citizens Committee on Displaced Persons (CCDP), 111-12, 148
Clark, Tom, 119
class differences, as source of conflict, 165-72
Clay, Lucius D., 271n80
clergy: in DP camps, 75-77, 82, 269-70n65; and New Emigration, 145; Polish Saturday schools and, 138
Coburg DP camp (Germany), 67, 99
Cohen, Robin, 245n24
Cold War: and DP anticommunism, 156-57; DP camps and, 58; and DP question, 111; and DP school curriculum, 86-87; exile mission and, 72, 102, 109, 193-94, 222; exile politics and, 198-99; Katyń Massacre and, 199-201; and Wyrwa affair, 192
Colombia, 24
Committee for Polish Relief, 41
Committee for the Care of Poles Remaining in Ingolstadt, Germany, 143
Committee of Central and Eastern Europe, 198
Committee of National Defense, 35, 190-91
Community and War Chests, 42
community building in DP camps, 64, 71-82, 278n182; American Polonia press reporting on, 153; camp administration,

348 | Index

community building in DP camps (*cont.*) 71–75; citizens' court and, 81–82; DP organizations and, 98–99; exile mission and, 101–3; need for, 70; PU and, 77–80; religion and, 75–77, 270n66; welfare associations and, 80–81

concentration camp prisoners, Polish: as DPs in Germany, 60–61; organizations formed by, 23, 92, 101; and WWII diaspora, 21–23

concentration camps, Nazi, 18, 23, 248n5

Conference of Eastern and Central European Countries, 197–98

Congress of Free Polish Culture, 209–10, 310n52

Congress of Industrial Organizations (CIO), 11, 47, 258n111

Congress of Polish Culture in Exile, 232

Congress of Polish Science and Culture in Exile, 232

Connecticut, 138–39, 231, 290n120

Council of National Unity, 197, 215

Council of the Three, 110, 195, 197

culture, Polish: and diasporic unity, 231–32, 239; in DP camps, 95–98, 277n160; exile mission and, 14, 226; during interwar period, 5, 6–7; as source of collaboration, 176–79, 226, 239

Curie, Ewa, 34

Curzon Line, 49–50

Cwojdziński, Antoni, 37–38

Czechoslovakia: communist control of, 107–9; Stalinist liberalization in, 202; Velvet Revolution in, 239

Czereśniewski, Wawrzyniec, 261–62

Czermański, Zdzisław, 35

Ćwiklinski, Jan (Capt.), 207

Dachau concentration camp (Germany), 18, 23

D'Antonio, Guy J., 125

Dąbski, Kazimierz, 115, 124, 153

Defilada, 91

Democratic Movement, 109, 196

Democratic Party, 11, 201, 208, 213

Denmark, 237

Deszcz, Zofia, 188

détente, 204–5, 212, 225

Detroit, 130, 283n38

Dever, Paul, 120

diaspora, defined, 245n24

diaspora, Polish: and state in exile concept, 51; unity of, and exile mission, 223–24; during WWII, 16–31, 249n10

diaspora, Polish postwar: creation of, 104–10; economically motivated, 228–30; government in exile and, 109, 110; historical significance of, 241–42; origins of, 8, 19–20; political influence of, 305–6n174; post-October, 228–29; post-Solidarity, 229; unity of, and exile mission, 230–32, 314nn11–12. *See also* exile community in U.S., Polish; resettlement program (U.S.)

displaced persons: ethnic separation of, 62–64; international resettlement of, 8–9, 104; non-Polish, and exile mission, 237–39; numbers of, 59; repatriation of, 59–61, 262nn3–4; and social displacement syndrome, 163–65; Ukrainian, 246n27; unresettled, 262–63n9. *See also* displaced persons, Polish

displaced persons, Polish: anticommunism of, 156–57; conflicting media images of, 147–57; imprisonment of, 296n36; numbers of, 62, 251n31, 263–64n12; occupational skills of, 62, 63, 246n29, 264n16; resettlement of, 9–10, 104–10; resourcefulness of, 297n66; Ukrainian DPs classified as, 265n22; UNRRA mistreatment of, 149–50; vital statistics of, 61–62; vocational training for, 272n97. *See also* resettlement program (U.S.)

Displaced Persons Act (1948), 112–13; agricultural criteria in, 126; expiration of, 118; Jews admitted under, 245–46n26; Polish immigrants admitted under, 281n28; Polish veterans and, 29–30, 188; and Polonia propaganda campaign, 156–57; public charge feature of, 132; refugee influx following, 225

Index | 349

displaced persons camps: American Polonia and, 43, 147–57; Catholic clergy in, 269–70n65, 270n66; citizens' court at, 81–82; conflict in, 70–71, 266n25, 295n26; crime in, 154–55; cultural life in, 95–98, 277n160; education in, 85–88, 272n97, 273n115; elections in, 73–74; ethnic separation in, 62–64; exile mission in, 71–72; formation of, 8–9, 58–64; German/Polish name changes, 103; governance of, 72–75, 269n57, 295n26; Jews in, 265n19; leadership in, 72, 77–82, 102; libraries in, 93–94, 276n143; map, 59; New Emigration aid to, 142–43; newspapers/journals in, 89–93, 274–75n129, 275n132, 275–76n141; political parties in, 101; population transfers among, 67–68, 263–64n12, 267n35, 295n25; publications in, 93–95; religious life in, 75–77; sports in, 98; unresettled refugees remaining in, 262–63n9; and WWII diaspora, 26–28. *See also* community building in DP camps; organizations, DP; *specific camp*

displaced persons camps, conditions in, 64–71, 268n46; and American Polonia propaganda campaign, 149–50; clothing, 69, 267n41; food, 68, 267n36; health concerns, 69–70; of Jews, 265n19; and population transfers, 266n25; strikes against, 267n36, 295n26

Displaced Persons Commission (DPC), 112–13, 117, 118–19, 127, 281–82n28

Division for Vocational Training (Sekcja Szkolenia Zawodowego), 272n97

Dobczyński, Serafin, 166

Dobraczyński, Jan, 95

Dobrzański, Henryk (Maj.), 185, 304n154

Dodatko, Jan Zygmunt, 255n65

Dulles, John Foster, 204

Durzyń DP camp (Germany): DP organizations in, 77, 84; governance of, 74, 269n59; living conditions in, 65–66, 267n38; Ogiński Choir formed in, 136–37; women's circle in, 99–100

Dyczok, Marta, 265nn19, 22

Dymek, Franciszka (Frances), 118, 132, 134

Dziennik Chicagoski, 186, 187–88, 189–90, 314n11

Dziennik Dla Wszystkich, 173

Dziennik Informacyjny, 91

Dziennik Ludowy, 244n11

Dziennik Polski (Detroit): and New Emigration/Old Polonia conflict, 169; and Piłsudski Institute, 35; and Wyrwa affair, 187, 188, 190–91

Dziennik Polski (London): DP propaganda campaign of, 154; and New Emigration/Old Polonia conflict, 168–69; and reevaluation of exile mission, 218; and Wyrwa affair, 187, 189–90

Dziennik Związkowy, 120; conflicting images of DPs in, 165; DP propaganda campaign of, 153, 154, 295n26; on DP welcome ceremonies, 119; and New Emigration, 143, 145; on "Polonian" dialect, 172–73; and resettlement-related conflict, 162; on Wyrwa affair, 186, 187–88

Dziennik Żołnierza, 91, 110, 218

Dzienny Biuletyn Radiowy, 91

Dziewońska-Krzemieńska, Elżbieta, 137

Eastern Archives of the "Charta" Center, 241

Ebensee DP camp (Austria), 66, 149, 294n14

Echo Dnia, 91

education. *See* schools/schooling

Eisenhower, Dwight D., 197, 200–201, 204, 205

Ellis Island (N.Y.), 116

employment/employment problems: of intellectuals, 128–29, 288n94, 298–99n83; job hopping, 129–30; and parish membership, 292n145; in rural areas, 121–28; unemployment/underemployment, 128–29, 298–99n83; in urban areas, 128; of WWII refugees, 24

endecja, 101, 109

Epstein, Julius, 200

Erdmans, Mary Patrice, 293n1

Exhibition of Polish Cultural and Educational Publications Printed in the American, British, and French Zones of Germany (Wiesbaden, 1946), 94 exile community in U.S., Polish: in American military, 185–92, 305–6n174, 306n176; American Polonia and, 39–57; and diasporic unity, 230–32; exile mission and, 14–15, 135; nineteenth-century, 2–4; organizational separation in, 182–85, 236–37; parish-based structure of, 3–4; and party politics, 302n138; and Poland as imagined community, 247–48n42; political influence of, 305–6n174; post-October immigrants and, 228–29; post-Solidarity immigrants and, 229; residential patterns of, 292n145; and Soviet intervention in Hungary, 217–18; during WWII, 24–25, 31–39. *See also* New Emigration; New Emigration/Old Polonia conflict; New Emigration/Old Polonia cooperation

exile mission: American Polonia and, 15, 39, 204–5, 219, 226; anticommunism and, 179–80, 221–23; Catholic clergy and, 76; communist liberalizations and, 204–5; and cultural leadership, 177–79, 226; and diasporic unity, 223–24, 230–32, 314nn11–12; and DP community building, 71–72, 102–3; DP organizations and, 77, 82, 83, 100–101; DP publications and, 90, 94–95; future goals of, 239–41; government in exile and, 109, 110; and historical memory, 14; historical significance of, 241–42; Lelewel on, 54; national celebrations and, 96; New Emigration and, 12–15, 141–42; and New Emigration/Old Polonia relations, 12–15, 147, 242; of non-Poles, 237–39; and obligation to homeland, 2–3, 13–14; political elements of, 221–23; and Poznań Massacre, 215; reevaluations of, 5–7, 204–11, 218–21, 224–27; Romantic roots of, 1–2, 223, 225; *Wolna Polska* and, 206–7; WWII and, 8–9, 30–31; WWII exile community and, 33, 55–57; Wyrwa affair and, 185–94. *See also* political activism

Facts About the Polish War Relief, The (Rada Polonii), 42

Fallingsbostel DP camp (Germany), 100, 278n175
family life: in American Polonia, 3–4; in DP camps, 99; exile mission and, 14–15
Federation of Sport and Gymnastic Associations, 92
Fiedler, Arkady, 34
First Armored Division Veterans Association, 141
First Independent Parachute Brigade, 61
First Polish Armored Division, 20, 61, 241
First Polish Corps, 20
Flossenburg concentration/DP camp (Germany), 23, 67, 140
Floyar-Rajchman, Henryk, 35, 47, 57
Ford Motor Company, strike against, 258n111
France, 24, 41, 106, 236–37
Frank, Hans, 17
Freedom for Poland, 229
Fundusz Obrony Narodowej (National Defense Fund; FON), 40
Fundusz Społeczny (Social Fund), 67
Fundusz Społeczny Kompanii Wartowniczych (Welfare Fund of the Polish Guards), 79
Fundusz Społeczny Stowarzyszenia Polskich Weteranów (Welfare Fund of the Polish Veterans Association), 79–80
Fundusz Wysiedleńczy (DP Fund), 133

Gawlina, Józef (Bishop), 75
Gdynia (Poland), 6
Gebert, Bolesław, 11
Geesthacht DP camp (Germany), 65, 72, 85
General Black (ship), 119
Generalna Gubernia (General Government), 17
Geneva Summit (1955), 204–5
Germanization, Poles intended for, 22, 60
Germany: Berlin Wall destroyed in, 239; concentration camps in, 23; deportations of Poles to, 21–23, 250n18; DP camps in, 58, 59; illegal border crossings into, 296n36; invasion/occupation of Poland, 16–21; organizational consoli-

dation in, 236; persecution of Polish Catholic clergy, 75
Gerö, Erö, 216
Gertler, Władysław, 235–36
ghettoization, 175–76, 180
Giedroyć, Jerzy, 198
Gierat, Stanisław, 183, 219, 234, 313n107
Gieysztor, Władysław, 55–56
Giller, Agaton, 2–3
girl scouts, 139, 251n26
Głos Ludowy, 48
Głos Polski, 275n132
Główna Komisja Porozumiewawcza Środowisk Polskich (Main Commission for the Coordination of Polish Communities), 77
Goetel, Ferdynand, 95
Goisern (Austria), 295n26
Goldring, Henryk, 95
Gombrowicz, Witold, 232
Gomułka, Władysław, 201, 216, 218
gomułkowszczyzna (Gomułka-sponsored liberalization), 218
government in exile, Polish: American Polonia and, 226; antirepatriation propaganda of, 71; diplomatic efforts of, 249n9; disbandment of (1989), 239; and DP school curriculum, 86–87; establishment of, 16; inflexibility of, 203, 218; internal divisions within, 109–10, 181, 196–97, 207; and Katyń Massacre investigation, 248n43; maximum demands concept of, 218; naturalization discouraged by, 51; and New Emigration/Old Polonia conflict, 180–81; and Polish independence, 218; and provisional Polish government, 107; PU and, 79, 82; relevance of questioned, 215, 226; unrecognized in West, 43, 50–51; WWII aid efforts, 45; and Wyrwa affair, 190
Grabski, Władysław, 6
Grayson, Wilmer, 125
Graz (Austria), 274n119
Great Britain: party politics in, 302n138; Polish exile community in, 24–25, 41, 224, 225–26; Polish-language press in, 219; Polish veterans resettled from, 286n72
Great Depression, 11, 247n34
Great Emigration. *See* Wielka Emigracja
Grey Ranks, 19
Gross, Feliks, 228
Gross-Rosen concentration camp (Germany), 21–22, 23
Grot-Kwaśniewski, Jerzy, 94
Grydzewski, Mieczysław, 32
Grygorcewicz, Wacław, 290n120
Gubala, Tadeusz, 22
Gunther, Blair F., 118
Gurda, Leon M., 283n38
Guzłowski, John, 267n35
Gwardia Ludowa (People's Guard), 19

Habielski, Rafał, 224
Haiman, Miecislaus, 10–11
Halecki, Oskar, 36, 210
Hall, Dudley S., 287n82
Haller, Józef (Gen.), 4
Haller's Army, 34, 40, 184
Hamtramck (Mich.), 11
Hanke, Hugon, 203, 308n31
harcerstwo. See Związek Harcerstwa Polskiego
Haren (Germany), 66
Harrison, Earl G., 265n19
Head Office for Polish Schools in Germany, 86, 87
Heberle, Rudolf, 287n82
Hebrew Sheltering and Immigration Aid Society, 114
Heilbronn DP camp (Germany), 89
Herald-American, 186
Herling-Grudziński, Gustaw, 232
Hertz, Aleksander, 179
Higgins, Lawrence E., 125
Hofmański, Bogdan, 95
Hohenfels (Germany). *See* Lechów DP camp (Germany)
Holborn, Louise W., 281n28
Holocaust Museum (Washington, D.C.), 242
Holocaust survivors, and Jewish Americans, 238–39

352 | Index

Holy Cross Brigade (Brygada Świętokrzyska), 60–61
Home Army. *See* Armia Krajowa
Home Army Veterans Association, 141
Hoover, Herbert, 41
housing, for resettled DPs, 121
Hrabyk, Klaudiusz: on DP political parties, 278n180, 302n138; on DP resourcefulness, 297n66; on DP underemployment, 298–99n83; and *Polska*, 90; and reevaluation of exile mission, 205, 219–20; repatriation to Poland, 203; resignation from Congress of Free Polish Culture, 210; on women in DP press, 277–78n171; and Wyrwa affair, 187, 305n169
Hubal (Maj.). *See* Dobrzański, Henryk
Hulme, Kathryn, 66, 104–5, 267n38, 269n59
Hungary: communist control ends in (1989), 239; communist control of, 107–9; DPs from, and exile mission, 238; liberalization in, 202, 313n104; Polish exile community in, 24, 41; Soviet military intervention in (1956), 216–18, 225
"Hymn of Poles in Exile" (Lechoń), 242

Iciek, S. A. (Rev.), 53
identity, Polish. *See* assimilation, as source of conflict
Iłłakowiczówna, Kazimiera, 32
immigrants, Polish, 229; in American military, 185–92, 305–6n174; American Polonia and, 31–32, 135–36; economically motivated, 228–30; as emigrants, 243n6, 248n45; exile mission and, 103; and interwar restrictions, 5; and naturalization, 313nn104, 107; nineteenth-century, 1–4, 225; numbers of, 3, 9, 31, 228, 281–82n28; political vs. economic, 301n129; post-October, 228–29; post-Solidarity, 229; postwar, 264–65n18; quotas for, 245n25; during WWII, 9, 31–39, 254n53. *See also* exile community in U.S., Polish; resettlement program (U.S.)
Immigrants' Protective League, 131
Immigration and Naturalization Service (INS), 9, 31, 254n53, 281n28

immigration laws: American Polonia and, 112, 147–48; and mortgaging against quotas, 281n23. *See also* Displaced Persons Act; sponsorship; Truman Directive
immigration procedures, 120–21
Independence and Democracy (NiD), 109, 199
India, 27
Industrial Workers of the World, 244n11
Informacja Prasowa, 91
Ingolstadt DP camp (Germany): cultural life in, 97, 277n160; library in, 94, 276n143; New Emigration aid to, 143; patriotic celebrations in, 95–96; and Polonia propaganda campaign, 153; sports in, 98
Instytut Literacki, 29
intelligentsia: anticlericalism of, 76; and diasporic unity, 231–32; as DP leadership, 72, 102; and DP publications, 95; during interwar period, 6–7; Nazi extermination of, 17–18; New Emigration and, 144–45; occupational skills of, 62, 106–7, 166; and Polonia/DP class differences, 166–72; and Polonian cultural life, 177–79; and reevaluation of exile mission, 220; and repatriation pressure, 202–3, 220; resettlement problems of, 128–29, 288n94, 298–99n83; in WWII diaspora, 34–35; in WWII exile community, 9–10, 55
International Bureau for DP Collaboration (Międzynarodowe Biuro Porozumiewawcze DP), 64
International Committee of DPs and Political Exiles in Germany, 98
International Refugee Organization (IRO): and ACRPDP, 117; and DP camp administration, 73; and DP camp conditions, 69, 263–64n12, 295n25; and DP Olympic competition, 98; and DP repatriation, 60, 61–62, 63–64; and DP resettlement, 104, 123, 128, 246n27; and DP schools, 87; PU and, 79, 264n16, 271n79; and unresettled DPs, 262–63n9
International Women's League, 277n170
International Workers Order, 47

Iran, 26–27
Irons, Peter H., 258n110
Italy, 58
Iwańska, Alicja, 299n83
Iwaszkiewicz, Jarosław, 32

Jagiellonian Troop, 89
Jagiellonian University (Kraków), 17
Janda, Wiktoria, 34
Janta, Aleksander, 54; on American Polonia and Polish language, 173, 174, 300n107; on Polonian cultural life, 176–77; on Polonian organizational rigidity, 182; on WWII exile community, 38
January Uprising (1863), 1
Januszewski, Frank, 35, 47, 52
Janusz, Grzegorz, 271n79
Jaroszewski, Wł., 277n170
Jews: in DP camps, 63, 265n19; and Holocaust survivors, 238–39; Nazi extermination of, 18; resettlement of, 245–46n26, 280–81n21
Jeż, Tomasz Teodor, 223
Jędrzejczak, Wacław, 21
Jędrzejewicz, Wacław, 35, 47, 51–52
job hopping, 129–30
journals. *See* newspapers/journals
Józef Piłsudski Institute for Research in the Modern History of Poland, 35, 52, 254–55n65
Jur-Sten, Jerzy, 276n143
Jutro Pracy, 91

Kaczmarek, Józef, 188
Kaczorowski, Ryszard, 239
Kádár, János, 217
Kania, Józef, 114, 181
Karasiewicz, Joseph, 187, 190–91
Karcz, Walerian (Rev.), 118
Karpińska-Gierat, Ewa, 231, 313n107
Karyntia (Austria), 72
Katyń Massacre, 25;; American Polonia and, 199–201, 207, 208; London exile community and, 204; political impact of, 47–48, 248n43
Kenya, 27

Khrushchev, Nikita, 201–2, 204–5
Kister, Hanna, 34
KNAPP. *See* Komitet Narodowy Amerykanów Polskiego Pochodzenia
koła akowskie (Home Army soldiers' circles), 101
Koło Artystów Sceny Polskiej (Polish Actors' Circle), 36–37
Koło Byłych Wychowawców i Wychowanków Polskich Szkół Średnich z Niemiec (Circle of Former Teachers and Pupils of the Polish High Schools from Germany), 140
Koło Kobiet (Women's Circle), 278n176
Koło Profesorów i Asystentów Polaków (Circle of Polish Professors and Teaching Assistants), 85, 273n105
Kołpak, Jan, 130–31
Kombatant w Ameryce, 142
komendanci, DP camp, 72–73
Komitet Narodowy Amerykanów Polskiego Pochodzenia (National Committee of Americans of Polish Descent; KNAPP): leadership of, 167; political activism of, 47–48, 49, 51–52; significance of, 55
Komitet Niesienia Pomocy Polakom Pozostałym w Ingolstadt (Niemcy) (Committee for the Care of Poles Remaining in Ingolstadt, Germany), 143
Komitet Obrony Narodowej (Committee of National Defense; KON), 35, 190–91
Komitet Pomocy Uchodźcom, 80
Komitet Wolnej Europy (National Committee for a Free Europe; KWE), 196, 198, 202–3, 210
Kompanie Wartownicze (Polish Guards): demobilization of, 266n32; as DPs in Germany, 294n16; journal published by, 67, 92, 93; and PU, 271n78; resettlement in U.S., 122–24, 286n71; training centers for, 66–67, 276n143; welfare fund of, 79
Komski, Jan, 95
Konarski, Feliks, 138
Koncius, Joseph B., 125
Kopański, Stanisław (Gen.), 106

Koprowska, Irena, 24
Korboński, Stefan, 109–10
Korczak, Władysław, 44
Korean War, 201, 305n174; Wyrwa affair and, 185–94
Korpus Przysposobienia i Rozmieszczenia (Polish Resettlement Corps; KPR), 106–7
Kosciuszko Foundation, 5, 41, 234
Kosciuszko League, 47
Kosidowski, Zenon, 33
Kosiński, Jerzy, 232
Kossak-Szczucka, Zofia, 203
Kościuszko, Tadeusz, 227
Kowalik, Jan, 154
Kowalski, Jan, 255n65
Kozielsk POW camp (Soviet Union), 25
Kraj (radio station), 202
Krasiński, Zygmunt, 2
Krawiec, Jan (John), 233, 274–75n129
Kronika, 92–93, 271n81, 277–78n171, 278n175
Kronika Dnia, 91
Krzemieński, Lucjan, 137, 290n121
Krzemińska, Julia, 278n175
Krzycki, Leo, 11, 46–47, 50, 244n11
Kucharzewski, Jan, 36
Kukiel, Marian, 196
Kulig, 231
Kulpiński, Piotr, 255n65
Kultura (Paris): and communist repatriation propaganda, 203; and diasporic unity, 198, 232, 314n11; and exile intellectuals, 220–21, 225; founding of, 29
Kuncewicz, Jerzy, 138–39
Kunz, Egon F., 313n104
Kuryer Codzienny (Boston), 186, 188
Kuryer Polski (Milwaukee), 136, 173–74, 188, 213
Kusielewicz, Eugene, 234, 315–16n22
Kwaśniewski, Stanisław, 13, 247n41

Labor Movement (SP), 101, 109, 196
labor unrest, 4, 11, 128, 258n111
Lagodzinska, Adela, 118, 134
Landowska, Wanda, 34
Lane, Arthur Bliss, 200, 201
Lange, Oskar, 47, 48–49, 259n121
Langiewicz, Jan, 169
language, Polish vs. Polonian, 172–74, 300n107
Latvian immigrants, 237, 317–18n36
Lauenberg DP camp (Germany), 266n25
leadership, Polish: cultural, 177–78; in DP camps, 72, 77–82, 102; Nazi extermination of, 17
League of Poland's Independence in Germany, 101
Lechoń, Jan: as exile in New York, 168; as exile mission symbol, 227; "Hymn of Poles in Exile," 242; and Piłsudski Institute, 35; as Skamandrite, 32; suicide of, 57, 211; and *Tygodnik*, 34, 38, 52–54, 56–57
Lechów DP camp (Germany): community building in, 278n182; cultural life in, 97–98; governance of, 74; living conditions in, 67; religious life in, 76; welfare committee at, 80
Lednicki, Wacław, 36, 178
Legion Młodych Polek (Legion of Young Polish Women), 41, 145
Lelewel, Joachim, 2, 54
Lesinski, John, 48, 123
Lewandowski, Robert, 138
libraries, 93–94, 175
Liga Niepodległości Polski w Niemczech (League of Poland's Independence in Germany), 101
Lilpop-Krancowa, Felicja, 34
Literary Club, 276n143
Lithuania/Lithuanian immigrants, 41, 237
Little Poland in exile: in DP camps, 102; Maczków as capital of, 66; PU and, 82; and repatriation, 71
London: Polish exile community in, 225–26; Polish exile demonstrations in, 204; Polish press in, 110. *See also* government in exile, Polish
Long Island Operations, 123–24
Lorentowicz, Irena: and American Polonia, 55; as member of WWII exile community, 24, 38, 56, 255n65; repatriation to Poland, 57; and *Tygodnik*, 34

Los Angeles, 138
Louisiana, DP resettlement in, 124-25, 287n82
Louisiana State DP Commission, 125
Louisiana State University, 287n82
Ludwigsburg DP camp (Germany), 71, 74, 100

łapanki (manhunts), 21
Łuczak, Czesław, 249nn10-11, 250n18, 251n26, 277n170
Łukaczyński, Zbigniew, 155
Łukomski, Kazimierz, 233, 234-35

Machcewicz, Paweł, 305n174
Machrowicz, Tadeusz, 206
Mackiewicz, Stanisław, 195, 203
Maczek, Stanisław (Gen.), 20, 61
Maczków (Germany), 66
Main Commission for the Coordination of Polish Communities, 77
Maiski, Ivan, 46
Malenkov, Georgi, 201
Malinowski, Bronisław, 36, 57
Małkowski, Andrzej, 89
Mannheim-Kafertal DP camp (Germany), 67
Marine Flasher (ship), 120
Markeles, Lazar, 45
Massachussetts DP Commission, 128-29
Matuszewski, Ignacy, 35, 47, 57, 167
Mauthausen concentration camp (Germany), 23, 251n26
maximum demands concept (*żądania maksymalne*), 218, 219, 225
Mazewski, Aloysius A., 233, 234, 235-36
McCarthyism, 199, 307-8n18
McNamara, John Michael, 214
mental illness, 130-31, 289n105
Mexico, 24, 28, 43
Miami, 124
Michalski, Jan, 65, 72, 267n38
Michalski, Stanisław, 193
Mickiewicz, Adam, 1-2, 177, 227
Mickiewicz Centennial (1953), 36
Middle East, crisis in, 215

Mieroszewski, Juliusz, 220-21, 232
Międzynarodowe Biuro Porozumiewawcze DP, 64
Migała, Bonawentura, 121
migration, psychological effects of, 163-65
Mikołajczyk, Stanisław: American Polonia and, 198-99; and communist takeover of Poland, 107; and exile politics, 109-10, 181, 195-96; and Katyń Massacre investigation, 200; as prime minister, 48
military, Polish: under British command, 20; as DP community, 66-67; in Germany, 60-61; newspapers/journals of, 91-92; resettlement in U.S., 112, 117, 122-24, 140-41, 282n28, 286n72; in Russia, 26; theater company supported by, 97; in WWII, 28-30, 249n9, 250n16, 252-53n44; and Wyrwa affair, 185-92. *See also* Anders Army; Armia Krajowa; Haller's Army; Kompanie Wartownicze; veterans organizations; *specific corps*
Milwaukee (Wis.), 135-36, 177, 283n38
Miłosz, Czesław, 232
Minnesota DP Commission, 130
Mississippi, 287n82
Młody Polak, 91
Moc, Aleksander, 188
Mochnacki, Maurycy, 2
Modelski, Tadeusz, 252-53n44
Modzelewska, Maria, 34, 37
Montana, 124
Morawski, Ignacy, 190
Mostwin, Danuta, 246n29, 264-65n18, 292n145, 302n138
Mościcki, Ignacy, 109
Mówią Wieki (scouting journal), 89
Mruk, Joseph, 48
Muhlstein, Anatol, 34
Munich DP camp (Germany), 99, 273n105
Murnau incident, 152
Mury (underground girl scouts), 251n26
Mutual Aid Association of the New Polish Emigration, 135, 136

Nagórski, Zygmunt, 168-69, 182

Nagy, Ferenc, 198
Nagy, Imre, 216
Nahurski, Francis J., 130
Nakoneczna, Zofia, 37
Narodowe Siły Zbrojne (National Armed Forces), 19, 60-61
Naród Polski, 75
Nasza Reduta (theater group), 137-38
Nasze Myśli, 91-92
Nasze Życie, 91
Na Szlaku, 92
National Armed Forces, 19, 60-61
National Catholic Welfare Conference (NCWC): aid to DP camps, 69; and DP resettlement, 113, 122-23, 282n32; founding of, 114; Louisiana resettlement cases reviewed by, 125; PIC and, 117; PU and, 79; War Relief Services, 114; WWII aid efforts, 43-44, 257n94
National Committee for a Free Europe. *See* Komitet Wolnej Europy
National Committee of Americans of Polish Descent. *See* Komitet Narodowy Amerykanów Polskiego Pochodzenia
National Councils in Exile, 196
National Defense Fund, 40
National Democratic Movement, 101, 109
nationalism, 2-3, 243n3
National Origins Act (1924), 245n25, 281n23
National Resettlement Council (NRC), 114, 282n32
National Union of Agricultural Workers, 106
National Union of Mineworkers, 106
National War Fund, 42
naturalization, 51, 313nn104, 107
NCWC. *See* National Catholic Welfare Conference
Nestorówna, Lunia, 37
Netherlands, 106
Neuengamme concentration camp (Germany), 23
Neue Zeitung, Die, 154
New Deal, 11
New Emigration: aid to DP camps, 142-43; compared to London exile community, 225-26; cultural organizations, 136-38; and exile mission, 12-15, 204-5, 219; First Convention of, 13; historical records of, 241; lay character of, 144-45; organizational consolidation by, 143-44; and reestablishment of community, 135; scouting troops, 138-40; self-help organizations, 135-36; and tourism in Poland, 203-4; veterans organizations, 140-42
New Emigration/Old Polonia conflict: and assimilation, 172-76, 226; and class differences, 165-72; and cultural life, 176-79; and differing needs, 293n1; exile mission and, 12-15; and historical misconceptions, 157-61; and international Polonia congress, 233-34; later-generation Polonians and, 236; and media images of DPs, 147-57; and organizational separation, 182-85, 236-37; and party politics, 180-82; and resettlement process, 161-65; significance of, 15, 192-94; and social displacement syndrome, 163-65; and Wyrwa affair, 185-92, 305n169
New Emigration/Old Polonia cooperation, 145-46; anticommunism and, 179-80, 193-94, 239; communist liberalizations and, 204-5; exile mission and, 15, 225-27, 242; and international Polonia congress, 235-36; and PAC leadership, 232-33; and political activism, 195-205, 209-10, 225-27, 232-33, 239; and Poznań Massacre, 212-15, 226-27
New Orleans, 119, 125
newspapers/journals: in DP camps, 89-93, 274-75n129, 275n132, 275-76n141; and exile mission, 94-95; of Polish Guards, 67; of radical organizations, 244n11. *See also* press, Polish; press, Polish-American; *specific publication*
New York: aid to refugees in, 45; DP welcome ceremony in, 119-20; New Emigration theater in, 138; Pułaski Day parade in (1956), 227; refugee associations in, 44-45; WWII exile community in, 9-10, 33-34, 36-37, 38-39

New York Times, 205
New Zealand, 28
Niepodległość i Demokracya (Independence and Democracy; NiD), 109, 199
niezłomność (uncompromising political attitude), 110
Nixon, Richard M., 308n22
Norwid, Cyprian Kamil, 2
November Uprising (1830), 1
Nowak, Stanley, 11
Nowak-Jeziorański, Jan, 198
Nowakowski, Tadeusz, 151, 268n46
Nowakowski, Zygmunt, 187
Nowicka, Stanisława, 37
Nowicki, Stella, 11
Nowiny Polskie, 175
Nowotarska, Róża, 99, 277n171
Nowy Świat: and aid to DP camps, 143; and Americanization, 175; and anticommunism, 179–80; and diasporic unity, 314n11; DP propaganda campaign of, 150–53, 294n16, 295n26, 296n36; and DP resettlement, 123, 126; and Polonia/DP class differences, 166, 167–69, 171–72; on reevaluation of exile mission, 205; on Wyrwa affair, 187–88, 190

Oberlangen POW camp (Germany), 58
Obertyńska, Beata, 34
Obrębski, Jan, 153
Ochab, Edward, 206
O'Connor, Edward M., 132
O'Dwyer, William, 119
Oflagen. *See* prisoners of war, Polish
Ogiński Choir, 136–37
Ognisko Restaurant (New York), 38
Okólnik, 70–71
Okręg Armii Krajowej na Stany Zjednoczone (Home Army Veterans Association in the United States), 141
Olejniczak, Jan (John), 127
Oleńska, Nina, 138
Olszewski, Witold, 91
Operation Spotlight, 197, 307n9
Organisation Todt, Polish deserters from, 250n16

organizations, American Polonia: and DP resettlement, 113–18; exile community and, 182–85, 236–37; fraternal, 4, 5, 40; libraries of, 175. *See also* American Committee for the Resettlement of Polish DP's; Polish American Congress; Rada Polonii Amerykańskiej; *specific organization*
organizations, DP: and Catholic clergy, 76–77; and civic leadership, 77–82; political parties, 101, 278n180; professional, 84–85; schools, 85–88; scouting, 88–89; trade unions, 82–84; veterans organizations, 100–101; welfare work of, 79–81; women's circles, 99–100, 277–78n171, 278n176. *See also specific organization*
organizations, exile: American Polonia and, 182–85, 236–37; and cultural exchanges, 315–16n22. *See also* New Emigration; *specific organization*
Orlemański, Stanisław, 47, 48–49, 259n121
Ormsby, J. Stanley, 124
orphans, Polish, 43–44, 257n94
Orzechowski, Emil, 291n123
Orzeł Biały, 78, 205, 218
Ossetyński, Leonidas Dudarew, 168, 175, 182
Ostaszków POW camp (Soviet Union), 25
Ostatnie Wiadomości, 67, 92, 93
Oświęcim Nazi concentration camp (Poland), 18, 248n5

PAC. *See* Polish American Congress
Paczkowski, Jerzy, 56
Paderewski, Ignacy Jan, 4
Pająk, Antoni, 218
Paraguay, 106
parish, in exile community, 3–4, 144, 292n145
Parnicki, Teodor, 203
Passowicz, Jan, 80
Pastorałka (Christmas play), 37–38
patriotism: Catholic clergy and, 76; in DP cultural life, 95–96; in DP school curriculum, 87; exile mission and, 2–3; immigrant anticommunism and, 199; Polish

patriotism (cont.)
    Saturday schools and, 138; scouting and, 88–89; Wyrwa affair and, 187
Pawlikowska-Jasnorzewska, Maria, 32
Pawłowski, Józef, 118
Peasant Battalions, 19
Pennsylvania Commission on Displaced Persons, 129
People's Guard, 19
People's Movement "Freedom," 101, 109
Peretiakowicz, Hanna, 137–38
Pestki (Women's Auxiliary Service), 31
Philadelphia, PAC convention in (1948), 316n25
PIASA. *See* Polish Institute of Arts and Sciences in America
PIC. *See* Polish Immigration Committee
Pienkos, Donald, 256n82
Piłsudskiites, 47, 52, 109
Piotrowska, Irena, 34
Piskorski, Florian, 97
Pismo Żołnierza, 91
Pittsburgh, 238–39
Plater-Zyberk, Maria, 171
Plusdrak, Edward E., 118, 132
PNA. *See* Polish National Alliance
Podkopacz, Helena, 16, 25, 28, 104
Pokrzywy, 92
Poland: American Polonia and, 4–5; Catholicism persecuted in, 208; Central Industrial Region in, 6; communist control ends in (1989), 239; communists seize power in, 107–9; Constitution (1935), 109; cultural exchanges with, 315–16n22; Curzon Line, 49–50; economic aid to, 213–14, 227; exile archives transferred to, 241; as imagined community, 247–48n42; independence and exile mission, 4–5, 13–14, 221–23, 224–25; independence of (1918), 5; interwar modernization in, 6–7; liberalization in, 201–2, 214, 218–19, 227, 228, 313n104; Nazi concentration camps in, 18, 248n5; Nazi deportations from, 21–23; Nazi-occupied, 16–21; Nazi/Soviet invasions of, 7–8, 16–17; opposition forces in, 224–25; Polish October (1956), 205–6, 216–21, 225; post-October emigration from, 228–30; provisional government of, 50, 107; relations restored with Soviet Union, 46; repatriation to encouraged, 202–3, 308–9n31; Solidarity movement in, 229; Soviet-occupied, 25–26; tourism in, 203–4, 220–21, 227; U.S. intelligence efforts in, 197, 307n9; and Yalta agreement, 49–50; *złoty* currency introduced in, 6
Poland's Children (Rada Polonii), 42–43
Pole Jump, 107
Polish Academic Association, 140
Polish Academy of Arts and Sciences, 36
Polish Actors' Circle, 36–37
Polish Airborne Forces Veterans Association in America, 141
Polish Air Force, 241
Polish American Congress (PAC), 113; aid to Poland, 227; and American administration, 198–99; and anticommunism, 180; and diasporic unity, 316n25; DP mistreatment reported to, 152; DP propaganda campaign of, 149–50, 155; and DP resettlement, 115, 117–18, 120–21, 123, 133; and exile mission, 15, 205, 209–10; founding of, 11, 49, 53, 259n121; and government in exile, 181, 207–10; and international Polonia congress, 234–36; and Katyń Massacre investigation, 199–201; KNAPP and, 55; leadership in, 183, 232–33; and New Emigration/Old Polonia relations, 183, 232–33; opposition to UNRRA, 111–12, 149–50; and party politics, 180–81, 207, 302n138; and PIASA, 36; and Poles in American military, 190; and Poznań Massacre, 211–13; Yalta opposed by, 50, 111, 213
Polish American Historical Association (PAHA), 35, 36
Polish American Labor Council, 182
Polish Americans. *See* Polonia, American
Polish American Studies, 36
Polish Armed Forces in the West, 140–41
Polish Army in France, 4–5
Polish Army in Russia, 26
Polish Army Veterans Association in

America (SWAP). *See* Stowarzyszenie Weteranów Armii Polskiej
Polish Artists' Theater, 37-38
Polish Arts Clubs, 5
Polish Association of ex-Political Prisoners in the United States, 142, 241
Polish Association of Former Political Prisoners of German Concentration Camps, 92, 101
Polish Association of Former Soviet Political Prisoners, 200
Polish Catholic Academic Association "Veritas," 145
Polish Central Advisory Council, 87
Polish Council of Trade Unions, 82-83
Polish Cultural Clubs, 174, 176
Polish Guards. *See* Kompanie Wartownicze
Polish Immigration Committee (PIC): aid to DP camps, 143; and DP resettlement, 113, 115-17, 122-23; Polish War Refugee Association and, 46; and Poznań Massacre, 212; and resettlement of Hungarian freedom fighters, 217
Polish Institute of Arts and Sciences in America (PIASA), 35, 36, 52, 210
Polish Labor Party, 47
Polish Military Mission (USFET-Frankfurt/M), 272n97
Polish Museum of America, 5, 54
Polish National Alliance (PNA): censor office in, 246n30; and exile mission, 2-3; members in American military, 259n112; and PAC Illinois division, 133; and Poznań Massacre, 212; PRCU and, 2; and Rada, 256n79; scout troops organized by, 291n126; WWII aid efforts, 41, 43-44
Polish National Catholic Church Relief and Resettlement Center, 114
Polish National Democratic Committee, 195-96
Polish National Theater, 36-37
Polishness. *See* assimilation, as source of conflict
Polish October (1956), 205-6, 216-21, 225

Polish Peasant Party, 107, 109-10, 196
Polish Red Cross, 69, 79, 80
Polish Repatriation Mission, 92
Polish Resettlement Corps (PRC), 106-7
Polish Roman Catholic Union (PRCU), 2-3, 256n79, 259n112, 291n126
Polish Sappers Veterans Association of the USA, 141
Polish Singers Alliance of America, 137
Polish Socialist Party (PPS), 101, 109
Polish Society of Arts and Sciences Abroad, 241
Polish Students Association, 88, 274n119
Polish Technical College (Esslingen, Germany), 83, 88
Polish Union in Germany (PU). *See* Zjednoczenie Polskie w Niemczech
Polish Union in the American Zone of Occupation in Germany, 77
Polish Veterans Association, 79-80, 92
Polish Victory Service, 18-19
Polish War Refugee Association, 44-46
Polish War Relief. *See* Rada Polonii Amerykańskiej
Polish Welfare, 80
Polish Women's Alliance (PWA), 41, 256n79, 259n112
Polish Work Abroad, 97
political activism: of American Polonia, 2-3, 40, 46-52, 112, 147-48, 205-11, 258n110; anticommunism and, 179-80, 221-23; exile mission and, 179, 181-82, 195-205; as source of collaboration, 195-205, 209-10, 225-27, 232-33, 239
Political Council, 110, 181, 195, 198-99, 307n9
political parties: American Polonia and, 226, 302n138; in DP camps, 101, 278n180; and exile politics, 195-96; government in exile and, 109-10; inflexibility of, 218; and New Emigration/Old Polonia conflict, 180-82; PAC and, 207. *See also specific party*
political prisoners, Polish: DP publications of, 92; organizations formed by, 101, 142, 200; PAC and, 208; and WWII diaspora, 21-22

360 | Index

Polonia: defined, 243n4; international congresses of, 233-36; transformation of exiles into, 240-41
Polonia, American: aid to DP camps, 110-11; aid to Hungary, 217; aid to Poland, 4-5, 11, 213-14; in American military, 11, 46, 256n82, 258-59n112; assimilation of, 11-12, 175, 247n39; and closing of DP schools, 273n115; cultural life of, 176-79; diplomatic efforts of, 249n9; DP propaganda campaign of, 147-57; and DP resettlement, 12, 113-18, 120-21, 133-34, 282-83n36; and DP welfare problems, 81; and exile mission, 15, 39, 204-5, 219, 226; and government in exile, 207-8; Great Depression and, 247n34; historical records of, 241; and immigration law, 112, 147-48; during interwar period, 5-7; Katyń Massacre and, 199-201; labor activism of, 4, 244n11; and McCarthyism, 307-8n18; and media images of DPs, 148; New Emigration and, 135-36; nineteenth-century debate within, 2-3; opposition to UNRRA repatriation policies, 111-12; parish-based structure of, 3-4, 292n145; parish-centered organizations of, 144; and party politics, 302n138; and Polish language, 172-74, 300n107; political activism of, 2-3, 40, 46-52, 112, 147-48, 205-11, 258n110; post-Solidarity immigrants and, 229; and Poznań Massacre, 211-15; and Republican Party, 308n22; and tourism in Poland, 203-4; working class roots of, 4, 165-66, 244n11; WWII exile community and, 10-11, 31-32, 39-57. See also New Emigration/Old Polonia conflict; New Emigration/Old Polonia cooperation; organizations, American Polonia
Polonian (dialect), 172-74
Polonia 1978—Polonia Jutra, 235-36
Polonia of the Free World, 233-36
Polonia Paderewski Choir, 290n120
Polonia's Heart, 217
Polska, 90-91
Polska Akademia Umiejętności (Polish Academy of Arts and Sciences; PAU), 36
Polska Chrystusowa, 92
Polska Macierz Szkolna (Polish schools in exile), 110
Polska Partia Socjalistyczna (Polish Socialist Party; PPS), 101, 109
Polska Pomoc Społeczna (Polish Welfare), 80
Polska Rada Zawodowa (Polish Council of Trade Unions), 82-83
Polskie Katolickie Stowarzyszenie Uniwersyteckie "Veritas" (Polish Catholic Academic Association "Veritas"), 145
Polskie Stowarzyszenie Byłych Więźniów Politycznych w Stanach Zjednoczonych (Polish Association of ex-Political Prisoners in the United States), 142, 241
Polskie Stronnictwo Ludowe (Polish Peasant Party; PSL), 107, 109-10, 196
Polskie Towarzystwo Naukowe na Obczyźnie (Polish Society of Arts and Sciences Abroad), 241
Polski Instytut Naukowy w Ameryce (Polish Institute of Arts and Sciences in America; PIN), 35, 36
Polski Komitet Imigracyjny (Polish Immigration Committee), 117
Polski Narodowy Komitet Demokratyczny (Polish National Democratic Committee; PNKD), 195-96
Polski Teatr Artystów (Polish Artists' Theater), 37-38
Polski Teatr Narodowy (Polish National Theater), 36-37
Polski Związek Akademików (Polish Academic Association), 140
Polski Związek byłych Więźniów Politycznych Niemieckich Obozów Koncentracyjnych (Polish Association of Former Political Prisoners of German Concentration Camps), 92, 101
Pomocnicza Służba Kobiet (Women's Auxiliary Service; PSK; *Pestki*), 31
Pomocnicza Służba Wojskowa Kobiet (Women's Auxiliary Military Service; PSWK), 31
POMOST, 229

Poznań Massacre, 211-15, 226-27
Pragier, Adam, 51
Preparatory Commission of the International Refugee Association (PCIRO), 60
press, Polish: in DP camps, 89-93, 274-75n129, 275n132, 275-76n141; on DP resettlement experiences, 121-22; exile mission and, 110; women in, 277-78n171; WWII diaspora and, 31
press, Polish-American: and diasporic unity, 230-31, 314n11; DP propaganda campaign of, 147-48, 150-57, 295n25; on DP resettlement experiences, 123; and DP welfare problems, 81; and economic aid to Poland, 213-14; during interwar period, 5; and job-hopping, 129-30; on Lechoń's suicide, 211; and organizational separation, 182, 184; and party politics, 180-81; "Polonian" dialect used by, 173; and Polonia-WWII exile relations, 52-54; and reevaluation of exile mission, 219; Republican Party propaganda in, 201; and WWII diaspora, 35; on Wyrwa affair, 186-88. See also specific publication
Preyss, Adelina, 41
prisoners of war, Polish: American Polonia aid to, 41-42; as DPs in Germany, 60-61; extraditions of, 249n11; living conditions of, 23; numbers of, 20; in Soviet camps, 25
professionals, underemployment of in U.S., 128-29, 298-99n83
Promyczek Szczęścia, 91
Proudfoot, Malcolm, 251n31, 262n4
Provisional Council of National Unity, 207
Provisional Government of National Unity, 50, 107
Przegląd Dwutygodniowy, 275n132
Przegląd Sportowy, 92
Przekroje, 273n105
przetrwanie (endurance), exile mission and, 223
Ptakowski, Jerzy, 90
PU. See Zjednoczenie Polskie w Niemczech
publishing: in DP camps, 76, 93-95; and New Emigration/Old Polonia conflict, 174-75; Second Polish Corps and, 29; WWII diaspora and, 31, 34
Pula, James S., 5
Pulaski Transport Line, 206
Pułaski Day Parade (1956), 227

Raczkiewicz, Władysław, 109, 224
Raczyński, Edward, 197
Rada Jedności Narodowej (Council of National Unity), 197, 215
Rada Narodowa (National Council), 196
Rada Polityczna (Political Council), 110
Rada Polonii Amerykańskiej (Polish American Council), 69, 282-83n36; aid to DP camps, 111; DP mistreatment reported to, 152; and DP resettlement, 113, 115, 116, 121, 126, 128; and economic aid to Poland, 214; founding of, 256n79; Immigration Committee, 116; and job-hopping, 129-30; KNAPP and, 47, 52; and organizational separation, 182, 283n38; political centrism of, 47; propaganda campaigns of, 42-43, 148-49, 257n94; PU and, 79-80; WWII aid efforts, 39-46, 256n80
Rada Trzech (Council of the Three), 110, 195, 197
radio: American Polonia and, 293n2; images of DPs, 148; "Polonian" dialect used by, 173; and Polonia-WWII exile relations, 53; and repatriation pressure, 202
Radio Free Europe (RFE)/Radio Wolna Europa (RWE), 198, 207, 216, 225
Radiowy Teatr Wyobraźni, 138
Radkiewicz, Stanisław, 201
Ravensbrück concentration camp (Germany), 23, 140, 251n26
Rawski, Czesław, 290n121
Reagan, Ronald, 308n22
Red Cross. See American Red Cross; Polish Red Cross
"Refugee's Religion" (Nowakowski), 151
Regional Advisory Councils, 87

Reit DP camp (Germany), 295n26
religion: in DP camps, 75-77; New Emigration and, 145. *See also* clergy; Roman Catholic Church
Remiarz, Stefan, 27-28
repatriation: communist pressure for, 202-3, 220, 308-9n31; and DP community building, 101-2; forced, 111; government in exile and, 71; numbers of, 262n4; SHAEF and, 262n3; UNRRA and, 60, 61, 62-64, 101, 111, 273n105
Republican Party, 49, 201, 208, 213, 308n22
resettlement program (U.S.): American Polonia and, 9, 12; children, 43-44; conflict resulting from, 161-65; costs of, 132-33; and DP community building, 101-2; DP welfare problems resulting from, 70-71, 81; employment problems, 121-30; health problems, 130-31; immigration procedures, 120-21; Jews admitted under, 245-46n26; as mental process, 118-19; mobility and, 129-30; organization of, 110-18; Polish immigrants admitted under, 281-82n28; in rural areas, 121-28, 286nn71-72, 287n82; sponsorship and, 131-32, 161-63; success of, 133-34; welcome ceremonies, 119-20. *See also* New Emigration
resistance organizations, Polish, 18-19, 139-40, 251n26, 304n154
reunions, and diasporic unity, 231
Ripa, Karol, 45
Robakiewicz, Feliks, 276n143
Robotnik Polski, 244n11
Rockland County Operation, 124
Rogozenski, Ben, 137
Roman Catholic Church: and centrality of parish, 3-4, 144, 292n145; New Emigration and, 144-45; persecuted in Poland, 208. *See also* clergy
Romania, 24, 41, 239
Roosevelt, Franklin Delano: American Polonia and, 46, 47-48, 258n111; and Katyń Massacre, 48; Krawiec's criticism of, 274n129; signs Yalta agreement, 49-50
Rosenfield, Harry N., 124-25

Roszkowska, Magdalena, 171
Rowinski, Leokadia, 58
Rozmarek, Charles (Karol): and aid to Poland, 214; and closing of DP schools, 273n115; criticism of Yalta agreement, 50, 207; and DP resettlement, 121; and exile mission, 207; and government in exile, 181; and Katyń Massacre investigation, 199-200; opposition to UNRRA, 111-12, 150; and PAC founding, 49; and Polonia cultural activities, 54; and Poznań Massacre, 211-13; and Świetlik, 115; and tourism in Poland, 204; WWII aid efforts, 43-44. *See also* Polish American Congress
Rozmarek, Wanda, 121, 124, 132, 134
Rój (publishing house), 34
Ruch Chrzescijańsko-Społeczny (Christian Social Movement), 101
rural areas, DPs resettled in, 121-28, 286nn71-72, 287n82
rural pacification, Nazi, 18
Rybij, Mary Gracille, 257n94

Sachsenhausen concentration camp (Germany), 18, 23
Safran, William, 245n24
Salicz-Płoskoń, Władysław, 138
Samodzielna Brygada Spadochronowa (First Independent Parachute Brigade), 61
Samopomoc Marynarki Wojennej (Polish Navy Veterans Association of America), 141
Samopomoc Nowej Emigracji (Mutual Aid Association of the New Polish Emigration), 135, 136
Santa Rosa refugee camp (Mexico), 28, 43
Scandinavia, 236-37
Schiller, Leon, 96-97
schools/schooling: in DP camps, 85-88, 272n97; exile mission and, 110; parish, 3; Saturday, 138; "walking," in concentration camps, 23, 251n26; WWII diaspora and, 31
Scotland, Polish reserve corps in, 250n16

scouting movement. *See* Związek Harcerstwa Polskiego
Second Polish Armored Division, 97
Second Polish Corps, 28–30, 208, 241, 275–76n141
Sekcja Szkolenia Zawodowego, 272n97
self-help organizations, 135–36
Sepucha, Charles, 120
Serafinowicz, Leszek. *See* Lechoń, Jan
Serce Polonii (Polonia's Heart), 217
Shade Tobacco Operation, 124
Shutten, Carl, 124
Sikorski, Władysław (Gen.), 46, 47–48, 258n111
Siwik, Anna, 218
Skamander, 32
Skamandryci (Skamandrites), 32
Skiba, Jerzy, 272n97
Skrowaczewski, Stanisław, 232
slave laborers, Polish, 208; as DPs in Germany, 60; living conditions, 23; and WWII diaspora, 20–21
Slavik, Juraj, 197–98
Slovenia, 238
Słonimski, Antoni, 32, 57
Słowacki, Juliusz, 1
Słowo Katolickie, 93
Słowo Polskie, 92
Służba Zwycięstwu Polski (Polish Victory Service), 18–19
Smosarska, Jadwiga, 37
social class, as source of conflict, 165–72, 239
Social Committee to Aid Polish Citizens in Germany, 78, 79
social displacement syndrome, 163–65
Sokoł (sports/patriotic organization), 98
Solidarity, 229
Sosnkowski, Kazimierz (Gen.), 196–97, 200, 218–19
South Africa, 27
Soviet Union: and détente, 204–5; German invasion of, 46; invasion of Poland, 7–8, 16–17; and Katyń Massacre, 47–48, 200, 248n143; liberalization in, 201–2; military intervention in Hungary (1956), 216–18; 225; and repatriation pressure, 202–3; Twentieth Party Congress (1956) in, 205; Warsaw offensive, 19
Soviet Union, Polish deportees in: American Polonia aid to, 41; living conditions of, 8, 25–26, 251–52n35; numbers of, 25, 251n31; repatriation of, 203, 204, 207; WWII agreement allowing departure of, 46
Spackenberg DP camp (Germany), 65, 266n25
Spadochron, 91
Spellman, Francis (Cardinal), 119–20
SPK. *See* Stowarzyszenie Polskich Kombatantów
Społeczny Komitet Pomocy Obywatelom Polskim w Niemczech (Social Committee to Aid Polish Citizens in Germany), 78, 79
sponsorship: for agricultural work, 126; and immigration procedures, 120–21; as immigration requirement, 113, 131–32; New Emigration and, 143; as source of conflict, 161–63
sports, in DP camps, 98
Sprawa Polska, 191
sprawa Wyrwy (Wyrwa affair), 185–92, 305n169
Squadron 303 (Fiedler), 34
Stahl, Zdzisław, 205
Stalinism, 205
Stalin, Josef, 49–50, 194, 201, 274n129
Stanek, Jan A., 118
Starczewski, Tadeusz, 91
Starobielsk POW camp (Soviet Union), 25
Stars and Stripes, 154
Starzyński, Stefan, 17
Starzyński, Teofil A., 40
State, Department of, 43, 200, 256n80, 305n174
state in exile concept, 51. *See also* government in exile, Polish; Little Poland in exile
Sterner, Wacław, 64–65, 266n25
Stevenson, Adlai, 197
Stoessinger, John George, 262–63n9, 288n94

Stowarzyszenie Artystów Sceny Polskiej (Association of Polish Performing Artists), 85
Stowarzyszenie Byłych Żołnierzy 1. Dywizji Pancernej (First Armored Division Veterans Association), 141
Stowarzyszenie Inżynierów Polskich w Argentynie (Association of Polish Engineers in Argentina), 236
Stowarzyszenie Lotników Polskich (Association of Polish Pilots), 141
Stowarzyszenie Nowych Amerykanów (Association of New Americans), 135–36, 177
Stowarzyszenie Polskich Kombatantów (Association of Polish ex-Combatants; SPK): and cultural exchanges, 315–16n22; in DP camps, 100–101; and exile mission, 100–101, 110; New Emigration and, 140–41; and Polish Saturday schools, 138; SWAP and, 141, 183–85, 192, 227, 303–4n148
Stowarzyszenie Polskich Weteranów (Polish Veterans Association), 79–80, 92
Stowarzyszenie Prawników Polskich w Stanach Zjednoczonych (Association of Polish Jurists in the United States), 140
Stowarzyszenie Samopomocy Nowej Emigracji, 143
Stowarzyszenie Saperów Polskich w USA (Polish Sappers Veterans Association of the USA), 141
Stowarzyszenie Weteranów Armii Polskiej (Polish Army Veterans Association in America; SWAP), 163; and DP/Polonia conflict, 141; SPK and, 141, 183–85, 192, 227, 303–4n148
Stratton, William G., 112
Strażnica, 91
strikes: American Polonia and labor movement, 4, 11, 258n111; in DP camps, 267n38, 295n26; and DP unemployment, 128
Stronnictwo Demokratyczne (Democratic Movement; SD), 109, 196
Stronnictwo Ludowe "Wolność" (People's Movement "Freedom"), 101, 109
Stronnictwo Narodowe (National Democratic Movement; *endecja*), 101, 109
Stronnictwo Pracy (Labor Movement; SP), 101, 109, 196
Strzecha, 278n176
Strzetelski, Stanisław, 34, 210
student associations, Polish, 88
Studia Irańskie, 27
Suez Canal crisis, 215
Suffolk County (N.Y.), 123
Supreme Committee for the Liberation of Lithuania, 237
Supreme Headquarters Allied Expeditionary Force (SHAEF) Displaced Persons Branch, 60, 64, 262n3
Swanstrom, Edward E., 114
SWAP. See Stowarzyszenie Weteranów Armii Polskiej
Świętosławski, Wojciech, 36
Switzerland, 24–25, 41, 236–37
Syndicate of Polish Journalists, 84, 93
Syracuse (N.Y.), 126
Szare Szeregi (Grey Ranks), 19, 139
szkoła chodzona (walking school), 23, 251n26
Szwajdler, Franciszek, 203
Szymczak, Robert, 200, 259n121

Śliwowski, Jan (Rev.), 126
Śpiewak, Wacław, 188–89
Światowy Związek Polaków z Zagranicy (Światpol; World Union of Poles from Abroad), 10
Świetlica Kompanii Wartowniczych, 92
Świetlik, Francis (Franciszek) X.: on American Polonia, 10; and Felix Burant, 117; political centrism of, 47; and Rada propaganda campaign, 149; and Rada resettlement program, 111, 115; and Rada's WWII aid efforts, 40, 42, 45. See also Rada Polonii Amerykańskiej

Tadeusz G. (Home Army soldier), 22, 29, 314n11

Talks with Polonia (radio show), 53
Tanganyika, 27–28
Taubenschlag, Rafał, 36
Teatr Aktora, 138
Teatr Dramatyczny, 138
Teatr Ref-Rena, 138
Teatr Zjednoczenia Polskiego (Theater of the Polish Union), 96
Texas Chamber of Commerce, 286n72
Texas Operation, 124, 286n72
theater, 36–38, 97, 137–38, 290n121
Tiche, Karin, 37
Titoism, 209
Tontarski, Feliks, 168
Toruń, University of (Poland), 241
Towarzystwo Łączności z Wychodźstwem Polskim "Polonia" (Association for Cooperation with Polish Emigration "Polonia"), 202
Towarzystwo Studiów Irańskich (Association of Iranian Studies), 27
Truman Directive: Jews admitted under, 280–81n21; Polish immigrants admitted under, 31, 281n28; Rada and, 114; significance of, 111
Truman, Harry S., 109–10, 111, 120, 125, 265n19
Trunk, Chil, 45
Tubielewicz, Jan, 26
Tubielewicz, Olga, 26, 28, 314n12
Tubielewicz, Roma, 28
Tubielewicz, Zygmunt, 29–30
turyści (tourists), 230
Tuwim, Julian, 32, 57
Tygodnik Polski, 32, 33–35, 37–38, 52–54, 56–57
Tygodniowy Przegląd Literacki Koła Pisarzy z Polski, 33–34
Tymczasowy Rząd Jedności Narodowej (Provisional Government of National Unity; TRNJ), 50, 107

Uganda, 27
Ukrainian immigrants, 237–38, 265n22
unemployment/underemployment, 128–29, 298–99n83

Union of Poles in America, 144
Union of Polish Artisans and Workers, 84
Union of Polish Centers in Northern Bavaria, 77, 267n41
Union of Polish Farmers, 84
Union of Polish Refugees in Germany, 79
Union of Polish War Emigration (ZPUW), 79, 271n81
Union of Polish Writers in Germany, 85
unions: American Polonia and, 46–47, 244n11; British, anti-Polish discrimination by, 106; in DP camps, 82–84; and Yalta agreement, 50
United Auto Workers, 258n111
United Kingdom, 106–7. *See also* Great Britain
United National Committees and Councils in Exile, 198
United Nations High Commissioner for Refugees (UNHCR), 60
United Nations Relief and Rehabilitation Administration (UNRRA), 69; and DP camp administration, 73, 269nn57, 59, 295n26; and DP camp conditions, 68, 69–70, 263–64n12, 266n25, 267n36; and DP journals, 90–91; and DP repatriation, 60, 61, 62–64, 101, 111, 273n105; and DP schools, 87, 273nn105, 115; PAC opposition to, 111–12, 149–50; PU and, 79
United States: conscription of foreign residents in, 190; and détente, 204–5; and exile politics, 198–99; non-Polish immigrants in, 237–39; political impact of Polish-Soviet split on, 48; Polonian political influence in, 226, 258n110; WWII neutrality declared by, 40. *See also* exile community in U.S., Polish; Polonia, American; resettlement program (U.S.)
United Ukranian American Relief Committee, 114
Universal Military Training and Service Act (1951), 306n176
University of Toruń (Poland), 241
UNRRA. *See* United Nations Relief and Rehabilitation Administration
Uruguay, 24

Uśmiechnij się Giocondo (Peretiakowicz), 137–38

Venezuela, 106
Versailles, Treaty of, 1
veterans organizations: in DP camps, 100–101; New Emigration/Old Polonia split in, 183–85, 234; Second Corps and, 29; in U.S. exile community, 140–42. *See also* Stowarzyszenie Polskich Kombatantów; Stowarzyszenie Weteranów Armii Polskiej; *specific organization*
Vistula Troop, 89

Wachtl, Karol, 5
wakacjusze (vacationers), 230
Wałęsa, Lech, 239
Walter, Francis E., 123
Wandycz, Piotr, 240
Wańkowicz-Erdman, Marta, 34
Wańkowicz, Melchior, 179, 180, 203, 210, 232
War, Department of, 48
war invalids, organizations of, 142–43
War Relief Services (WRS), 114. *See also* National Catholic Welfare Conference
Warsaw Uprising (1944), 8, 19, 20, 22, 49, 56
Wasilewski, Thaddeus, 48
Watenstadt DP camp (Germany), 89–90
Wawer (Poland), 18
Wazeter, Franciszek (Francis), 53, 293n2
Wczoraj i Jutro, 91
Wehrmacht, Polish deserters from, 250n16
Weiden-"La Guardia" DP camp (Germany), 67, 74, 98
Weintraub, Wiktor, 221
welfare organizations/committees, 79–81
Werten, Maria, 34
Wesoła Czwórka, 138
Wesoła Lwowska Fala, 138
Westward Ho!, 107
Węgrzynek, Maksymilian F., 35, 47, 52
WHOM (radio station), 293n2
Wiadomości, 91
Wiadomości Literackie, 32, 34, 110, 218, 241
Wiadomości Polskie, 33, 275n132, 275–76n141

Wiadomości Prawnicze, 92
Wichrowski, Bolesław (Gen.), 118
Wiedzielski, Kazimierz, 188
Wielka Emigracja (Great Emigration), 1–2, 33, 56–57, 223
Wieniawa-Długoszewski, Bolesław, 47, 57
Wierzyński, Kazimierz: and exile mission, 33, 34; and exile/Polonia conflict, 55; and *Kultura*, 232; Paczkowski on, 56; and Piłsudski Institute, 35; as Skamandrite, 32
Wilczówna, Janina, 37
Wildflecken (Germany). *See* Durzyń DP camp (Germany)
Wisconsin, 237, 283n38, 317–18n36
Wittlin, Józef, 32; and exile mission, 34, 177–78; and *Kultura*, 232; and publishing in Poland, 221; and *Tygodnik*, 38
Wojciechowska, Władysława, 139–40
Wojciechowski, Marian, 140
Wolna Polska (ship), 206–7, 217
women, Polish: in DP camps, 99, 277n170, 277–78n171, 278n175; Nazi deportations of, 22, 277n170; occupational skills of, 62; in Polish army, 30; resettlement in U.S., 44, 127; and scouting movement, 139–40; in WWII diaspora, 34–35
women, Polish American, 3–4, 134
Women's Auxiliary Military Service, 31
Women's Auxiliary Service, 31
Women's Circle, 278n176
Woodbridge, George, 269n57
World Lithuanian Community, 237
World Union of Poles from Abroad, 10
World War I, 4–5
World War II: and American Polonia, 247n39; diaspora during, 7–9, 16–31; and exile mission, 30–31, 225; German-Soviet war, 26, 46; Polish army in, 28–30; Polish resistance during, 18–19, 139–40, 251n26, 304n154; Polish scouting during, 140; Polonia-exile relations during, 39–57; quota immigration during, 9; U.S. Polish exile community during, 31–39; victims' associations, 142–43; Warsaw Uprising, 8, 19, 20, 22, 49, 56. *See also* Katyń Massacre

writers, exiled, 177–78, 220, 276n143
Wróbel, Elżbieta and Janusz, 257n94
Wspólnymi Siłami, 92
Wyman, Mark, 265n19
Wyrwa affair (*sprawa Wyrwy*), 185–92, 305n169
Wyrwa, Józef, 185–86, 189, 306n181
Wyrwa, Tadeusz, 185–92, 226, 240
Wyszyński, Stefan (Cardinal), 204, 207, 216
Wytrwal, Joseph A., 247n39, 258–59n112

Yalta agreement: American Polonia and, 49–50, 111, 201, 207, 213; exile mission and opposition to, 8–9, 102, 179–80, 221–23; political stability of, 225; and postwar diaspora, 8–9; provisional government decided at, 50, 107; Wyrwa affair and, 187, 188, 191
Yolles, Peter P., 133, 167–72, 187, 225

Zachariasiewicz, Walter, 123
Zagórski, Stefan, 44
Zajączkowski, J. P., 175–76
Zaleski, August, 109–10, 181, 195–97, 215
Zaleski, Henryk, 123
Załoga, 82–83
Zamek, 110, 195
Zaremba, Zygmunt, 215
Zbierzowska-Frydrych, Wanda, 138
Zgoda, 218, 314n11
Zjednoczenie Polaków w Ameryce (Union of Poles in America), 144
Zjednoczenie Polskich Uchodźców w Niemczech (Union of Polish Refugees in Germany), 79
Zjednoczenie Polskiego Uchodźstwa Wojennego (Union of Polish War Emigration; ZPUW), 79, 271n81
Zjednoczenie Polskie w Amerykańskiej Strefie Okupacji Niemiec (Polish Union in the American Zone of Occupation in Germany), 77
Zjednoczenie Polskie w Niemczech (Polish Union in Germany; PU): citizens' court established by, 81–82; conflict within, 271n79; and DP camp name changes, 103; and DP cultural life, 96; and DP women, 99, 277n170; financial difficulties of, 270–71n78; formation of, 77–78; and IRO data, 264n16; legalization of, 271n80; membership of, 78–79; and national celebrations, 96; and Polish press, 92–93; and Polonia propaganda campaign, 153; structure of, 78; welfare work of, 79–80
złoty (currency), 6
Zrzeszenie Artystów Plastyków Polskich (Association of Polish Artists), 85
Zrzeszenie Kół Techników Polskich (Association of Circles of Polish Technicians), 83
Zrzeszenie Ośrodków Polskich Bawarii Północnej (Union of Polish Centers in Northern Bavaria), 77, 267n41
Zrzeszenie Polskich Nauczycieli na Wychodźstwie w Niemczech (Association of Polish Teachers in Emigration in Germany), 86
Zrzeszenie Prawników Polskich (Association of Polish Lawyers), 84, 92
Zrzeszenie Przyjaciół Żołnierza Polskiego (Association of Friends of the Polish Soldier), 152
Zrzeszenie Uchodźców Wojennych z Polski w Stanach Zjednoczonych (Polish War Refugee Association), 44–46
Zrzeszenie Wydawców i Księgarzy (Association of Publishers and Booksellers), 84, 93
Zubrzycki, Jerzy, 240, 250n16, 301n129
Związek Akademików Polskich (Association of Polish Academicians; ZAP), 274n119
Związek Harcerstwa Polskiego (Polish scouting; ZHP): American Polonia and, 291n126; Catholic clergy and, 145; in DP camps, 27, 88–89; exile mission and, 110; girl scouts, 139–40, 251n26; historical records of, 241; New Emigration and, 138–40; Szare Szeregi organized by, 19
Związek Lekarzy Polskich na Wychodźstwie (Association of Polish Physicians in Exile), 140

Związek Młodzieży Polskiej (Association of Polish Youth), 138–39
Związek Pisarzy Polskich na Obczyźnie (Association of Polish Writers in Exile), 220, 221
Związek Pisarzy Polskich w Niemczech (Union of Polish Writers in Germany), 85
Związek Polskich Spadochroniarzy w Ameryce (Polish Airborne Forces Veterans Association in America), 141
Związek Rolników Polskich (Union of Polish Farmers), 84
Związek Rzemieślników i Robotników Polskich (Union of Polish Artisans and Workers), 84
Związek Studentów Polaków (Polish Students Association), 88, 274n119

żądania maksymalne (maximum demands, doctrine of), 218, 219, 225
Żeromski, Stefan, 294n14
Żyłka, Józef, 120

www.ingramcontent.com/pod-product-compliance
Lightning Source LLC
Chambersburg PA
CBHW020637300426
44112CB00007B/139